Middle Eastern Monarchies

This monograph explores the dynamics of ingroup identity in the foreign policymaking of Middle Eastern monarchies from the evolution of the regional system after the world wars until the present. Using an innovative theoretical framework that combines foreign policy analysis in the context of authoritarian regimes and social identity theory, the book theorizes the origins and inner workings of a "monarchic peace" among hereditary regimes in the Middle East, including the Gulf monarchies, Jordan, and Morocco.

While the phenomenon of the "democratic peace" is well established in political science, this book argues that like the examined monarchic peace, it is in fact a sub-case of a broader similar political systems peace (SPSP). The theory posits that monarchies do not wage war against each other, because they recognize each other as members of the same "ingroup", which allows for other mechanisms of conflict resolution – behavior that is allowed against outsiders might be prohibited against members of the same club or "family". The theory is illustrated with numerous case studies that look at overall regional dynamics as well as four crucial cases of monarchic interstate conflict: Bahraini-Qatari relations, the Saudi-Hashemite rivalry, and the relations between Kuwait and Iraq and between Iran and the United Arab Emirates (UAE).

This in-depth account of the foreign policies and community connecting Middle Eastern monarchies will be of interest to readers in international relations, authoritarianism studies, and Middle Eastern and Persian Gulf politics.

Anna Sunik focuses on Middle East politics and authoritarianism. She studied political science, Islamic studies and cultural anthropology in Heidelberg and Paris and has worked in the Middle East Institute of the GIGA Global Institute of Global and Area Studies and the German Federal Foreign Office.

Routledge Studies in Middle Eastern Politics

The Decline of Democracy in Turkey
A Comparative Study of Hegemonic Party Rule
Kürşat Çınar

Ethnicity and Party Politics in Turkey
The Rise of the Kurdish Party during the Kurdish Opening Process
Berna Öney

Religion and Hezbollah
Political Ideology and Legitimacy
Mariam Farida

Erdoğan's 'New' Turkey
Attempted Coup d'état and the Acceleration of Political Crisis
Nikos Christofis

The Iraqi Kurds and the Cold War
Regional Politics, 1958–1975
Hawraman Ali

Islam, Jews and the Temple Mount
The Rock of Our/Their Existence
Yitzhak Reiter and Dvir Dimant

Saudi Interventions in Yemen
A Historical Comparison of Ontological Insecurity
Caroline F. Tynan

Middle Eastern Monarchies
Ingroup Identity and Foreign Policy Making
Anna Sunik

For a full list of titles in the series:
www.routledge.com/middleeaststudies/series/SE0823

Middle Eastern Monarchies
Ingroup Identity and Foreign
Policy Making

Anna Sunik

LONDON AND NEW YORK

First published 2021
by Routledge
2 Park Square, Milton Park, Abingdon, Oxon OX14 4RN

and by Routledge
52 Vanderbilt Avenue, New York, NY 10017

Routledge is an imprint of the Taylor & Francis Group, an informa business

© 2021 Anna Sunik

The right of Anna Sunik to be identified as author of this work has been asserted by her in accordance with sections 77 and 78 of the Copyright, Designs and Patents Act 1988.

All rights reserved. No part of this book may be reprinted or reproduced or utilised in any form or by any electronic, mechanical, or other means, now known or hereafter invented, including photocopying and recording, or in any information storage or retrieval system, without permission in writing from the publishers.

Trademark notice: Product or corporate names may be trademarks or registered trademarks, and are used only for identification and explanation without intent to infringe.

British Library Cataloguing-in-Publication Data
A catalogue record for this book is available from the British Library

Library of Congress Cataloging-in-Publication Data
Names: Sunik, Anna, author.
Title: Middle Eastern monarchies : ingroup identity and foreign policy making / Anna Sunik.
Description: Abingdon, Oxon ; New York, NY : Routledge, 2021. | Series: Routledge studies in Middle Eastern politics; 103 | Includes bibliographical references and index.
Identifiers: LCCN 2020012503 (print) | LCCN 2020012504 (ebook) | ISBN 9780367443160 (hardback) | ISBN 9781003008934 (ebook) | ISBN 9781000164442 (adobe pdf) | ISBN 9781000164541 (epub) | ISBN 9781000164497 (mobi)
Subjects: LCSH: Middle East—Foreign relations. | Monarchy—Middle East. | Authoritarianism—Middle East. | Political stability—Middle East. | Middle East—Kings and rulers.
Classification: LCC JZ1670 .S86 2021 (print) | LCC JZ1670 (ebook) | DDC 327.56—dc23
LC record available at https://lccn.loc.gov/2020012503
LC ebook record available at https://lccn.loc.gov/2020012504

ISBN: 978-0-367-44316-0 (hbk)
ISBN: 978-1-003-00893-4 (ebk)

Typeset in Times New Roman
by Apex CoVantage, LLC

For my parents

Contents

	List of tables and figures	viii
	List of abbreviations and glossary	ix
1	Introduction: explaining the dynamics of "monarchic peace"	1
2	Moving beyond democratic exceptionalism: the peace among similar political systems	18
3	Middle East monarchies from the Arab Cold War to the Arab Spring	62
4	When monarchies collide: case studies of "near misses" of monarchic war	91
5	From monarchy to republic – from peace to war?: "Quasi-experiments" of collapsed monarchic couples	152
6	The limits of SPSP: deviant cases?	218
7	Conclusion: toward a peace among similar political systems	229
	Index	245

List of Tables and Figures

Tables

1.1	Monarchies and Participation in International Wars Since 1945	2
1.2	MENA Wars and Monarchy Involvement 1945–2003	3
1.3	MIDs in the Middle East 1945–2001	6
4.1	The Hawar Islands Dispute	117
4.2	The Saudi-Hashemite Conflict	142
5.1	Deterioration of Iraqi-Kuwaiti Relations	173
5.2	Deterioration of Iranian-UAE Relations	208

Figures

2.1	Causal chain links and steps 1–4	38

Abbreviations and glossary

ACC	Arab Cooperation Council (Jordan, Iraq, Egypt, and North Yemen)
AFU	Arab Federation/Union/Federal Union between the Hashemite monarchies of Jordan and Iraq in 1958
CP	Comparative Politics
DP/DPT	democratic peace/democratic peace theorem
FPA	foreign policy analysis
GCC	Gulf Cooperation Council
Darak	Gendarmerie
Ikhwan	"Brotherhood", Wahhabi tribal force in early period of KSA expansion
Khaleeji	Referring to the Persian Gulf, particularly to GCC members
KSA	Kingdom of Saudi Arabia
ME	Middle East
MENA	Middle East and North Africa
MP	Monarchic Peace
NRCC	National Revolutionary Command Council (Iraq)
PFLOAG	Popular Front for the Liberation of the Occupied Arabian Gulf
SIT	social identity theory
SNSC	Supreme National Security Council of Iran
SPSP	similar political systems peace
Takfir	the labeling of other Muslims as nonbelievers
UAE	United Arab Emirates
UAR	United Arab Republic (merger between Egypt and Syria 1958–1961)
UK	United Kingdom
'Ulama	Religious scholars (singular: 'alim)
UNSC	United Nations Security Council
US	United States
USSR	United Soviet Socialist Republic

1 Introduction

Explaining the dynamics of "monarchic peace"

Almost half a century ago, Huntington seemed convinced that authoritarian monarchies were a thing of the past, claiming that the "future of the existing traditional monarchies is bleak. . . . The key questions concern simply the scope of the violence of their demise and who wields the violence" (Huntington 1968, 191). The "king's dilemma" (cf. also: Huntington 1966) became the new paradigm in authoritarianism research: the monarch's choice was only between increasing repression or increasing irrelevance. Huntington's quote embodies the sentiment that the word "monarchy" often invokes to this day – "an anachronism in the modern world of nations" (Hudson 1977, 166) that is likely to disappear soon. In light of waves of democratization and the founding of new states as republics, they seem to be relics of the "zeitgeist of an earlier era" (Maddy-Weizmann 2000, 37). Such an ancient and obsolete form of government may seem a fitting topic for historians and nostalgic audiences but hardly relevant to the politics of the modern world in the 21st century.

Yet this peculiar type of political system has survived in one region in particular: the Middle East and North Africa, the home of eight of about 15 remaining authoritarian monarchies worldwide (Friske 2008). In this region, almost half of all states are monarchies – from Morocco in the utmost west of North Africa to Oman on the Persian Gulf in the east.

The transformation of the region following the Arab Spring has reignited popular and scholarly interest in this group of states, because they proved remarkably resilient in contrast to their republican neighbors. No monarch was overthrown amid the disturbances that brought down four (or five, including both regime changes in Egypt) presidents, with another one fighting in a vicious civil war in Syria to conserve his rule.

While scholars have focused on the monarchies' seemingly unique resilience, they have so far overlooked an even-more-puzzling feature of monarchic foreign policy: *monarchies in the Middle East do not wage war against each other*. However, they sometimes go to war against other types of states. These patterns mirror those found in the foreign policy of a different group of political systems: democracies.

How can the fact that there has not been a *single* case of interstate war between monarchies in a region so highly accustomed to military conflict be explained?

2 Introduction

After all, the Middle East witnessed 11 major interstate wars since 1948, and monarchies have always formed a large share of all states –even the majority until the 1960s.

This book argues that this monarchic peace has the same explanation as the democratic peace: similar political systems do not go to war against each other. Instead of a peculiar democratic or monarchic pacifism, it is that when weighing their choices on war and peace, an important part of the calculation of states is who their counterpart is and whether it is part of their ingroup or an outsider. The rules on conflict management inside an ingroup differ strongly from rules toward those on the outside. The foreign policy patterns of Middle East monarchies help uncover this similar political systems peace (abbreviated here as SPSP) that trumps monarchism and democracy alike.

1.1 The empirical puzzle: are monarchies more peaceful?

What are the patterns of *monarchic* foreign policy? The first indications of monarchic idiosyncrasies can be discerned in descriptive statistical data on interstate war on the global level.

Table 1.1 summarizes some of the more interesting patterns relating to war and conflict internationally that seem to distinguish monarchies and republics. For instance, in relation to republics, monarchies are proportionally less involved in wars globally ("Participation") and are less likely to initiate wars ("Initiation") or even merely participate in them on the side of the aggressor ("Initiator party"). Much more significantly, however, after World War II, there has not been a *single* case of a war where monarchies fought against each other ("Intragroup war").

Table 1.1 Monarchies and Participation in International Wars Since 1945[1]

Out of 38 interstate wars	Participation	Initiation	Initiator party	Intragroup war	Share of all states
Monarchy	6 (15.7%)	2 (5.2%)	4 (10.5%)	0 (0%)	~10%–20%
Republic	38 (100%)	36 (94.7%)	37 (97.4%)	36 (94.7%)	~80%–90%

1 "Participation" indicates the number and share of interstate wars in which monarchies participated out of all 38 interstate wars in the correlates of war (CoW) data set between 1945 and 2003 (Sarkees and Wayman 2010; Stinnett et al. 2002). "Initiation" refers to the number and share of interstate wars in which a monarchy/republic was the initiator. "Initiator party" lists the number and share of interstate wars in which monarchies/republics participated on the side of the war initiator. "Intragroup war" refers to the number and share of intra-monarchic/intra-republican war. Of the two wars when a republic did not fight a fellow republic, one is the Falkland War, thus referring to the democratic UK. Excluding democratic monarchies (that are outside of the scope conditions of this book) would thus again further strengthen the existing tendency. "Share of all states" refers to the share of monarchies/republics out of all existent states. Due to the increase in the number of states and regime changes during the time scope of the data set (1945–2003), only a rough average share of monarchies/republics is noted in this table. The asymmetric distribution of especially war initiation and intragroup war is nonetheless evident.

Introduction 3

Since the Second World War, monarchies formed about 10%–20% of all states (Geddes, Wright, and Frantz 2011, 12–14)[1] and thus seem to be underrepresented concerning war involvement and initiation. Surprisingly, in the MENA (Middle East and North Africa) region, an especially conflict-ridden place, where monarchies accounted for two-thirds to slightly less than half all states,[2] we find the same tendency even reinforced.

Table 1.2 shows a more detailed breakdown of interstate wars, this time only for the Middle East. The overview shows additional hints of a monarchy–republic gap. Middle East monarchies appear less likely in general to initiate or support the initiator of a war, or even to merely participate in an interstate war compared to republics and their share of states in the region.

The only outlier was the Gulf War 1990–2001, when Iraq under Saddam Hussein attacked and occupied Kuwait, a monarchy. At that time, four monarchies (Kuwait, Oman, Qatar, and UAE) participated for the first and only time (together with two more experienced others) in a war, uniting almost all monarchies in the region to liberate their fellow monarchy. Two other monarchies (Egypt and Iraq in their monarchic periods)[3] also only participated in a war once, while the same

Table 1.2 MENA Wars and Monarchy Involvement 1945–2003[1]

Total 11 interstate wars			*Monarchy*	*Republic*
Arab-Israeli War 1948	*Egypt, Israel, Iraq, Jordan, Lebanon, Syria*	Participation/overall[2] Initiation/initiator ally Share	50%/50% Yes (Jordan)/50% 66.7% (6 out of 9)	50%/100% No /33.3% 33.3% (3 out of 9)
Suez War 1956	*Egypt, FR, Israel, UK*	Participation/overall Initiation/initiator ally Share	0%/0% No/0% 58.3% (7 out of 12)	100%/16.7% Yes/100% 41.7% (5 out of 12)
Ifni War 1957–1958	*FR, Morocco, ES*	Participation/overall Initiation/initiator ally Share	33.3%/14.3% Yes/33.3% 58.3% (7 out of 12)	66.7%/0% No/0% 41.7% (5 out of 12)
Six-Day War 1967	*Egypt, Israel, Jordan, Syria*	Participation/overall Initiation/initiator ally Share	25%/16.7% No/0% 42.8% (6 out of 14)	75%/37.5% Yes/25% 57% (8 out of 14)
War of Attrition 1969–1970	*Egypt, Israel*	Participation/overall Initiation/initiator ally Share	0%/0% No/0% 40% (6 out of 15)	100%/22.2% Yes/50% 60% (9 out of 15)

(*Continued*)

4 *Introduction*

Table 1.2 (Continued)

Total 11 interstate wars			Monarchy	Republic
Yom Kippur War 1973 Egypt, Iraq, Israel, *Jordan*, Syria, *KSA*		Participation/ overall Initiation/initiator ally Share	33.3%/22.2% No/33.3% 47.3% (9 out of 19)	66.7%/40% Yes/50% 52.6% (10 out of 19)
Iran–Iraq War 1980–1988 Iran, Iraq		Participation/ overall Initiation Initiator ally Share	0%/0% No 0% 42.1% (8 out of 19)	100%/18.2% Yes 50% 57.8% (11 out of 19)
Lebanon War 1982 Israel, Syria		Participation Overall Participation Initiation/initiator ally Share	0% 0% No/0% 42.1% (8 out of 19))	100% 18.2% Yes/50% 57.8% (11 out of 19)
Aouzou Strip War 1986–1987 Chad, Libya		Participation/ overall Initiation/initiator ally Share	0%/0% No/0% 42.1% (8 out of 19)	100%/18.2% Yes/50% 57.8% (11 out of 19)
First Gulf War 1990–1991 Egypt, Iraq, *Kuwait, Morocco, Oman, KSA, Qatar*, IT, FR, CAN, Syria, *UAE*, UK, US		Participation/ overall Initiation/initiator ally Share	42.9%/75% No/0% 44.4% (8 out of 18)	57.1%/30% Yes/7.1% 55.6% (10 out of 18)
Second Gulf War 2003 AUS, Iraq, UK, US		Participation/ overall Initiation/initiator ally Share	0%/0% No/0% 44.4% (8 out of 18)	100%/10% Yes/75% 55.6% (10 out of 18)
Overall participation: *never* *Once* *More than once*			4 Libya, N Yemen, Iran, Bahrain 6 KWT, Oman, Qatar, UAE; Egypt, Iraq 3 Jordan, Morocco, KSA	3 Algeria, Tunisia, S Yemen 3 Iran, Lebanon, Libya 4 Egypt, Iraq, Israel, Syria
Overall participation w/o Gulf War: *never* *Once* *More than once*			6 4 1	3 3 4
Sum (share) out of 36 war parties from MENA (49 in total, including external participants)			13 (36.1%)/13/ (26.5%)	23 (63.9%)/36 (73.5%)

Total 11 interstate wars	Monarchy	Republic
Sum (share) of initiations by MENA countries	2 (18.2%)	7 (<u>63.6%</u>)
Average initiator alliance	21.2%	44.5%
Average share of regimes in the region	*48.8%*	*51.2%*

1 The data source is the same as in the previous table (CoW and GPRD), the names of the wars correspond to their names in the CoW data set. All interstate wars in the Middle East where at least one Middle Eastern state was a direct participant are included in the table. The last-recorded war is the Iraq War, or Second Gulf War, of 2003; later wars were excluded because they were asymmetric wars fought between a state and non-state actor and thus are of limited utility here. Including them would further strengthen the evidence in favor of monarchies (here in italics) given that the wars were fought by republics.

2 "Participation": of all *warring parties*, how many are monarchies/republics. *Overall participation*: of all the *existing monarchies/republics* in the region, how many took part in the war. "Initiation": was the initiator of the war a monarchy/republic? "Initiator ally": of all warring parties, how many monarchies/republics took part on the initiator's side. "Share": how much is the overall share of monarchies/republics in the region at the onset of the war. The <u>underlined</u> numbers indicate an over-representation in relation to the overall share of monarchies/republics in the region.

is true for just three republics: Iran, Lebanon, and Libya (Lebanon, however, was embroiled in an intense civil war for 15 years). Libya, North Yemen, and Iran (in their monarchic periods) and Bahrain, four monarchies altogether, have not participated in an international war since 1945, a balance only three republics (Algeria, Tunisia, and South Yemen) can produce (two of which once again were preoccupied with civil or colonial war during a large part of their existence). Republics are overrepresented in most of the relevant categories concerning war, although because of the rarity of war, these differences are not statistically significant.

The more interesting finding is that globally – and even in the Middle East, where 11 of all 38 interstate wars between 1945 and 2003 took place (29%) – **no single one has seen two monarchies clash**.[4]

Interstate wars are relatively rare in general. Consequently, researchers in the democratic peace theorem (DPT) paradigm have tested whether the general tendencies held true in a wider set of similar cases by analyzing militarized interstate disputes (MID) that did not reach the threshold defined for war – democratic MID dyads, albeit present, were highly underrepresented (Russett and Oneal 2001). If we do the same for the monarchic peace, the statistical evidence points in the same direction and is even more compelling (Table 1.3).

Of 444 post-1945 MIDs in the Middle East, only 139 contain monarchies among the participants – that is, 31% – as opposed to 432 disputes made up of at least one republican participant, or 97%, of all MIDs. This again shows considerable underrepresentation, but not enough to statistically confirm a monadic reading of the monarchic peace – that monarchies are more peaceful in general.

In dyadic terms, when taking into account the counterpart, the evidence is cogent. The share of MIDs with monarchies on opposite sides is miniscule and includes 14 conflicts or about 3%. In comparison, democratic intergroup dispute is a slightly higher: 4.5% (cf. disaggregated numbers in Maoz and Abdolali 1989, 22).

6   Introduction

Table 1.3 MIDs in the Middle East 1945–2001[1]

Out of 444 MIDs in the MENA	Involvement	Intragroup dispute	Share of all states[2]
Monarchy	139 (31%)	14 (3%)	42%–67% (av. 53%)
Republic	432 (97%)	305 (69%)	33%–60% (av. 47%)

1 The summary statistics are based on the CoW MID 3.0 data set, which defines MIDs as "a set of interactions between or among states involving the threat, display, or use of military force in short temporal intervals," which is overt, non-accidental, government sanctioned, and government directed (Maoz and Abdolali 1989, 13) and includes MIDs from 1945 to 2001.
2 Due to the increase in the number of states in the regional system and five regime changes from monarchy to republic during the time scope of the data set (1945–2001), the maximum range of shares of monarchies/republics is noted in this table, although to slightly restrict the range as to not skew the share, the period is adapted to start in 1948 (as, except for Lebanon, all states that became independent before 1945 were monarchies). That is, at any given time, no fewer than 42% and no more than 67% independent monarchies were ever in the regional system. See previous table for exact shares at given time periods.

Furthermore, the figure for monarchic intergroup dispute includes MIDs in which one opponent monarchy was the UK or monarchic Spain. Given that both are (former) colonial powers in the region and democracies, they do not fall in the same category as the Middle East monarchies but rather belong outside of the scope of the analysis. If we exclude British and Spanish participation, intra-monarchic MIDs are cut in half, to only 7, or about 1.6% of all MIDs in the region throughout the period. Contrasted against the number of purely intra-republican conflict, 69%, it looks almost negligible.[5] In general, the monarchic MID dyads also produced fewer or no registered fatalities.[6] So monarchies do not just refrain from fighting one another, if they do so, but are also less aggressive toward each other and always keep it below the level of war.

These tendencies are not artifacts of idiosyncratic coding, because similar tendencies hold in other conflict data sets as well: the UCDP Dyadic data set (Version 1–2011) codes 29 dyadic interstate armed conflicts[7] in the Middle East from 1948 to 2003, *none* of which is jointly monarchic and only 6 (20.7%) of which have monarchic participants at all (in contrast, all conflicts entail at least one republican participant).[8] Only four of these (or just under 14%), reach the highest intensity level of war – that is, over 1000 battle-related deaths – which make up 20 (69%) of all coded dyads and are all conflicts with at least one (main) republican participant (Harbom, Melander, and Wallensteen 2008).

1.2 Overhauling the SPSP concept

The patterns that form the monarchic peace have in the past been overshadowed by more-salient features of monarchic politics in the Middle East. Monarchies are rarely studies as a regime type, because of the prolonged academic "unspoken consensus that monarchy is passé" (Anderson 2009, 1). Although monarchies have crumbled everywhere in the world since at least the turn of the 20th century,

Introduction 7

with revolutions or the establishment of new states invariably producing republics, they have survived in the Middle East. The consequence was a widespread belief of the irrelevance and obsolescence of monarchy with remnants of contemporary monarchy research surviving only in scholarship on the Middle East. Due to this "exceptionalism", Middle East scholars focused their attention on explaining monarchic resilience ever since the rise of modernization theory by Huntington and Halpern (Halpern 1963; Huntington 1968) while neglecting other possible characteristics of monarchies.

A broad range of aspects were considered as explanation: the interweavement of Islamic-Arabic culture and the monarchic system (Sharabi 1988), the reinvention of tradition by monarchies to stabilize their rule (Anderson 2009; Demmelhuber 2011), the shaping of a political culture enabling credible commitment by their institutions (Menaldo 2012), the capacity of monarchs to employ an effective *divide-et-impera* policy (Byman and Green 1999; Frisch 2011), the stabilizing effect of oil wealth (Gause 1994), and various combinations of these and other factors (Bank, Richter, and Sunik 2015; Yom and Gause 2012). Factors relating to foreign policy and international relations like external support and geostrategic position have also been deployed (Frisch 2011; Gause 1994; Maddy-Weizmann 2000), but only to explain stability (or democratization/liberalization), and the patterns of foreign policy itself have been overlooked. The strong emphasis on the societal level and the regime level in both theorized cause and effect follows the traditional embeddedness of the research tradition mainly in comparative politics (CP).

The "natural" discipline to explain war and peace and foreign policy in general, international relations (IR) with its sub-field of foreign policy analysis (FPA), is confined mostly to the two levels of *state* – that is, the foreign policy of individual states (see e.g. Hinnebusch and Ehteshami 2002; Al-Khalili 2009) – and (regional or global) *system* (Buzan and Gonzalez-Pelaez 2009; Fawcett 2009; Gause 2010; Halliday 2011), if they are not preoccupied with overarching issues of security, hegemony, terrorism, and the like (Henry and Springborg 2001; Roskin and Coyle 2003; Rubin and Rubin 2004). Only rarely are second-image explanations of internal factors like the domestic political system considered on the level of *groups of states* or through the prism of regime type or state form like monarchies. Two of the most important research programs in international relations, the (neo-) realist school and the democratic peace theorem (DPT), contributed to this effect, stymieing research on monarchies: the former because it neglected regime type as a germane factor in favor of the view of states as "like units", the latter because it brought this factor back into focus as an account of democracy–autocracy opposition, neglecting the greater diversity of autocracies. When non-democracies are studied, they are usually lumped together under the generic catch-all category of autocracies or authoritarian regimes.[9] The emphasis on quantitative methods, especially in the DPT literature, led to a neglect of these numerically insignificant cases. The Middle East monarchy research, on the other hand, was situated mostly in CP and largely neglected foreign policy behavior.

8   Introduction

The patterns of war and peace among Middle East monarchies parallel those of democracies in various ways. And we can benefit from the extensive literature around the DPT. Filling in the blanks that still remain is one of the tasks of this book.

There are strong indications that the empirical phenomenon of the democratic dyadic peace is better conceptualized as a subtype of the larger phenomenon of a peace among similar political systems, which would make the monarchic peace a parallel subtype to the DPT. Another blind spot of the DPT literature, as a research tradition grounded in the study of democracies following a specific path-dependent history of democratic institutions, it has a Eurocentric (or rather Western-centric) bias that should be balanced by engaging with area-specific approaches and topics outside of the Western world. In addition, its predominantly quantitative orientation leaves much room for qualitative analyses of the specific causal mechanism that leads to peace among similar political systems.

Such a causal mechanism that could apply to a democratic peace as well as to a monarchic peace is inspired by social identity theory (SIT), which posits that similar states band together in ingroups in which the use of violence to achieve individual aims has been ruled out. It is an inherently dyadic pathway and thus applicable to all kinds of states, both democratic and autocratic, regardless of the specificities of their institutions. In the shortest possible terms as applied to the monarchic peace, this book claims that **monarchies do not fight each other, because they recognize each other as members of the same ingroup – a "royal club".**

Because the examination of the features of democratic foreign policy is firmly established in IR and FPA, autocracies are often reduced to mere mirror images of democracies. There is a growing trend criticizing this conception of autocracies and advocating the development of the study of autocratic foreign policy. This budding field borrows heavily from research on authoritarian regimes from the field of CP to formulate sophisticated concepts of autocracy. Because it is a newly emerging field, not every subtype of autocracy has been examined. Seminal work has so far focused on the cooperation potential of different subtypes of autocracy (Erdmann et al. 2013; Mattes and Rodríguez 2014; Weeks 2014b), including authoritarian solidarity aimed to prevent regime change, liberalization, or destabilization, much of which is grounded in area studies (Bader 2015; Odinius and Kuntz 2015; Way 2015). Other classic FPA topics like war initiation propensity (Weeks 2012, 2014a) and the stamina of dictators in interstate conflict (Sirin and Koch 2015) have also been examined. Most of these studies, however, ignore monarchies altogether or lump them together with other distinct subtypes of autocracies like the "machines" analyzed by Weeks – which refer to dynastic monarchies and to single-party regimes (Weeks 2012, 331). Furthermore, many of these approaches are based on institutionalist explanations like selectorate theory and audience costs (Mattes and Rodríguez 2014; Sirin and Koch 2015; see e.g. Weeks 2012).

In contrast, the focus on monarchic peace provides an opportunity to not just discover patterns previously obscured by different lenses but also further uncover

Introduction 9

mechanisms behind well-known but still-unexplained phenomena like the democratic peace and at the same time advance the emerging research field of autocratic foreign policy.

This adds to at least three main bodies of literature, some area-specific and some general – Middle East monarchy research, Middle East–specific IR/FPA, and general IR/FPA – by bringing together a focus on autocratic monarchies, foreign policy, and area expertise to the respective fields where these aspects have so far been neglected and to help address the resulting biases. From this fusion, an updated SPSP concept emerges that is based on a modified conceptualization and specification and has more explanatory power, being applicable to dyads beyond democracies. This also adds to the emerging field of the study of the foreign policy of autocracies.

Of course, the study of monarchies is also relevant from a strictly empirical point of view. Before the "waves of democratization" (Huntington 1991) made the distinction between democracies and autocracies (or rather non-democracies) dominant, the main and most salient differentiation between different states was the state form – the distinction between monarchies and republics (cf. Friske 2007, 5). Machiavelli emphasized the relevance of this difference when he wrote that "All states, all powers, that have held and hold rule over men have been and are either republics or principalities" (Machiavelli 2006).

The two world wars constitute the threshold when the monarchy–republic division lost its importance, while the democracy–autocracy division increasingly gained meaning. With the rising trend of the overthrow and abolishment of monarchies and the establishment of republics, monarchy slowly disappeared as the main category, becoming increasingly "synonymous with irrelevance, ossification, and obsolescence" (Ben-Dor 2000, 71). The republic, on the other hand, went from forming one part of a triad (monarchy–aristocracy–republic) to becoming the opposite of monarchy (cf. Friske 2007, 12–44). Monarchy theory, once part and parcel of every theory of constitutions and a main field of political philosophy since at least Aristotle, has declined in the same degree as the phenomenon of monarchy declined with the triumphal procession of republicanism.

Of the current 193 UN member states, 43 are formal monarchies (Friske 2007, 6–7), but the number of *authoritarian* monarchies is far smaller, ranging from 12 to 18 depending on the definition of either "authoritarian" or "monarchy", with most concentrated in the Middle East.[10] While this might not seem like much, other subtypes of political systems are just as isolated but generate a significant amount of scholarship. Additionally, due to its large share of states in the Middle East, monarchism is of great significance for the politics of this region.

Focusing on monarchies helps to uncover other interesting contemporary patterns of foreign policy in the region apart from war – like their heightened foreign policy activity since 2011. Even in light of the global decrease of interstate war (cf. Malešević 2014), an examination of monarchic war and peace thus contributes to illuminating broader aspects of foreign policy.

10 *Introduction*

The regime data set by Hadenius, Teorell, and Wahman, for instance, counts 14 military regimes, seven single-party regimes, and one theocracy (Iran) in 2010 (Wahman, Teorell, and Hadenius 2013), whereas the data set by Geddes, Wright, and Frantz records only two military regimes and 15 single-party regimes (Iran is registered as a non-defined sui generis system) (Geddes, Wright, and Frantz 2011). And yet there is ample scholarship on military dictatorships (see e.g. Acemoglu, Ticchi, and Vindigni 2010; Geddes 1999; Martín 2006), single-party regimes (see e.g. Hess 2013; Malesky, Abrami, and Zheng 2011), and, of course, the political system of the Islamic Republic of Iran (Amjad 1989; Moshaver 2003; see e.g. Mozaffari 1993).

Authoritarian monarchies form a small subset of existing states, but they also clearly represent a phenomenon that deserves to be studied in its own right, adding to our knowledge about political systems and their relation to other aspects of state and society.

1.3 Patterns of monarchic peace – monadic or dyadic?

Mirroring the early findings and discussion of the democratic peace, two variants of a monarchic peace emerge: a *monadic* variant linking monarchies in general to greater pacifism and a *dyadic* variant linked to only two interacting monarchies who refrain from war in times of conflict. In another parallel to the DPT discussion, the evidence for the monadic effect is weak. War is a rare event, and there are only a handful of monarchies left in the postwar era, so this effect is not statistically significant. In other words, there are not enough instances of war to filter out unambiguous significant distinctions between monarchies and republics per se, regardless of the opponent.

Of much greater interest is the dyadic variant: why have monarchies (after WWII) never gone to war against one another, neither globally nor on the smaller scale of the Middle East with its abundance of both monarchies and war? To get to the core of the *dyadic* phenomenon – jointly peaceful monarchies – a dyadic explanatory mechanism is called for – in other words, a mechanism which kicks in only when a monarchy encounters another monarchy.

The similar patterns of the separate peace among monarchies and democracies suggest a shared or at least similar explanation instead of a monarchy-specific one. If there is indeed a shared explanatory factor involved, it cannot be based on the specific institutional features of democracy or monarchy alone. Instead, the explanation would have to fit both equally. This suggests an ideational or constructivist approached based on a broader concept of political similarity that is not intrinsically tied to, for example, the openness of the democratic system or the hereditary succession of monarchies.

As has become evident from the foregoing preliminary descriptive statistical data, there is an intriguing empirical puzzle to match the theoretical research gaps which calls for a focus on monarchies and their foreign policy. Without the prism of monarchism, these empirical patterns might not have been uncovered.

1.4 Questions, hypotheses, and concepts

Given the context of the research problem and the gaps in existing literature outlined earlier, the overarching research question is, what are the typical patterns of monarchical foreign policy in the Middle East, and how can they be explained? This in turn can be broken down into three sub-questions relating to interstate conflict, ingroup relations, and changes in the patterns of making of monarchic foreign policy:

1   What factors shape the interplay between domestic structure and external state behavior in MENA monarchies, especially relating to war and war avoidance?
2   How do MENA monarchies engage in interstate conflict and cooperation?
3   What factors shape the pattern of MENA monarchy interaction over time?

The units of analysis or subjects of investigation are *independent authoritarian monarchical nation-states in the MENA region*, which applies to **Bahrain, Jordan, Kuwait, Morocco, Oman, Qatar, Saudi Arabia**, and the **United Arab Emirates**, which still persist, and the historic monarchical periods of **Egypt, Iraq, Yemen, Libya**, and **Iran** up to the 1950s through to the 1970s. A *monarchy*, originally and etymologically the "rule by one", is here understood as a political system with "a hereditary head of state with life tenure and wide-ranging powers", adapting the definition of Merriam-Webster.[11] Excluded are therefore all 15 Commonwealth monarchies and the 11 European kingdoms, principalities, and grand duchies and other formal monarchies where the head of state performs merely ceremonial functions, such as Japan.[12]

The focus lies on war avoidance patterns of monarchies and intra-monarchic solidarity. The core thesis is that **monarchies do not go to war against one another, because they identify as one ingroup wherein violence has been eliminated as an appropriate method of conflict resolution**. This allows us to situate this monarchic peace inside the broader phenomenon of the similar political systems peace (SPSP). The SPSP is explained through a social identity theory (SIT) approach, which posits that states identifying as members of a shared "community", or ingroup, are restrained from war by ingroup norms. Inside an ingroup, violence has ceased to be a viable option as "interaction has literally eliminated defection (war) as a possibility-where there exists the 'impossibility of imagining violence'" (Abdelal et al. 2006, 697). In view of the small number of both monarchies and interstate wars, the chosen approach is a qualitative comparative multiple case study analysis.

To analyze the monarchic peace as a subtype of the SPSP, the theoretical framework needs to be adapted for monarchies. To answer our main research questions addressing monarchic foreign policy in the region, we connect the empirical observation that no war between two monarchies has ever taken place since 1945 with a SIT-centric theoretical framework that leads to the following hypotheses.

12   *Introduction*

Primary implications of a monarchic peace via SIT – *war* – are supplemented by secondary implications of a monarchic ingroup – *alliance and monarchic solidarity*.

General patterns of foreign policy and the nexus between political system structure and foreign policy behavior:

1   What factors shape the interplay between domestic structure and external state behavior in MENA monarchies, especially relating to war and non-war?

   Hypothesis H_1: monarchies recognize each other as equal and part of the same ingroup, which encourages distinct types of behavior for monarchies toward one another and toward other regimes.

2   How do MENA monarchies engage in interstate conflict and cooperation?

   Hypothesis H_2: ingroup identity leads to ingroup favoritism (but not necessarily outgroup hostility).
   Hypothesis H_{2a}: ingroup favoritism leads to the de-escalation of severe conflicts and crises and thus prevents war.
   Hypothesis H_{2b}: ingroup favoritism leads to monarchic alliance or solidarity beyond ad hoc coalitions.

Change of foreign policy behavior:

3   What factors shape the pattern of MENA monarchy interaction over time?

   Hypothesis H_3: MENA monarchy interaction is shaped by the salience of monarchic ingroup identification, which varies over time.
   Hypothesis H_{3a}: the salience of monarchic ingroup identification is raised in times of crisis when monarchies face a common threat and when they form a (decreasing) minority of states in the region.[13]
   Hypothesis H_{3b}: the salience of monarchic ingroup identification is lowered by a divisive ideology among monarchies.
   Hypothesis H_{3c}: even in periods of low salience, the ingroup bond precludes military action in intra-monarchic conflicts.

There is no clear theoretical expectation of a weighting or ranking of the factors. They are therefore assumed to have equal importance and effect.

To eschew oversimplification and reductionism, monarchism is not meant to be a mono-causal explanation for peace and war in the region but an additional understudied aspect that helps in illuminating previously obscured features. Indeed, omitted factors like resource wealth, geostrategic location, alliance structure, and size go a long way to explaining foreign policy in the region, both of monarchies and of republics. Nevertheless, the lens of regime type difference can explain some of the variance left hitherto unexplained by other shared qualities of the group of states in focus.

Introduction   13

Why should we search for an explanation on the political system level at all? First, as shown earlier, there are group differences in foreign policy behavior and especially war between Middle East monarchies (and even monarchies in general) and Middle East republics. These group differences align more clearly with the monarchy–republic distinction than other overlapping similarities that the respective states share, such as capabilities, economic system, and Western alliance, which also happen to cluster in monarchies. Second, neither this difference nor possible explanations have been explicitly covered in the previously mentioned research literature still marked by the tenacious assumption of monarchic obsolescence. Most importantly, Middle East monarchies fit the ideal type of similar political systems, which makes them a fitting candidate for a test of the SPSP.

In conclusion, we expect to see a less-hostile attitude of monarchies toward other monarchies than toward republics, especially relating to war. We would also expect to see a difference in monarchic solidarity, depending on the overall salience of the monarchic distinction, conditioned by the level of threat toward monarchies, their share in the system, and the presence or absence of a divisive ideology.

1.5 Outline of the book

The book proceeds as follows: Chapter 2 presents the theory and its scope and addresses methodological questions and alternative explanations. The empirical analysis in the form of a multiple comparative case study design applies the theoretical framework in Chapters 3, 4, 5, and 6. Chapter 3 introduces the Middle East monarchies and their interstate and inter-societal relations and presents a plausibility probe of monarchic cohesion in periods of a common threat – the Arab Cold War in the 1950s and 1960s and the Arab Spring after 2011. Because of the high threat level, not only was a shared identity among monarchies especially likely, but it was so strong that it not only impeded war between them but also made them ally against their opponents. This chapter contextualizes the monarchies' conflict and alliance patterns on the regional level and illustrates the theory. Chapter 4 presents two case studies where war between two monarchies was close and a real possibility for external observers, "near misses" of monarchic conflicts, and shows how monarchic ingroup identity contributed to de-escalation. The first case, that of Bahraini-Qatari relations, shows this process between two similar and close monarchies with an established joint identity that therefore shows a particularly clear case of ingroup identification, while the second explores the scope conditions to such an identification and illustrates the emergence of a common identity from previous rivals and even enemies. The two case studies of Chapter 5 conduct "quasi-experiments": if shared monarchy is important for peace, what happens when one monarchy in the pair breaks down and changes its political system? These cases therefore serve to separate the effect of joint monarchism from other factors. Again, the first case is a "more likely" case of ingroup

14 *Introduction*

identification and subsequent breakdown of relations after regime change, namely Iraqi-Kuwaiti relations, which led to an all-out war in the post-monarchic period. The second case explores the limits of monarchic ingroup identification for a dyad that had strong asymmetries even during their jointly monarchic period in the case of Iran and the UAE but still had more cooperative relations than they had after regime change. In Chapter 6, two cases that merit examination and explanation will be shortly discussed: the Saudi–Yemeni War of 1934 and the Qatar Crisis that erupted in 2017. The findings will be summarized and discussed in the final chapter.

Notes

1 Counting only authoritarian monarchies, if all formal monarchies (including the democratic monarchies) are counted, the number is far higher, about 34%–22% (Friske 2007, 125).
2 The data is based on a regional definition that excludes Mauretania, Sudan, and Turkey. Adding these (conflict-prone) republics would provide even stronger evidence of monarchic restraint.
3 Given that the contributions by Jordan and Saudi Arabia to the war effort in the Yom Kippur War of 1973 were merely symbolic (Pollack 2002, 348–350, 433), there is an argument to be made to exclude them, which would put Saudi Arabia in the "once" category, further bolstering the overall tendency.
4 The CoW data set on interstate conflict formed the basis of this paragraph as well, in this case comprising all interstate wars in the Middle East where at least one Middle Eastern state was a direct participant.
5 This is not an indictment of republics in general, because there are various differing subtypes among them that have widely differing rates of conflict participation and initiation (see e.g. Weeks 2012).
6 The uncertainty arises from the missing fatality numbers for the disputes between Egypt and Jordan in June 1948 and between (North) Yemen and Britain in 1949 and 1956–1958.
7 The UCDP defines "armed conflict" as "a contested incompatibility that concerns government and/or territory where the use of armed force between two parties, of which at least one is the government of a state, results in at least 25 battle-related deaths in a year" (Harbom, Melander, and Wallensteen 2008, 700).
8 Even if we include the UK, which for the just-noted reasons belongs to a different category of state, the number merely increases to ten mixed dyads, including one monarchic participant. Six of those reach the highest intensity level of war.
9 Although there is some debate on the differentiation between the two concepts, they will be used here interchangeably (cf. Kailitz and Köllner 2013, 9).
10 Outside the Middle East, further authoritarian monarchies are found in Africa (Lesotho and Swaziland), Asia, and the Pacific (Bhutan, Brunei Darussalam, Cambodia, Malaysia [a federal electoral monarchy], Thailand, and Tonga). Controversial cases include the Vatican and Samoa (cf. Riescher and Thumfart 2008).
11 The contemporary definition of monarchy, as exemplified by the Merriam-Webster encyclopedia is "a government having a hereditary chief of state with life tenure and powers varying from nominal to absolute" (monarchy 2012). Although that definition is somewhat Eurocentric in that it is skewed toward Commonwealth and European monarchies and excludes elective monarchies, of which the UAE (or Malaysia) is a representative, it is sufficiently conceptually narrow to serve as the basis for definition in this work.

Introduction 15

12 A monarchy is considered authoritarian if it scores below 7 on the Polity IV scale or "not free"/"party free" in the Freedom House categorization respectively. The United Arab Emirates is a slightly deviant case in that it is a federation of seven "mini-monarchies", each with its own ruling families; the highest posts are the president and the prime minister and are selected. Still, it is a distinction without a difference for the analysis because the de jure "elected" head of state (president) and head of government (prime minister) of the federation are de facto hereditary since they are customarily occupied by the (hereditary) emirs of Abu Dhabi and Dubai respectively.

13 The two elements can be independent. Because a common threat is as much a matter of perception as of material reality, a decrease in monarchies might enhance the feeling of threat. However, there is no necessary connection since there might be no clear common threat but a decreasing number of monarchies in the region – e.g. when the number of republics rises because of a wave of independence in new states.

References

Abdelal, Rawi, Yoshiko M. Herrera, Alastair Iain Johnston, and Rose McDermott. 2006. "Identity as a Variable." *Perspectives on Politics* 4(4): 695–711.

Acemoglu, Daron, Davide Ticchi, and Andrea Vindigni. 2010. "A Theory of Military Dictatorships." *American Economic Journal: Macroeconomics* 2(1): 1–42.

Al-Khalili, Majid. 2009. *Oman's Foreign Policy*. Westport, CT: Praeger Security International.

Amjad, Mohammed. 1989. *Iran: From Royal Dictatorship to Theocracy*. New York: Greenwood Press.

Anderson, Lisa. 2009. "Absolutism and the Resilience of Monarchy in the Middle East." In *Politics of the Modern Arab World. Critical Issues in Modern Politics. Volume I: State, Power and Political Economy*, ed. Laleh Khalili. London and New York: Routledge.

Bader, Julia. 2015. "Propping up Dictators? Economic Cooperation from China and Its Impact on Authoritarian Persistence in Party and Non-Party Regimes." *European Journal of Political Research* 54(4): 655–72.

Bank, André, Thomas Richter, and Anna Sunik. 2015. "Long-Term Monarchical Survival in the Middle East: A Configurational Comparison, 1945–2012." *Democratization* 22(1): 179–200.

Ben-Dor, Gabriel. 2000. "Patterns of Monarchy in the Middle East." In *Middle East Monarchies – The Challenge of Modernity*, ed. Joseph Kostiner. Boulder, CO; London: Lynne Rienner Publishers, 71–84.

Buzan, Barry, and Ana Gonzalez-Pelaez. 2009. *International Society and the Middle East : English School Theory at the Regional Level*. Basingstoke; New York: Palgrave Macmillan.

Byman, Daniel L, and Jerrold D Green. 1999. "The Enigma Of Political Stability in the Persian Gulf Monarchies." *Middle East Review of International Affairs* 3(3): 20–37.

Demmelhuber, Thomas. 2011. "Political Reform in the Gulf Monarchies. Making Family Dynasties Ready for the 21st Century." *Orient* 52(I): 6–10.

Douglas Stinnett, Jaroslav Tir, Paul Diehl, Philip Schafer, and Charles Gochman. 2002. "The Correlates of War (COW) Project Direct Contiguity Data, Version 3.0." *Conflict Management and Peace Science* 19(2): 59–67.

Erdmann, Gero, André Bank, Bert Hoffmann, and Thomas Richter. 2013. *International Cooperation of Authoritarian Regimes: Toward a Conceptual Framework*. GIGA. www.econstor.eu/handle/10419/77916 (November 11, 2015).

16 Introduction

Fawcett, Louise L'Estrange. 2009. *International Relations of the Middle East*. Oxford; New York: Oxford University Press.

Frisch, Hillel. 2011. "Why Monarchies Persist: Balancing Between Internal and External Vulnerability." *Review of International Studies* 37(1): 167–84.

Friske, Tobias. 2007. "Staatsform Monarchie. Was Unterscheidet Eine Monarchie Heute Noch von Einer Republik?" www.freidok.uni-freiburg.de/volltexte/3325/.

———. 2008. "Monarchien – Überblick Und Systematik." In *Monarchien*, eds. Gisela Riescher and Alexander Thumfart. Baden-Baden: Nomos, 14–23.

Gause, F. Gregory, III. 1994. *Oil Monarchies: Domestic and Security Challenges in the Arab Gulf States*. New York: Council on Foreign Relations Press.

———. 2010. *The International Relations of the Persian Gulf*. Cambridge: Cambridge University Press.

Geddes, Barbara. 1999. "What Do We Know About Democratization After Twenty Years?" *Annual Review of Political Science* 2(1): 115–44.

Geddes, Barbara, Joseph Wright, and Erica Frantz. 2011. "Authoritarian Regimes: A New Data Set."

Halliday, Fred. 2011. *The Middle East in International Relations: Power, Politics and Ideology*. New edition. Cambridge: Cambridge University Press.

Halpern, M. 1963. *The Politics of Social Change in the Middle East and North Africa*. Princeton: Princeton University Press.

Harbom, Lotta, Erik Melander, and Peter Wallensteen. 2008. "Dyadic Dimensions of Armed Conflict, 1946–2007." *Journal of Peace Research* 45(5): 697–710.

Henry, Clement, and Robert Springborg. 2001. *Globalization and the Politics of Development in the Middle East*. Cambridge: Cambridge University Press.

Hess, Steve. 2013. "Single-Party Regimes." In *Authoritarian Landscapes*. New York; Heidelberg; Dordrecht; London: Springer, 41–52.

Hinnebusch, Raymond A., and Anoushiravan Ehteshami. 2002. *The Foreign Policies of Middle East States*. Boulder, CO: Lynne Rienner Publishers.

Hudson, Michael C. 1977. *Arab Politics*. New Haven [u.a.]: Yale University Press.

Huntington, Samuel P. 1966. "The Political Modernization of Traditional Monarchies." *Daedalus* 95(3): 763–88.

———. 1968. *Political Order in Changing Societies*. New Haven: Yale University Press.

———. 1991. *The Third Wave: Democratization in the Late Twentieth Century*. Norman: University of Oklahoma Press.

Kailitz, Steffen, and Patrick Köllner. 2013. "Theorien Und Modelle Der Autokratieforschung" eds. Steffen Kailitz and Patrick Köllner. *Politische Vierteljahresschrift* 47(Sonderheft "Autokratien im Vergleich"): 9–34.

Machiavelli, Nicolo. 2006. *The Prince*. http://gutenberg.org/files/1232/1232-h/1232-h.htm

Maddy-Weizmann, Bruce. 2000. "Why Did Arab Monarchies Fall? An Analysis of Old and New Explanations." In *Middle East Monarchies: The Challenge of Modernity*, ed. Joseph Kostiner. Boulder, CO; London: Lynne Rienner Publishers, 37–52.

Malešević, Siniša. 2014. "Is War Becoming Obsolete? A Sociological Analysis." *The Sociological Review* 62(2_suppl): 65–86.

Malesky, Edmund, Regina Abrami, and Yu Zheng. 2011. "Institutions and Inequality in Single-Party Regimes: A Comparative Analysis of Vietnam and China." *Comparative Politics* 43(4): 409–27.

Maoz, Zeev, and Nasrin Abdolali. 1989. "Regime Types and International Conflict, 1816–1976." *Journal of Conflict Resolution* 33(1): 3–35.

Martín, Félix. 2006. *Militarist Peace in South America: Conditions for War and Peace.* 2006 edition. New York: Palgrave Macmillan.

Mattes, Michaela, and Mariana Rodríguez. 2014. "Autocracies and International Cooperation." *International Studies Quarterly* 58(3): 527–38.

Menaldo, Victor A. 2012. "The Middle East and North Africa's Resilient Monarchs." *The Journal of Politics* 74(3): 707–22.

"Monarchy." 2012. *Merriam-Webster.*

Moshaver, Ziba. 2003. "Revolution, Theocratic Leadership and Iran's Foreign Policy: Implications for Iran-EU Relations." *Review of International Affairs* 3(2): 283–305.

Mozaffari, Mehdi. 1993. "Changes in the Iranian Political System After Khomeini's Death." *Political Studies* 41(4): 611–17.

Odinius, Daniel, and Philipp Kuntz. 2015. "The Limits of Authoritarian Solidarity: The Gulf Monarchies and Preserving Authoritarian Rule During the Arab Spring." *European Journal of Political Research* 54(4): 639–54.

Pollack, Kenneth Michael. 2002. *Arabs at War: Military Effectiveness, 1948–1991.* Lincoln, NE [u.a.]: University of Nebraska Press.

Riescher, Gisela, and Alexander Thumfart. 2008. *Monarchien. Eine Einführung.* Baden-Baden: Nomos.

Roskin, Michael, and James J. Coyle. 2003. *Politics of the Middle East: Cultures and Conflicts.* Upper Saddle River: Pearson/Prentice Hall.

Rubin, Barry, and Judith Colp Rubin. 2004. *Anti-American Terrorism and the Middle East: A Documentary Reader.* Oxford: Oxford University Press.

Russett, Bruce, and John R. Oneal. 2001. *Triangulating Peace: Democracy, Interdependence, and International Organizations.* New York: W. W. Norton & Company.

Sarkees, Meredith Reid, and Wayman. 2010. "Resort to War: 1816–2007. Correlates of War Database." www.correlatesofwar.org

Sharabi, Hisham. 1988. *Neopatriarchy. A History of Distorted Change in Arab Society.* Oxford: Oxford University Press.

Sirin, Cigdem V., and Michael T. Koch. 2015. "Dictators and Death: Casualty Sensitivity of Autocracies in Militarized Interstate Disputes." *International Studies Quarterly* 59(4): 802–14.

Wahman, Michael, Jan Teorell, and Axel Hadenius. 2013. "Authoritarian Regime Types Revisited: Updated Data in Comparative Perspective." *Contemporary Politics* 19(1): 19–34.

Way, Lucan A. 2015. "The Limits of Autocracy Promotion: The Case of Russia in the 'Near Abroad'." *European Journal of Political Research* 54(4): 691–706.

Weeks, Jessica. 2012. "Strongmen and Straw Men: Authoritarian Regimes and the Initiation of International Conflict." *The American Political Science Review* 106(2): 326–47.

———. 2014a. *Dictators at War and Peace.* 1st edition. Ithaca; London: Cornell University Press.

———. 2014b. "Why Cooperate? Authoritarian Cooperation in the International System." *International Studies Quarterly Online.* www.isanet.org/Publications/ISQ/Posts/ID/284/Why-Cooperate-Authoritarian-Cooperation-in-the-International-System (March 12, 2016).

Yom, Sean L., and F. Gregory Gause III. 2012. "Resilient Royals: How Arab Monarchies Hang On." *Journal of Democracy* 23(4): 74–88.

2 Moving beyond democratic exceptionalism

The peace among similar political systems

2.1 Evolution of a concept

We have seen that monarchies are more peaceful toward each other but not necessarily toward other types of systems. To explain both sides of monarchic foreign policy, we need an explanation that is *dyadic*: one that takes both conflict actors into consideration at the same time. Dyadic explanations do not necessarily depend on the specificities of the two regimes that interact but rather focus on characteristics of the interaction itself. If there are different sets of behaviors of monarchies toward other monarchies than toward republics, the conflicting sides must at first recognize the other as different or similar to themselves. This means that they might adapt their behavior depending on what they *know* of their opponent. Given that knowledge is not an objective and unchangeable monolith but highly constructed, social constructivist factors need to be taken into account. This book therefore uses approaches based on social identity theory (SIT). SIT's advantage is that it is not restricted to the specificities of monarchism but instead enables the explanation of a broader phenomenon – the similar political systems peace (SPSP) – of which the monarchic peace (MP) and the related democratic peace (DP) are subtypes.

SPSP approaches, mostly derived from the DPT literature, have been proposed numerous times by various scholars but could not gain traction because of a **misleading specification and operationalization** relating to the understanding of "autocracy" as a type of political system and "similarity". This book is based on an adapted alternative that uses a more nuanced concept of autocracy as well as clearly defined criteria for (political system) similarity.

The democratic peace is the closest thing "we have to an empirical law in international relations" (Levy 1988, 662), or "one of the strongest nontrivial and nontautological generalizations that can be made about international relations" (Russett 1990, 123). It is possibly the most strongly established empirical phenomenon in international relations (IR). All the more surprising, then, that there is still no consensus or even cautious agreement on why it exists (Choi 2016; Ember, Ember, and Russett 1992). This suggests that while the empirical phenomenon persists, the framing and specification might be misconceived and should be re-examined. These previous misspecifications are in large part to blame for the

Moving beyond democratic exceptionalism 19

inability of the alternative conceptualization of the SPSP theorem to reach a wider consensus. The following is an attempt to construct an SPSP concept that does more justice to the empirical phenomenon and thereby revitalizes the concept that can in turn be used to explain the monarchic peace.

After the phenomenon that no two democracies go to war against one another was established as a virtually undisputed empirical fact, the most frequent criticism of DPT revolved around the question of misspecification. The criticism was clustered mostly along three varieties: confounding; (horizontal) special case; and (vertical) sub-case.

The confounding-factor critics have claimed that the democratic peace is not that after all but in fact a capitalist peace (Gartzke 2007), a trade and development peace (Mousseau, Hegre, and O'neal 2003), a cold war or common-interest peace (Farber and Gowa 1995, 1997), or a stable border peace (Gibler 2014): better explained by *third, confounding factors* that are usually found among democratic states without necessarily being directly related to democracy.

The second type of misspecification criticism is that the DPT may be one *special case* of many geographical and historical "zones of peace" (Kacowicz 1998, Ch. 1), e.g. in Northern Europe (Archer 1996), East Asia (Kelly 2012), Africa (Herbst 1990), or South America (Martín 2006), as democracies are also highly clustered geographically (cf. Gartzke and Weisiger 2013, 173).

This book ascribes to the third type of criticism, which asserts that the DPT may be part of a broader phenomenon of which it is a *sub-case*, a peace among politically similar systems (Peceny, Beer, and Sanchez-Terry 2002; Souva 2004; Werner 2000). This concept is referred to here as similar political systems peace (SPSP).[1] The SPSP is a more encompassing theorem than is the DPT, and it can explain a larger universe of cases and events and leads to discoveries of regularities among other than democratic dyads. Therefore, Imre Lakatos's criteria for a "progressive" research program to supersede an older one are met (Lakatos 1970) and the explanatory power of the DPT should be reevaluated.

This by no means implies that we need to throw out all the research and insights that the DPT has helped to uncover with the bathwater of its narrow scope on a subset of a larger class of instances. As Bennett correctly points out, the DPT might still have idiosyncratic features that could be understood and studied independently of the general SPSP (2006, 317). Even if the DPT were a special sub-case of the SPSP, it would not become obsolete, just as Newtonian mechanics has rightly remained in school curricula after the discovery of Einstein's relativity theory. However, the SPSP provides a broader framework helping explain a larger universe of cases of peaceful groups of dyads.

The SPSP is not a novel theory. First hints are already found in early reviews of the DPT literature where a joint institutional similarity effect is found even for dyads that are not democracies. Studies since the 1990s have found evidence of an autocratic peace (e.g. Gleditsch and Hegre 1997; Raknerud and Hegre 1997).

In a 2000 article, Werner made that link explicit and analyzed "political similarity", finding a strong effect even when controlling for joint democracy (Werner 2000). Peceny, Beer, and Sanchez-Terry looked at subtypes of autocracies and

20 *Moving beyond democratic exceptionalism*

found evidence of a dictatorial peace comparable in effect to democratic dyads at least among some subtypes of dictatorships (Peceny, Beer, and Sanchez-Terry 2002). Souva later found that economic similarity is also important for peacefulness, even among politically dissimilar states (Souva 2004). Henderson asserts in probably the strongest terms that the DPT is "simply a subset of peace among politically similar states" (Henderson 2002, 42), after modifying a classic DPT study to include a measure for political dissimilarity. Gartzke and Weisiger provide a more nuanced argument of the dynamic nature of democratic and autocratic peace relative to the overall frequency of democracies or autocracies in the system (2013).

However, the SPSP phenomenon has encountered controversy, with criticism running the gamut from highlighting the greater impact of democratic similarity to a dismissal of the phenomenon altogether. It can be divided into three main groupings: First, an SPSP effect is discernable, but considerably smaller than that of joint democracy (Bennett 2006; Conrad and Souva 2011; Maoz and Abdolali 1989). A second, often overlapping criticism identifies strong regime similarity effects for "coherent" systems, i.e. among highly autocratic or highly democratic regimes (N. Beck, King, and Zeng 2004; Bennett 2006; Kinsella 2005) with a U-distribution. The third group of critics deny any SPSP effect altogether (Bausch 2015; Ray 2005).[2]

This mixed picture points us to the central problem of the specification and operationalization of what scholars referred to as political system similarity (Werner) or institutional similarity (Souva). Werner and Souva, along with most authors who did not find a separate effect of an autocratic or SPSP, do not actually operationalize similar political systems or institutions, but only different degrees of autocracy/democracy, on the basis of the polity scale data set (Marshall, Gurr, and Jaggers 2014 and previous versions). Even-more-recent articles still employ this measure even if they recognize this shortcoming themselves (see e.g. Choi 2016; Dafoe, Oneal, and Russett 2013). Despite various modifications of this measure,[3] none of it is a valid operationalization of political similarity, because it merely differentiates between the degree of authoritarianism.

Authoritarian regimes, however, are highly diverse, much more so than democracies. Since the DPT is still paramount in IR, along with the realist dictum that is blind toward regime differences in general, autocracies are rarely studied with the same degree of nuance and sophistication as democracies are, in striking difference to the sub-field of CP.[4]

Most democracies (especially "coherent" ones) undoubtedly share various similarities, being politically pluralist and participatory, with similar institutions, mostly Western and mostly economically powerful states, clustering in certain geographic regions. This gives rise to the frequent criticism invoked at the beginning that it is a (confounding-factor) similarity different from "democraticness" that induces dyadic peacefulness.

Looking beyond the democratic backyard, there is not nearly the same level of similarity among systems as diverse as North Korea, Morocco, or the misleadingly named Democratic Republic of Congo. What has long been recognized and

Moving beyond democratic exceptionalism 21

ameliorated in autocracy research, namely that the great scope and heterogeneity of the different systems make their grouping together as autocracies or authoritarian states inadequate to explain their behavior and vulnerabilities (Geddes 1999; cf. Levitsky and Way 2002; Schedler 2006), has so far not taken hold in IR and FPA literature. Geddes's famous dictum that "different kinds of authoritarianism break down in characteristically different ways" (Geddes 1999, 117) is applicable to foreign policy behavior as well: "different kinds of authoritarianism make war and peace in characteristically different ways" too.[5] The criticism that autocracy is more diverse and heterogeneous than democracy and cannot be adequately covered by a dichotomous or continuous operationalization was already voiced as early as 1995 by Hermann and Kegley (1995, 519–520), before even the first consolidated SPSP study, but could so far not shake the deficient operationalization along the democracy–autocracy continuum or dichotomy. Bridging the fields of international relations and comparative politics is therefore an important task.

This misspecification explains the mixed review that the SPSP received in IR literature and the common finding that the effect is strongest on the edges – highly jointly democratic and highly jointly autocratic states – itself another hint of the lack of differentiation among autocratic regimes. While extremely autocratic regimes might indeed resemble each other more since a high level of autocratic control and lack of audience costs might produce structurally similar, e.g. personalists systems, this would not apply to less-autocratic regimes per se, which would still be more heterogeneous.

In the words of Steve Chan, "how similar or different the regimes in a dyad are from each other offers itself as a relevant factor for future analysis" (Chan 1997, 83). But what exactly constitutes difference or similarity? Since autocracies are more heterogeneous than democracies are, we must find more adequate measures for similarity by looking at different regime subtype dyads as possible other subcases of the SPSP, along with the DPT. Two of the studies most favorably disposed toward a possible SPSP are, as would be expected from the argument made earlier, those with a more sophisticated understanding of similarity.

Peceny et al., following Geddes (1999), break up the autocracies into three types: personalist, military, and single party (2002). Because the Geddes data set used by the authors does not yet include monarchies, they are excluded or lumped into the "mixed" category. The results show evidence for a sort of dictatorial peace, especially among military and personalist systems. The caveats that the authors apply are related mainly to the rarity of war and some of the regime subtypes and therefore the tenuousness of the statistical effect, not to any lack of effect per se.

Souva then reverts to the polity scale to measure political similarity but employs an additional measure of economic similarity and finds that systems that are both politically and economically similar are especially unlikely to confront each other militarily (2004). Having two measures of similarity enhances the chances of having a valid depiction of similar regimes as it adds more markers of similarity. Using such a broadened measure of similarity would therefore clearly distinguish between regimes like Saudi Arabia and North Korea, which have similar

22   *Moving beyond democratic exceptionalism*

polity scores but dissimilar economic (and political) systems. While presenting a more valid and robust operationalization for large-n studies that necessitate broad encompassing categories, it is still far from a fleshed-out concept of similarity.

There is a limited number of studies critical of the SPSP that recognize and tackle this major problem. The most nuanced critique is provided by Conrad and Souva (2011), who only find consistent results for joint democracy but inconsistent results for other kinds of joint similarity. Recognizing the problems in lumping all autocracies together, the authors test not only joint coherence, on the basis of polity scores, but also two other operationalizations – that is, institutional regime similarity, on the basis of a typology consisting of democracy, monarchy, single-party system, military dictatorship, and personalist system, and audience costs, on the basis of a slightly different typology with mixed non-democracy replacing personalist and dynastic monarchy replacing monarchy. This leads to a more nuanced although still-not-determining picture: the evidence points to peaceful effects among socialist dyads, single-party dyads, and monarchic dyads, although they are not seen across all models and specifications employed, due mostly to the small number of cases in some types of non-democratic dyads.[6] The weaker evidence for other kinds of SPSP is therefore a problem of data availability, not of lack of effect per se. Joint democracy is always significant, in part because there is a far larger set of onset cases to draw inferences from. A lack of significance might thus rather be a consequence of the data in use than of a random distribution.[7]

AN SPSP concept based on social identity theory: ingroup/outgroup identification influences foreign policy behavior

In light of the discussed methodological problems, the evidence against SPSP does not seem that strong after all. To obtain a valid test, we need to adapt the specification and operationalization of political similarity among autocracies. Reconceptualizing the empirical patterns as SPSP and respecifying similarity might help retest the SPSP in quantitative studies similar to those already conducted with the old conceptualization. It is, however, not enough to revitalize the struggling theorem; a convincing causal pathway is called for. Distinct approaches attempting to explain an SPSP are circulating, many of them adopted and adapted from the DPT.

If there is a common mechanism that explains DP and MP, it cannot be exclusively applicable to democracy (or monarchy).[8] Conrad and Souva identify three strands of theoretical approaches applicable to other than just joint democracies:

1   Institutional coherence approaches (similar level of autocracy – separate peace)
2   Audience costs approaches (similar level of audience costs generated – separate peace)
3   Institutional political similarity (similar systems – separate peace) (2011, 8).

Coherence approaches have already been shown to inadequately portray the heterogeneity in autocratic systems. Audience cost approaches are additive and

Moving beyond democratic exceptionalism   23

not inherently dyadic. In general, normative and institutionalist approaches are mostly democracy-specific and exhibit an additive effect – not an inherently dyadic one.[9]

Ideational or social constructivist approaches, embedded in the political similarity literature, have the greatest potential to explain dyadic behavior because they explicitly entail the dimension of interaction and mutual perception. Theorists of this brand of IR assume that "soft" factors like identity, role, and norms are at least as important for the behavior of states as are institutions and power relations (Reus-Smit 2009; Wendt 1992).

How states act toward each other and in general is significantly shaped by their self-image/identity and their image of their interaction partner, the "other". The most likely candidate to explain behavior driven by identity is social identity theory (SIT) (Conrad and Souva 2011; Gartzke and Weisiger 2013; Hermann and Kegley 1995; Tajfel 1974, 1982; Weart 1998). Social identities are "sets of meanings that an actor attributes to itself while taking the perspective of others, that is, as a social object" (MCCall and Simmons 1978, 61–100, cited in: Wendt 1994, 385) or, following a liberalist view a "set of preferences shared by individuals" that shapes a set of interests representing these rational actors' preferences (Moravcsik 1997, 517, 525).

Originally a micro-level psychological concept, the point of departure of SIT is that identity is constructed against a "significant other" with collective identity distinguishing between the ingroup and the outgroup (Dovidio, Gaertner, and Validzic 1998; Tajfel 1974). And "apparently, the mere fact of division into groups is enough to trigger discriminating behavior", even when that division is based on arbitrary factors such as a preference for the modern painters Paul Klee or Wassily Kandinsky (Tajfel 1970, 96) or in which of two buses one happened to arrive (Sherif 2010). This concept can be applied to large-scale social groups, including nations and states – as Tajfel intended from the outset (Robinson and Tajfel 1996, 66). This lends itself handily to an analysis of groups of similar political systems who form the ingroup, while non-similar states are conceptualized as the outgroup.

These processes are set in motion even without direct contact or even personal knowledge of the other, designation as other being enough. As self-worth is linked more closely to the group identity, the incentive to protect the group becomes stronger (cf. Hermann and Kegley 1995, 517–518). Group identity has real behavioral consequences, with ingroup favoritism and outgroup discrimination and hostility often occurring simultaneously – ingroup "love" and outgroup "hate", in Marilynn Brewer's terms (1999, 442). Although outgroup hostility is not an unavoidable outcome of ingroup identity building (Brewer 1999; Oakes 2002), it can accelerate in the event of a common threat or a salient external pressure (cf. Gibler, Hutchison, and Miller 2012, 1657), which has to be perceived "by the population at large as a serious societal danger" (Gibler, Hutchison, and Miller 2012, 1659). External pressure does not mean here that the threat cannot have an internal source, even if it has been triggered from outside. This is especially germane for the Middle East, where regional foreign policy was "chiefly used to

24 *Moving beyond democratic exceptionalism*

counter domestic threats: either regimes used anti-imperialistic rhetoric to shore up their fragile legitimacy or they sought protection from the Western powers against domestic opposition" (Hinnebusch and Ehteshami 2002, 34).

Inside an ingroup, violence has ceased to be a viable option because "interaction has literally eliminated defection (war) as a possibility-where there exists the 'impossibility of imagining violence'" (Abdelal et al. 2006, 697), with the potential to explain peace inside the monarchic ingroup. Ingroup bias is greater the more important the relevant attribute to the social identity of its members is and the more comparable the outgroup is to the ingroup (Tajfel 1978, 250), a finding that can be applied to political systems and regime types that are easily compared to each other.

However, an ingroup identity does not depend on complete sameness or assimilation; rather, intragroup differences exist and are vital for the individual members. Belonging to an ingroup also does not mean that every member is equally important or that the group is acephalous (see e.g. Hogg 1996, 80–83). In short, the sameness is perceived in terms of an "equality in kind", not an "equality in power" or importance.

Transferring a micro-level concept onto the state level

But how can a psychological or sociological theory for groups of individuals be translated from the first to the third image (Waltz 2001) – as states are not just "people, too"? Under certain conditions, applying anthropomorphous traits to states can be appropriate. First, Tajfel himself intended his theory of intergroup relations to apply to large-scale social groups, including nations, from the outset (Robinson and Tajfel 1996, 66). Second, social constructivist theoreticians in IR have already applied social identity theory to states – Alexander Wendt explicitly notes the possible impact of collective identification, i.e. "*identification* with the fate of the other" (Wendt 1994, 385, emphasis in original) through "shared norms and political culture" (1994, 386). This can form a positive collective identity – the basis for "friendship" (Wendt 1999, ch. 7). The literature on security communities takes this at its point of departure (Deutsch 1957) and recognizes the importance of identity building against an "other" (Adler and Barnett 1998, 56). Michael Barnett carved out the importance of group identities for the Arab alliance system (Barnett 1996), and transnational and subnational identities have been shown to affect foreign policy in the Middle East (Telhami and Barnett 2002). Role-theoretical analyses also apply these group-centered identification processes to state behavior (cf. Harnisch, Frank, and Maull 2011).

Ingroup–outgroup explanations have been used explicitly by proponents of DPT and SPSP (Gartzke and Weisiger 2013; Hermann and Kegley 1995; Souva 2004; Weart 1998). As Owen states, "democracies recognize one another and refuse to fight on that basis" (J. M. Owen 1994, 96). One of the most extensive and comprehensive accounts of the DPT takes ingroup identification as the primary explanatory prism and claims that certain states are peaceful toward each other because they recognize each other as equal (in kind) (Weart 1994). This examination also shows that ingroup–outgroup identification is not exclusive to

Moving beyond democratic exceptionalism 25

democracies. Spencer Weart claims in his work, elaborated in a course of extensive historical examination and covering sources from antiquity to the present, that established territorial republics of the same type, democracy or oligarchy, (almost) never wage war against one another (1998, 14).[10]

In addition, empirical findings from other fields substantiate the effect of large-group similarity on foreign policy behavior. Experiments confirm that popular acceptability to use force against a country becomes stronger when it is not perceived as "one of their kind" (Mintz and Geva 1993), leading back to the original micro-foundation of SIT. This conforms to the findings on the tendency to ally and refrain from force among politically similar (via common culture or common regime type) systems (Lai and Reiter 2000; Siverson and Emmons 1991), which is corroborated for democracies and for autocracies (Koschut 2012).

Finally, micro-level approaches are directly applicable to *leader-centric analysis* and *regime-centric analysis*, as is the case here. The importance of individual leaders is often underestimated in IR (Hermann and Kegley 1995; Lebow 2010). This is particularly true for autocracies, because ultimately, the leaders' perception is decisive.

This is one of the reasons why Middle Eastern monarchies lend themselves especially well to SIT-style approaches. Since they exhibit an especially high level of personalization, comparable only to the "presidents for life" in some Arab republics (R. Owen 2012), they are especially suited to a leader-centric analysis. Monarchs often stayed in power for decades, shaping the modern states decisively and rarely delegating too many powers. Personal relationships often form the basis of agreements and formal relations, and thus, the human traits of the monarch and their inner foreign policy circle are more easily transferrable to the state level. In addition, the monarch is also usually the prime decision maker, especially in foreign policy. Even in more open and liberalized states, foreign policy is usually conducted by a small circle of people; this is even more true for the highly untransparent authoritarian monarchies in the MENA. As Ayubi states, "Foreign relations are obviously a domain reserved exclusively for the family", where even the office of the foreign and defense minister is in general either occupied by the monarch or by a close relative (Ayubi 1995, 230). In this analysis, the monarchs and their immediate regime members are the identification actors because *their perception of their counterparts* counts in foreign policy decision-making, especially in times of crisis.

This work therefore follows the call by Valerie Hudson: since the particularities of decision makers are vital to understanding foreign policy choice they "should not remain as undigested idiosyncrasies (as in traditional single-country studies) but should rather be incorporated as instances of larger categories of variation in the process of actor-specific theory-building" (Hudson 2005, 7).

A definition of political similarity

INSTITUTIONAL SIMILARITY

But what exactly could constitute an ingroup among states? How is an "other" constructed? In other words, what constitutes political systems similarity that

26 *Moving beyond democratic exceptionalism*

engenders peace? The first criterion is the most obvious one and one that recurs in large parts of the earlier-cited research: politically similar regimes must be *institutionally similar*. This does not mean, however, that their degree of democraticness or autocraticness is the primary distinction or of any importance at all. Rather, a more complex view of institutional similarity revolves around the specificities of the political system. Second, regimes must be *ideationally similar*, which includes immaterial factors such as a common culture, history, religion, etc. Third, and most importantly, they must recognize each other as similar – *perception of similarity* becoming the third criterion.

The *type of political system* or regime (sub)type is a particularly salient similarity characteristic and therefore a relevant criterion of difference and similarity for various reasons. First, it is clearly visible across borders and combines "malleability and staying power" (Gartzke and Weisiger 2013, 175).[11] Second, a rival or enemy with a different type of political system than one's own can appear particularly threatening. As illustrated by Stalin's infamous dictum "Whoever occupies a territory also imposes his own social system on where his army arrives. It could not be any different",[12] such an opponent is a double threat: to both the territorial integrity of the state and the stability of the regime. They can do this by military conquest, by increasing "the costs of enforcing the state's particular set of institutions" (Werner and Lemke 1997, 532), or by promoting the interests of internal rivals of the leader (Werner and Lemke 1997, 533). Third, given that similar institutions are either the consequence of or the origin of a similar worldview or ideology, institutionally similar states have a similar outlook on the world and thus simply fewer issues of disagreement (Souva 2004; Werner 2000). Fourth, regime stability as a prime driver of foreign policy is tied to regime legitimation: the imperative to be seen as a "good" system is important for regime survival. This leads not only to war avoidance but also to alliance: if regimes are "good", then helping out a similar system must be good too. Also, being part of a broader movement or club bolsters legitimacy because it justifies its own political principles as accepted and prevalent (Walt 1985, 20). A last but crucial point why regime type similarity rather than any other important similarity between two states should be examined within this particular framework is that regimes are responsible for conducting foreign policy and are thus especially likely to be a reference for decision makers who are responsible for foreign policy and ultimately for war and peace.

But bare institutional similarity is not enough: Conrad and Souva emphasize that to better account for similarity, instead of preference similarity from similar political institutions "a broader institutional similarity, common culture, shared threat, economic wealth, or some combination of these factors may better influence preference similarity and the likelihood of conflict" (Conrad and Souva 2011, 26).

IDEATIONAL SIMILARITY

Some of these immaterial traits have been studied as a basis for a feeling of commonality and explanatory lenses for bilateral relations, such as the classic

Moving beyond democratic exceptionalism 27

Anglo-American special relationship. Cultural and linguistic commonality was invoked: "though the American people are very largely foreign, both in origin and in modes of thought, their rulers are almost exclusively Anglo-Saxons, and share our political ideas" (Lord Cecil 1917, cited in: Reynolds 1985, 2). *Common history* was also invoked: "History, tradition, affinity have been crucial to the alliance, rather than peripheral" (Dawson and Rosecrance 1966, 41).

A study focusing on the Confucian Long Peace, from 1644 to 1839, finds a separate peace between the similar political systems of China and its Confucian neighbors (Kelly 2012). Kelly claims that their common culture generates a "we-ness", a self-perception of an "imagined community" that, combined with the Confucian anti-war ethic, leads to peaceful behavior within this group of states not present in encounters outside the group. The author even mentions the Arab state system as a possible candidate for another "zone of peace" via cultural similarity and finds corroborating evidence. However, the evidence is weak, because all the different types of Arab states are lumped together. While pointing to the importance of a cultural link, this strengthens the argument that common culture, language, and history are apparently not sufficient for a separate peace, same as institutional "coherence".

PERCEPTION OF SIMILARITY AND SALIENCE

Institutional and ideational or cultural similarity need to be combined to find similar political systems. In the end, however, the only definitional hallmark of political similarity is whether the leaders of states (or their publics) consider their counterpart as similar to themselves or not (cf. Hermann and Kegley 1995) – *perception* of similarity – under the condition that they "believe" that ideology shapes international alignment (Walt 1985, 25). The other criteria merely help delimitate where to look for this perception but only form can necessary, not sufficient, definitional conditions.

Perception of similarity would be sufficient to classify the members of a dyad as politically similar, but it is notoriously hard to study and prove. Nevertheless, it has also been highlighted in DPT literature when controversial cases of possible war among democracies were resolved by establishing that the rivals did indeed not recognize each other as democracies, a perception contributing to war (J. M. Owen 1994; Weart 1998).

States can be similar in countless ways, e.g. culturally, linguistically, by religion, by geography and climate, economically, by political organization, by institutions, and by culture. But the perception of similarity is crucial to understanding which commonality is salient enough to affect foreign policy behavior in the particular context at the particular time under consideration. It is one characteristic that can help us distinguish and understand when to use a typology consisting of military, single-party, personalist, and monarchic regimes, when to look at Muslim, Catholic, or Hindu identities, and when at Russophone and Ukrainophone polities.

Even when looking exclusively at different regime types for the reasons just cited, *salience*, i.e. the simultaneous existence of a comparable or contrasting

28 *Moving beyond democratic exceptionalism*

category (Turner and Oakes 1986), defines when a democracy/non-democracy difference has become politically relevant or when regime subtype distinctions matter more. If an identity has a higher salience, it is more likely to be acted on. A higher salience of a shared quality enhances the perception of belonging to that category with others. Fluidity and amenability to change with different identities alternating and overlapping is an essential characteristic of ingroup and outgroup identity. and capturing this change is a prime challenge to any theoretical framework.

In the following case studies, political system similarity pertaining to the structural dimension of similarity as opposed to perception will be operationalized by three indicators, to capture a multidimensional similarity between two states (or, more precisely, their ruling and decision-making elites). In case of dissimilarity, numerous dimensions are absent or underdeveloped. This step is important because identity, while constructed, is not infinitely flexible but rather is based on and restricted by physical and material attributes that are resistant to change, including geography, size, language, ethnicity, etc. (Chafetz, Spirtas, and Frankel 1998, xi). The three indicators are as follows:

1.1 Shared language, culture, history and religion
1.2 Similar political system (monarchy)

> In the cases analyzed here, a similar political system is defined by regime subtype. For monarchies, this implies that their heads of state have a hereditary title and rule and reign (authoritarian monarchies). Other state institutions, such as parliaments or consultative assemblies, might be present but must be subordinated to the monarch and/or the ruling family.

1.3 Similar economic system

> A comparable economic system often goes hand in hand with a similar political system. Nevertheless, having a similar economic system helps in establishing clear expectations by ingroup members and fostering similar interest preferences.

Constraints and catalysts to monarchic salience: the waxing and waning of the "royal club"

Although neither institutional similarity nor a common culture necessarily brings about a perception of similarity, three main conditions can be identified that either catalyze or obstruct the perception of similarity of institutionally similar systems and thus condition the salience of the type of political system shared by the ingroup members:

1 *Common threat*. This binds an ingroup together against a common enemy and induces a "rally-around-the-flag" (or, in this case, throne) effect. A common threat against monarchies either threatens the survival of their states

or the survival of their regimes or ruling dynasties and thus can have external (e.g. radical pan-Arabism incited by republican presidents) or internal sources (e.g. opposition groups that aim to overthrow the monarchy). In case of mixed dyads in the "quasi-experiment" cases, this category indicates whether there is a common threat against the group of states of the alternative potentially shared identity post-regime change (e.g. against Arab or Muslim states). Although this factor is often emphasized in the literature, it is not a necessary condition for a shared identity to emerge (Chafetz, Spirtas, and Frankel 1998, xiii).

2 *Divisive ideology.* This posits a hierarchy inside a community and thus legitimizes the leadership of one member over the others, which prevents identification as equals and incited conflict over hegemony (Walt 1985, 21–23).[13] Since this posited hierarchy threatens regime survival for all other members, even the most institutionally similar political systems are less likely to develop a shared perception of similarity and therefore refrain from escalation. This effect explains the harsh rivalries among many communist and pan-Arabist regimes, such as the Ba'th-ruled Iraq and Syria (Walt 1985, 21–23) and the Sino-Soviet border conflict of 1969. Walt admits that it is absent among democracies and monarchies (Walt 1985, 23), which are thus predisposed to the development of an ingroup.

3 *Overall distribution of difference and sameness.* If the ingroup expands to an extent that there are barely any "others" left against which to build an *ego* identity, alternative identifications are likely to emerge – this is an argument behind the claim that the democratic peace will subside if the quantity of democracies rises above a certain threshold (Gartzke and Weisiger 2013, 175). To measure the effect of this condition, monarchic salience is assumed to heightened if monarchies constitute a minority and/or a decreasing share of states in the reference regional system.

This principle of dynamic shifting allegiances via varying identification is further backed by ethnographic evidence and known as "fission and fusion" (Neel and Salzano 1967) in cultural anthropology. It is best embodied in the Arab proverb "me against my brother, me and my brother against my cousin, me and my cousin against the stranger"[14] and refers to the dynamics of large units and subunits in interaction with internal or external units where allegiances change as the reference category changes, usually in tribal or clan societies consisting of multiple lineages.[15] Who bonds together is thus determined by who the "other" is in the given context.

Summing up the first step of the causal mechanism, **similar political systems are characterized by similar regime types; a common culture, language, and history; a similar economic system; and the perception of belonging into the same category.** Furthermore, **a shared threat, a low prevalence of the respective type of political system, and lack of divisive ideology strengthen that perception**, although not all factors have to be present at all times. This definition is a highly flexible one, characterized by a Wittgensteinian family resemblance

30 *Moving beyond democratic exceptionalism*

rather than by a monothetic classification. This makes perceived political similarity a multidimensional concept combining institutional and ideational elements that can accommodate and explain changes over time better than static approaches can.

When we apply this definition to the monarchic peace, authoritarian monarchies in general undoubtedly become similar political systems. They share a regime type, a political culture, a common alliance with the West, and for the most part similar economic systems. In the Middle East, the area with the highest remaining concentration of monarchies, they also accrue a common history, religion, culture, and (excluding monarchic Iran) language.

But that does not automatically mean that monarchy becomes a salient joint characteristic. In case of a low salience of monarchic identity, other communalities might be more relevant for foreign policy behavior (Arab ethnicity, Islam, local or tribal identities, etc.), and the monarchic identity does not necessarily translate into foreign policy behavior of any kind. If its salience is high, it is expected to influence foreign policy behavior, most notably vital decisions like war initiation. The higher the salience, the more politically relevant the identity becomes. This raises the likelihood that foreign policy decisions of a lower level are also affected, resulting in secondary implications of a monarchic peace, such as monarchic solidarity. As there is no clearly defined threshold for salience "sufficient" for an ingroup identification to arise, and the effect of the enumerated factors is additive, with none expected to be automatically stronger than the others; any combination of them might be sufficient for a salient monarchic (or otherwise similar in case of studies of mixed dyads) identity to emerge.

How that translates into perception of similarity and how this perception is developed and affirmed will be examined in the following section and illustrated empirically in Chapter 3.

How ingroup identification leads to de-escalation

While the statistics in the introduction showed a clear negative peace as an absence of war, the SPSP framework also implies a positive definition of a stable peace as "a situation in which the probability of war is so small that is does not really enter into the calculations of any of the people involved" (Boulding 1978, 13). If similar political systems do not wage war against each other, they must either have less conflictual relations (e.g. due to fewer issues of disagreement, as prior SPSP researchers suggested [Souva 2004; Werner 2000]) or, as is the interpretation followed by this book, have additional ways to de-escalate crises in existing conflicts that dissimilar systems do not necessarily possess.

This second interpretation is easier to trace because fewer cases are needed and because the comparison of levels of non-military conflict would pose significant methodological and ontological challenges, but more importantly, it emphasizes that **absence of war does not mean absence of conflict** – even with fewer conflict issues, there always remains the possibility of at least a few serious conflicts

Moving beyond democratic exceptionalism 31

to arise, which seems to conform to reality. The Middle East, and especially the Arabian Peninsula, is a highly conflict-ridden region – yet conflicts still fail to escalate into wars. Third, SIT implies a different code of conduct *in case of conflict* rather than the elimination of conflict issues – as "interaction has literally eliminated defection (war) as a possibility-where there exists the 'impossibility of imagining violence'" (Abdelal et al. 2006, 697) inside an ingroup. **It is not the absence of conflict that calls for an explanation – the actual puzzle is why all of these conflicts have never escalated to the extent of overstepping the threshold of war and rarely led to any sort of military confrontation, whereas other conflicts in the region frequently did.**

Given that war is a rare event – even among the most dissimilar of systems – there are, of course, multitudes of pathways toward peace. Ingroup identification is only one additional path to de-escalation. It is not non-war per se that needs explaining but rather the "concentration" or "overrepresentation" of non-war among certain types of states. Escalation to war is not a given for dissimilar dyads in the same way that alliance is not a given for similar ones. In fact, the conflicts on the Arabian Peninsula often hamper intra-monarchic alliances: "Cooperation among the Gulf monarchies themselves – a natural thing given their common domestic backgrounds, regional vulnerabilities, and international orientation – is complicated by historical disputes among the dynasties" (Gause 1994, 120–121). However, the same mechanism that supports de-escalation should also make cooperation and long-term alignment among ingroup members more likely, albeit not assured. To trace the effects of a different code of conduct inside the ingroup, we need to identify the *social processes of ingroup identification*. Once there are enough structural similarities and monarchic identity is salient, an ingroup (via perception as equals) is likely to develop. Once it develops, it needs to be sustained to remain relevant. To ascertain whether this development has indeed taken place, indicators capturing both **ingroup development and affirmation** need to be found. Given that perception is difficult to measure, the indicators should be highly varied to allow for an intersubjective analysis. The numbered elements here follow a general causal and roughly chronological sequence, as expected from the theoretical framework.

1 Mutual recognition

Mutual recognition is often the first step toward an ingroup development because it indicates an acceptance and recognition of equality of status between two states. Yet it is not a sufficient condition for ingroup development, because it is the default in international relations, regardless of the level of conflict between states. States that mutually recognize each other diplomatically might still see each other as illegitimate or fair game. Recognition is preceded by the consolidation of borders and state institutions, which is a scope condition (see section 2.3). Before the consolidation of the nation-state, imperial expansionary logic trumps nation-state territorial logic and makes conflict much more likely even in the case of an existing ingroup identification.

32   *Moving beyond democratic exceptionalism*

In the case of regime change, this indicator also clarifies whether there has been a cut or downgrading of diplomatic relations. Similar to the limited expressiveness of the absence of mutual recognition, a rupture might merely be a short-lived escalation that does not indicate longer-term deterioration of relations in a dyad, but merely a restricted crisis. A withdrawal of recognition is still a strong indicator of escalation, but an existing recognition is a weak indicator of a joint identification.

2   *Personalization of bonds between ruling elites (especially rulers)*

Personalized bonds between rulers and other decision makers are the basis that fosters ingroup development. Intensive personal bonds regularize and normalize interaction and are instrumental in clearing misunderstandings directly before they can become detrimental to the bilateral relationship. There are numerous avenues by which personalization happens, but the analysis will focus on the following three:

Frequent high-level state visits

Frequent high-level indicate regular and normalized contact between elites. The more personal interactions on the political level, the easier it is for other types of bonds, like intermarriage and friendship, to ensue. On the other hand, other types of bonds might induce more frequent visits. If bilateral relations sour, particularly among dissimilar regimes that have little incentive to prioritize cooperation over conflict, less-direct exchange between rulers or their representatives is expected. However, this is a weak indicator only for a rupture because visit frequency in general depends on the quality of bilateral relations at a given time. Explicitly boycotting visits indicate tense relations.

Kinship, intermarriage, and friendship bonds

Personalized bonds beyond the political sphere entangles political elites, who become more interdependent, and if groups of people overlap, the similarities between different polities and regimes are heightened as well, and thus, alliance becomes more likely. Intimate bonds also humanize the "other", and trust can develop more easily, especially in personalized political systems like monarchies in the Middle East, where personal relations are valued more highly than institutional formalities and official positions and ranks. Each of these makes violence more likely to be seen as an illegitimate instrument as the other becomes part of an actual or metaphorical "family". It is no accident that marriages were often pursued for political reasons, both in the high times of European monarchies and among royal elites in the Middle East today.

The personalization level between ruling elites also decreases if no or little new close unofficial relations develop among them or if old existing relations rupture. This is especially likely in the case of monarchic breakdown, because monarchies often exhibit a degree of intermarriage that is not continued by republican elites.

Shared socialization

Personal relationships and a shared education system or process shape the worldview of the decision-making elite, leading to a more similar outlook and ruling ideology among individuals who went through the same socialization. It shapes perceptions of the other and fosters common ideas, preferences, and conflict-resolution approaches (Peceny, Beer, and Sanchez-Terry 2002, 19). This in turn makes ingroup identification more likely. Socialization can take place in palace schools, the military, or traditional education, forging elite solidarity at the top (cf. Ayubi 1995, 245).

There are two main ways that the socialization of (ruling) elites are hampered after a regime change in one member of a dyad. First, the new ideology used to legitimize the new system is incompatible with prior ways of preparing, e.g. future monarchs for ruling (e.g. the changes in power access, recruitment, social composition, and desirable traits and values brought about by the installation of Arab nationalist ideologies after coups). Second, there is a different predisposition toward the prestige of education institutions (e.g. the sending of political elites to British educational facilities preferred by the monarchs was transformed into a preference for education facilities in Arab nationalist states, e.g. Egypt, in the first decades following anti-monarchic and anticolonial revolutions).

3   *Affirmation (or denial) of commonality*

Because identification is a fluid and social process, it is not a given once it has developed, but rather, it has to be strengthened and reaffirmed to remain normatively relevant. Affirmation serves the double purpose of signaling to oneself and others (both other ingroup members and sometimes outgroups) who belongs together and on what grounds and of reaffirming and reifying an existing community or ingroup.[16] It defines and shapes common identity over time. There are many ways that a shared identity can be reified, and the following three will form the main indicators used here.

The breakdown of the dyadic relationship not only means a passive lack of reification of communality but in general also an active othering process, i.e. the negation of similarity and the emphasis and consolidation of difference.

Kinship and family references

"Family" is one of the most exclusive and solidarity-demanding "clubs" there is. Such references between elites are therefore vital to identifying where such a solidarity club has formed. Of special importance are repeated appeals to family membership toward rivals or opponents. To enable war against an "other", a process of "othering" must take place, usually in a dehumanizing or demonizing manner. If, however, opponents consistently refer to each other as family, especially in fraternal terms (as these imply equality in contrast to, e.g., parents–offspring asymmetry), de-escalation is more likely. Family members might be rivals, but not

34 *Moving beyond democratic exceptionalism*

enemies, and therefore, military attack is unacceptable to them, but it may be possible against outsiders. It is especially often found among the Gulf monarchies, who "resort to 'organic' concepts such as family, kind, neighborhood and community, in the attachment to custom and tradition, and in the nostalgia for the past" (Ayubi 1995, 244), but it can be seen across other states as well.[17]

Family rhetoric toward populaces, a frequent occurrence in republics rather than between regimes and its elites, serves a different function and is therefore not counted as an instance of kinship rhetoric here. Popular interests are different from regime interests and can be played against each other, which does not necessarily preclude interstate conflict.

Emphasis on similarity over difference

Similar arguments can be used for this indicator as a somewhat weaker measure of "friendship" instead of "family". An othering discourse and following escalation are far less likely if acknowledged similarities outweigh perceived and acknowledged differences. If the level of conflict rises, usually differences are accentuated more than similarities. If this does not occur, the ingroup must be sufficiently well developed to recognize that conflict is present but can (and should) be contained. The valuing of similarity over difference can be seen in, e.g., refraining from othering by, e.g., emphasizing different ethnic or confessional differences.

The opposite, and an indicator for the breakdown of ingroup identity, are instances of othering, e.g. excommunication of the community and, at the most extreme, dehumanizing and demonizing rhetoric. In these cases, differences are more likely to be emphasized or exaggerated, especially along salient identity lines like ethnicity or sect/religion.

References to shared historical narratives

The importance of this indicator lies in that it is not merely the mere historiographic past and similar events that foster a joint identity but how the past is pictured and perceived, i.e. if historical narratives, such as about (anti)colonialism and shared alignment patterns, are similar. Monarchies and republics in the Middle East have highly intertwined histories but interpret and value different events and developments differently. This is a result of a different worldview that might hinder ingroup identification. A similar worldview will more likely result in more similar alliance patterns and political priorities fostering mutual peacefulness. A shared view of history leads to a similar outlook on the future and possibly even a "community of fate". Given that the worldview shapes preferences and identity, it is an important factor in determining whether regimes are similar enough to develop a shared identity.

In mixed dyads with no ingroup identification, another indicator for disassociation is the use of competing constructions of identity, especially in historical narratives.

Moving beyond democratic exceptionalism 35

Common ceremonies and shared institutions based on identity
To make up for the problems associated with measuring similarity perception via public speeches, another type of indicator is also used: the affirmation of common bonds via shared ceremonies that reify shared identity. As Lisa Wedeen notes, spectacles, a subtype of public ceremonies, are "systems of signification and community" and "functional strategies to enforce dominance and construct community" (Wedeen 1999, 13). Ceremonies and rituals can vary in their level of regulation and structure. They can be singular events, like the Persepolis Celebrations of the Shah of Iran, celebrating, defining, and reifying monarchic tradition or regular events with established protocols, like succession festivities, royal weddings, or funerals. On the most institutionalized end of the spectrum, rituals, ceremonies, and protocols can find regularized expression in common institutions and organizations whose memberships are at least partly defined by identity, e.g. the Gulf Cooperation Council.

Connecting the first step in the SPSP pathway to its predicted outcome, we can claim that **similar political systems that develop the perception of belonging to the same group do not go to war against one another, because this option is eliminated as unacceptable inside an ingroup**.

This does not preclude members from going to war against "outsiders", where violence is not ruled out. If the ingroup identity is particularly strong, the same mechanisms could also lead to ingroup alliance. This perspective not only explains peace among democracies but, in addition, peace among dyads of other political systems, such as monarchies.

Once ingroup identity has been established and affirmatively sustained, it is expected that the ingroup members share core norms of behavior, most notably nonviolence toward ingroup members. If the identity is especially central or if there is a strong common threat, positive norms might become guiding principles as well and lead to sustained cooperation and mutual support. To test nonviolence norms, it is insufficient to look at general relations. Decisive for the strength of a norm is whether it still holds in circumstances when strong circumstances or interests (e.g. survival or hegemony) play against it. For the norm on nonviolence, this would be a serious crisis, which might emerge even among "family" members. In that case, ingroup identity enables and prioritizes de-escalation and cooperation, whereas a lack thereof makes escalation to war more likely. The following three main indicators serve to measure these different possible outcomes:

1 Military restraint
This first and foremost means refraining from military action – war and MID – and disavowal of violence in general within the ingroup. Generally, the definitions of the CoW and MID data sets will be employed to define the military clashes to include in the analysis. The CoW data set uses the threshold of 1000 battle-related deaths in the span of a year to record a war,

36 *Moving beyond democratic exceptionalism*

whereas the definition of "MID" is "a set of interactions between or among states involving the threat, display, or use of military force in short temporal intervals" that is overt, non-accidental, government sanctioned, and government directed (Maoz and Abdolali 1989, 13). Only MIDs with a hostility level of at least 4 (which means "use of force", whereas 5 means "war") will be considered instances of military actions, although others are still noted in the analysis.[18]

2 *Non-military restraint*

War and even militarized disputes are rare in interstate interaction, whether of similar or dissimilar political systems, and we thus need additional indicators to measure restraint from escalation of monarchic elites. They are only the most dramatic culminations of escalation spirals and crisis slides. This set of indicators serves to identify the actions that are most likely to lead to an escalation to war by analyzing dynamics just below the threshold for interstate violence. It is rare that war breaks out without any previous signs or buildup and consistently poor prior relations. Rather, severe militarized conflict is usually preceded by some of the following steps: delegitimization, subversion, and rhetorical escalation. Secondary implications of monarchic de-escalation thus would be refraining from such measures and instead framing the conflict in terms of disagreements instead of existential incompatibility.

Refraining from delegitimizing the opponent's regime

To legitimize an act of war against an opponent usually also means justifying one's own cause and delegitimizing the other to ensure backing by the populace and allies. The delegitimization of the opponent's regime at the least (or, in some cases, the whole state) indicates a break of ingroup norms in that it legitimizes its removal or transformation altogether, acting directly against the prime drive of all leaders: regime survival. It is distinct from mere criticism of individual policies or personal criticism of the ruler or some of their individual associates. The personal delegitimization of the ruler is also strongly confrontational, but the removal of the ruler without the removal of the regime might (and in Middle East monarchies often does) mean mere retirement and often comfortable asylum in the near abroad. Removing the regime, however, often means incarceration or death and the discontinuation of the rule of all the ruler's allies (and, in case of a monarchy, relatives altogether). SIT posits that a mutual recognition of equality (in kind, not in power) is a hallmark of ingroup identification. The theoretical expectation is thus that once ingroup identification is present, delegitimizing the regime or revoking previous recognition of legitimacy of the regime should be unacceptable inside an ingroup because it would also mean a pars pro toto delegitimization of the club itself. Delegitimization can take place on the basis of the disavowal or discrediting of the ruling ideology, on the basis of sovereignty of a regime ("puppet regime" or foreign agent) or on the state level by claims that the state itself is not a viable or "real" state.

Moving beyond democratic exceptionalism 37

It is impossible to clearly separate this indicator from the indicators for social identity processes, because there is a feedback effect between the successful settling of a conflict or de-escalation and an affirmation of monarchic identity. Similarly, there is also a feedback loop between military escalation and the othering of an opponent. For the sake of the concision of the analysis, these feedback effects are ignored. In general, social-process indicators (especially the emphasis of similarity over difference) are taken to mean "typical" behavior in "normal" times, whereas the delegitimization of regime or the refraining from doing so is measured during ongoing crises.

Refraining from subverting the opponent's regime
For the same reason, subversion, i.e. the attempt to undermine and change the regime/political system of the other, via e.g. coups or the support of subversive opposition groups in the target country, should also be off the table in the case of a monarchic ingroup. If threats to state and regime survival are the prime threats that foreign policy decision makers have to cope with, subversion as being directed against regime security is one step removed from militarized action (directed against state integrity).

Rhetorical restraint
Casting the conflict in non-existential terms helps prevent escalation spirals with rhetorical reprisals that might spill over into action. This restraint might be, e.g., in territorial conflicts seen when staking claims to small parts of the opponent's territory, but not the whole, emphasizing that the disagreement is over issues, not over identity or mutual incompatibilities or a question of essential security and refraining from threats of violence. Escalating rhetorically and securitizing a conflict raises the stakes for all parties and can lead to conflict escalation. In contrast, rhetoric restraint signals that it can be solved peacefully and is a de-escalatory tactic that favors cooperation and compromise.

In contrast to ingroup members who tend to frame conflict issues in de-securitizing ways, ruling elites who perceive each other as belonging to different groups are more likely to inflate, securitize, and dramatize conflict issues.

3   *Alliance and solidarity*
Although the focus lies on the de-escalation of conflict and therefore an *ex negativo* concept of non-war, an important consequence of ingroup identification is positive – namely monarchic solidarity, expressed e.g. in persistent alliances (in contrast to ad hoc coalitions that merely indicate convergence of interest) (for the difference between alliances and coalitions, cf. Kober 2002, 1). The key difference between overlapping interests and joint ingroup identification resulting in a foreign policy convergence and coordination and nonviolent dispute resolution is that the former is episodic and ephemeral, i.e. it can disappear as soon as the interest convergence vanishes. The latter, however, can bridge difficult periods when members of the same "club" have

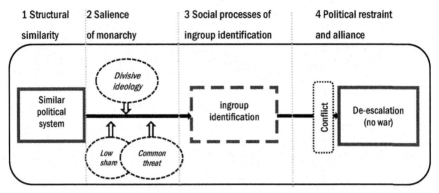

Figure 2.1 Causal chain links and steps 1–4

clashes over interests and still refrain from violent escalation. One example of ephemeral interest convergence is the foreign policy of Iraq under Saddam Hussein, which was highly cooperative toward the Gulf monarchies during periods of shared interests, e.g. during the Iran–Iraq War, but it attacked one of its major supporters and funders, Kuwait, after the war and the convergence of interests passed.

According to the underlying theoretical expectations, a longer-term alliance (in contrast to an ad hoc coalition due to interest convergence) is less likely to occur and persist among mixed dyads (but evidently not impossible). Especially strong indications of a "club" are an institutionalized form of security and defense-related formal alliances, e.g. intragovernmental organization with security-related provisions.

The causal mechanism as adapted for the MP and broken up into four causal chain links as a subtype of the SPSP is illustrated in Figure 2.1.

2.2 Existing approaches: why it is not oil, imperialism, or repression

Since monarchies are rare and concentrated in one region, they share a plethora of other characteristics apart from their political system, and to disentangle their effect from monarchism is a challenge. How do we know that it is not merely one of these similarities that explains monarchic foreign policy behavior instead of the political system?

Complementary confounding factors: geography and kinship

Especially the monarchies of the Persian Gulf share a broad range of commonalities – geographical proximity and institutions; a common culture and historical trajectory; and, in most cases, an economic system. However, while they pose problems for the analysis, because they complicate the isolation of the effect of the political system per se, they are complementary rather than competing explanations. This is because they are not necessarily a separate factor, nor do they always have the same direction of effect as a SIT-based mechanism.

Except for Oman,[19] all of the Gulf monarchies are *dynastic* (see Herb 1999), meaning family dynasties form the ruling class and the pool of higher-level political personnel. These dynasties are further connected with each other via various marriage, family, and tribal relations and shared common identities while forming a regional subsystem constituted by kinship and alliance.

Far from being an alternative to a SIT-centered explanation, these shared features make monarchies are a likely case of it. Family and tribal ties are generally more likely to be found among monarchies given that intermarriage is rarer between or with republics. The especially close bond that the Gulf states share intensifies the ingroup identification among the members of the subgroup of the Gulf monarchies as forms part of their shared similarity. The commonalities of the Gulf monarchies would thus not constitute a separate explanatory factor but rather form part of the monarchic traits of the system. Also, close ties alone have not discouraged countries from waging war against one another in the past, as the prewar (pre-world-war) European monarchies plainly show.

This also applies to *geographical clustering*, which makes the monarchic peace even more puzzling, because it should raise the possibility of war. While geographic proximity or contiguity can have an ambivalent causal effect on war and peace, for most except the major powers, it is a necessary condition for a war to occur (Diehl 1985) and at least contributes to war (Diehl 1991) – which is why it is recommended as a control variable to avoid overestimating the probability of war. Nonetheless, although it may be necessary, it is not sufficient for war. Military escalation is not inevitable for neighbors, if they find alternative ways to solve their conflicts (cf. Vasquez 2009, 161). Therefore, concentrating the study on the Middle East is the most promising course of action – not only has it the largest concentration of remaining authoritarian monarchies, providing them with opportunities for conflict absent between more distanced monarchies, but it also provides an ample concentration of another rare phenomenon: interstate war. Between 1948 and 2003, 11 such wars occurred here.

Rival confounding factors: small states, oil, alliance and coup-proofing

There are other traits that cluster among Middle East monarchies that might make them more peaceful without being linked to their political system per se. The first

40 *Moving beyond democratic exceptionalism*

such commonality is their size. Most monarchies are also *small states*, especially if measured by citizen population.[20] Small states have only limited foreign policy options at their disposal compared to larger and thus generally more-powerful states (Baker Fox 1959; Keohane 1969; Peterson 2006). Two main expectations for foreign policy derive from the limitations that small states (or micro-states) face (cf. Peterson 2006):

1 A more defensive stance
2 A more effective alliance-building.

Both might preclude (offensive) war. A situation wherein Qatar attacks Saudi Arabia, more than 14 times its size in population, is almost inconceivable, even during the tensions since the beginning of the blockade. One the other hand, the reverse is possible in such a case, making a small and wealthy statelet like Qatar a low-hanging fruit to any larger states to pick, including other monarchies, thus raising the possibility of military conflict. However, most of the broken-down monarchies, as well as Jordan and Morocco, are medium or even large territorial states. In addition, many studies have shown that small states can still conduct a varied and confident foreign policy, including conflict participation (see e.g. Al-Khalili 2009 for the case of Oman; and Kamrava 2013 for the case of "smart power" Qatar).

Apart from belonging to the same subregion and mostly exhibiting small-state characteristics, the Gulf monarchies are also *rentier states* (Beblawi and Luciani 1987; M. Beck 2009) with a high dependence on resource export and the ensuing high income. Analogous to a common critique of the DPT (Gartzke 2007), this fact suggests that the driving force of external behavior is not regime type but rather economy or wealth: rich states tend to be saturated status quo powers, i.e. "states that seek only to keep their resources and for whom the costs of war exceed the gains from nonsecurity expansion" (Schweller 1997, 46), and pursue a comparatively more conservative and thus risk-averse policy. In addition, external powers dependent on the exported resources have a high interest in the protection of the exporting states.

However, oil is not a necessary explanation for peacefulness, as the existence of the resource-poor monarchies Jordan and Morocco as well as their former brethren Egypt and North Yemen in their monarchical periods show. It is also not sufficient, as Iraq under Saddam Hussein repeatedly demonstrated. Some of the most "radical" or confrontational states in the high times of pan-Arabism and anti-imperialism were rentier states like Algeria, Libya, Iraq, and Iran.[21]

On the contrary, oil can lead to conflicts because the wealth-induced heightened military capabilities raise the probability of military success and therefore also the probability of war (Gause 2010). Furthermore, the search for oil can lead to more territorial conflicts, of which most wars encompass at least an element of (Vasquez 2009, 166). Thus, there is no clear causal expectation for rentierism or oil wealth. Fred Halliday even asserts that "oil has no significant causative relation" to most interstate conflicts in the region (2011, 271, FN 31).

Moving beyond democratic exceptionalism   41

In addition, the state of saturation can be achieved only if the allocation and cooptation of societal groups enabled by the resource export (Ross 2001) works. Changing oil prices can affect this ability. If oil wealth were the defining factor for monarchical peacefulness, *boom* and *bust* periods would directly relate to foreign policy behavior. Instead, we find that monarchic war involvement is consistently low and peaks only in the First Gulf War, when (oil-rich) Iraq attacked monarchic (and even more oil-rich) Kuwait and the fellow monarchies flocked to its aid. In addition, if oil wealth ameliorated conflict, the expectation for the resource-poor monarchies of Jordan and Morocco would be higher war-proneness. Although those are also the only monarchies to initiate conflict, they also never fought against other monarchies – in contrast to oil exporters Iran and Iraq, which did fight each other.

Due to their lesser wealth, Morocco and particularly Jordan are highly depend-ent on the *external support by Western powers*, but this is a commonality that all monarchies share to some extent. This phenomenon even holds true on a global scale, as every monarchy since the Second World War has been a Western ally, but it is even more salient for the Middle Eastern monarchies that were mostly created, or at least shaped, by the British.

Alliance structure is an important determinant of foreign policy behavior, and a possible monarchical peacefulness could therefore be an artifact of the Cold War and the bloc structure. If all monarchies are Western allies, there should be no need or opportunity to attack one other. Furthermore, they might feel safer because of the promise of external protection and therefore less prone to preven-tive or preemptive wars. (Defensive) alliance ties are also able to deter potential aggressors (Leeds 2003). This is a strong argument, especially because it is dyadic in nature with the outcome of depending on the alliance affiliation of both mem-bers of a dyad.

Nevertheless, it is not sufficient grounds for dismissing other theoretical approaches. The extent of Western support differed over time and was never an absolute determination for the choice of foreign policies by Middle Eastern rul-ers. Even close Western allies show significant autonomy. This is most drasti-cally emphasized by Jordanian refusal to fight Iraq despite pressure from the whole Western bloc and most of its own Arab neighbors in the First Gulf War of 1990–1991, which also illustrates the failure of deterrence by alliance. In addi-tion, Saddam Hussein's invasion of Kuwait as well as Arab-Israeli wars show other instances when Western alliance alone was not a sufficient explanation to keep two (or more) Western-backed states from waging war against one another. Furthermore, ally entanglement in wars can lead to higher conflict participation (cf. Christensen and Snyder 1990).

There is sufficient ground to argue that Western alliance is in fact not so much an explanation for the foreign policy behavior of monarchies as it is the outcome of the same properties of monarchies that also account for other features of the foreign policy behavior of monarchies. Monarchies are almost always Western allies, an anomaly that can be explained in part by monarchic specificities mak-ing monarchies particularly suitable for alliance with external Western powers

42   *Moving beyond democratic exceptionalism*

(cf. Sunik 2015). It thus cannot be considered separately from factors relating to the political system of these states.

When thinking about what factors could account for a difference in conflict initiation in the Middle East, the role of the *military* stands out. Due to the historic threat of military coups – in fact, four of the five post-WWII MENA monarchies have been removed by military coups d'état – the surviving monarchies tried to coup-proof their regimes by fragmentation, redundancy, and narrowing the loyalty bounds of their militaries (Quinlivan 1999). Power-sharing and balancing purposes were additional drivers of these processes that weaken military power in the monarchies. In Saudi Arabia under King Abdallah, for instance, the king ran the National Guard, Crown Prince Sultan controlled the air force and was minister of defense, and Crown-Prince-in-waiting Nayif commanded the interior forces (Billingsley 2009, 64).

A possible conclusion would be that since the military is not an integral part of the regime, military options become less likely. Since leaders with a military background tend to be more war-prone (Horowitz and Stam 2014), this could explain the difference between the republican presidents who mostly share a military background and monarchs who usually (but not universally, as King Hussein of Jordan or Sultan Qaboos of Oman demonstrate) do not. Military socialization normalizes war as an option and tilts the cost–benefit analysis of employing military violence abroad while pacifist leanings are often penalized in a military junta context (Brecher 1996; Debs and Goemans 2010; Huntington 1957; Posen 1986). Therefore, if the military is part of the regime, military options might be more widespread. Civilian monarchies would thus not be more pacific per se. Instead military republics would be more belligerent, which would account for the monarchy–republic divide.

There are a few caveats to this explanation, however. First of all, there are studies disputing a greater bellicosity in military personnel (Betts 1991; Feaver and Gelpi 2005; Sechser 2004). Not only might military leaders not differ much from civilian leaders in war-proneness, but also Martín shows in his extensive analysis of the South American "zone of peace" between military republics that common military socialization can in some circumstances even impede armed conflict (Martín 2006).

Even if we concede a greater propensity for military conflict in military regimes, other objections remain: coup-proofing was not implemented to the same extent in all monarchies – in the linchpin monarchies of Jordan and Morocco, the military played a greater role than in the dynastic monarchies. There were purges following military unrest and coup attempts there, but the military was never neutralized like in the Gulf states and continues to form an important pillar of the stability of the regime, especially in Jordan (cf. Pollack 2002). Also, coup-proofing was never an exclusive monarchic tactic; on the contrary, it was most pronounced in republican military regimes such as Iraq and Syria, where coup-experienced leaders saw enough iterations to gain in-depth knowledge on how to prevent them and used that knowledge to stabilize their own rule (Heller 1977; Lutterbeck 2013). The

Moving beyond democratic exceptionalism 43

belligerence of military regime would thus at most be an incomplete explanation for a monarchic peace.

In summary, it appears that most shared characteristics of monarchies in the Middle East discussed earlier are static and, though they certainly can explain some events, cannot explain dynamics and changes. With the exception of Western alliance, the majority of these explanations is monadic and can also explain only war or peace, but not both. In contrast, a SIT-centered explanation is dyadic and can explain changes over time as well as wars with non-monarchies and peace among monarchies.

A more comprehensive explanation always encompasses theoretical synthesis to an extent. The aforementioned factors have been covered at length in previous works. They are not dismissed for the benefit of a SIT-centered explanation but complement it.

But what can we say about other monarchy-related explanations of their conflict behavior? Although monarchy research has rarely explicitly aimed to explain foreign policy behavior, there are some indications that monarchies are special in numerous ways.

Monarchic pacifism from an institutionalist perspective

Monarchy research is a valuable source of explanation for a *monadic* effect of monarchism – i.e. if there is something about monarchic systems in general that generates greater peacefulness or lesser belligerence in contrast to other types of systems, such as juntas, personalist dictatorship, or single-party systems, it should be found here. What sets monarchies apart from other political systems are specific monarchic institutions – most obviously the position of the head of state, the monarch. The nature of the institution of the monarch enables a greater pragmatism, especially in foreign policy, and restricts ideological chain ganging and brinkmanship.

Despite the limiting concentration on the survival of monarchical authoritarianism, research on the Middle Eastern monarchies bears many fitting leads for research on their foreign policy as well. Lisa Anderson (see e.g. 2000) points to the special advantages of monarchies which are not bound to a specific overreaching ideology, an aspect that she attributes to the prerequisites of state building. Whereas presidents are per definition always part of a particular political group or party and – especially in the Arab world (in religious terms also in Iran) – came to power through ideology-driven revolutions, monarchs, whether they be kings, emirs, or sultans, are formally above everyday politics and mostly do not have a pronounced political ideology, in particular not one directed externally (Anderson 2000; Lucas 2004; Waterbury 1970).

Monarchy also brings advantages for legitimation. Many monarchies allow for parliaments occupied with the concrete design of laws, while monarchs issue mere directives or royal decrees. Thus, they can employ *divide-et-impera* policies among their political rivals much more easily (Byman and Green 1999) and

44 *Moving beyond democratic exceptionalism*

can delegate responsibility for unpopular or failed decisions to the legislative. Because of the comparatively broad basis of their legitimacy, they are less bound to certain allied elites and can choose among different groups more freely (Anderson 2000; Ben-Dor 2000).

Also, they are less vulnerable to open contradictions than republics are. Etymologically and historically, as res publicae, the latter's legitimacy is officially derived from popular sovereignty, forcing their elites to at least nominally fight against nepotism, closed elites, and a lack of transparence and participation in the political system. De facto, of course, as authoritarian regimes, they are tolerating or even fostering these phenomena to solidify their rule. For monarchies, on the other hand, those issues are an accepted or at least tolerated part of dynastic systems, and no jarring open contradiction arises (see also R. Owen 2004, 41–44). Since decision-making processes usually do not have to be justified or openly displayed, monarchies are more independent from the populace in their decisions. They thus have fewer veto players that must be included in the decision-making process, putting them on another level of political accountability.

At the same time, monarchies are not subject to comparably strict ideologies, as republics are: "[M]onarchs can stand above tribal, religious, ethnic, and regional divisions by acting as the linchpin of the political system" (Lucas 2004, 106). Friske calls that the ability to act as a *pouvoir neutre* (Friske 2007, 79). They are not the leader of a particular party but rather "mediators" between different societal groups (Frisch 2011; Waterbury 1970, 267–274).

Ideology is a greater restriction for republican presidents. Republics in the region came into being mainly from social-revolutionary regime changes and, at least in the first decades of their existence, based their legitimation on ideology and revolutionary values (cf. Hinnebusch and Ehteshami 2002, 335–337). For this reason, their political maneuvering is heavily restricted, even more so on foreign policy. The basic tenants of pan-Arabism, the central revolutionary ideology of the period of decolonization, are related to foreign policy: solidarity among Arab states and hostility toward (neo-)imperialism and the "Zionist entity" Israel. These tenants form unambiguous principles that form a moral imperative and thereby considerably restrict the foreign policy choices of leaders. Open alliances between these states and their ideological enemies become almost impossible. Even informal ones are complicated, as their uncovering would have serious consequences for the legitimacy of a regime based on pan-Arabist principles. It implies both less flexibility in allowing alliances with their ideological enemies and possible chain ganging deriving from the pan-Arab solidarity (Christensen and Snyder 1990). If pan-Arabism under Nasser at first bolstered Egypt's influence, it later became a burden to the president, who was bound by the role of the "Arab hero", which led to confrontations with the West and Israel and eventually chain ganged him into the catastrophic 1967 war (Hinnebusch and Shama 2014, 87).

The lack of ideological rigor in Middle East monarchies leads to moderation with no clear enemies but also no clear friends: "But when the crisis passes, they once again seek some regional middle ground, avoiding, if at all possible, friendships that are too close and also enmities that are too intense" (Gause 1994, 121).

Moving beyond democratic exceptionalism 45

Both can serve to prevent war – because there is no clear and demonized enemy to attack and because having fewer prescribed friendship responsibilities means that it is unlikely to be dragged into a war of a "friend's" making.

The monarchies, during the period of the "Arab Cold War" on the side of the "reactionary" and "counter-revolutionary" powers, do not have those legitimacy problems to the same extent. This does not mean that they can completely disregard the opinion of their people sympathizing with the ideological currents dominating certain periods. However, there is no open contradiction between the base of their legitimacy, mostly detached from foreign policy, and their actual foreign policy and alliance behavior that does not directly threaten said legitimacy (cf. R. Owen 2004, 41). This presupposes more freedom in foreign policy behavior since ideological friend–fiend schemes are less decisive for alliance or conflict. Foreign policy can thus become more "pragmatic" (cf. also: Kühnhardt 2012).

The preference for pragmatism over ideology partially explains alliances of monarchs with Western hegemons as well as the more relaxed relationships with Israel – policies almost unthinkable for most social-revolutionary republics with strong and explicit anti-(neo)colonial rhetoric. As fervent pan-Arabism has declined significantly even in former revolutionary republics and as they have taken on other characteristics of monarchies, hybridizing from "*jumhuriyya*" (republic) to "*jumlukiyya*", a portmanteau combining the Arab terms for monarchy and republic, such alliances became more open in practically all states of the region (Ibrahim 2000). Nonetheless, the ideological underpinnings of republican rule as well as core institutional differences could not be shed. To the contrary, the transformation from socialist republics into hereditary autocracies ultimately undermined their rule because it went counter to their foundation (cf. R. Owen 2012). If ideology plays a lesser role in monarchies than in republics, it can explain both enmity and amity. Monarchies should be less prone to be dragged into wars along ideological lines.

But there are also ideological differences among monarchies. The lack of ideology is not equally spread out among all of them (the same, of course, applies to republics) – a case in point is Saudi Arabia, which has strong ideological underpinnings due to the importance of Wahhabism for the regime's legitimacy. Therefore, the pragmatism of Saudi foreign policy is restricted. First, it is one of only three monarchies that never established any kind of open relations with Israel; because of the domestic pressure, the US moved their air force base from the Prince Sultan Air Base to al-Udeid in Qatar in 2003 (Blanchard 2011; Rasheed 2007, 8, 83–95, 135). Second, along with Jordan and Morocco, it is also one of the three monarchies in the region that participated in more than one war.

First indications that there might be some truth to these arguments are the remarkably good relations of the monarchies with Israel, even before the consequences of the Arab Spring solidified Iran as the common enemy. If there are significant group differences in the levels of ideology and pragmatism between monarchies and republics, they should exhibit themselves more clearly in issues that are highly contested and ideologically loaded, like relations with Israel and the Arab-Israeli conflict. The more ideologically committed, the harder it would

46 *Moving beyond democratic exceptionalism*

be for Arab states to maintain cooperative relations with Israel. Indeed, on the spectrum of cooperation intensity, monarchies have consistently less-hostile and more-"normalized" relations with Israel than republics do, not just since the Arab Spring period but historically as well. Although only Jordan has a peace treaty, the monarchies often hosted trade missions and even had mutual visits (see Alpher 2015, 114; Melman 2011; Roth 2015).

Although the sheer accumulation of the monadic effect might lead to the patterns seen in dyadic interaction, we should still see an independent effect of monarchic peacefulness, even in interactions with republics. If the small difference in general bellicosity presented in the tables from earlier would prove to be a statistical artifact, there would not be much left to explain. This book therefore focuses on a dyadic explanation of joint monarchism.

2.3 Scope conditions and case studies

Scope conditions: autocracy, independence, and statehood

The monarchic peace is set in the scope of *independent authoritarian nation-state monarchies*. The assumption underlying these scope conditions is that these monarchies have a distinct functional logic. The weight of regime type overrides the importance of state form in democratic regimes. Formal or "democratic" monarchies where royalty mostly entails a merely ceremonial or representative role have many more similarities with their republican democratic neighbors than with authoritarian monarchies in that the power is shifted away from unelected royalty toward democratic institutions, such as parliament, the prime ministry, parties, and courts. The Netherlands is usually best compared to Germany or Austria, not Saudi Arabia or Swaziland.

All MENA monarchies are unanimously considered *authoritarian*, thus obliterating potential definitional problems here. This region is best suited to a comparative analysis because it hosts the only remaining significant concentration of ruling *and* reigning monarchs in the world. The restriction to *nation-state* monarchies is essential for two reasons: it sets apart these monarchies from sub-state monarchies that persist today (mostly in Africa – e.g. in Ghana, Namibia, Togo, and Uganda) and it fills the timeframe cutoff at 1945 with meaning, as most nation-states outside the Western world consolidated after the Second World War.

Starting long-range analysis after World War II has become a default and sometimes arbitrary option for political scientists. Regarding an analysis of monarchic foreign policy, it also mows down the number of cases significantly and thus restricts the analysis. Before the world wars, monarchies constantly waged war against one another, negating the notion of any sort of monarchic peace. However, in this case, there are valid reasons for the cutoff that trump any potential confirmation bias. In fact, setting the cutoff at 1945 does not exclude many potential cases, because the monarchies and their context are too different to make meaningful comparisons for three main reasons, which follow.

Moving beyond democratic exceptionalism 47

First, before 1945 (and especially before 1914), monarchies tended to be empires to which a different functional logic applied. This fact has wide-ranging theoretical implications. Empires are defined by vague and fluid borders and thus an inherent expansionary drive, making them prone to territorial irredentism via expansion and invasion by or of other territories. Territorial conflicts and wars are thus much more likely for empires and have, in fact, constituted the largest share of wars during the era of empires (see e.g. Wimmer and Min 2006).

Their relations between foreign and domestic politics is different from that of modern nation-states, which are based on a delimitated (even if contested) territory, and there are therefore far fewer territorial disputes. Military aggression for territory has become largely delegitimized in recent decades because the international law norm of territorial integrity has become more ingrained in state interactions; in fact, military disputes resulting in a major change in territory have sharply dropped since the second half of the 20th century (Zacher 2001). When this principle is encroached upon, an immediate and strong reaction follows. One obvious example is the reaction to Saddam Hussein's invasion of Kuwait, and another, more-recent one is the international outrage over the annexation of Crimea by the Russian Federation in 2014.

In the "age of nationalism", territorial conflict resulting in militant revisionism is much less likely than it was in the "age of dynasties", to follow John Vasquez's terminology, because ethnolinguistic boundaries are more stable than dynastic (imperial) rule that hinges on a particular ruler's persona, ambitions, and power from which an empire's borders are derived. In "dynasty-era" monarchies, every succession left borders open to renegotiation, sometimes by violent means; the fact that the successor could also be an outsider if they produced a legitimate claim or could force their way on the throne was a further destabilizing factor (Vasquez 2009, 161–165). This is by now almost unconceivable. Even the succession pool of the traditionalist conservative Arab monarchies in existence today is, however indeterminate, not questioned by outsiders.[22] By setting the limit on 1945, we thus eliminate empires and their inevitable territorial claims as accepted casus belli, allowing for a clearer analysis.

Second, this delimitation applies even more for the Middle East monarchies as most of them had not even come into existence before the 20th century, much less formed states, nation-states or otherwise. State building and institutional and territorial consolidation had not achieved for the Gulf monarchies and Jordan until well into the 20th century. Before, they were societies governed by tribal law and (semi-)nomadicism (Zahlan 2002, 24). The multi-centennial dynastic tradition of monarchies such as Egypt and Iran was affected heavily by external influence and control by colonialist powers, making them states, but often not sovereign. The nation-state condition also largely overlaps with the scope condition of independence in the region. Foreign policies of states that are controlled by foreign powers cannot be analyzed without addressing colonial dynamics first.[23] The first part of the following case study on Saudi-Hashemite relations illustrates the importance of this scope condition.

48 *Moving beyond democratic exceptionalism*

The third reason is related to the main theoretical claim of this work regarding inter-monarchical behavior. It centers on the argument that the reason why monarchies don't fight each other is because of a strong *ingroup identification* and the existence of different codes of conduct inside and outside the ingroup. However, such an ingroup develops in a differential process of *othering* only in contrast to other groups consequently defined as outgroups. As illustrated earlier, this happens only when the ingroup is not the "default" category anymore and can thus be considered a salient category, as ingroup solidarity can take hold only then. A sense of common threat accelerates the process. Before 1945 and especially 1914, when most states were monarchies, monarchy was hardly a defining ingroup, because it was the "default" category. States tended to bond along different lines such as Protestantism or Catholicism during the age of the Wars of Religion, a cleavage embedded even in the names of the two blocs: the Protestant Union and the Catholic League. When in the 20th century monarchies started to be successively replaced by republics and the monarchs were robbed of their power or acquiesced into transferring it to a parliamentarian system, it started to consolidate into a meaningful category once again; only then were the conditions for a monarchic peace to occur met.[24]

The following analysis will focus on the regime or the ruling elite of the monarchies, not on the state per se nor on the level of the population. *Government, regime*, and *state* are not interchangeable. In the definition of Robert Fishman, a regime is

> the formal and informal organization of the center of political power, and of its relations with the broader society. A regime determines who has access to power, and how those who are in power deal with those who are not. . . . Regimes are more permanent forms of political organization than specific governments, but they are typically less permanent than the state. The state, by contrast, is a (normally) more permanent structure of domination and coordination including a coercive apparatus and the means to administer a society and extract resources from it.
>
> (Fishman 1990, 428)[25]

Here the relevant decision makers of the regime are identified as core members of the ruling family (usually including, but not limited to, the monarch, the heir apparent, and ruling family members in prime and foreign minister positions). Sometimes commoners can be included as well if they wield a significant amount of power and have decision-making capabilities inside the monarchic framework, especially in linchpin monarchies, where the ruling family is too small to control the regime on its own. An example is the iconic role played by Nuri al-Said, the long-time prime minister of Hashemite Iraq.

The definition of the "Middle East" is not consistent in everyday language or academic use. There are different levels of broadness of the concept with the broadest including even North Africa (thus making MENA a pleonasm). The relevant past and present (independent) monarchies that at some point have

Moving beyond democratic exceptionalism   49

constituted part of a regional system are Morocco since 1956; Libya 1951–1969; Egypt 1922–1952; Jordan since 1946; Iraq 1932–1958; Iran 1941–1979;[26] Kuwait since 1961; Saudi Arabia since 1932; the United Arab Emirates, Bahrain, Qatar, and Oman since 1971; and North Yemen 1918–1962.[27] Therefore, a broad definition of the Middle East will be used to cover the countries from Morocco to Iran.[28]

Multiple comparative case study approach

A case study approach is used for the following analysis for methodological and epistemological reasons: given that both monarchies and war are rare, medium-n or small-n approaches lend themselves more easily to the task than large-n studies. They can also serve to better solve the "too many variables, too few cases" problem that imposes itself in view of the many shared complementary factors laid out earlier. Therefore, we must find analytical units that are separable to untangle the complex web of shared traits, transnational diffusion, and interdependence, which is more difficult in a large-n-framework.

Furthermore, as shown earlier, some theoretical shortcomings are the consequence of an overreliance on large-n comparisons. A major reason for the preference of a case study framework is the prime motivation of the book – theory building and the laying out of the causal mechanism – to which such a framework is especially well suited.

For this purpose, a qualitative *comparative-historical case study* approach (Gerring 2007, 27–28) consisting of multiple, both synchronic and diachronic, case studies is chosen as the basis of the analysis, which, following George and Bennett, is also specified as a "building block" case study that serves to identify common patterns of particular types or subtypes of more-general phenomena (2005, 76) – here the monarchic peace as a subtype of the SPSP.

Since monarchies in the Middle East share so many features and therefore form similar political systems, monarchic foreign policy behavior in the Middle East is an especially likely case of an SPSP, rendering it in a good position for a plausibility check of the theory. To buttress the analysis and given data access problems associated with studies on the Middle East and authoritarian regimes in general (Ahram and Goode 2016), different case study designs and diversified data sources (statistical data, primary and secondary sources, and field interviews conducted in Qatar in April 2013 and Jordan in September 2015) are used for methodological triangulation.

The comparative case study consists of two main parts. The first entails an overview over Middle East monarchies and a "most likely" case that serves to *plausibilize* the mechanism of ingroup identification leading to ingroup favoritism under exceptionally favorable conditions, when monarchies face a common threat and contextualize the monarchic peace in a *regional* context. During periods of common threat to monarchies, ingroup identification is expected to be especially high and war therefore highly unlikely. Instead, secondary implications of ingroup favoritism are seen clearly in patterns of alliance and monarchic solidarity. The case study serves to illuminate the theorized mechanism of a strong coalescent

50 *Moving beyond democratic exceptionalism*

effect of external threats on ingroup formation and the ingroup favoritism that follows it. The cases chosen are two periods when monarchies faced a strong common threat not as individual states but as monarchies, which promises a particularly strong effect on monarchic cohesion: first, during the Arab Cold War in the 1950s and 1960s, and second, following the wave of rebellions and instability sweeping the region from 2011 to 2015.

The second part consists of two-by-two case studies that serve to *trace* the mechanism in less-favorable conditions for ingroup identification, namely during intragroup conflict between *dyads* (a triad in the Saudi-Hashemite case). All four are set in a context of intra-monarchic conflict. The study combines cross-case and within-case inference. While the four case studies form a most dissimilar case design to enhance generalizability (cross-case comparison), each case will be based on *theory-testing process tracing* (Beach and Pedersen 2011), to identify the causal mechanism responsible amid other possible pathways (within-case comparison). Following the advice of Goertz, both pairs start with a typical case where the causal mechanism can be expected to work best to clarify the causal process. The "subsequent case studies then explore the limits of the causal mechanism: how general is it?" (Goertz 2017, 71). The last two of the case studies further try to disentangle the effect of the monarchic political system from other factors by juxtaposing two periods of dyadic relations in which one monarchy broke down.

The four cases were also chosen to cover a set that is as diverse as possible to enhance the generalizability of the findings. They feature at least eight countries (Bahrain, Qatar, Saudi Arabia, Jordan, Iraq, Kuwait, Iran, and UAE) that span over two subregions (Persian Gulf and Levante), cover a wide time period covering different stages of the development of the regional system (from the 1940s to the 2000s), have different issues at their core (territory vs. national power and regional hegemony), and include different types of monarchies: rentier and non-rentier states, dynastic and linchpin monarchies, major regional powers, and small states in different arrangements (from small-small Bahrain-Qatar to large-large Saudi-Hashemites). They also include Iran as a non-Arab, non-Sunni state to refine the concept of similarity and isolate the shared monarchism as the relevant feature.

Two additional episodes of intra-monarchic conflict will be examined in a shorter fashion: the Saudi–Yemeni War of 1934 and the Qatar Crisis since 2017.

"Near misses": conflicts that failed to escalate into wars

Because there are no cases of inter-monarchic war since the consolidation of the Middle East state system and because proving a negative is demanding, other approximations to war and the monarchic effect on it must be found to further analytically separate political system effects from other factors.

Therefore, the first pair of case studies will be "near misses" of inter-monarchic war in Chapter 4, cases where monarchies have de-escalated major conflicts before they erupted into wars. This approach has been fruitfully applied in the

Moving beyond democratic exceptionalism 51

examination of the democratic peace theory, which also lacks instances of contradictory cases (inter-democratic war) (see Layne 1994). The chosen cases must be from among cases of monarchic dyads that experienced "close calls" of conflicts severe enough that war or at least militarized dispute can be seen as a realistic possible outcome. They show how important the institutional similarity was vis-à-vis other factors for decisions not to escalate.

"Quasi-experiments": monarchic breakdown leading to escalation

Despite the attempts to entangle monarchic effects from other possible confounding factors in the previous case studies, there is still a degree of overlap that needs to be further separated. Two case studies of Chapter 5 therefore look at two "quasi-experiments" in a *diachronic study*: pairs of monarchies where one experiences regime change. A regime change by revolution or coup would hardly affect oil wealth, geographic location, and capabilities in terms of balance-of-power approaches; however, it is likely to change alliance patterns and possibly the militarism of the new regime. From a perfectly controlled environment, though, it is a valuable method to gauge the effect of the political system. Large-n studies with a similar basis have been successfully conducted for the DPT (Hensel, Goertz, and Diehl 2000).

Notes

1 "Political system" is used here as an overarching concept that includes both state form (monarchy-republic) and regime form (democracy-autocracy), to ensure a broader applicability, not just for autocracies and democracies (see Chapter 2).
2 The end of this spectrum is formed by Petersen, who concludes that joint democracy is the driver behind political similarity, joint autocracy being statistically insignificant (2004), in exact opposition to Henderson (2002).
3 Mostly differing between a dichotomous measure of democracy and a democracy–autocracy continuum with differing cutoff points.
4 This is hardly surprising given that autocracy research originated in this field (Art 2012; Diamond and Program 1988; Friedrich and Brzezinski 1965, see e.g.; Geddes 1999; Levitsky and Way 2002; Schedler 2002).
5 See Petersen (2008) for a more extensive elaboration on the problems linked to a one-dimensional conceptualization of autocracy.
6 There are other caveats to their analysis: because three widely differing data sets on rivalries are used, and the overall frequency of rivalry onset among similar dyads is small, results are not always significant (though in almost all cases in the expected direction). Also, their dependent variable is not war or armed conflict but "rivalry", which is a more entrenched and sustained hostile relationship (Conrad and Souva 2011, 2). Although it may be possible that democracies are provisioned with special capabilities allowing them to deal with prolonged rivalries better than other similar systems can, it does not automatically follow that the same factors lead to a stronger or even a unique general peacefulness in democratic dyads compared to other politically similar dyads.
7 When looking at the small number of monarchic rivalries, the informative value is further questioned. Of the three data sets, one does not include any monarchic rivalries, while the others have two (Egypt–Jordan, starting in 1948; Saudi Arabia–Qatar starting

52 *Moving beyond democratic exceptionalism*

in 1992) and three (Egypt–Jordan, starting in 1946; Jordan–Saudi Arabia starting in 1946; Bahrain–Qatar starting in 1986) respectively, with only one overlap (Egypt–Jordan, but with differing start dates). None of the four enumerated rivalries ever resulted in war or severe military conflict, and one (Bahrain–Qatar) was even resolved by arbitration by the International Court of Justice (Wiegand 2012). This is an especially rare process for the region and resembles conflict resolution among mature democracies more than among autocratic states, and it is therefore hardly evidence for a lesser ability to solve conflicts. The evidence for an SPSP among monarchies (and some other regime subtypes) being a fitting representation is thus stronger than could be expected by the cautious phrasing of the results by the authors.

8 This does not mean that the DPT and other kinds of SPSP cannot have separate explanations. Given the strong empirical parallels, it is, however, a likely proposition that there is a common explanation for both (also see Gartzke and Weisiger 2013, 173).

9 Theoretically, additive factors can lead to stronger effects in similar than mixed dyads, accounting for (at least a weak) dyadic effect, but only if there is also a clear monadic tendency. In addition, there are institutionalist and explanations that claim a dyadic effect kicking in once a democracy "knows" the regime type of its adversary (Conrad and Souva 2011, 4). Since knowledge directly involves the perception of the "other", these explanations can also be subsumed under the following social constructivist approaches.

10 Republics here do not correspond to the opposite of monarchy, as is usually the case, but refer to the regime type, wherein Weart echoes Kant (and to an even greater extent Montesquieu), who also subdivides republic into the two categories: aristocracy (which Weart calls oligarchy) and democracy (Montesquieu 2002, 35, II, ch. 2). Middle East monarchies would fall under Weart's definition of "oligarchy", as he notes himself of "Arab-tribal monarchies" (1998, 71–72). Regardless whether this characterization is overstretching the concept of republic, the core arguments remains: regimes that recognize each other as similar or equal do not fight each other militarily.

11 Gartzke and Weisiger, as most other anglophone authors, conflate regime type to include both the variance of systems across the democracy–autocracy distinction and specific regime subtypes that vary along the state form (like authoritarian monarchies). For consistency, this is how "regime type" will also be used here, although "political system" would be the more correct description.

12 In a conversation with Yugoslav politician Milovan Djilas in April 1945 (Djilas 1960).

13

> When the ideology calls for the members to form a centralized hierarchical movement obeying a single authoritative leadership, the likelihood of conflict is increased. This somewhat paradoxical result occurs for several reasons. First, because the ideology is a source of legitimacy for each member regime, each must at a minimum affirm its universal validity. But when the ideology calls for a single leader, then all regimes save the one that emerges on top will find their autonomy threatened by the other members of the same movement. Second, because the authority of the leadership rests on its interpretation of the common ideology, ideological quarrels are quite likely. They are also likely to be intense, because rival factions can defend their own interpretation only by portraying rivals as traitors or heretics.
>
> (Walt 1985, 21)

14 "*ana 'ala akhuy wa-ana wa-akhuy 'ala ibn 'ammi wa-ana wa-ibn 'ammi 'ala l-gharib*".

15 Functionalist anthropologist Edward Evan Evans-Pritchard described this complementary opposition in the segmentary society of the Nuer clan in Sudan:

> Its lineages are distinct groups only in relation to each other. . . . There is always fusion of collateral lineages of the same branch in relation to a collateral branch. . . . Hence two lineages which are equal and opposite are composite in relation to a

Moving beyond democratic exceptionalism 53

third, so that a man is a member of a lineage in relation to a certain group and not a member of it in relation to a different group. Lineages are thus essentially relative groups, like tribal sections, and, like them, also are dynamic groups. Therefore, they can only be described satisfactorily in terms of values and situations.

(Evans-Pritchard 1940, 285–286)

16 Although a broad term, "affirmation of commonality" is preferred to the somewhat awkward opposite of "othering", "saming", which is not broadly used and which, distractingly, has additional meanings (Bruce and Yearley 2006, 266).

17 Family rhetoric is a suitable indicator because it is a special category and not an automatism in harmonious periods. "Friendly" states outside the inner ingroup are usually referred to as friends or neighbors. Family as a category is more demanding.

18 The cutoff is chosen because including lower-level MIDs on the levels of "display of force" or "threat of use of force" would inflate the category into meaninglessness. Those lesser forms of confrontations are better captured by the following indicator of "non-military restraint". Otherwise, it might mean classing instances like former Tory leader Michael Howard's assertion in April 2017 that the UK would go to war against Spain for Gibraltar (Asthana 2017) in the same category as actual war between democracies.

19 If the Middle East monarchies are subdivided into linchpin monarchies and rentier monarchies, Oman falls in between, making it a hybrid "linchtier" monarchy (Bank, Richter, and Sunik 2014).

20 There is significant disagreement on what constitutes a small state or a micro-state. Many definitions seem overly broad; e.g. Baker Fox's approach applies the concept to everyone except global powers. Even Turkey, Egypt, and Iran, the largest states in the region by territory and population, are counted as "small states" in her work (Baker Fox 1959, 2), a problematic definition for a study of Middle Eastern states. Other early studies suffer from similar definitional problems (Keohane 1969). Elman conceptualizes small states as "weak states" and thus includes the US in the 19th century in his study (Elman 1995, 191–192). On the other end of the scale, some definitions are overly narrow. Especially definitions used by large data sets look at population size, with different cutoff points of 1 (as does the UN), 3, or 5 million inhabitants while micro-states may range from under 100,000 to under 1 million (Peterson 2006, 734–735). By the older, broadest definitions, all Middle Eastern monarchies (and almost all republics) would be small states, and by the later, most restrictive, 1 million threshold, no monarchies (except Bahrain and Qatar, but only if disregarding the expatriate population) would be considered small states, thus providing an exceedingly broad range.

21 Also, as Schweller demonstrates, given the right circumstances, even status quo states can wage wars of aggression (1997, 48–56).

22 In contrast to earlier eras and even the vestiges of European monarchies of the present, as in the peculiar case of Monaco, where until a legal change in 2002, a lack of dynastic offspring would have resulted in the principality's sovereignty being returned to France.

23 This is still an early delimitation – Lawson even argues that only by the mid 1950s did the Arab state system adopt "Westphalian features" that would conform to the scope conditions outlined here (Lawson 2006, 141).

24 However, the first indications of a monarchic (or imperial) bloc can already be traced back to the Holy Alliance (1815) and the Conference of Münchengrätz (1833).

25 For the study of Middle East monarchies, however, the differences often tend to blur, especially in the case of the Gulf states, where the incorporation of the dynasty into the state structure has become so entrenched that a regime change might also result in state breakdown or fragmentation, typical for "Sultanistic" regimes (cf. Fishman 1990, 428).

54 *Moving beyond democratic exceptionalism*

26 Iran was an independent monarchy for centuries or even millennia, but the installment of Shah Reza Pahlavi instead of his father during the Second World War in 1941 will be taken as a pragmatic cutoff point to adhere to the post-WWII limes.

27 Tunisia is excluded because its monarchical period was mainly during colonial times. Monarchies at the periphery of the system were Ethiopia until 1974 and Afghanistan until 1973; these cases are excluded here because they only rarely directly interacted in the regional system of the Middle East and are better attributed to other regions.

28 To ease legibility, Arabic names and words as already established in English-language sources are used whenever possible (e.g. Gamal Abdel Nasser instead of Ǧamāl ʿAbd an-Nāṣir, Hussein instead of Ḥusayn); in all other cases, a simplified version of the transliteration employed by the *International Journal of Middle East Studies* (*IJMES*), without diacritical marks, is used. The definite article is transliterated in its non-assimilated form as "al-" while "Al" is reserved for the Arab concept of dynasty or family (e.g. Al Saud, Al Thani etc.).

References

Abdelal, Rawi, Yoshiko M. Herrera, Alastair Iain Johnston, and Rose McDermott. 2006. "Identity as a Variable." *Perspectives on Politics* 4(4): 695–711.

Adler, Emanuel, and Michael Barnett. 1998. *Security Communities*. Cambridge: Cambridge University Press.

Ahram, Ariel I., and J. Paul Goode. 2016. "Researching Authoritarianism in the Discipline of Democracy: Authoritarianism in the Discipline of Democracy." *Social Science Quarterly* 97(4): 834–49.

Al-Khalili, Majid. 2009. *Oman's Foreign Policy*. Westport, CT: Praeger Security International.

Alpher, Yossi. 2015. *Periphery: Israel's Search for Middle East Allies*. Lanham; New York; Bolder; Toronto; London: Rowman & Littlefield.

———. 2000. "Dynasts and Nationalists: Why Monarchies Survive." In *Middle East Monarchies. The Challenge of Modernity*, ed. Joseph Kostiner. Boulder, CO: Lynne Rienner Publishers, 53–70.

Archer, Clive. 1996. "The Nordic Area as a 'Zone of Peace'." *Journal of Peace Research* 33(4): 451–67.

Art, David. 2012. "What Do We Know About Authoritarianism After Ten Years?" *Comparative Politics* 44(3): 351–73.

Asthana, Anushka. 2017. "Theresa May Would Go to War to Protect Gibraltar, Michael Howard Says." *The Guardian*. www.theguardian.com/politics/2017/apr/02/britain-and-eu-worse-off-without-brexit-deal-says-michael-fallon (April 25, 2017).

Ayubi, Nazih N. 1995. *Over-Stating the Arab State: Politics and Society in the Middle East*. London: I.B. Tauris.

Baker Fox, Annette. 1959. *The Power of Small States. Diplomacy in World War II*. Chicago: Cambridge University Press.

Bank, André, Thomas Richter, and Anna Sunik. 2014. "Durable, Yet Different: Monarchies in the Arab Spring." *Journal of Arabian Studies* 4(2): 163–79.

Barnett, Michael. 1996. "Identity and Alliances in the Middle East." In *The Culture of National Security*, ed. Peter J. Katzenstein. Columbia University Press, 400–47.

Bausch, A.W. 2015. "Democracy, War Effort, and the Systemic Democratic Peace." *Journal of Peace Research* 52(4): 435–47.

Beach, Derek, and Rasmus Brun Pedersen. 2011. *What Is Process-Tracing Actually Tracing? The Three Variants of Process Tracing Methods and Their Uses and Limitations.*

Moving beyond democratic exceptionalism 55

Rochester, NY: Social Science Research Network. SSRN Scholarly Paper. http://papers.ssrn.com/abstract=1902082 (June 30, 2016).

Beblawi, Hazem, and Giacomo Luciani, eds. 1987. *II The Rentier State*. London: Croom Helm.

Beck, Martin. 2009. "Rente Und Rentierstaat Im Nahen Osten." In *Der Nahe Osten Im Umbruch: Zwischen Transformation Und Autoritarismus*, eds. Martin Beck, Cilja Harders, Annette Juenemann, and Stephan Stetter. Wiesbaden: VS-Verlag, 25–49.

Beck, Nathaniel, Gary King, and Langche Zeng. 2004. "Theory and Evidence in International Conflict: A Response to de Marchi, Gelpi, and Grynaviski." *American Political Science Review* 98(2): 379–89.

Ben-Dor, Gabriel. 2000. "Patterns of Monarchy in the Middle East." In *Middle East Monarchies – The Challenge of Modernity*, ed. Joseph Kostiner. Boulder, CO; London: Lynne Rienner Publishers, 71–84.

Bennett, D. Scott. 2006. "Toward a Continuous Specification of the Democracy – Autocracy Connection." *International Studies Quarterly* 50(2): 313–38.

Betts, Richard K. 1991. *Soldiers, Statesmen, and Cold War Crises*. Morningside edition. New York: Columbia University Press.

Billingsley, Anthony. 2009. *Political Succession in the Arab World: Constitutions, Family Loyalties and Islam*. London: Routledge.

Blanchard, Christopher M. 2011. *Saudi Arabia: Background and U.S. Relations*. Washington, DC: Congressional Research Service.

Boulding, Kenneth Ewart. 1978. *Stable Peace*. Austin: University of Texas Press.

Brecher, Michael. 1996. "Crisis Escalation: Model and Findings." *International Political Science Review/Revue internationale de science politique* 17(2): 215–30.

Brewer, Marilynn B. 1999. "The Psychology of Prejudice: Ingroup Love and Outgroup Hate?" *Journal of Social Issues* 55(3): 429–44.

Bruce, Steve, and Steven Yearley, eds. 2006. *The SAGE Dictionary of Sociology*. Los Angeles; London; Singapore; Washington: SAGE.

Byman, Daniel L, and Jerrold D Green. 1999. "The Enigma of Political Stability in the Persian Gulf Monarchies." *Middle East Review of International Affairs* 3(3): 20–37.

Chafetz, Glenn, Michael Spirtas, and Benjamin Frankel. 1998. "Introduction: Tracing the Influence of Identity on Foreign Policy." *Security Studies* 8(2–3): 7–22.

Chan, Steve. 1997. "In Search of Democratic Peace: Problems and Promise." *Mershon International Studies Review* 41(1): 59–91.

Choi, Seung-Whan. 2016. "A Menace to the Democratic Peace? Dyadic and Systemic Difference." *International Studies Quarterly* 60(3): 573–577.

Christensen, Thomas, and Jack Snyder. 1990. "Chain Gangs and Passed Bucks: Predicting Alliance Patterns in Multipolarity." *International Organization* 44(2): 137–68.

Conrad, Justin, and Mark Souva. 2011. "Regime Similarity and Rivalry." *International Interactions* 37(1): 1–28.

Dafoe, Allan, John R. Oneal, and Bruce Russett. 2013. "The Democratic Peace: Weighing the Evidence and Cautious Inference." *International Studies Quarterly* 57(1): 201–14.

Dawson, Raymond, and Richard Rosecrance. 1966. "Theory and Reality in the Anglo-American Alliance." *World Politics* 19(1): 21–51.

Debs, Alexander, and H.E. Goemans. 2010. "Regime Type, the Fate of Leaders, and War." *The American Political Science Review* 104(3): 430–45.

Deutsch, Karl Wolfgang. 1957. *Political Community and the North Atlantic Area: International Organization in the Light of Historical Experience*. Princeton: Princeton University Press.

56 *Moving beyond democratic exceptionalism*

Diamond, Larry Jay, and Hoover Institution on War Program Revolution, and Peace International Studies. 1988. *Beyond Authoritarianism and Totalitarianism: Strategies for Democratization*. Redwood City: Hoover Institution, Stanford University.

Diehl, Paul F. 1985. "Contiguity and Military Escalation in Major Power Rivalries, 1816–1980." *The Journal of Politics* 47(4): 1203–11.

———. 1991. "Geography and War: A Review and Assessment of the Empirical Literature." *International Interactions* 17(1): 11–27.

Djilas, Milovan. 1960. *The Face of Totalitarianism. Conversations with Stalin (Lico Totalitarizma. Razgovory so Stalinom)*. Samizdat.

Dovidio, John F., Samuel L. Gaertner, and Ana Validzic. 1998. "Intergroup Bias: Status, Differentiation, and a Common In-Group Identity." *Journal of Personality and Social Psychology* 75(1): 109.

Elman, Miriam Fendius. 1995. "The Foreign Policies of Small States: Challenging Neorealism in Its Own Backyard." *British Journal of Political Science* 25(2): 171–217.

Ember, Carol R., Melvin Ember, and Bruce Russett. 1992. "Peace Between Participatory Polities: A Cross-Cultural Test of the 'Democracies Rarely Fight Each Other' Hypothesis." *World Politics* 44(04): 573–99.

Evans-Pritchard, Edward Evan. 1940. "The Nuer of the Southern Sudan." In *African Political Systems*, eds. Meyer Fortes and Edward Evan Evans-Pritchard, Oxford: Oxford University Press, 272–97.

Farber, Henry, and Joanne Gowa. 1995. "Polities and Peace." *International Security* 20(2): 123–46.

———. 1997. "Common Interests or Common Polities? Reinterpreting the Democratic Peace." *The Journal of Politics* 59(2): 393–417.

Feaver, Peter, and Christopher Gelpi. 2005. *Choosing Your Battles. American Civil-Military Relations and the Use of Force*. Princeton: Princeton University Press.

Fishman, Robert. 1990. "Rethinking State and Regime: Southern Europe's Transition to Democracy." *World Politics* 42(3): 422–40.

Friedrich, Carl Joachim, and Zbigniew Brzezinski. 1965. *Totalitarian Dictatorship and Autocracy*. 2nd edition. Cambridge: Harvard University Press.

Frisch, Hillel. 2011. "Why Monarchies Persist: Balancing between Internal and External Vulnerability." *Review of International Studies* 37(1): 167–84.

Friske, Tobias. 2007. "Staatsform Monarchie. Was Unterscheidet Eine Monarchie Heute Noch von Einer Republik?" www.freidok.uni-freiburg.de/volltexte/3325/.

Gartzke, Erik. 2007. "The Capitalist Peace." *American Journal of Political Science* 51(1): 166–91.

Gartzke, Erik, and Alex Weisiger. 2013. "Permanent Friends? Dynamic Difference and the Democratic Peace." *International Studies Quarterly* 57(1): 171–85.

Gause, F. Gregory, III. 1994. *Oil Monarchies: Domestic and Security Challenges in the Arab Gulf States*. New York: Council on Foreign Relations Press.

———. 2010. *The International Relations of the Persian Gulf*. Cambridge: Cambridge University Press.

Geddes, Barbara. 1999. "What Do We Know About Democratization After Twenty Years?" *Annual Review of Political Science* 2(1): 115–44.

George, Alexander L., and Andrew Bennett. 2005. *Case Studies and Theory Development in the Social Sciences*. Cambridge; London: MIT Press.

Gerring, John. 2007. *Case Study Research: Principles and Practices*. New York: Cambridge University Press.

Gibler, Douglas M. 2014. "Contiguous States, Stable Borders, and the Peace Between Democracies." *International Studies Quarterly* 58(1): 126–9.

Gibler, Douglas M., Marc L. Hutchison, and Steven V. Miller. 2012. "Individual Identity Attachments and International Conflict: The Importance of Territorial Threat." *Comparative Political Studies* 45(12): 1655–83.

Gleditsch, Nils Petter, and Håvard Hegre. 1997. "Peace and Democracy Three Levels of Analysis." *Journal of Conflict Resolution* 41(2): 283–310.

Goertz, Gary. 2017. *Multimethod Research, Causal Mechanisms, and Case Studies: An Integrated Approach*. Version 6. Princeton University Press. http://www3.nd.edu/~ggoertz/qmir/goertz2016pupv6.pdf (March 5, 2017).

Halliday, Fred. 2011. *The Middle East in International Relations: Power, Politics and Ideology*. New edition. Cambridge: Cambridge University Press.

Harnisch, Sebastian, Cornelia Frank, and Hanns W. Maull. 2011. *Role Theory in International Relations: Approaches and Analyses*. London; New York: Routledge Chapman & Hall.

Heller, Mark. 1977. "Politics and the Military in Iraq and Jordan, 1920–1958 The British Influence." *Armed Forces & Society* 4(1): 75–99.

Henderson, Errol Anthony. 2002. *Democracy and War: The End of an Illusion?* Boulder; London: Lynne Rienner Publishers.

Hensel, Paul, Gary Goertz, and Paul F. Diehl. 2000. "The Democratic Peace and Rivalries." *The Journal of Politics* 62(4): 1173–88.

Herb, Michael. 1999. *All in the Family: Absolutism, Revolution, and Democracy in the Middle Eastern Monarchies*. Albany: State University of New York Press.

Herbst, Jeffrey. 1990. "War and the State in Africa." *International Security* 14(4): 117–39.

Hermann, Margaret G., and Charles W. Kegley Jr. 1995. "Rethinking Democracy and International Peace: Perspectives from Political Psychology." *International Studies Quarterly* 39(4): 511–33.

Hinnebusch, Raymond A., and Anoushiravan Ehteshami. 2002. *The Foreign Policies of Middle East States*. Boulder, CO: Lynne Rienner Publishers.

Hinnebusch, Raymond A., and Nael Shama. 2014. "The Foreign Policy of Egypt." In *The Foreign Policies of Middle East States*, eds. Raymond A. Hinnebusch and Anoushiravan Ehteshami. Boulder, CO: Lynne Rienner Publishers, 75–103.

Hogg, Michael. 1996. "Intragroup Processes, Group Structure and Social Identity." In *Social Groups and Identities: Developing the Legacy of Henri Tajfel*, eds. William Peter Robinson and Henri Tajfel. Oxford: Psychology Press.

Horowitz, Michael C., and Allan C. Stam. 2014. "How Prior Military Experience Influences the Future Militarized Behavior of Leaders." *International Organization* 68(3): 527–59.

Hudson, Valerie. 2005. "Foreign Policy Analysis: Actor-Specific Theory and the Ground of International Relations." *Foreign Policy Analysis* 1: 1–30.

Huntington, Samuel P. 1957. *The Soldier and the State: The Theory and Politics of Civil-Military Relations*. Cambridge: Harvard University Press.

Ibrahim, Saad Eddin. 2000. "Iqtirah Bi-Insha' Malakiyyat Dusturiyya Fi l-Jumhuriyyat al-'arabiyya 'ala l-Umma an Tudhif Mustalah 'jumlukiyya' Ila Qamusiha l-Siyasi'." *al-Majalla*. www.eicds.org/arabic/publicationsAR/saadarticles/03/nov-dec/gomlokeya.htm.

Kacowicz, Arie Marcelo. 1998. *Zones of Peace in the Third World: South America and West Africa in Comparative Perspective*. Albany: SUNY Press.

58 *Moving beyond democratic exceptionalism*

Kamrava, Mehran. 2013. *Qatar: Small State, Big Politics*. Ithaca, NY: Cornell University Press.

Kelly, Robert E. 2012. "A 'Confucian Long Peace' in Pre-Western East Asia?" *European Journal of International Relations* 18(3): 407–30.

Keohane, Robert O. 1969. "Lilliputians' Dilemmas: Small States in International Politics." *International Organization* 23(2): 291–310.

Kinsella, David. 2005. "No Rest for the Democratic Peace." *The American Political Science Review* 99(3): 453–7.

Kober, Avi. 2002. *Coalition Defection: The Dissolution of Arab Anti-Israeli Coalitions in War and Peace*. Westport: Greenwood Publishing Group.

Koschut, Simon. 2012. "Friedlicher Wandel Ohne Demokratie? Theoretische Und Empirische Überlegungen Zur Bildung Einer Autokratischen Sicherheitsgemeinschaft." *Zeitschrift für Internationale Beziehungen* 19(2): 41–69.

Kühnhardt, Ludger. 2012. "The Arab Spring Revisited: How the Arab Monarchies Can Survive." *World Security Network*. www.worldsecuritynetwork.com/showArticle3.cfm?article_id=18594 (February 3, 2012).

Lai, Brian, and Dan Reiter. 2000. "Democracy, Political Similarity, and International Alliances, 1816–1992." *Journal of Conflict Resolution* 44(2): 203–27.

Lakatos, Imre. 1970. "Falsification and the Methodology of Scientific Research Programmes." In *Criticism and the Growth of Knowledge: Proceedings of the International Colloquium in the Philosophy of Science, London, 1965*, eds. Imre Lakatos and Alan Musgrave. Cambridge: Cambridge University Press, 91–197.

Lawson, Fred Haley. 2006. *Constructing International Relations in the Arab World*. 1st edition. Redwood City: Stanford University Press.

Layne, Christopher. 1994. "Kant or Cant: The Myth of the Democratic Peace." *International Security* 19(2): 5–49.

Lebow, Richard Ned. 2010. *Why Nations Fight: Past and Future Motives for War*. Reissue edition. Cambridge, UK; New York: Cambridge University Press.

Leeds, Brett Ashley. 2003. "Do Alliances Deter Aggression? The Influence of Military Alliances on the Initiation of Militarized Interstate Disputes." *American Journal of Political Science* 47(3): 427–39.

Levitsky, Steven, and Lucan A. Way. 2002. "The Rise of Competitive Authoritarianism." *Journal of Democracy* 13(2).

Levy, Jack S. 1988. "Domestic Politics and War." *The Journal of Interdisciplinary History* 18(4): 653–73.

Lucas, Russell E. 2004. "Monarchical Authoritarianism: Survival and Political Liberalization in a Middle Eastern Regime Type." *International Journal of Middle East Studies* 36(1): 103–19.

Lutterbeck, Derek. 2013. "Arab Uprisings, Armed Forces, and Civil – Military Relations." *Armed Forces & Society* 39(1): 28–52.

Maoz, Zeev, and Nasrin Abdolali. 1989. "Regime Types and International Conflict, 1816–1976." *Journal of Conflict Resolution* 33(1): 3–35.

Marshall, Monty, Ted Robert Gurr, and Keith Jaggers. 2014. *Polity IV Project. Political Regime Characteristics and Transitions, 1800–2013. Dataset Users' Manual*. Center for Systemic Peace. www.systemicpeace.org/inscr/p4manualv2013.pdf (March 13, 2016).

Martín, Félix. 2006. *Militarist Peace in South America: Conditions for War and Peace*. 2006 edition. New York: Palgrave Macmillan.

Melman, Yossi. 2011. "Bahrain King Boasted of Intelligence Ties with Israel." *Haaretz*. www.haaretz.com/print-edition/news/haaretz-wikileaks-exclusive-bahrain-king-boasted-of-intelligence-ties-with-israel-1.354728 (January 20, 2014).

Moving beyond democratic exceptionalism 59

Mintz, Alex, and Nehemia Geva. 1993. "Why Don't Democracies Fight Each Other? An Experimental Study." *Journal of Conflict Resolution* 37(3): 484–503.

Montesquieu, Charles de Secondat, ed. 2002. *De l'esprit Des Lois.* Chicoutimi: J.-M. Tremblay. http://classiques.uqac.ca/classiques/montesquieu/de_esprit_des_lois/de_esprit_des_lois_tdm.html (October 22, 2012).

Moravcsik, Andrew. 1997. "Taking Preferences Seriously: A Liberal Theory of International Politics." *International Organization* 51(4): 513–53.

Mousseau, Michael, Håvard Hegre, and John R. O'neal. 2003. "How the Wealth of Nations Conditions the Liberal Peace." *European Journal of International Relations* 9(2): 277–314.

Neel, J.V., and F.M. Salzano. 1967. "Further Studies on the Xavante Indians. X. Some Hypotheses-Generalizations Resulting from These Studies." *American Journal of Human Genetics* 19(4): 554–74.

Oakes, Penelope. 2002. "Psychological Groups and Political Psychology: A Response to Huddy's 'Critical Examination of Social Identity Theory'." *Political Psychology* 23(4): 809–24.

Owen, John M. 1994. "How Liberalism Produces Democratic Peace." *International Security* 19(2): 87–125.

Owen, Roger. 2004. *State, Power and Politics in the Making of the Modern Middle East.* London; New York: Routledge.

———. 2012. *The Rise and Fall of Arab Presidents for Life.* Cambridge: Harvard University Press.

Peceny, Mark, Caroline Beer, and Shannon Sanchez-Terry. 2002. "Dictatorial Peace?" *American Political Science Review* 96(1): 15–26.

Petersen, Karen K. 2004. "Laying to Rest the Autocratic Peace." Presented at the Journeys in world Politics, University of Iowa.

———. 2008. "There Is More to the Story than 'Us-Versus-Them': Expanding the Study of Interstate Conflict and Regime Type Beyond a Dichotomy." *Peace Economics, Peace Science and Public Policy* 14(1). http://works.bepress.com/karen_petersen/2 (June 1, 2014).

Peterson, J.E. 2006. "Qatar and the World: Branding for a Micro-State." *Middle East Journal* 60(4): 732–48.

Pollack, Kenneth Michael. 2002. *Arabs at War: Military Effectiveness, 1948–1991.* Lincoln, NE [u.a.]: University of Nebraska Press.

Posen, Barry R. 1986. *The Sources of Military Doctrine: France, Britain, and Germany Between the World Wars.* Ithaca, NY: Cornell University Press.

Quinlivan, James T. 1999. "Coup-Proofing: Its Practice and Consequences in the Middle East." *International Security* 24(2): 131–65.

Raknerud, Arvid, and Håvard Hegre. 1997. "The Hazard of War: Reassessing the Evidence for the Democratic Peace." *Journal of Peace Research* 34(4): 385–404.

Rasheed, Madawi al-. 2007. *Contesting the Saudi State: Islamic Voices from a New Generation.* Cambridge, UK; New York: Cambridge University Press.

Ray, James Lee. 2005. "Constructing Multivariate Analyses (of Dangerous Dyads)." *Conflict Management and Peace Science* 22(4): 277–92.

Reus-Smit, Christian. 2009. *The Moral Purpose of the State: Culture, Social Identity, and Institutional Rationality in International Relations.* Princeton: Princeton University Press.

Reynolds, David. 1985. "A 'Special Relationship'? America, Britain and the International Order Since the Second World War." *International Affairs (Royal Institute of International Affairs 1944-)* 62(1): 1–20.

60   *Moving beyond democratic exceptionalism*

Robinson, William Peter, and Henri Tajfel. 1996. *Social Groups and Identities: Developing the Legacy of Henri Tajfel*. Oxford: Psychology Press.

Ross, Michael L. 2001. "Does Oil Hinder Democracy?" *World Politics* 53(3): 325–61.

Roth, Daniel J. 2015. "Israel, Saudi Arabia Admit Secret Diplomacy for First Time." *The Jerusalem Post*. www.jpost.com/Israel-News/Israel-Saudi-Arabia-admit-secret-diplomacy-for-first-time-405123 (June 9, 2015).

Russett, Bruce. 1990. *Controlling the Sword: The Democratic Governance of National Security*. Cambridge: Harvard University Press.

Schedler, Andreas. 2002. "The Menue of Manipulation." *Journal of Democracy* 13(2): 36–50.

———. 2006. *Electoral Authoritarianism: The Dynamics of Unfree Competition*. Illustrated edition. Boulder: Lynne Rienner Publishers.

Schweller, Randall L. 1997. *Deadly Imbalances: Tripolarity and Hitler's Strategy of World Conquest*. New York: Columbia University Press.

Sechser, Todd S. 2004. "Are Soldiers Less War-Prone than Statesmen?" *Journal of Conflict Resolution* 48(5): 746–74.

Sherif, Muzafer. 2010. *The Robbers Cave Experiment: Intergroup Conflict and Cooperation. [Orig. Pub. as Intergroup Conflict and Group Relations]*. Middletown: Wesleyan University Press.

Siverson, Randolph M., and Juliann Emmons. 1991. "Birds of a Feather. Democratic Political Systems and Alliance Choices in the Twentieth Century." *Journal of Conflict Resolution* 35(2): 285–306.

Souva, Mark. 2004. "Institutional Similarity and Interstate Conflict." *International Interactions* 30(3): 263–80.

Sunik, Anna. 2015. "The Royal Special Relationship. Großbritannien und die arabischen Monarchien." In *Sonderbeziehungen als Nexus zwischen Außenpolitik und internationalen Beziehungen*, Außenpolitik und Internationale Ordnung, eds. Sebastian Harnisch, Klaus Brummer, and Kai Oppermann. Baden-Baden: Nomos, 55–80.

Tajfel, Henri. 1970. "Experiments in Intergroup Discrimination." *Scientific American* 223: 96–102.

———. 1974. "Social Identity and Intergroup Behaviour." *Social Science Information/sur les sciences sociales* 13(2): 65–93.

———, ed. 1978. *Differentiation between Social Groups: Studies in the Social Psychology of Intergroup Relations*. London; New York: Published in cooperation with European Association of Experimental Social Psychology by Academic Press.

———, ed. 1982. *Social Identity and Intergroup Relations*. Cambridge; Paris: Cambridge University Press; Editions de la Maison des sciences de l'homme.

Telhami, Shibley, and Michael Barnett. 2002. *Identity and Foreign Policy in the Middle East*. Ithaca: Cornell University Press.

Turner, John C., and Penelope J. Oakes. 1986. "The Significance of the Social Identity Concept for Social Psychology with Reference to Individualism, Interactionism and Social Influence." *British Journal of Social Psychology* 25(3): 237–52.

Vasquez, John A. 2009. *The War Puzzle Revisited*. Cambridge: Cambridge University Press.

Walt, Stephen M. 1985. "Alliance Formation and the Balance of World Power." *International Security* 9(4): 3–43.

Waltz, Kenneth N. 2001. *Man, the State, and War: A Theoretical Analysis*. Revised edition. New York: Columbia University Press.

Waterbury, John. 1970. *The Commander of the Faithful: The Moroccan Political Elite – a Study in Segmented Politics*. New York: Columbia University Press.

Weart, Spencer. 1994. "Peace Among Democratic and Oligarchic Republics." *Journal of Peace Research* 31(3): 299–316.

———. 1998. *Never at War: Why Democracies Will Not Fight One Another*. New Haven: Yale University Press.

Wedeen, Lisa. 1999. *Ambiguities of Domination: Politics, Rhetoric, and Symbols in Contemporary Syria*. Chicago: University of Chicago Press.

Wendt, Alexander. 1992. "Anarchy Is What States Make of It: The Social Construction of Power Politics." *International Organization* 46(2): 391–425.

———. 1994. "Collective Identity Formation and the International State." *The American Political Science Review* 88(2): 384–96.

———. 1999. *Social Theory of International Politics*. Cambridge: Cambridge University Press.

Werner, Suzanne. 2000. "The Effects of Political Similarity on the Onset of Militarized Disputes, 1816–1985." *Political Research Quarterly* 53(2): 343–74.

Werner, Suzanne, and Douglas Lemke. 1997. "Opposites Do Not Attract: The Impact of Domestic Institutions, Power, and Prior Commitments on Alignment Choices." *International Studies Quarterly* 41(3): 529–46.

Wiegand, Krista E. 2012. "Bahrain, Qatar, and the Hawar Islands: Resolution of a Gulf Territorial Dispute." *The Middle East Journal* 66(1): 78–95.

Wimmer, Andreas, and Brian Min. 2006. "From Empire to Nation-State: Explaining Wars in the Modern World, 1816–2001." *American Sociological Review* 71(6): 867–97.

Zacher, Mark W. 2001. "The Territorial Integrity Norm: International Boundaries and the Use of Force." *International Organization* 55(2): 215–50.

Zahlan, Rosemarie Said. 2002. *The Making of Modern Gulf States: Kuwait Bahrain Qatar, The United Arab Emirates and Oman*. Reading: Ithaca Press.

3 Middle East monarchies from the Arab Cold War to the Arab Spring

3.1 A brief history of monarchism in the Middle East

Monarchism in the region

The Middle East is the last region in the world where more than a few (authoritarian) monarchies have persisted. Although a common narrative is to describe monarchies as the oldest and most traditional form of government on earth, most of the monarchies currently in existence are, in fact, modern creations (Anderson 2009). For instance, many areas controlled by Great Britain before independence were turned into newly established monarchies (like Libya, Jordan, and Iraq). In other cases, pre-existing (semi-hereditary) practices of succession were formally institutionalized into nation-state form with British help, like in the smaller Gulf states. Some of the monarchies did not survive for long: the Federation of Southern Yemeni Emirates and Tunisia were short-lived monarchies that collapsed shortly after independence, while France hindered the establishment of the newly formed Kingdom of Syria in 1920.

One the one hand, monarchies represented a political innovation in the region: even the title of king, usually translated as *malik* in Arabic, was not in widespread use before the 20th century and often entailed a negative connotation. The first modern Muslim ruler declaring himself king was Sharif Hussein bin Ali, the father of the founders of the Hashemite dynasties of Iraq and Jordan, who in 1916 proclaimed himself King of the Hijaz. Later Middle Eastern monarchs taking that title usually signaled their sovereignty and independence from colonial rule. Kuwait, Qatar, the UAE, and Bahrain until 2002 used the designation of emir (Arabic for prince), while Oman is a sultanate and North Yemen had an imamate instead.

On the other hand, monarchy as a form of rule by hereditary succession had a long tradition in the region, going back to the early days of Islam and sometimes to the pre-Islamic period. In many countries, monarchism was the dominant form of political rule, and republicanism arrived much later: the first Muslim republic was Azerbaijan, installed in May 1918 (Ayalon 2000; Lewis 2000). Saudi Arabia, Oman, Morocco, (North) Yemen, and Iran, for instance, already had long histories of monarchical rule, as did Egypt, for centuries an integral part of the Ottoman Empire – itself another (imperial) monarchy.

But while the legacy of monarchism in the region is as old as its European counterpart, Middle Eastern monarchies have always differed from them in their institutional setup and their deployment of religious legitimization. For instance, while none of the current eight monarchies in the Middle East could be described as parliamentary (although Morocco, Jordan, and Kuwait are sometimes called constitutional monarchies) – because the powers of the parliaments are largely symbolic, while those of the monarchs are vast – they are also by no means "absolute" in the European understanding shaped by 17th-cenury to 18th-century Louis Quatorzian absolutism.

In the Middle Eastern monarchy, the family rules instead of a single absolute sovereign. Consequently, these states are very much constrained not only by their population, which may revolt, but by the balance of power within the political elite and other elites. This includes the military, which might stage a coup, but especially the royal family itself and the old Arab principles of *shura* and *ijma'* (Herb 1999; Lewis 2000). Monarchies with a parliament and a constitution, such as Morocco, Jordan, and Kuwait (and Egypt and Iraq in their monarchical periods), also have important veto players in the form of societal, tribal, or socioeconomic groups that must be considered. Middle Eastern monarchies also exhibit much more diverse and flexible systems of succession that were only exceptionally based on primogeniture, as was typical of European monarchies.

In addition, the role of religion differed starkly from the European medieval principle of rule by divine right. Only Saudi Arabia can be said to combine religious and profane authority at the core of the state and regime. However, even there, the royal Al Saud depend on the *ulama'*, the Islamic scholars, as well as on the Al Shaikh, the descendants of Mohammad ibn Abd al-Wahhab, to legitimize their rule in religious terms. In other words, the dynasty does not claim to derive its right to rule directly from God. While neither royal family nor the monarch is members of a particular political current (although there are certainly political factions within the family), the monarch is a representative of the particular brand of Islam in the country and the custodian of the two holy sites (*khadim al-haramain*), Mecca and Medina. This religious role sometimes substitutes political divisions for religious ones (cf. e.g. Rasheed 1998; Vassiliev 2013).

In other cases, religious legitimacy is based on Sharifian descent (descent from the Prophet), as by the Moroccan and Jordanian royal families as well as the Sanoussis of Libya, the Hamid al-Din imams of Yemen, and the Hashemites of Iraq. Nonetheless, even Sharifian rulers never claimed a direct divine link that makes their rule inevitable or God given. The other monarchs do not claim any religious legitimacy at all, although they also serve as protectors of the faith and religious role models in terms of public piety (Ben-Dor 2000; Krämer 2000; Maddy-Weizmann 2000).

Monarchies as similar political systems

Middle East monarchies are "similar", in both structure and institutions, connected by strong personalized links and public displays of solidarity showing that they perceive each other as such. The links that they create through personal and family relationships, their shared political vocabulary, and attempts to institutionalize the common "club" show the social processes of ingroup identification. Prolonged interpersonal contact, common elite socialization, and kinship ties form a strong ground for a common identity, which can be expressed in referring to the closeness of the other, e.g. as "family", a proxy for perception of sameness.

While monarchic solidarity makes monarchs recognize each other as equals, some are more equal than others. Not all monarchic relationships are alike. The "club of monarchies" varies in time, size, and relevance. It is a continuum rather than a strictly bounded and clearly delimitated and defined group. The more qualities are shared by two members, the closer their connection becomes. They form a core in the group that can consist of multiple layers of increasingly weaker links. The dynastic Gulf monarchies constitute such a core in that they share family and cultural ties, a common history and experience, similar worldviews, religious outlooks, political systems, language, and alliance structure. The extra-regional monarchies of Jordan and Morocco still share many of these traits, including the core features of the political system, the Arab culture, shared cultural and historical heritage, and a distinct Sharifian ancestry linking them to the Arabian Peninsula. On the other hand, they have fewer family ties, limited geographic proximity (or none at all), and different historic experiences and trajectories. Other monarchies had even less in common with the core, such as pre-revolutionary Iran, a Persian and Shiite state. At the periphery of this monarchic core, one might situate non-authoritarian and non-Islamic monarchies such as the United Kingdom.[1] This common identity of the MENA monarchies was formed over decades, if not centuries. Most existing monarchies have a common history as British creations. The Hashemite dynasties of Jordan and Iraq were "imported" by the British from what is now Saudi Arabia, while the smaller Gulf monarchies, now known as Bahrain, Kuwait, Qatar, and the UAE, were created almost from scratch. To this day, Jordan is sometimes referred to as "the very epitome of artificiality in the region" (Krämer 2000, 269). Today's borders, flags, dynasties, and even the succession regulations were either created or at least defined by Britain (Lawson 1989; Zahlan 2002). Libya, which consists of the three formerly separated provinces of Tripolitania, Cyrenaica, and Fezzan, an Italian colony from 1912 to 1919, was united under British administration and spearheaded by King Idris as it gained its independence in 1951 (Wright 1983).

Only Egypt, Iran, (North) Yemen, and of the current monarchies Morocco, Oman, and (in some respects) Saudi Arabia, could look back at a more or less autochthonous, though not unbroken, dynastic tradition. Still, even the Egyptian Khedive and the Pahlavi, Al Saud, and Al Bu-Said dynasties at times survived only with British (later also US) support against rebellions and coup attempts like the coup in Iran in 1953 (Owen 2004, 7). Merely Morocco

From the Arab Cold War to the Arab Spring 65

remained free from British control – because it was already a protectorate of another European colonial power, France, from 1912 to 1956. In contrast to the republics, the monarchies, not having lived through revolutions or regime changes, have not broken with the past, which is still an important part of their identity and perceived commonality. Despite decolonization movements, sometimes led by the monarchs themselves (especially in Morocco and Jordan), they have consistently remained Western allies. Common channels allow them to keep the ties with the former imperial powers as well as each other alive (Sunik 2015).

This *shared history* has shaped institutions and traditions of the states, linking them together and resulting in a *shared socialization* of the political elite. Up to this day, most of the monarchs and a large share of other ruling family members continue to be educated in British "royal education facilities" such as Harrow School, formerly also the Victoria College in Cairo, and especially the Royal Military Academy of Sandhurst. Sometimes, these are the locations where the royal youth met each other for the first time. Palace schools, where ruling family members learn about the principles and responsibilities of being a ruler, often by example from other monarchies, are another arena where a shared royal identity is fostered and reified (Yom 2013). Said bin Taimur, the father and predecessor of Sultan Qaboos in Oman, visited the Mayo College in India, also known as the College of Princes, as it was an education facility for local aspirants for future rule under British regency (Allen and Rigsbee 2000, 2). Sandhurst has a special status as the military forge of kings, and many personal relationships between royals date back to the period of their joint years of study. Even for monarchs who attended at different times, it is a unifying trait.[2] Almost all of the Jordanian royal family since Talal bin Abdallah's times – the first Arab Officer Cadet there (Shlaim 2009, 38) – and a large part of the rulers in the Gulf or at least their close relatives received their education at the military academy, along with the progeny of European monarchies (Teller 2014). The Bahraini king, Hamad bin Isa Al-Khalifa, is the patron of the board of trustees of Sandhurst's alumni organization, Sandhurst Trust (Sandhurst Trust 2013).

This common socialization of the elite during a crucial period of personality development is vital for shaping perceptions of the other as well as common ideas, preferences, and conflict-resolution approaches (cf. the common socialization as an explanation for the peace among military dictatorships: Peceny, Beer, and Sanchez-Terry 2002). This intensive contact led to a strong level of *personalization of ties*, even in comparison to personalized republics, and raised the cooperation to a more personal and emotional level, making friends out of political counterparts from different countries.[3] According to a data set, from 1980 to 2013, that was assembled by Sean Yom, monarchs interacted with each other significantly more than with presidents, even when including Egypt, which accounted for a quarter of all interactions because of its hosting of the Arab League headquarters. This is not just a matter of proximity – even a periphery monarchy like Morocco attracted more visits by Saudi royals than any other locale, except the neighboring emirate of Dubai (Yom 2014, 59–60).

66 *From the Arab Cold War to the Arab Spring*

Consequently, many personal and political links across boundaries arose, in many cases also family ties through marriage, which in turn led to more intensive and extensive interaction, creating a feedback loop. Especially the Gulf monarchies, but also Jordan and Morocco and even historical monarchical families, exhibit a huge amount of intermarriage, like European monarchies until the 20th century (Yom 2014, 59). The emirates of the UAE are heavily intermarried; Jordanian princes and princesses married into the Ottoman Empire and the Dubai ruling family; the Saudi king's daughter is married to a son of the king of Bahrain; Fawziya Fu'ad, the wife of Shah Mohammed Reza Pahlavi of Iran, was the sister of Egyptian King Faruq, while his son, the last king of Egypt, married the granddaughter of Mohammed Zahir Khan, the last king of Afghanistan. Some family connections go even further back. The first kings of Iraq and Jordan were brothers, and they, as well as the king of Morocco, the Sanoussis from Libya, and the Imams of the Kingdom of Yemen, derive their ancestry from the Prophet Mohammad.[4] The ruling families of Kuwait and Bahrain share an ancestry of the *'Utub*, a central Arabian tribe and a branch of the *'Aniza*, from which also the Saudi royal family descends ('Abd al-Hakim al-Wa'ili 2002a, 1515, 2002b, 1283). All three plus the Qatari Al Thani derive their ancestry from the Najd region in central Arabia.

There is no comparable extent of personal exchange and linkage between presidents and their inner circle or between republican leaders and dynasties (Yom 2014, 59–60). Although British and especially US higher education facilities are popular among the latter as well, there are no comparable focal points or centers of political socialization. All this "regularized social interaction" shaped the monarchic elites of the Middle East into an "epistemic community" that shared and allowed for a diffusion of ideas (Yom 2014, 59). For instance, after the shah had supported the Omani sultan against rebels in Dhofar, the two exchanged ideas and talked about introducing a "White Revolution-like" reform in the separatist region, on the basis of the Iranian model, during the shah's visit in late 1977 (Goode 2014, 461).

Monarchs often recognize this commonality through family rhetoric, a key indicator for the presence of a strong ingroup identification. The founder of the UAE and its president until 2004, Shaikh Zayed bin Sultan Al Nahyan, claimed in 1972 that any differences with Saudi Arabia were merely differences of opinion as "such things even happen between brothers" and in a later interview in November that year that there were "no differences with Saudi Arabia in any real sense" (cited in: Alkim 1989, 118). He later proclaimed that the "UAE, Saudi Arabia and the Gulf are one family and share the same heritage, history and a common future" during a state visit by Saudi King Khalid on March 27, 1976 (cited in: Alkim 1989, 124), and Khalid reciprocated. UAE Foreign Minister al-Suwaidi brought the term "two sisters" into circulation in 1975 for its relation with Saudi Arabia, which has since been customary (Alkim 1989, 123). During a state visit to Saudi Arabia of Omani Sultan Qaboos in December 1971, King Faisal issued a statement recognizing the Omani sultan by addressing his "royal brother" and the "brotherly people of Oman", followed by a confidential note to

From the Arab Cold War to the Arab Spring 67

raise the Sultanian address from *Adhamat* (Highness) to the more regal *Jalalat* (Majesty) (Al-Khalili 2009, 73).

Although they can acknowledge actual distant family links, for the most part, family references are metaphorical and were at times even extended to monarchs who were clearly not kin even in the broad encompassing sense of ethnicity. The Iranian shah, for instance, considered the Omani sultan a brother (Goode 2014), despite belonging to unconnected dynasties, different ethnicities, and Islamic sects. He also wrote in his memoirs about his fellow monarch in Jordan: "As for King Hussein of Jordan, I cannot praise him enough. He is not only a friend, but a brother. His qualities as a man and his goodness of heart are enhanced by great courage and a true love of his country" (Pahlavi and Waugh 1980, 146). This closeness marked the continuation of Pahlavi-Hashemite relations between the shah and Hussein's grandfather, King Abdallah, who also referred to the shah as a brother of "a sister Muslim country". After a visit to Iran in which royal medals, the Iranian Royal Collar, and the Collar of Hussein bin Ali were exchanged, King Abdallah described how the monarchs "embraced as father and son or as brothers" while "exchanging expressions of Islamic brotherhood" (Abdallah I King of Jordan 1954, 63–64).

Similar recognitions were sometimes bestowed upon other Arab states, although they were mostly confined to the level of the state or the populace instead of individual ruler or the regime. This distinction is often visible by the more abstract appellation to "sisterhood"[5] (e.g. "sisterly Arab countries" referring to Egypt and Iraq by Kuwaiti ruler Shaikh Abdallah Salim (Joyce 1998, 56)), instead of the more personal and individual "brother". External allies, especially the Western states, were merely referred to as "friends". The following case studies unearth more of such references and the circumstances of their employment among the examined dyads.

As this section has shown, the dynasties of the Middle East monarchies are bound together by more than just structural similarity: they are intimately linked by a close-knit personal network that is shaped by bonds of kinship, marriage, common socialization, and historical path dependence, which is the foundation on which common norms regarding nonviolence toward each other are developed. But this "monarchic club" by far surpasses the relevance of a mere alumni association of the Academy of Sandhurst: in times of crisis, vague bonds of kinship and familiarity would develop into much-more-formalized practices of ingroup solidarity, both during the Arab Cold War and the Arab Spring, as shown in the following sections.

3.2 Monarchies in crisis

What does a monarchic peace look like in action in an active regional context? We have established in the previous section that monarchies in the Middle East are similar systems (structural similarity) that are often recognized and acknowledged by their leaders and elites (social processes of ingroup identification). But how does this lead to a distinct foreign policy behavior? This section focuses on

68 *From the Arab Cold War to the Arab Spring*

these effects in a most likely case – that is, during times of a strong common threat that forces monarchies to hang together or to hang apart. If ingroup identification is particularly strong, we should see not just the absence of war but also active intra-monarchic solidarity, a much stronger requirement. This is shown for two periods with particularly strong threats toward monarchies: the Arab Cold War in the 1950s and 1960s and a shorter period following the Arab Spring during 2011–2015. The rallying together and pronounced solidarity among monarchies during these time periods plausibilizes the theoretical assumptions and illustrates the macro-dynamics conditioned by salience of monarchism as an identifying factor.

When monarchies fight: the Arab Cold War 1952–1970

It is no coincidence that many monarchies broke down from the 1950s to the 1970s. In the aftermath of decolonization, Arab nationalism was widespread. The revolutionary wave against hereditary regimes enhanced the perception of the MENA monarchies as an endangered group that should stick together against any challenges, foreign and domestic. In those days, far from the solid rock of the Arab Spring period, the monarchies seemed close to extinction.

The distinction between conservative monarchies and radical republics turned into the dominant cleavage among the states of the region, thereby propelling monarchism to the highest possible salience, culminating in the depiction of the period by Malcolm Kerr as a bipolar Arab Cold War (Kerr 1971). The threat was directed not only toward individual monarchs or their regimes but also toward monarchies as a group. The two main blocs were revolutionary Arab socialist republics such as Egypt, Syria, and Iraq and "reactionary" traditional monarchies, first and foremost Saudi Arabia and Jordan, because the small Gulf states had not yet achieved their independence.

The challenge of the Six-Day War in 1967 and the humiliating defeat of Nasser's pan-Arabism significantly reduced inter-Arab conflict, but isolated episodes between the two camps continued until the 1970s, e.g. with the Black September clashes in Jordan in 1970.

Common threat from internal opposition and its support by outgroup members

In the 1950s and 1960s, four monarchies were toppled by coups d'état by socialist-minded and Arab nationalist–minded "Free Officers" – Egypt (1952), Iraq (1958), Yemen (1962), and Libya (1969), before the last monarchy to fall, Iran, was engulfed in a major popular revolution in 1979.

But the survivors also struggled against internal opposition. Attempted coups and assassinations against the kings shook Jordan, Morocco, and Saudi Arabia. The internal enemies were not isolated; in some cases, they even reached deep into the royal elite itself, like the "Free Princes" faction led by Saudi Prince Talal bin Abd al-Aziz, which supported pan-Arabism and called for constitutional reform in the kingdom (Rogan and Aclimandos 2012, 156–157).

From the Arab Cold War to the Arab Spring 69

In addition, the domestic opponents were often supported by regional rival republics. Apart from the funding of the existent opposition group, the secret services of the hostile parties employed subversion to destabilize their enemies' regimes, escalating to a "covert war" (Rathmell 2014).

The threat level was not uniform. There were periods of détente and of increased tensions as when King Hussein ended his rapprochement with Syria and Egypt after dismissing the country's first democratically elected parliament in 1957 in anticipation of a palace coup (Shlaim 2009, 132). Jordan and Saudi Arabia were the monarchies targeted most intensively. After a failed rapprochement in 1957, there was intense Syrian and Egyptian secret service activity in Jordan (Rathmell 2014, 132–133). US reports spoke of an Egyptian-sponsored plot to assassinate Hussein and of an alleged planting of a bomb in one of King Saud's palaces. Syria and Egypt stepped up their campaign of anti-royalist black propaganda and terrorism aimed at destabilizing Jordan and strengthening the popular opposition. The recruitment of agents who would be willing to bomb government and Western targets was combined with a whispering campaign that King Hussein would bow to popular pressure and reinstate the elected government. Anti-royalist propaganda leaflets were distributed by Egyptians. The Deuxième Bureau, as the Syrian military intelligence was known until 1969, toured Jordan recruiting agents who dropped off bombs in Amman, Hebron, Irbid, and Ramallah. After bombs went off outside the Turkish embassy and the house of the military governor of Amman in September, Jordanian security forces began discovering caches of weapons smuggled in from Syria. Syrian agents were prosecuted and Syrian diplomats expelled from Jordan while Syria set up a Jordanian government-in-exile (Rathmell 2014, 134–135). After a major bombing targeting Jordanian Prime Minister Hazza Majali in August 1959, the two suspects fled to the UAR, which denied extradition requests and whose media portrayed the attack as the laudable work of a Jordanian opposition movement, rebelling against the "oppressive monarchy" (Rathmell 1996).

The sponsoring of a terrorism campaign inside Jordan did not cease in the 1950s. After the ninth coup in 17 years on February 23, 1966, Syrian leaders escalated their policy against "reactionary" states. A few weeks before the outbreak of the 1967 war, a car bomb killed 21 Jordanians at the Ramtha border post on May 21. For King Hussein, this was evidence that Syrian enmity toward Jordan was greater than that toward the nominal common foe, Israel, so he subsequently cut diplomatic relations (Shlaim 2012, 104, 121). In 1983, there were attacks against Jordanian embassy personnel in four countries. Bombings and other terrorist tactics "became the primary ones of Syrian foreign policy in this period" and not just against Jordan (Rathmell 1996).

Jordan also feared destabilization by Palestinian activities, particularly by Fedayeen from their territory while Syria acted as their protector. After Hussein's crackdown on Palestinians in what became known as the Black September, when the Palestinian Liberation Organisation (PLO) under Yassir Arafat attempted to take over the state and overthrow the monarchy in 1970, Syrian armored column crossed into Jordan and engaged, although Syria claimed that they were Palestine

70 *From the Arab Cold War to the Arab Spring*

Liberation Army (PLA) units. Qadhafi also threatened to send his army to Jordan and broke off diplomatic relations. Libya, but also Kuwait, withdrew their aid to the monarchy (Kerr 1971, 149–150).

Saudi Arabia was also vulnerable and was targeted particularly in relation to the proxy war in Yemen. In 1962, the kingdom cut relations with Egypt after it had tried to smuggle weapons into the Hijaz, and Egyptian soldiers allegedly tried to infiltrate the country while dressed as pilgrims (Gause 1990, 60–61). In 1963, nine Saudi pilots sent to fight in Yemen defected to Egypt, and the opposition not only was found among military circles in Saudi Arabia but covered broader societal sections, including bourgeoisie and reformists (Ayubi 1995, 282). The Yemeni Civil War was a large battlefield between royalist and republican supporters, fighting a hot proxy war amid the regional cold war. When Nasser renewed his threats against Saudi bases in Yemen in March 1966, the tentative détente was reversed, so tensions flared up again (Kerr 1971, 109). A series of explosions hit the kingdom between December that year and April 1967, with evidence pointing to Egyptian involvement (Gause 1990, 70).

The tensions of the period go back to the transnational ideology of pan-Arabism at its zenith at that time. The ideology was inextricably tied to republics, especially those with a revolutionary recent history – embodied in Muhammed Hussanein Heikal's distinction of Egypt as a state and Egypt as a revolution (Ajami 1978, 356). Pan-Arabism was in its height, promoting Arab unity that was tied to ideas of anticolonialism and revolutionary socialism, both incompatible with the less-ideological monarchies and their system. Pan-Arabism rejected the pro-Western support of the monarchies and called for revolution and ultimately the dismantlement of the "reactionary" conservative monarchies (Kerr 1971, 1–7).[6] The pan-Arabist current of Ba'thism explicitly "advocated the destruction of traditional monarchies and the end of Shaikhly rule" (Joyce 1998, 131). Promoted by republican pan-Arabist rulers and popular among the populations inside their realism, the ideology further heightened the feeling of vulnerability of the monarchs.

The threat toward Middle Eastern monarchies during the period of the Arab Cold War was immediate and direct, and it targeted not only individual states but rather monarchies as a group. This increased the salience of monarchy as a commonality that could be used for mobilization and alliance.

Although the 1970s offered some brief respite, the next period of confrontation and common threat was ushered in soon by the Islamic Revolution and its accompanying rise of pan-Islamic ideology, which was also directed against "un-Islamic" (in contrast to "un-Arab") monarchies. Combined with the threat by republican Ba'thist Iraq, the rise of the Islamic Republic led to the formation of the Gulf Cooperation Council (GCC) as a Gulf monarchy solidarity club (cf. Kostiner 2009, 56).

Ingroup favoritism: solidarity, alliance and institutionalization of community

The vulnerability of MENA monarchies at that time induced a sort of "rally-around-the-crown" effect, leading to an ingroup favoritism that was expressed by

From the Arab Cold War to the Arab Spring 71

mutual diplomatic, financial, and military support and to the formation of formal and informal alliances, including attempts at formalizing these alliances into institutionalized "clubs" among monarchies with exceptionally close ties.

Although Jordan and Saudi Arabia had been bitter rivals up to the 1950s, they buried the hatchet and directed their ire against the republics, bound together by a persistent though unofficial alliance that lasts to this day. Other monarchies also started to join this tacit alliance. Many of the instances of ingroup favoritism were symbolic, consisting of promises and token support by monarchs to each other, but other forms of support and alliance were more tangible.

After the revolution in Iraq, which almost took its Jordanian sister dynasty with it, King Hussein went on a world tour between February and May when he visited the monarchies of Iran, Morocco, and Ethiopia, along with some (mostly African) republics. His visit to Ethiopia was particularly symbolic in that Emperor Haile Selassie – also called the Lion of Judah – gave King Hussein, known as the Lion of Jordan, two lion cubs as a gift and symbol of friendship (Shlaim 2009, 175).

When monarchic alliance patterns grew stronger in 1957, Jordan's ties with Saudi Arabia and the US strengthened, and Jordan could participate in what one UK official termed "the Monarchistic Trade Union" (cf. Shlaim 2009, 132). At the beginning of the Yemeni Civil War, Jordan stood by the side of its "sister Kingdom of Saudi Arabia", and King Hussein proclaimed that his country regarded aggression against Saudi Arabia as a direct aggression against Jordan (Rogan and Aclimandos 2012, 157). During the intense subversion campaign aimed at destabilizing the monarchy in the late 1950s, King Hussein asked Iraq and the US for help. King Faisal obliged, dispatching Iraqi troops to Jordan (Moubayed 2000, 173).

Finally, there were increasing attempts at formalized alliance and even institutionalized community, especially among core sets of similar political systems. The Hashemite sister kingdoms of Jordan and Iraq attempted to institutionalize their alliance and relationship. An early attempt was the Treaty of Brotherhood and Alliance signed in March 1947, but the formation of the United Arab Republic (UAR) on February 1, 1958, by Egypt and Syria boosted these efforts. The Hashemite kingdoms, ruled by cousins at that time, formed the Arab Federation (or Arab Union, AFU) as a reaction to the UAR a fortnight later. They also invited Kuwait, which they perceived as sharing their pro□Western and conservative outlook (Khadduri and Ghareeb 2001, 45–54). Despite assertions that these unions were balancing Israel, inter-Arab conflict and especially Nasser's struggle against the monarchies was of prime importance to both of them (Podeh 1999, 39–48).[7]

Other attempts to institutionalize an alliance followed. King Faisal's alignment of Muslim states, referred to by himself as an Islamic "conference" and by his foes as an Islamic "pact", professed to include all Muslim countries but was de facto an alliance of similar conservative states, mostly monarchies. The "conference" was kicked off by Faisal's visit to the shah in 1965, followed by visits to Jordan, Morocco, Libya, and Kuwait. He also visited Turkey, Sudan, Pakistan, and Tunisia and, as Kerr notes, "rather oddly" to Nasser's allies in Guinea and Mali (Halliday 2011, 115; Kerr 1971, 110–112). This is also how the republican bloc perceived the alliance. Nasser criticized members of the Islamic Alliance, the

72 *From the Arab Cold War to the Arab Spring*

three Kingdoms of Saudi Arabia, Jordan, and Iran, of colluding with the enemy and ruled out coordination with them (Laqueur and Rubin 2008, 98).

Although the frontlines between the two clearly delineated blocs sometimes blur and republics could at times be found in the monarchic camp,[8] the monarchies clung together, even across ethnic lines. While pan-Arabist ideology was a threat to the monarchies, all Arab leaders at least at times paid lip service to its ideals. Nevertheless, the monarchic bond prevailed over Arabist goals. Iran is an unlikely monarchic ally, due to its non-Arab identity and long-standing territorial conflicts with Gulf monarchies – especially Iran's occupation of Abu Musa and the two Tunb islands of the UAE on the eve of the independence of the UAE, which received a remarkably restrained response from its Arab monarchic neighbors (see also in Chapter 5.2 of the Iran–UAE case study). Yet the Arab monarchs' relations with the Persian shah were closer and friendlier than those with most Arab republics. King Hussein even saw the shah as a mentor and often visited for consultation or vacation at Iranian royal retreats on the Caspian Sea or on Kish Island in the Gulf (Goode 2014, 449).

Even while the shah's position was weakened by massive domestic protests and a surging Iraq, the ties to Arab monarchies, especially Kuwait and Saudi Arabia, intensified instead of weakening, as would be expected if they were a mere ad hoc cooperation based on common interests. The archrivals of today, Saudi Arabia and Iran, cooperated intensely before the revolution, especially between 1972 and 1978, to counter Iraq's support of various radical movements in the Gulf (Cordesman 1984, 419). Even amid the revolutionary turmoil and mass protests in 1978 and 1979, Saudi Arabia issued official statements in favor of the shah, and King Khalid continued to proclaim that "the Shah's regime is legitimate and Saudi Arabia supports it" even after the shah announced his intention to leave in January 1979 (cited in: Alkim 1989, 126) and at the same time accused Ayatollah Khomeini of advocating "wrong subversive ideologies" (Korany 1984, 252). The victory of the Islamic Revolution then prompted the founding of the GCC (cf. Boghardt 2006, 53). Even in the Arab-Israeli conflict, monarchic solidarity prevailed in that the Gulf monarchies chose to finance only those "Islamic" fighters (*fidayin*) against Israel which did not attack Jordan (Kerr 1971, 139).

Of course, the level of solidarity differed strongly. While the cooperation and mutual support were most pronounced between Hashemite sister monarchies Jordan and Iraq and noticeable with and between Saudi Arabia and Kuwait, the monarchies on the periphery – Morocco, Libya, Yemen, and Oman – were somewhat less involved. This is explained in part by their geographical distance and in some cases their relatively recent introduction into the Middle East regional system (Morocco and Libya became independent only in 1956 and 1951, respectively). Despite these complications, there was extensive cooperation between the Moroccan and especially Jordanian monarchy, particularly during the long reigns of Hassan II (1961–1999) in Morocco and Hussein in Jordan (1952–1999), who even got matching nicknames as the Plucky Little King (Hussein) for his courage and the Cocky Little King because of his "superb self-assurance in adversity and his angry reactions to criticism" (S. O. Hughes 2001, 5). The shah and the kings of

From the Arab Cold War to the Arab Spring 73

Saudi Arabia had also been "close friends" of King Hassan as well, despite "enormous differences" (S. O. Hughes 2001, 5; cf. Pahlavi and Waugh 1980, 145). Even the cooperation with the peripheral (and idiosyncratic) monarchies of Yemen and Oman was strong, and both were supported in their civil wars by other monarchs.

Monarchies fighting republics: military action, subversion, and delegitimization

In this period, ingroup favoritism was not the only outcome of the consolidation of a "monarchic club". In the presence of a common threat perceived "as a serious societal danger" (Gibler, Hutchison, and Miller 2012, 1659), outgroup hostility can be catalyzed (cf. Gibler, Hutchison, and Miller 2012, 1657), which is exactly what happened in this period. It shows that monarchies are not inherently peaceful, having had no qualms to oppose and destabilize republics.

Outgroup hostility during the Arab Cold War took the form mainly of subversion, but it also resulted in proxy wars. The latter are also indicative of monarchic solidarity given that the monarchies supported "similar" local monarchic allies, while the republics did the same for republicans.

The covert war described earlier was not a one-sided republican subversion of monarchies; it was a highly symmetric affair. Especially in the 1950s, Jordanian and Syrian intelligence sought to carry out terrorist operations against one another. In July 1957, Jordanian intelligence sent a Muslim Brotherhood agent, Adib ad-Dessuki, to Syria to assassinate leftist leaders and kidnap Jordanian exiles. There also were reports of Jordanian arms provision to the Druze and Alawites in Syria, who were challenging the central government (Rathmell 2014, 134). Saudi Arabia also used subversive tactics and even initiated an ill-conceived assassination attempt against Nasser in 1958 (Rathmell 2014, 148). King Saud was also accused of bankrolling Syrian rebels who plotted secession from UAR during 1961, to which Egypt responded with calls for the overthrow of the monarchy (Rogan and Aclimandos 2012, 156). A renewal of tensions in the feud between Syria and Jordan was launched with (Saudi-encouraged) Jordanian broadcast calls for the overthrow of the Syrian and Egyptian rulers by their people in 1960. Anti-republican attacks grew increasingly direct. In May 1960, Amman Radio admonished "small dictators" and "Pharaonic rulers". On June 26, King Hussein directly attacked Nasser and prophesied his collapse (Rathmell 1996).

The tension built up into an imminent military confrontation. By September 12, 1959, Jordan had mobilized troops and was "ready for a military move against Syria" (Rathmell 1996). It took a good measure of British attempts at convincing and restraining to step back from this threat. Instead, Jordan decided to pay back in kind and started recruiting and training agents who conducted bombings in Damascus and on UAR targets. The covert war ended with Nasser's acceptance of King Hussein's truce offer in March 1961 (Rathmell 1996).

The tensions had a history before Nasser, as Hashemite efforts to extend their influence had already led King Hussein's grandfather, King Abdallah, to support "monarchist movements" to realize "Greater Syria". In fact, most coup plot

74   From the Arab Cold War to the Arab Spring

warnings in 1947 were linked to this movement, and Syrian officers then reported that a majority of the military would support such a coup or were already allied with Abdallah. The main recruiting source were ethnic and religious minorities such as the Druze, who had once asked Abdallah to annex their territory to Jordan (Landis 2001, 178, 181–183). This was then already perceived as a conflict between monarchies and republics. Syrian Prime Minister Jamil Mardam blamed the monarchs for not intervening in Palestine before the first Arab-Israeli War of 1948: "So long as the position of the Kings and Amirs is one of caution and plots, this [i.e. the formation of a volunteer army instead of direct military intervention] is the only sound policy" (cited in: Landis 2001, 192).

Under Nasser, Egypt was a main target of monarchic destabilization attempts due to his leader's role in fostering revolutionary ideologies. Jordan withdrew its ambassador to Cairo when Nasser called Hussein "a debauched king, the adulterer of Jordan", in February 1967 (Shlaim 2012, 117). Jordanian propaganda against Egypt was escalated in the period of 1966–1967 in the period before the Six-Day War (Shlaim 2012, 105). The level of distrust in this period is starkly illustrated by Nasser's rejection and ignoring of King Hussein's warnings of an impending Israeli military strike. On the eve of the war, Nasser disregarded the king's message twice because, as he later admitted, he did not believe him. Nasser's failure to take countermeasures led to the disastrous defeat of the Egyptian air force, securing Israeli victory (Shlaim 2012, 111–112).

The most striking embodiment of the bipolar regional system were the proxy wars, most notably in Yemen from 1962 to 1967. Yemen served as a battleground for an indirect war of the two camps of the Arab Cold War similar to the Angolan and Greek civil wars during the "global" Cold War.

The coup in Yemen formed an opportunity to showcase Nasser's allegiance to pan-Arabism. Five thousand Egyptian troops arrived in Sana'a mere days after the overthrow of Yemen's Imam Muhammad al-Badr, to later grow into a force of 50,000, of which 26,000 were killed in the five years of war (Pollack 2002, 48, 51, 56). Egypt supported republican revolutionists and the "Free Officers", inspired by and named after the same movement that brought Gamal Abdel Nasser and his allies to power (Badīb 1986; Kerr 1971). Iraq, Syria, and Lebanon recognized the revolutionaries, while Saudi Arabia and Jordan supported the royalists "out of dynastic solidarity", as Kerr states (Kerr 1971, 40–141).

Imam Ahmad's son and successor, Muhammad al-Badr, had initially been sympathetic to Nasserism but also proved an incompatible ally with Nasser's shift to Arab socialism in 1961. He then "found himself lumped together with conservative monarchs as a bastion of Arab reaction" (Rogan and Aclimandos 2012, 151–152), a triumph of ingroup perception over potential interest convergence. Identity and ideological bonds were apparently more dominant and durable than interest-based ones.

The Cold War rhetoric died down after the Six-Day War of 1967, in which both sides were implicated and failed miserably. As the ideological fervor of pan-Arabism abated and Hussein was severely weakened by the war, a renewed and more persistent rapprochement became a reality, especially after the evaporation

From the Arab Cold War to the Arab Spring 75

of the Yemen threat to Saudi Arabia because of Egypt's withdrawal in November. King Hussein cut his affiliation with the Islamic Alliance in the hope of Egyptian Patronage, and Saudi Arabia recognized the Republic of North Yemen in 1970 (cf. Kerr 1971, 128–130).

This did not imply the elimination of the old fault lines. The Arab-Israeli conflict remained a sore spot and a source of trouble; the ideological conflict between the systems lingered on. In an unguarded moment during a meeting with King Hussein in 1969, Nasser delighted at the news that another Arab king had been overthrown in Libya. Hussein took it personally and confided to a friend that "[t]hat scene will be forever engraved in my memory" (Kerr 1971, 148; Rouleau 1970).

The Yemen War was not the only proxy war in the region; a less known one was conducted in neighboring Oman, where a royalist axis consisting of Britain, Jordan, and Iran allied against challengers to the Sultan's rule and their external backers, revolutionist South Yemen (G. Hughes 2015; Jones 2011). Although the longest period of Oman's Dhofar rebellion, 1965–1975, is set after the main period of the Arab Cold War, it is a telling example of monarchic alliances. Not only did the Jordanian Air Force and the British Royal Air Force (RAF) help the Sultan to retain power, one "can hardly overemphasize the role Iran played in wining [*sic*] the war in Dhofar" (Al-Khalili 2009, 77). The Persian shah had supported the Omani sultan with military aid since 1973 and sent troops (4000 at the height of the conflict), while Jordan came to Oman's side despite the popular pressure against siding with Iranians against fellow Arabs (Al-Khalili 2009, 78).

The old sultan, Said bin Taimur, was unpopular among his neighbors and isolated his country, in a similar way to Imam Ahmad in Yemen – one reason why both remained at the periphery of the "royal club". His son Qaboos, who took power in a coup in 1970 with British support, was at first an unknown entity, but he quickly won the support of his fellow monarchs, who were the prime targets of his quests for support. After waiting three months after the coup, the shah invited the sultan to the celebrations of 2500 years of Iranian monarchy at Persepolis in October 1971. Diplomatic relations were established soon after. At the celebrations, he met other monarchs and royals for the first time, which in the case of King Hussein, resulted in a material offer of support. Jordan sent several senior police officers for training Omanis and later a special forces battalion. King Hussein's role was especially important for the success of the fight against the insurgency because he also mediated between the shah and Arab monarchs, notably Shaikh Zayed of Abu Dhabi, president of the UAE at their inception in December 1971. Hussein sent Jordan's head of military intelligence, General Amr Ammash, to Zayed to convince him to normalize relations with Iran. Jordan also actively fostered the stability of the UAE and Qatar in the early 1970s (Goode 2014, 447–449).

The first contacts with Saudi Arabia were also made at the Persepolis festivities when Qaboos met Saudi Prince Nawaf bin Abd al-Aziz, a brother of the king (Takriti 2016, 226). Although the kingdom was also slow to extend recognition to the new Omani ruler, diplomatic relations were established after the sultan's visit

76 *From the Arab Cold War to the Arab Spring*

to Riyadh in late 1971. While they supported Oman against the Dhofar rebels, their material assistance was minimal, and they refused to extend military support (Goode 2014, 456–458). Even this reservation stood in sharp difference to the Arab republican reaction: while Arab Gulf monarchies issued reserved criticism of the Iranian involvement, Libya threatened to "turn the region into a second 'southeast Asia'" if British, Iranian, and Jordanian involvement were not immediately withdrawn (cited in: Goode 2014, 460).

Meanwhile, the Persepolis festivities symbolize how monarchism shapes common bonds. An occasion of royal celebrations led to the personalization of the relations between monarchies, ultimately leading to cooperation even across ethnic and linguistic lines. Monarchic solidarity trumped ethnic identity and pan-Arabism.

The divisive ideology that kept the republics from uniting to fight monarchies

The monarchies were not alone in forming blocs and alliances; the republics also often coalesced, most often around some incarnation of Arab unity like the UAR, which united Syria and Egypt for three years from 1958 to 1961. After the fall of the Libyan monarchy, the Libyan junta joined with UAR, Sudan, and Syria in a plan for an eventual union in 1970 (Kerr 1971, 130).

However, the bipolar structure could not veil the fragmentation inside the republican camp, especially when juxtaposed with monarchic solidarity. The "revolutionary front" was far from united or cohesive. Factional struggles between Ba'thists and Nasserists as well as intra-Ba'th struggles (Kerr 1971, 118–119) defined this period, expressed in particular in Iraq and Syria with multiple coups and coup attempts and a "kind of domestic cold war" in Syria (Seale 1965).

Republics were also faced with a common monarchic threat and directly attacked and subverted by monarchies, as shown in the previous section, which were often just as concerned with destabilizing and overcoming the enemy as the revolutionary republics were. They also were similar systems in that they had similar institutions, had a similar trajectory from revolution to state- and regime-consolidation, and shared the core tenets of pan-Arabism. The asymmetry of ingroup cohesion among monarchies and among republics nevertheless shows that monarchic solidarity is not reducible to a shared threat per se but that it took an identification with "similar" states.

In the social constructivist reading of this book, common threat is only one of three factors that governs monarchic relations with each other by conditioning the salience of the common trait (here monarchy) – the others being the overall share in the regional system and the absence of a divisive ideology. Although republics were also faced with a common threat, their numbers were growing and soon formed a majority in the regional system. Most importantly, their ideology was as much a unifying as a divisive factor, leading to a struggle for dominance and leadership and feuds over the correct interpretation of the doctrine and the identification of heretics. The republican camp was therefore more fragmented

From the Arab Cold War to the Arab Spring 77

and not inclined to solidarity but to fewer obstacles to military aggression toward members of the same camp.

Although the Syrian Ba'th was at times more ideological than Nasser's Egypt, before 1958 it also used to collaborate with the "reactionaries" while struggling with ideological opponents in its own camp. After the revolution in Iraq, the inter-republican relations were tested again with the emergence of Qasim as a new ideological rival to Nasser's leadership role, forcing Nasser into rapprochement with the monarchies – Jordanian-UAR diplomatic relations were restored in August 1959; two weeks later, King Saud officially visited Egypt. The diplomatic thaw was not to last: Nasser later broke off relations again and denounced the reactionary monarchs, but this was not followed by a stronger cohesion inside the republican camp. Until then, the Kuwait crisis further wedged the socialist bloc apart, pitting the anti-imperialists and anti-monarchists against the anti-Qasimists. The disappearance of the Iraqi monarchy also called the UAR into question, which ultimately broke apart in 1961 (Kerr 1971, 9, 17–20).

Apart from ideological squabbles, there were military clashes among the republics, but none among the monarchies. In the period between the Egyptian Revolution and the beginning of the 1967 Arab-Israeli War, the high tide of the Arab Cold War, there were 16 MIDs among Middle East republics, many including actual use of force (some with but most without monarchic intervention), while there were only two inter-monarchic MIDs in the same period (Iraq vs. Iran in 1953 and a Saudi-Jordanian altercation in 1956) without actual use of force (Ghosn, Palmer, and Bremer 2004). This is a highly disproportionate distribution, given that monarchies accounted for the majority of states until 1962. Clearly, the nonviolence norm was not as established among republics as among monarchies.

These confrontations continued well into the 1970s. In 1976, "Sadat was determined to march on Tripoli to oust Qadhafi. Thus, it seems that he was only prevented from attacking by the unpreparedness of his army" (Pollack 2002, 133). In the Egyptian-Libyan dispute of 1977, about 500 were killed (400 Libyans and 100 Egyptians), and both sides accused the other of attempts to overthrow the other's regime (Pollack 2002, 137, 363).

The political struggles between the Arab nationalist republics with their highly ideological factionalism spoke volumes about the lack of unity or alliance inside the republican camp: whether it was *qawmiyya* (pan-Arab nationalism) and *qutriyya* (local nationalism) and *wataniyya* (country-specific nationalism) or the *infisali* (secessionist) Syrians or the *shu'ubi* (defamatory of Arabism) Iraqis (Kerr 1971, 29–33), the ideology led to more division instead of (Arab) unity.

When monarchies ally: the Arab Spring 2011–2015

In contrast to the period of the Arab Cold War, the main threat of the Arab Spring that ushered in a comparable period of tensions, earning the moniker of the New (Arab) Cold War (Bank and Valbjørn 2010; Khoury 2013; Stephens 2017, a.o.), derived not from rival elites but from mass uprisings. It evinced a similar sense of common threat for the rulers in 2011. While republics around them broke down

78 *From the Arab Cold War to the Arab Spring*

or collapsed into civil war, monarchies remained stable and were (except for Bahrain) not vitally affected by the uprisings. While their durability was based on many pillars, one important element was an extensive sense of "monarchic solidarity" that was expressed via mutual support in financial (toward Bahrain, Oman, Jordan, and Morocco) and sometimes military terms (toward Bahrain) (cf. Bank, Richter, and Sunik 2014; Yom and Gause 2012).

Nabeel Khoury identifies the fronts of the New Arab Cold War as "conservative monarchies, transitioning republics and non-state Islamic groups" (Khoury 2013, 73). The monarchies felt threatened not just as individual regimes but also as a group of states, fearing a domino effect starting with just one fallen monarchy (cf. Yom 2013, 13). Their "unique 'pan-royal' identity that shared a singular fate" (Yom 2016) formed into a solidarity community that supported each other against the threats that they faced.

With the impact of growing sectarianism, the blocs have shifted toward a Sunna–Shia fault line (POMEPS 2016; Wehrey 2013), but many support mechanisms hinting at monarchic ingroup favoritism are still seen.

Revolution diffusion as a common threat

While regicide nowadays is not as common as it was in the distant past, when more than every fifth monarch met a violent end,[9] the wave of revolutions of the 1950 to the 1970s are well remembered in the monarchies until today: Hashemite King Faisal of Iraq and his family were shot to death, and assassination attempts (as well as actual assassinations, as in Saudi King Faisal's case) were common. The fate of Libyan leader and monarch-like "Arab President for Life" (Owen 2012) Mu'ammar Qadhafi did not serve to calm that fear.

The sentiment has been captured succinctly by Sean Yom in an interview with an (anonymous) member of the Alaoui royal family in Morocco during the period of turmoil in 2013:

> *Royal families do not live in an historical vacuum. . . . We know how rare it is to still think that blood matters more than ballots [emphasis his]. But when you grow up and attend the palace school with all those attendants, you learn history in a different way. You learn all about how other royal families lost everything because this person or that person couldn't solve certain problems and instead just killed or shot everyone. And nobody in my family, and I would imagine my cousins in Saudi Arabia or our friends in Jordan, wants to be counted among this club of kings without crowns. Also, remember that an ex-dictator lives in shame . . . like Ben Ali in Saudi Arabia now . . . but a deposed king has to face his family as well [emphasis his].*
>
> (Yom 2013, 13–14)

This quote encapsulates many elements of monarchic ingroup identification: the realization that monarchism is rare, decreasing, and fragile and that it forms a bond that outsiders cannot understand, because they do not share the same constraints

From the Arab Cold War to the Arab Spring   79

or experiences, and the fear for regime stability and survival. It also shows how this identity is constructed by inheritance, kinship, and shared socialization via education (palace school) and historical learning and experience and how it is affirmed in terms of family and "club membership". These bonds tie even the seemingly peripheral Moroccan ruling family into one "community of fate".

The uprisings led to four regime changes until 2013 – in Tunisia (2011), Egypt (twice, 2011 and 2013), Libya (2011), and Yemen (2012). Libya, Syria, Yemen, and Iraq were consequently embroiled in a civil war. But even the monarchs that were not in immediate danger to be directly overthrown faced calls for reform reaching demands for constitutional monarchy, threatening their hold on power, especially in Bahrain, where a Sunni royal family reigns over a Shia majority. Only Qatar and the UAE escaped demonstrations completely. These particular claims could not occur in republics and heightened the sense of community in the few authoritarian monarchies that still remain in the Middle East (Yom 2016).

Institutionalizing the "royal club"

The eight remaining monarchies in the region intensified their communication early on amid the rising tensions since 2011. High- and lower-level officials, kings, princes, and ministers met, talked, and consulted with each other on a more regular and intense basis than usual, including informal meetings and talks and formalized summits (Yom 2016). Up to March 2016, five joint ministerial summits of the foreign ministers of the GCC and Jordan and Morocco took place (MOFA Qatar 2016).

The monarchies have also stepped up their cooperation with various initiatives, including a joint military command, a joint police force, and, most recently, an Islamic anti-terror alliance led by Saudi Arabia, as well as a potential monarchic "military bloc" (Gaub 2016; Mustafa 2014). While some were restricted to GCC members, most also included Jordan and Morocco. Some include the GCC members and Jordan and Morocco exclusively, making them into monarchic clubs.[10]

The clearest sign of monarchic solidarity was the invitation of Jordan and Morocco to join the GCC in May 2011 and the strong financial support of the richer monarchies for the poorer monarchies of Jordan, Morocco, Oman, and Bahrain (Al Lawati 2011).[11] The invitation is not easily explained by geopolitical or economic needs – Jordan and Morocco would be financial burdens to the council and they cannot provide for the military security of the Gulf states. This is especially true for Morocco, which is geographically almost as distant from the Gulf of Mexico as from the Gulf of Persia. So why invite two non-Gulf states to the *Gulf* Cooperation Council, while Gulf and Arabian Peninsula applicants Iraq and Yemen are ignored?

Only the perspective of a formation of a pan-regional "Monarchical Bloc of Tranquility" (Barany 2012, 34–35) of alliance of systems of shared political values (Al Tamamy 2015) enables a deeper understanding of this unusual move, as an attempt to institutionalize the community, similar to previous such efforts during the period of the Arab Cold War.

80　*From the Arab Cold War to the Arab Spring*

The membership of the two monarchies would transform the GCC into a "club of monarchies" and include all MENA monarchies still in existence. While the invitation was retracted (or, in another interpretation, silently dropped) once the imminent domestic threat waned (Barany 2012, 35), most benefits, including mutual financial and military support, were continued well beyond the immediate period of turmoil. In 2014, the invitation was rekindled in the shape of a military union (Ryan 2014).

While the invitation seemed surprising at the time, it is consistent with GCC policy, which is "primarily concerned with the preservation of monarchism" (Bellamy 2004, 130). Bellamy goes on to elaborate on the three core tenets of the council, which point to a strong ingroup identification among the members: first, membership only for Gulf Arab monarchies that subscribe to traditional Islamic law; second, the recognition of the moral equality of each monarch and therefore the unanimous decision-making process; and third, the recognition of the sovereignty of each monarch, with no pre-determined path of integration or any other agenda (Bellamy 2004, 130).

This group identification is inherent in the GCC's own self-definition at its foundation. The communiqué of the pre-meeting by the organization's foreign minister in Ta'if on February 4, 1981, describes the unifying forces of the organization:

> out of consideration of their *special relations and joint characteristics* stemming from their joint creed, *similarity of regimes*, unity of heritage, *similarity of their political, social and demographic structure*, and their cultural and historical affiliation.
>
> (cited in: Kechichian 2001, 281, emphasis added)

In Kuwait's Minister of Information Saud Nasir Al Sabah's description, "there is one culture, one religion, one set of customs . . . it is a family". Former GCC secretary-general Abdallah Bishara similarly described its members as "like-minded countries, similar domestically, internationally, in their politics and their history and their culture" (interviews of 1997, both cited in: Priess 1998, 25). This similarity was based on the political system and political culture to a degree that allowed it to expand to more-distant fellow monarchies – at least temporarily.

While Jordan already expressed interest in membership, other states have sought membership for an even longer period, notably Yemen, since 1996 the only formal applicant, but also Iraq (Priess 1998). Priess considered Jordan the least likely to join the GCC in 1998 (Priess 1998, 24).[12]

Instead, 2011 witnessed a "fast tracking" of Jordan and Morocco, while Yemen and Iraq remained on the sidelines, apparently still excluded from membership because of their regime type, as it has been the case in the past (Bellamy 2004, 120; Holthaus 2010, 40). Although cooperation agreements have been signed with Yemen in 2002, they were never intended to lead to full membership, nor were they announced as such. The same applies to potential Iraqi affiliation (cf. Holthaus 2010, 52–53).

From the Arab Cold War to the Arab Spring   81

Apparently, out of the most important commonalities of the GCC states, political system trumped geography (Arabian Peninsula/Persian Gulf that could include Iran, Iraq, and Yemen), economic system (oil rentierism like in Iraq and Iran), and friendship in times of need (the friendly Yemeni regime was at least just as threatened by the turmoil of the period as the poorer monarchies were, forcing its ruler of 34 years, Ali Abdallah Salih, to resign).[13]

While actual access to membership has not been granted so far, in April 2014, the GCC invited Jordan and Morocco to form a monarchic military alliance. It was reported that Jordan and Morocco would provide up to 300,000 troops in return for the $5 billion aid package promised to the two countries in 2012. Jordan already trains some GCC members' militaries and sent gendarmerie (*darak*) forces to quell the uprising in Bahrain (EIU 2014).

Another form of monarchic solidarity just below the military level is what Sean Yom calls "cross-policing", monarchies prosecuting and criminalizing criticism and actions against other monarchies within their own borders to stabilize each other's regimes. The legal basis is a GCC agreement, the Joint Security Agreement in which Jordan and Morocco have been included, once more emphasizing the close alliance between all monarchies. Similar "anti-terrorism" laws have been passed in the eight countries. Jordan arrested Muslim Brotherhood official Zaki Bani Irsheid after he criticized the UAE on social media, and Kuwaiti parliamentarians have been detained and imprisoned for criticizing their Saudi, Emirati, or Bahraini neighbors (Yom 2016).

The intent to integrate more strongly spilled over from the political and security-related sphere into other fields, as indicated e.g. by the invitation of the two non-Gulf monarchies into the Gulf football cup (Dorsey 2014). Qatar and Jordan also signed a protocol of cooperation between their police sports federations in April 2016 (Ministry News 2016). On the fifth joint ministerial meeting between the GCC and Jordan and Morocco, the final communiqué lauded the signing of a memorandum of understanding (MoU) for cultural cooperation between the GCC and Jordan (MOFA Qatar 2016). The cooperation between Saudi Arabia and Jordan is intensive in all policy fields and marked by a high level of trust, and Jordan even replaced Saudi Arabia on the UN Security Council after Saudi Arabia rejected the seat (Nichols 2013). GCC-Moroccan cooperation is also intensifying, with the second GCC–Morocco summit and a repeated meeting of an economic working group between the countries planned for 2017 (Alaoui 2016; Le Maroc et les pays du CCG veulent renforcer leur coopération 2017).

It is in this context that the sending of the Peninsula Shield Force of the GCC to Bahrain in March 2011 becomes comprehensible – as an extreme act of monarchic solidarity, the military support of a fellow monarchy against a looming threat. When Bahrain's royal family seemed to be in danger of suffering the same fate as Ben Ali and Mubarak before them, the GCC states agreed to send a strong signal of support and solidarity to the Al Khalifa dynasty and each other (Guzansky 2014). Although most troops were Saudi, the UAE sent 500 police officers, and

82 *From the Arab Cold War to the Arab Spring*

token support was provided by Kuwait and Qatar as well, even though the troops were not actually involved in the crushing of the rebellion (Khatib 2013, 419).

Security cooperation was not restricted to the GCC and therefore not a limited *khaleeji* (Arab Gulf) affair – Jordanian police officers patrolled the streets in Bahrain even before 2011, and 700 Jordanian Darak officers were sent to support the GCC operation.[14]

The military operation in Yemen, initially termed Decisive Storm, is a further step toward bloc building – a security club employing military measures together, highly uncommon for the monarchic regimes that used to stay on the sidelines during wars or employing merely defensive tactics. The Decisive Storm coalition initially included ten states, five from the GCC (only Oman abstained); Pakistan, Egypt, and Sudan; and the two remaining monarchies, Jordan and Morocco. The monarchies and possibly Egypt are the most committed members of the coalition in commitment of personnel, fighter jets, and financial means (Mustafa and Mehta 2016; Shaheen and Kamali Dehghan 2015).

Saudi Arabia contributed the greatest number of resources to the coalition and reportedly deployed 100 fighter jets and 150,000 troops, while Qatar sent ten and Bahrain and Kuwait 15 jets in the first hours, in stark contrast to their nominal participation in the effort against the "Islamic State" (IS) (Shaheen and Kamali Dehghan 2015).[15] Except for Pakistan, where parliament resisted military participation, all the other initiative countries sent fighter jets as well, the UAE 30, and Jordan up to six (AFP 2015). Saudi Arabia and the UAE deployed Special Forces in July (Binnie 2015). Small numbers of Egyptians and Jordanians were conducting trainings in Aden (TSG 2015). As in the anti-IS coalition, Oman declined to join, instead focusing on humanitarian assistance while continuing to provide a mediation platform for Iran and the Houthis (Wilkin and Alarimi 2015). After the outbreak of the Qatar Crisis, the emirate dropped out of the coalition, in 2017.

Although not limited to monarchies, they were the main contributors in terms of financial and military resources and workforce. In other projects, Egypt also took a leading role, although most of these were bogged down quickly. The Joint Arab Force, planned mainly by Saudi Arabia and Egypt within the framework of the Arab League supposed to number 40,000 troops (Mustafa 2015), has not progressed since 2015. In sharp contrast, cooperation and coordination on a narrower monarchic scale seem more active. The Yemen War intervention coalition has seen a major surge in increased interoperability, cooperation, and coordination, showing high levels of trust among the active coalition members. Jordan and Morocco are also part of the Saudi-initiated Islamic Anti-Terror Alliance and participated in the Northern Thunder drill with Oman and nearly 20 other countries, the largest exercise in the region (Fouad 2015; Riedel 2016).

Others were limited to the Gulf monarchies. In its 34th summit in December 2013, the GCC had agreed on the establishment of a joint military command that was to be instituted alongside the Peninsula Shield Force and to have a force

From the Arab Cold War to the Arab Spring 83

of 100,000, half of which to be provided by Saudi Arabia (Saidy 2014). At the summit the following year, the institution of a joint police force (based in Abu Dhabi) and a joint navy (based in Bahrain) were decided. All these proposals tackle the problem of the lack of interoperability in the security sphere between the Gulf states (Vela 2014).

While a formal monarchic alliance or organization has not materialized so far, all of the numerous intense cooperation projects that were agreed on and implemented have a monarchic core membership. The only notable exception is Oman's abstention in the Yemen civil war intervention. This boosts the conclusion that in light of a common threat toward authoritarian political systems, those of a more equal composition – monarchies – cling together and support each other to strengthen and stabilize the ingroup as a whole.

Monarchic peace as an element of monarchic resilience

Because the threat has shifted toward the transnational level compared to the Arab Cold War period, there are no clear-cut state sponsors of domestic opposition movements inside the monarchies, and comparable to the Arab Cold War period, outgroup hostility is less pronounced because the outgroup is not as clearly constituted, as in the previous period.

Nevertheless, the result were proxy wars and support for opposition movements in republics (Libya, Syria, and partly Egypt) to various degrees and at different times. On the other hand, attention focuses on the fight against opposition movements inside monarchies (financially in Jordan, Oman, and Bahrain and militarily in Bahrain) and inside monarchic allies (Yemen). Although the ingroup is more or less defined, the outgroup is not as clear.

The geopolitical situation is far different from the Arab Cold War but parallels it in regard to the asymmetry between monarchic and republican solidarity. Then as now, no similar solidarity blocks have emerged among the republics. Although many of them were involved one way or the other in the uprisings, the republics mostly did not differentiate between the regime types of the targeted state of their support or opposition.

As the threat to the regimes since the wave of 2011 subsides, other identities might become more salient than the monarchic one is, like the Sunna–Shia divide. However, although there might already be a cohesive Shia bloc led by Iran, there is a highly fragmented bloc of Sunni states, inside which the monarchies have yet to form a more cohesive unit.[16]

Although much has changed in the regional context since the 1950s and the level of cooperation among monarchies has waxed and waned, their common bond always precluded open military conflict and regime destabilization attempts that might have led to the breakdown of a monarchy. To the contrary, such destabilization was seen as a common task to avoid, leading to mutual support among monarchies – something that cannot be said of the group of republics as a whole.

84 *From the Arab Cold War to the Arab Spring*

These initial findings will be systematically assessed in the following case studies, which show monarchic dyads (and one triad) in intragroup conflict. The case studies will show the following:

1 How ingroup identification among monarchies developed and how it helped keep disputes from escalating into war via an analysis of two cases of "near misses" that came close to war at some point in their relationship
2 How the change in regime type in a dyad of two monarchies transformed their bilateral relationship up to the point of war via a study of two "quasi-experiments".

Notes

1 Nonetheless, even among such systems, which are only tenuously "similar", ingroup formation is sometimes visible (see Sunik 2015 for an elaboration of the special relationship between the UK and Middle East monarchies).
2 See e.g. the descriptions of "fellow Sandhurst graduates" in the memoir of King Abdallah of Jordan:

> Hamad bin Isa Al Khalifa was a close friend of my father and I looked on him as an uncle. A fellow Sandhurst graduate, he smiled in recognition when I told him about the punishing training we were being put through. . . . I knew that the grandson of Sheikh Hamad, who had by then become king of Bahrain, would welcome the gift. He was attending Sandhurst and I had all too vivid recollections of what he was going through.
>
> (Abdallah II King of Jordan 2011, 45, also cf. 148)

3 Cf. the lengthy elaborations of King Hussein of Jordan in his memoirs (H. King of Jordan 1962, ch. 2 and 3).
4 Among non-monarchic rulers, only Saddam Hussein claimed a similar ancestry. The head of the Islamic State, Abu Bakr al-Baghdadi, who laid claim to territory from Syria and Iraq and beyond, is another rare example.
5 In Arabic, the use of the female grammatical gender for abstract concepts is common.
6 Kerr also notes at this point that anti-colonialism dominated until 1958, when it was overtaken in importance by revolutionary socialism (Kerr 1971, 1–7). Regardless of the particular "flavor" of the reigning ideology, it was consistently directed toward monarchies and the ideas and alliances that they represented.
7 Neo-realists like Stephen Walt dispute "any intrinsic affinity between monarchical regimes" in the unification of the Hashemite sister kingdoms and asserts that the "independent power of monarchical solidarity was probably slight", pointing to the rivalry of the dynasties (Walt 1990, 213). However, an approach based on ingroup identification is predicated not on intrinsic monarchic qualities but on mutual perception of similarity. Walt even notes that a monarchic solidarity did develop later, albeit on the basis of the common threat of revolutionary Arab nationalism. He also acknowledges that the ease with which the conservative Arabs maintained good relations with one another stood in sharp contrast to the behavior of the Arab nationalist states (Walt 1990, 213, fn 111). A common threat indeed is essential for the regional dynamics of that period, but if it were the only factor, the alliance would have broken up once that threat disappeared, which is not what can be observed.
8 Lebanon and Sudan are also sometimes considered to be part of the moderate camp otherwise comprised of monarchies.

From the Arab Cold War to the Arab Spring 85

9 According to Eisner, 15% of European monarchs from 600 CE to 1800 CE were murdered, and including other violent deaths, such as executions and battle deaths, raises the number to nearly 21% (excl. accidents) (Eisner 2011).

10 It was reported that Egypt was also considered for membership in the proposed military bloc; however, there was never a formal invitation, and a broader consensus among the monarchies for Egyptian membership seemed to be lacking (cf. Mustafa 2014).

11 When asked about the existence of a notion of monarchic solidarity and identity, most Jordanian officials from the military, government, and Hashemite Royal Court, interviewed by the author in Amman between September 7 and September 14, 2015, answered affirmatively while citing this incident.

12 Under the condition if Saddam Hussein would be removed from power in Iraq (which was fulfilled in 2003); otherwise, Iraq was considered the least likely candidate.

13 In an interview with a researcher, the Jordanian prime minister at the time of the formation of the GCC, Mudar Badran, recounted his conversation with his GCC counterparts on why Jordan could not join, showing the same priorization:

When it was established, I asked them, "Why just Saudi Arabia, Kuwait, Qatar, Bahrain, the Emirates, and Oman?" The answer was that the relations between these states were very close. Then I asked, "Why not Jordan? The relations between His Majesty and King Khaled are very close, relations are very friendly – we like you, you like us". They said, "Only the states of the Gulf". "But Iraq is a state of the Gulf". They said, "The regime is different, and [the GCC] is about the Arabian Peninsula". I asked, "Then why not Yemen? It is in the Arabian Peninsula". They answered, "The regime is different". I said, "Jordan has the same regime".

There was no reply (Priess 1998, 19).

14 Interview with former Jordanian military official, Amman, September 8, 2015, and former Jordanian government official, Amman, September 13, 2015.

15 All troop numbers are based on open-source media information only and should therefore be read with caution because they are probably highly exaggerated. More credible accounts put the numbers of Saudi combat troop numbers at about 3,500 (with 6,500 support personnel) (Mustafa and Mehta 2016). Although this is a far smaller number, it is still much more than in the anti-IS coalition, where there has been no commitment to ground troops yet.

16 However, the claim can be made that anti-Shiism is a defining characteristic of the common identity of the contemporary monarchic club (despite its one Ibadite member Oman) (cf. Yom 2014).

References

'Abd al-Hakim al-Wa'ili. 2002a. "'anaza." *Mawsu'a qaba'il al-'arab* 4.
———. 2002b. "'utub." *Mawsu'a qaba'il al-'arab* 3.
AFP. 2015. "Saudi Says Egypt, Morocco, Pakistan Joining Yemen Operation." *Daily Star.* www.dailystar.com.lb/News/Middle-East/2015/Mar-26/292153-saudi-says-egypt-morocco-pakistan-joining-yemen-operation.ashx (November 18, 2015).
Ajami, Fouad. 1978. "The End of Pan-Arabism." *Foreign Affairs* 57(2): 355–73.
Al Lawati, Abbas. 2011. "Strategic Value of GCC Expansion Plans Come under Scrutiny." http://gulfnews.com/news/region/strategic-value-of-gcc-expansion-plans-come-under-scrutiny-1.806700 (September 26, 2012).
Al Tamamy, Saud Mousaed. 2015. "GCC Membership Expansion: Possibilities and Obstacles." *Al Jazeera Centre for Studies.* http://studies.aljazeera.net/en/dossiers/2015/03/20153 3171547520486.html (April 7, 2017).

86 *From the Arab Cold War to the Arab Spring*

Alaoui, Mohamed Chakir. 2016. "Le 2ème Sommet Maroc-CCG En Mars Prochain à Bahreïn." *Le360*. http://fr.le360.ma/politique/le-2eme-sommet-maroc-ccg-en-mars-prochain-a-bahrein-99459 (April 7, 2017).

Al-Khalili, Majid. 2009. *Oman's Foreign Policy*. Westport, CT: Praeger Security International.

Alkim, Hassan Hamdan al-. 1989. *The Foreign Policy of the United Arab Emirates*. London: Saqi.

Allen, Calvin H., and W. Lynn Rigsbee. 2000. *Oman under Qaboos: From Coup to Constitution, 1970–1996*. London: Cass.

Anderson, Lisa. 2009. "Absolutism and the Resilience of Monarchy in the Middle East." In *Politics of the Modern Arab World. Critical Issues in Modern Politics. Volume I: State, Power and Political Economy*, ed. Laleh Khalili. London; New York: Routledge.

Ayalon, Ami. 2000. "Post-Ottoman Arab Monarchies: Old Bottles, New Labels?" In *Middle East Monarchies. The Challenge of Modernity*, ed. Joseph Kostiner. Boulder, CO: Lynne Rienner Publishers, 23–36.

Ayubi, Nazih N. 1995. *Over-Stating the Arab State: Politics and Society in the Middle East*. London: I.B. Tauris.

Badīb, Saʿīd M. 1986. *The Saudi-Egyptian Conflict over North Yemen, 1962–1970*. Boulder, CO: Westview Press.

Bank, André, Thomas Richter, and Anna Sunik. 2014. "Durable, Yet Different: Monarchies in the Arab Spring." *Journal of Arabian Studies* 4(2): 163–79.

Bank, André, and Morten Valbjørn. 2010. "Bringing the Arab Regional Level Back in. . . – Jordan in the New Arab Cold War." *Middle East Critique* 19(3): 303.

Barany, Zoltan. 2012. *The Arab Spring in the Kingdoms*. Doha: Arab Center for Research and Policy Studies. Research Paper. http://english.dohainstitute.org/release/907fb84b-4fc8-49be-baef-2252a8e605c4 (October 3, 2012).

Bellamy, A. 2004. *Security Communities and Their Neighbours: Regional Fortresses or Global Integrators?* Heidelberg: Springer.

Ben-Dor, Gabriel. 2000. "Patterns of Monarchy in the Middle East." In *Middle East Monarchies – The Challenge of Modernity*, ed. Joseph Kostiner. Boulder, CO; London: Lynne Rienner Publishers, 71–84.

Binnie, Jeremy. 2015. "Saudi, UAE Forces Deployed to Yemen." *IHS Jane's Defence Weekly 360*. www.janes.com/article/53117/saudi-uae-forces-deployed-to-yemen (November 18, 2015).

Boghardt, L.P. 2006. *Kuwait Amid War, Peace and Revolution*. New York: Palgrave Macmillan.

Cordesman, Anthony H. 1984. *The Gulf and the Search for Strategic Stability: Saudi Arabia, the Military Balance in the Gulf, and Trends in the Arab-Israeli Military Balance*. Boulder: Westview Press.

Dorsey, James M. 2014. "Gulf Soccer Diplomacy Highlights Regional Divisions." *The Turbulent World of Middle East Soccer*. http://mideastsoccer.blogspot.sg/2014/11/gulf-soccer-diplomacy-highlights.html (November 19, 2014).

Eisner, Manuel. 2011. "Killing Kings: Patterns of Regicide in Europe, AD 600–1800." *British Journal of Criminology* 51(3): 556–77.

EIU. 2014. "GCC Seeks Military Alliance with Jordan and Morocco." *The Economist*. http://country.eiu.com/article.aspx?articleid=81741392&Country=Saudi%20Arabia&topic=Politics&subt_5 (April 7, 2017).

Fouad, Ahmed. 2015. "What's Saudi's New Islamic Coalition Really Up To?" *Al-Monitor*. www.al-monitor.com/pulse/originals/2015/12/egypt-saudi-arabia-islamic-alliance-goals.html (September 23, 2016).

Gaub, Florence. 2016. *Saudi Arabia and the Islamic Alliance*. EUISS. www.iss.europa.eu/uploads/media/Brief_1_Saudi_Islamic_alliance.pdf (March 12, 2016).

Gause, F. Gregory, III. 1990. *Saudi-Yemeni Relations: Domestic Structures and Foreign Influence*. New York: Columbia University Press.

Ghosn, Faten, Glenn Palmer, and Stuart Bremer. 2004. "The MID3 Data Set, 1993–2001: Procedures, Coding Rules, and Description." *Conflict Management and Peace Science* 21: 133–54.

Gibler, Douglas M., Marc L. Hutchison, and Steven V. Miller. 2012. "Individual Identity Attachments and International Conflict: The Importance of Territorial Threat." *Comparative Political Studies* 45(12): 1655–83.

Goode, James F. 2014. "Assisting Our Brothers, Defending Ourselves: The Iranian Intervention in Oman, 1972–75." *Iranian Studies* 47(3): 441–62.

Guzansky, Yoel. 2014. "Defence Cooperation in the Arabian Gulf: The Peninsula Shield Force Put to the Test." *Middle Eastern Studies* 50(4): 640–54.

Halliday, Fred. 2011. *The Middle East in International Relations: Power, Politics and Ideology*. New edition. Cambridge: Cambridge University Press.

Herb, Michael. 1999. *All in the Family: Absolutism, Revolution, and Democracy in the Middle Eastern Monarchies*. Albany: State University of New York Press.

Holthaus, Leonie. 2010. *Regimelegitimität und regionale Kooperation im Golf-Kooperationsrat (Gulf Cooperation Council)*. Frankfurt am Main: Peter Lang Verlag.

Hughes, Geraint. 2015. "A Proxy War in Arabia: The Dhofar Insurgency and Cross-Border Raids into South Yemen." *The Middle East Journal* 69(1): 91–104.

Hughes, Stephen O. 2001. *Morocco under King Hassan*. 1st edition. Reading: Ithaca.

Jones, Clive. 2011. "Military Intelligence, Tribes, and Britain's War in Dhofar, 1970–1976." *The Middle East Journal* 65(4): 557–74.

Joyce, Miriam. 1998. *Kuwait, 1945–1996: An Anglo-American Perspective*. London; Portland, OR: Frank Cass.

Kechichian, Joseph A. 2001. "Unity on the Arabian Peninsula." In *Iran, Iraq and the Arab Gulf States*, ed. Joseph A. Kechichian. New York: Palgrave, 281–302.

Kerr, Malcolm H. 1971. *The Arab Cold War. Gamal 'Abd al-Nasir and His Rivals, 1958–1970*. 3rd edition. London: Oxford Univ. Press.

Khadduri, Majid, and Edmund Ghareeb. 2001. *War in the Gulf, 1990–91: The Iraq-Kuwait Conflict and Its Implications*. Oxford: Oxford University Press.

Khatib, Lina. 2013. "Qatar's Foreign Policy: The Limits of Pragmatism." *International Affairs* 89(2): 417–31.

Khoury, Nabeel A. 2013. "The Arab Cold War Revisited: The Regional Impact of the Arab Uprising." *Middle East Policy* 20(2): 73–87.

King of Jordan, Abdallah I. 1954. *My Memoirs Completed (al-Takmilah)*. Washington: American Council of Learned Societies.

King of Jordan, Abdallah II. 2011. *Our Last Best Chance: The Pursuit of Peace in a Time of Peril*. New York: Viking.

King of Jordan, Hussein. 1962. *Uneasy Lies the Head: The Autobiography of His Majesty King Hussein I of the Hashemite Kingdom of Jordan*. First Printing edition. New York: Bernard Geis Associates.

Korany, Bahgat. 1984. *The Foreign Policies of Arab States*. 1st edition. Cairo: American University in Cairo Press.

Kostiner, Joseph. 2009. *Conflict and Cooperation in the Gulf Region*. Wiesbaden: VS Verlag für Sozialwissenschaften. http://site.ebrary.com/id/10274811.

Krämer, Gudrun. 2000. "Good Counsel to the King: The Islamist Opposition in Saudi Arabia, Jordan, and Morocco." In *Middle East Monarchies: The Challenge of Modernity*, ed. Joseph Kostiner. Boulder, CO: Lynne Rienner Publishers, 257–88.

Landis, Joshua. 2001. "Syria and the Palestine War: Fighting King 'Abdallah's 'Greater Syria Plan'." In *The War for Palestine: Rewriting the History of 1948*, eds. Eugene L. Rogan and Avi Shlaim. Cambridge: Cambridge University Press, 176–203.

Laqueur, Walter, and Barry M. Rubin, eds. 2008. *The Israel-Arab Reader: A Documentary History of the Middle East Conflict*. 7th rev. and updated ed. New York: Penguin Books.

Lawson, Fred Haley. 1989. *Bahrain: The Modernization of Autocracy*. Boulder, CO: Westview Press.

"Le Maroc et Les Pays Du CCG Veulent Renforcer Leur Coopération." 2017. *Menara.ma*. www.menara.ma/fr/actualit%C3%A9s/economie/2017/02/14/2111154-le-maroc-et-les-pays-du-ccg-veulent-renforcer-leur-coop%C3%A9ration.html (April 7, 2017).

Lewis, Bernard. 2000. "Monarchy in the Middle East." In *Middle East Monarchies. The Challenge of Modernity*, ed. Joseph Kostiner. Boulder, CO: Lynne Rienner Publishers, 15–22.

Maddy-Weizmann, Bruce. 2000. "Why Did Arab Monarchies Fall? An Analysis of Old and New Explanations." In *Middle East Monarchies: The Challenge of Modernity*, ed. Joseph Kostiner. Boulder, CO; London: Lynne Rienner Publishers, 37–52.

Ministry News. 2016. "MOI – Protocol of Cooperation Between Qatar & Jordan PSF." *Ministry of Interior Qatar*. www.moi.gov.qa/site/english/news/2016/04/04/35783.html (April 7, 2017).

MOFA Qatar. 2016. "GCC, Jordan and Morocco Foreign Ministers Issue Final Communique." *News*. https://mofa.gov.qa/en/all-mofa-news/details/2016/03/09/gcc-jordan-and-morocco-foreign-ministers-issue-final-communique (April 7, 2017).

Moubayed, Sami M. 2000. *Damascus Between Democracy and Dictatorship*. Lanham: University Press of America.

Mustafa, Awad. 2014. "GCC Seeks to Form Military Bloc with Jordan, Morocco." *Defense News*. www.defensenews.com/article/20140414/DEFREG04/304140018/GCC-Seeks-Form-Military-Bloc-Jordan-Morocco (April 23, 2014).

———. 2015. "Arab League Sets New Defense Force at 40,000." *Defense News*. www.defense news.com/story/defense/policy-budget/warfare/2015/04/01/united-arab-emirates-defense-force-league/70786878/ (September 23, 2016).

Mustafa, Awad, and Aaron Mehta. 2016. "Syria: 'Quicksand' for Saudi Forces?" *Defense News*. www.defensenews.com/story/war-in-syria/2016/02/14/syria-quicksand-saudi-forces/80282096/ (March 12, 2016).

Nichols, Michelle. 2013. "Saudi Rejects U.N. Security Council Seat, Opening Way for Jordan." *Reuters*. www.reuters.com/article/us-un-saudi-jordan-idUSBRE9AB14720131112 (April 24, 2017).

Owen, Roger. 2004. *State, Power and Politics in the Making of the Modern Middle East*. London; New York: Routledge.

———. 2012. *The Rise and Fall of Arab Presidents for Life*. Cambridge, MA: Harvard University Press.

Pahlavi, Mohammad Reza, and Teresa Waugh. 1980. *The Shah's Story*. London: M. Joseph.

Peceny, Mark, Caroline Beer, and Shannon Sanchez-Terry. 2002. "Dictatorial Peace?" *American Political Science Review* 96(1): 15–26.

Podeh, Elie. 1999. *The Decline of Arab Unity: The Rise and Fall of the United Arab Republic*. Eastborne: Sussex Academic Press.

Pollack, Kenneth Michael. 2002. *Arabs at War: Military Effectiveness, 1948–1991*. Lincoln: University of Nebraska Press.

POMEPS. 2016. *The Gulf's Escalating Sectarianism*. POMEPS. POMEPS Briefing. http://pomeps.org/wp-content/uploads/2016/01/POMEPS_BriefBooklet28_Sectarianism_Web.pdf (April 23, 2017).

From the Arab Cold War to the Arab Spring 89

Priess, David. 1998. "The Gulf Cooperation Council: Prospects for Expansion." *Middle East Policy* 5(4): 17–26.

Rasheed, Madawi al-. 1998. "Political Legitimacy and the Production of History: The Case of Saudi Arabia." In *New Frontiers in Middle East Security*, ed. G. Martin Lenore. Houndmills: Macmillan, 25–46.

Rathmell, Andrew. 1996. "Syria's Intelligence Services: Origins and Development1." *Journal of Conflict Studies* 16(2). https://journals.lib.unb.ca/index.php/JCS/article/view/11815 (November 2, 2016).

———. 2014. *Secret War in the Middle East: The Covert Struggle for Syria, 1949–1961.* London: I.B. Tauris.

Riedel, Bruce. 2016. "Are Latest War Games Just a Face-Saver for Riyadh?" *Al-Monitor.* www.al-monitor.com/pulse/originals/2016/02/saudi-arabia-military-exercises-goal-iran-isis-yemen.html (September 23, 2016).

Rogan, Eugene L., and Tewfik Aclimandos. 2012. "The Yemen War and Egypt's War Preparedness." In *The 1967 Arab-Israeli War: Origins and Consequences*, Cambridge Middle East studies, eds. Avi Shlaim and William Roger Louis. Cambridge: Cambridge University Press, 149–64.

Rouleau, Eric. 1970. "Les Palestiniens Face Au Trône Jordanien, II: Faux Calculs." *Le Monde*.

Ryan, Curtis R. 2014. "Jordan, Morocco and an Expanded GCC." *Middle East Research and Information Project.* www.merip.org/jordan-morocco-expanded-gcc?ip_login_no_cach e=746bbc901ee2d67854d77bcdebad9496.

Saidy, Brahim. 2014. "The Gulf Cooperation Council's Unified Military Command." *Foreign Policy Research Institute.* www.fpri.org/article/2014/10/the-gulf-cooperation-councils-unified-military-command/ (September 23, 2016).

Sandhurst Trust. 2013. "Our Trustees." *Sandhurst Trust.* www.sandhursttrust.org/about/trustees/ (October 3, 2014).

Seale, Patrick. 1965. *The Struggle for Syria: A Study of Post-War Arab Politics 1945–1958.* 2nd edition. London: Oxford University Press.

Shaheen, Kareem, and Saeed Kamali Dehghan. 2015. "Gulf States Consider Yemen Ground Offensive to Halt Houthi Rebel Advance." *The Guardian.* www.theguardian. com/world/2015/mar/26/gulf-states-yemen-ground-offensive-to-halt-houthi-rebel-advance (November 18, 2015).

Shlaim, Avi. 2009. *Lion of Jordan: The Life of King Hussein in War and Peace.* New York: Vintage.

———. 2012. "Jordan: Walking the Tight Rope." In *The 1967 Arab-Israeli War: Origins and Consequences*, Cambridge Middle East studies, eds. Avi Shlaim and William Roger Louis. Cambridge: Cambridge University Press, 99–125.

Stephens, Michael. 2017. *The Arab Cold War Redux. The Foreign Policy of the Gulf Cooperation Council States since 2011.* Carnegie Endowment for International Peace. https://tcf.org/content/report/arab-cold-war-redux/ (March 4, 2017).

Sunik, Anna. 2015. "The Royal Special Relationship. Großbritannien und die arabischen Monarchien." In *Sonderbeziehungen als Nexus zwischen Außenpolitik und internationalen Beziehungen*, Außenpolitik und Internationale Ordnung, eds. Sebastian Harnisch, Klaus Brummer, and Kai Oppermann. Baden-Baden: Nomos, 55–80.

Takriti, Abdel Razzaq. 2016. *Monsoon Revolution: Republicans, Sultans, and Empires in Oman, 1965–1976.* Oxford: Oxford University Press.

Teller, Matthew. 2014. "Sandhurst's Sheikhs: Why Do So Many Gulf Royals Receive Military Training in the UK?" *BBC.* www.bbc.com/news/magazine-28896860 (October 3, 2014).

90 *From the Arab Cold War to the Arab Spring*

TSG. 2015. "The Balancing of Allegiances in Yemen." *The Soufan Group.* http://soufan-group.com/tsg-intelbrief-the-balancing-of-allegiances-in-yemen/ (November 18, 2015).

Vassiliev, Alexei. 2013. *The History of Saudi Arabia.* London: Saqi Books.

Vela, Justin. 2014. "GCC to Set Up Regional Police Force Based in Abu Dhabi." *The National.* www.thenational.ae/world/gcc/gcc-to-set-up-regional-police-force-based-in-abu-dhabi (September 23, 2016).

Walt, Stephen M. 1990. *The Origins of Alliances.* Ithaca: Cornell University Press.

Wehrey, Frederic M. 2013. *Sectarian Politics in the Gulf: From the Iraq War to the Arab Uprisings.* Cambridge: Cambridge University Press.

Wilkin, Sam, and Fatma Alarimi. 2015. "Iran, Oman Discuss Yemen War, Settle Maritime Borders." *Reuters.* www.reuters.com/article/2015/05/26/us-yemen-security-iran-oman-idUSKBN0OB1SF20150526 (November 18, 2015).

Wright, John. 1983. *Libya: A Modern History.* London: Croom Helm.

Yom, Sean L. 2013. "Royal Repression and Regime Resilience: The Middle Eastern Experience." In *APSA Annual Meeting,* Chicago.

———. 2014. "Authoritarian Monarchies as an Epistemic Community." *Taiwan Journal of Democracy* 10(1): 43–62.

———. 2016. "How Middle Eastern Monarchies Survived the Arab Spring." *Monkey Cage – Washington Post.* www.washingtonpost.com/news/monkey-cage/wp/2016/07/29/the-emerging-monarchies-club-in-the-middle-east/?utm_term=.4045a12771b4 (March 20, 2017).

Yom, Sean L., and F. Gregory Gause III. 2012. "Resilient Royals: How Arab Monarchies Hang On." *Journal of Democracy* 23(4): 74–88.

Zahlan, Rosemarie Said. 2002. *The Making of Modern Gulf States: Kuwait Bahrain Qatar, the United Arab Emirates and Oman.* Reading: Ithaca Press.

4 When monarchies collide

Case studies of "near misses" of monarchic war

A peace among similar political systems does not equal harmonious relations devoid of conflict. On the contrary, it allows us to exhibit a mechanism that contains and manages conflict rather than avoiding or negating it. The two following cases are thus chosen *because* they are cases of monarchic conflict and are some of the closest instances of Middle East monarchies going to war against each other. Before their consolidation into independent nation-states, war was a frequent occurrence. After developing an identity as a separate state and recognizing the other as equal, warfare stopped, even though their conflicts with each other continued.

Of the following two cases, the first is a likely case for ingroup identification and subsequent preference for de-escalating conflicts to better showcase the mechanism. The second is a harder case that attempts to establish the limits of the theory and the influence of confounding factors and generalizability.

The chapters show how the strong sense of commonality led to political and military restraint in the case of Bahraini-Qatari relations and how the consolidation of state borders and institutions and, later, a shared threat were necessary for an ingroup identification to arise, transforming the rivalry between the Al Saud and the Hashemites into a relationship based on cooperation rather than conflict.

4.1 Bahrain and Qatar – keeping conflict "in the family": the Hawar Islands dispute

Despite being counted among the "most serious disputes" (Khalaf 1987) on the Arabian Peninsula,[1] the conflict between Bahrain and Qatar also shows how a more developed and mature ingroup identification impedes conflict escalation.

Although a crisis slide into a full-out war was not likely even at the height of the conflict in 1986, it marked a shocking departure in the conflictual but usually nonviolent relations of the two statelets, thus fitting into the category of a "near miss". The case is also important because it shows an ingroup that, unlike the other case studies, had sufficient time to develop and is based on numerous more similarities than monarchy, heightening similarity in the dyad.

A formative aspect in Bahraini-Qatari relations was their territorial dispute about the 17 Hawar Islands and Zubarah, including the *fashts* (shoals/banks) of

92 *When monarchies collide*

Dibal and Jaradah. It lasted for 30 years since their independence until its resolution by the International Court of Justice (ICJ) in 2001, but its roots were significantly older.

The following analysis will therefore focus mainly on the trajectory of the conflict and the actions and reactions of the Bahraini and Qatari ruling elites. The complete period of analysis from independence in 1971 to the resolution of the territorial dispute by the ICJ in 2001 will be subdivided into two periods to ensure greater legibility and stronger homogeneity within periods. After a short pre-independence historical summary, the two main periods will be divided by crucial successions in the emirates that markedly influenced bilateral relations: the dividing line is formed by the palace coup in Qatar that brought Hamad bin Khalifa Al Thani to power in 1995. While the period between the two successions is especially fraught with tensions due to the incongruence of the worldviews of the rulers, once the generational change had transpired, the conditions for the resolution of the dispute were especially good. Even at the nadir of their relations, the tight bonds of similarity enabled a political (and ultimately military) restraint between Doha and Manama.

The context of the islands dispute

However small (the largest island, Hawar, is 11 miles long and two miles wide), the Hawar Islands were suspected to have offshore oil reserves and made up almost a third of Bahraini territory, making them strategically valuable (Cordesman 1997, 49). Their importance for Qatar is derived mainly from proximity – the Hawar Islands are located 1–7 km from the Qatari coast, but 20 km from Bahrain. Zubarah lies on the northwestern coast of Qatar (Lotfian 2002, 119; Wiegand 2012, 81).

During the 19th and early 20th centuries, Bahrain under the Al Khalifa was the dominant part of the dyad and even ruled over the Qatari peninsula until the Al Thani established their authority there. Bahrain used tribal relationships to extend their territory into Qatar: the Khalifa and Jalahma branches of the Utub tribe migrated from Kuwait to Zubarah on the northwestern corner of the Qatari peninsula in 1766 to set up fort in al-Murair. The Khalifa family became wealthy merchants there. After their relocation in 1786 (after they had evicted the Persian governor of Bahrain who had frequently attacked Zubarah, along with other tribes) and a power struggle, they became rulers of Bahrain and remain so until today (Wright 2012, 299). The Al Thani that would come to rule Qatar established themselves in the peninsula around the 1860s, later than most shaikhdom dynasties (cf. Peterson 2011, 31).

A short war with the Al Khalifa in Bahrain in 1867 ultimately led to the sack of eastern towns in Qatar by a united force from Bahrain and Abu Dhabi but also brought on the first agreement of the Al Thani with the British in 1868 (not yet a treaty of protection but a recognition of the Al Thani as the chiefs of Qatar). The Ottoman military presence since 1871 shielded the Al Thani from Bahraini challengers and the Al Saud (Wright 2012, 299). In 1872, Qatar recognized Turkish sovereignty and stopped paying tribute to the Al Khalifa. Struggles over territory followed (Cordesman 1997, 46). When the Ottomans were made to withdraw from the region amid the First World War, the Al Thani signed a treaty with the British to become a protected state in 1916, following in the footsteps of their neighboring shaikhdoms (Wright 2012, 300).

With the discovery of oil and the distribution of oil concessions, the question of territorial demarcation emerged with a greater urgency. In 1936, Bahrain angered Qatar by putting their flags on Hawar, Fasht al-Dibal, and Fasht al-Jaradah, which Qatar claimed as their territory (Wiegand 2012, 81–82). Britain then sided with Bahrain (Cordesman 1997, 46). Qatar claimed that the decision was biased because it did not have the chance to present its case on the same basis as Bahrain. While the latter had more developed administrative and legal institutions and could present its case in modern terms commonly used by the British arbitrators, the Qataris relied on traditional terms, which failed to impress (cf. Peterson 2011, 31).

After the initial settlement, numerous other variants were attempted under British mediation but did not lead to a final solution. Although the Zubarah fort had been destroyed in 1878, the Naim tribe of that region retained allegiance ties to the Al Khalifa, forming the basis for their claims of authority over Zubarah. They were defeated by Qatari Shaikh Abdallah bin Jassim Al Thani's armed forces in 1937, even though the British warned the Bahraini ruler Hamad bin Isa Al Khalifa not to step in (Cordesman 1997, 47). Charles Belgrave, the British chief advisor of the Shaikh of Bahrain, describes this incident in his memoirs. The Bedouin guard of Shaikh Abdallah attacked Naim tribespeople loyal to the Al Khalifa during a visit from a negotiation delegation from Bahrain, which resulted in about two dozen casualties. Belgrave asserts that this "incident exacerbated the feeling between Bahrain and Qatar and put an end to any hope of negotiating a settlement for many years to come" (Belgrave 1972, 156).

As these and other clashes before independence show, the norm against using violence was markedly absent, as were claims to authority and territory that were detached from tribal allegiance. The imperial expansionary logic still trumped the national-state territorial one, but it began to erode with the solidification of borders and states.

Following the states' independence in 1971, the dispute went through numerous ups and downs, accompanied by numerous attempts at GCC and Saudi Arabian mediation. The ebb was reached in April 1986, when the two countries clashed in the only instance of a recorded militarized interaction, and again in the second half of the 1990s, when diplomatic spats dominated the bilateral relations (cf. Wiegand 2012). Despite these tensions, the relations were marked by strong political restraint and a clear preference for cooperation over escalation at all times.

The ICJ finally ruled on March 16, 2001, according the Hawar Islands and al-Jaradah (now declared an island) to Bahrain and Zubarah, the Janan Islands, and al-Dibal (still considered a shoal) to Qatar. Each country received about half of the disputed territory (Wiegand 2012, 79).

94 *When monarchies collide*

State formation and territorial conflict (1971–1995) – neighbors, brothers, family: ingroup identification and the discovery of similarity

Structural similarities

In contrast to most of the other case studies, the similarities between the two members of the dyad are striking. Even among the relatively homogenous group of small Gulf monarchies, they stand out for their shared attributes.[2]

Bahrain and Qatar are contiguous neighbors, small countries that are practically city states – in fact, the smallest among the Gulf monarchies. In the timeframe of the analysis, both political systems were similar, with a dynastic system presided over by an emir (Hamad bin Isa Al Khalifa proclaimed himself king of Bahrain in 2002, i.e. after the settlement of the dispute) and ruling family members in most other key positions. Both the Al Khalifa in Bahrain and the Al Thani in Qatar legitimize their rule via tradition: they were the pre-eminent shaikhs at the time of the British arrival and became the dominant actors in the state-building process that followed the formative British presence and oil exploitation.

The comparatively modernized and liberalized polity of newly independent Bahrain and Qatar, in contrast to other small Gulf monarchies, led scholars to set them apart as examples of a slightly less paternalistic "modern paternalism", just after their independence in 1971 (Sadik and Snavely 1972, 143). Early on, Bahrain installed the National Assembly (*majlis al-watani*) and Qatar the Council of Ministers (*majlis al-nawwab*) and the Consultative Council (*majlis al-shura*) (Sadik and Snavely 1972, 143). While their neighbors have caught up in establishing participatory political institutions (and state institutions in general) besides traditional audience fora like *majalis* and *diwaniyyas*, another wave of liberalization, including a new constitution, followed the 1999 succession of Hamad bin Isa Al Khalifa in Bahrain and 1995 of Hamad bin Khalifa Al Thani in Qatar (the constitutions came into effect in 2002 in Bahrain and 2004 in Qatar). The position of ruling family remains dominant, and participation of other political actors is highly limited, but Bahrain's semi-elected National Assembly makes its system more competitive. Qatar has elections only for the municipal council, although elections for the consultative council have been announced for years (Bahry 1999; cf. Commins 2012, 197–199; Lawson 1989; Ulrichsen 2014).

Economically, both countries could follow a similar development path because they also both started oil exploration at a similar time, in the 1950s (oil was discovered in both countries in the 1930s), although Qatar quickly overtook Bahrain in the amount of production (Sadik and Snavely 1972, 145). Both have similar economies, being rentier states with a proportionally high non-citizen population of expat workers, although Qatar's share of expatriates is significantly higher. Since the 1980s, the two national economies have started to diverge as Bahraini oil dried up (Commins 2012, 203, 212).

However, before independence, the development was uneven because general education had been introduced much earlier in Bahrain and because its state institutions were more developed, not least due to the longer-entrenched British presence (Sadik and Snavely 1972, 145–147). This is reflected in the condescending attitudes of Bahrainis toward Qataris as "country cousins", noted by Qataris and their rulers as late as the 1950s (Belgrave 1972, 158) and the British asymmetric handling of the two shaikhs. A telling example is a 1948–1949 correspondence between the UK government and the Bahraini emir relayed in a US embassy cable of 1976, which, in a bracketed "FYI", quotes the UK's "contention that while Bahrain clearly had sovereign rights over Hawar island group, Jinan island to the south of Hawar belonged not to 'His Highness the Amir of Bahrain' but to 'His Excellency the Shaikh of Qatar'. End FYI" (Cable: Qatar-Bahrain Median Line 1976). The difference in styles makes the "amir" superior to the "shaikh". In stark contrast to "Highness", "Excellency" is a title used mostly for non-royals. This asymmetry initially impeded the recognition of equality, the basis for ingroup identification. With the development of modern state apparatuses and the consolidation of borders, the underlying causes for the asymmetry gradually eroded, and ingroup identification could follow.

In terms of kinship and culture, their ruling families share a descent from the Anaza tribal federation from the central Arabian Najd, as do the Kuwaiti Al Sabah and the Al Saud (in addition, the Al Khalifa and the Al Sabah descend from the same tribe of Utub) ('Abd al-Hakim al-Wa'ili 2002a, 2002b; Assiri 1990, 2). Due to the fluidity of borders and territorial proximity, there is a certain degree of intermarriage, even during periods of tense relations. For instance, a grandson of the Bahraini ruler Abdallah bin Ahmad Al Khalifa married a daughter of the "founder" of Qatar, Jassim bin Muhammad Al Thani, in the 19th century (Cooke 2014, 38–39). Sometimes, like among historical European monarchies, marriages were arranged for political reasons: to bind dynasties together (Rugh 2007, 82–95, 191, 227).

Their *khaleeji* (Arab Gulf) identity, which encompasses the Arabic language (and the specific *khaleeji* dialect), tradition, literature and poetry, and way of life, remains important to both rulers and populations until today although national identities have started to develop and be actively fostered by the governments (Diwan 2016; cf. Erskine-Loftus, Al-Mulla, and Hightower 2016).[3]

The main difference between the two, however, consists in the homogeneity of their populations. Qatar, especially compared to Gulf standards, is a highly homogeneous state regarding its citizen population, and even the previous economic divisions of *hadar* and *badu* (settled townspeople and nomads) have been blurred with its economic rise and development. Meanwhile, in Bahrain, the Sunni Arab Al Khalifa dynasty rules over a majority Shia population and a non-negligible share of citizens of Iranian descent (both Sunni and Shia). Consequently, the potential and actual level of internal conflict is much higher than in Qatar (cf. AlShehabi 2016).[4] Although societal conflict level influences external and internal threat perception, these dissimilarities did not impede the ingroup identification on the elite level.

Both states and especially their ruling elites, the Al Khalifa and the Al Thani, are more than sufficiently similar for the theorized ingroup to emerge. The ingroup similarity here encompasses a broader set of shared traits that goes far beyond

96   *When monarchies collide*

monarchism. In terms of case selection, this is both a weakness and a strength. Overlapping similarities make it harder to connect the building of the ingroup to the political system alone; however, if, as posited by the theoretical framework, it is the *perception of similarity* that induces de-escalative foreign policy behavior via a solidarity-prescribing ingroup norm, the higher degree of structural similarity could lead to a stronger such perception and represent a clearer mechanism illustrated by the case.

Salience: constraints and catalysts to ingroup identification

The wave of independence of the small Gulf monarchies in 1971 boosted the number of monarchies to nine out of 19, i.e. 47%, but also somewhat lowered the salience of monarchy. Despite the wave of independence of monarchies, they were still a minority in the system: one that had not quite overcome the threat by coups and revolutions. However, because the wave of independence also led the small Gulf monarchies to share a historical fate, the decrease of monarchic salience in 1971 might not have been too pronounced. The Iranian Revolution in 1979 again changed the picture, not just because it decreased the absolute number of monarchies in the Middle East (eight out of 19, or 42%) but also because the new revolutionary republic was bent on destroying and replacing monarchism and therefore posed a major threat to the Arab monarchies. This was the last change in the proportion of different types of political systems. During the first period, the salience of monarchy was moderately high but was at times overshadowed by the identification as part of the "*khaleej*", the Arab part of the Persian Gulf.

Before independence, the Al Khalifa had at times laid claim to all of Qatar, but this claim has gradually shrunk with the loss of control over territory and allied tribes and has in effect ceased to exist after independence. Therefore, a divisive ideology based on a hierarchy of relations cannot be discerned for the post-independence period between Bahrain and Qatar (or the Al Khalifa and Al Thani in particular).

Bahrain and Qatar, and the small Gulf states in general, were threatened both internally (via competing ruling ideologies from Iraqi Ba'thism, Pan-Arabism, and Iranian Pan-Islamism) and externally (by military aggression by Iran and Iraq). Whereas Iraq had been a potential threat before, Iran became one only after its revolution. Over a decade later, the military threat peaked again with the Iraqi invasion of Kuwait. The states felt threatened not only because they were much smaller and more vulnerable than Iran and Iraq but also because they were monarchies. Revolutionary ideology from both states was decidedly anti-monarchical.

While relations with the shah had mostly been good,[5] and the Gulf monarchies were reluctant to recognize the new Iranian regime that promoted an anti-monarchic propaganda (Alkim 1989, 126; Assiri 1990, 64). This found its immediate expression in a flurry of visits between the monarchs of the different Gulf states, e.g. the president of the UAE and the king of Saudi Arabia met more than 16 times between 1979–1983 (Alkim 1989, 235, EN 173).

When monarchies collide 97

Revolutionary leader Khomeini had dismissed the Gulf rulers as "mini shahs", equating them with the regime he had just overthrown (Boghardt 2006, 29) and delegitimized the monarchic system in general, even before the revolution. Already in the 1970s, he lectured that "Islam proclaims monarchy and hereditary succession wrong and invalid" (Khomeini cited in: Lafraie 2009, 67). From the other side across the Gulf, Ba'thist Iraq's ideology called for "the destruction of traditional monarchies and the end of Shaikhly rule" (Joyce 1998, 131). Iraq had supported internal radical movements against the monarchies, especially in the 1950s and 1960s. Although it eventually abandoned these subversion attempts, Iran remained a threat in the 1980s and 1990s, fostering Shia activism, especially just after the Iranian revolution. The 1981 coup attempt in Bahrain stood out. Bahraini authorities implicated 73 Shiites from different Gulf Arab states for the coup attempt that was linked to Iran. As a result, except Kuwait, all the GCC states signed bilateral security with Saudi Arabia (Boghardt 2006, 53–54). It was only then that Saudi Arabia and most smaller Gulf states aligned themselves with Iraq. In the 1980s, further attacks, bombings, and assassinations in the GCC states were carried out by Iran-, Iraq-, or Syria-linked groups or by Palestinian groups, and between 1987 and 1989, 142 international terrorist attacks were connected to Iran alone (Boghardt 2006, 54–56, 93, 130).

The heightened threat from both Iran and Iraq pushed the Gulf monarchies closer together and drove the formation of the GCC in 1981. The integration of the Gulf states into a regional security complex made the necessity to settle the dispute more urgent for both parties and increased the acceptability of Saudi Arabia as a mediator (cf. Calvert and Alcock 2004).

For Bahrain and Qatar, the Gulf War in 1991 was the first time that they engaged in a major military operation – an indication of the high level of the perceived threat. Qatar played an important role in the battle for Ras al-Khafji (Allison 2012, 122; Al-Musfir 2001, 318).

A common threat to a group of states that included Bahrain and Qatar as monarchies persisted throughout the period, although its level was not static. For example, most Gulf states openly supported Iraq in its war against Iran throughout its duration: 1980–1988. Post-revolutionary Iran, on the other hand, was not uniformly seen as a threat by all Gulf states, with Oman, Dubai, and Qatar having especially good relations with its neighbor across the Gulf. In 1992, Qatar alienated Bahrain and other GCC states the next month by moving closer to Iran in its signing three cooperation agreements with the republic in one month (Kostiner 2009, 135).

Social processes of ingroup identification

Once state borders and institutions had been cemented, the developing and strengthening of an ingroup with which Qatar and Bahrain identified could be discerned. Qatar renewed its claim to the islands and Zubarah after independence in 1971, when it became an international dispute between independent states

98   *When monarchies collide*

(Cordesman 1997, 47). The contention dominated Qatari-Bahraini relations, especially during the peaks of tension in 1986 and 1996 and kept them from establishing official diplomatic relations on an ambassadorial level. While a significant sign of disagreement, it is not tantamount to non-recognition, because both countries interacted and even cooperated freely in international fora like the UN, the Arab League, and the GCC.

While state institutions were still relatively new and developing, the independence in an era of virtual global monopoly of nation-states meant cementing the individual states' identity and security. The new states were attributed legitimacy as independent sovereign entities where the norms of territorial integrity and national sovereignty reigned over dynastic claims over group allegiance. While this marked the end of the transformation of the dispute over the islands and Zubarah from a dynastic rivalry into a territorial dispute, it did not spell its disappearance.

Regardless of the level of tensions, the personalization of bonds remained. Direct interaction never stopped, and the lack of ambassadorial representation did not preclude frequent high-level visits. To the contrary, after each severe incident (and especially the 1986 confrontation), a series of tripartite meetings with the conflict parties and Saudi Arabia ensued. The mediation resulted in compromise to put the case to the ICJ if Saudi mediation failed (Wiegand 2012, 85).

Informal meetings, provided by intra-monarchic protocol, were also important occasions for interaction and crisis-diffusion or prevention, an example being the visit of Muhammad bin Mubarak Al Khalifa, the foreign minister of Bahrain, to Qatar to pay condolences for the death of the Qatari minister of commerce, Nasir bin Khalid Al Thani, in 1986, shortly after the altercation over Fasht al-Dibal. GCC officials pushed to diffuse the crisis before the coming GCC heads of state meeting in the UAE in November that year (Consultations in progress on meeting of tripartite committee 1986). Apart from tripartite meetings and bilateral negotiations, the regular meetings of the GCC were natural fora for debate and negotiation.

Close contact was both enabled by and contributed to a similar worldview. Bahrain and Qatar exhibit many of the features associated with Ayubi's concept of "clannish democracy" (*dimuqratiyya 'asha'iriyya*) that he identified in Arab monarchies, for him a formula similar to consociationalism that cements elite solidarity at the top and aims at the erection of a modern state within a traditional society (Ayubi 1995, 245).

This joint conception is due to a shared traditional socialization in similar societies, often combined with British education. Their common outlook and common worldview were also decisively shaped by the Iranian Revolution in 1979 and by prior republican subversion that helped forge a shared view of history. After having reconciled with the shah once he had abandoned his claim to Bahrain, the Gulf monarchies distinguished themselves by forging a tight bond with the Persian monarchy. This contributed to their markedly tepid reaction to the Iranian seizure of islands claimed by two emirates of the UAE – so much that Iraq and other republics protested the weakness of the reaction and condemned them for it (Chubin and Tripp 2014, 44).

Regardless of the level of conflict, the two ruling families were continually eager to appeal to their shared traits and close ties and thus affirm and reaffirm their commonality. They perceived threats in a similar way and appealed to shared links and alliances and repeatedly emphasized the need for a "brotherly solution" between "sisterly countries", while de-emphasizing differences. This did not mean, however, that distrust had been eliminated between them but rather that there was no significant "othering" in that period.[6]

At the GCC summit in Doha in December 1990, the two sides agreed to withdraw the ICJ case "in the event of reaching a brotherly solution acceptable to both parties" (cited in: Al-Arayed 2003, 331) through continued bilateral negotiations and mediations. This was despite their disagreement on the best course of action to solve the dispute: Bahrain preferred arbitration by Saudi Arabia, while Qatar called for adjudication by the ICJ. This was accompanied by the compromise reached under the Saudi aegis, namely to attempt mediation and jointly refer the matter to the ICJ if this approach failed, pursued since the 1986 clash (Wiegand 2012, 85).

The two neighbors' shared historical trajectory led to a preference for Western alliance. This led them to frame threats in similar ways to each other and set them apart from non-monarchies where that link was broken by the revolutionary ideology of anti-imperialism. Their markedly different understanding of regional relations and readings of history from revolutionary republics regularly comes up in confrontations, e.g. with post-revolutionary Iran, a major political ideologue. Ideological republics that were antagonists of the shah, like Syria and Libya, allied with the Islamic Republic because both shared its anti-Western outlook.

Despite the density and strength of relationships between the Al Thani and Al Khalifa elites, there was still a significant amount of mutual distrust up to the 1990s. Diplomatic cables relay a July 1978 report by then–Commandant of Police Hamad bin Jassim Al Thani,[7] who claimed that his intelligence unit tried to warn Bahraini authorities about an impending attack on a Bahraini journalist, but they did not believe him, because they thought Qatar was trying to "sow discontent". Hamad bin Jassim claimed that the Bahrainis changed their minds after the attack, fostering bilateral cooperation (Cable: Qatari Police Chief on Qatar Police 1978).

Foreign policy restraint and de-escalation in periods of crisis

The strengthening of bilateral ties inside the club of Gulf monarchies helped contain the conflict and prevent escalation into a war or warlike clash, although a major confrontation happened in 1986 – which was, however, quickly resolved.

The period until 1995 was marked by multiple altercations (most notably in 1978, 1982, 1986, and 1991) and provocations by both sides. Accusations of lacking commitment to conflict resolution surfaced from time to time (Lawson 1989, 133). Still, the diplomatic avenue was the most important for both countries,

100 *When monarchies collide*

which shared the desire to settle the dispute by mediation. The level of a militarized conflict (although far from a war) was reached only once, in 1986, which did not result in any casualties and was quickly diffused by the decision makers. Despite the importance of the issue, the 1986 events mark the absolute height of the strife, and no militarized altercation was recorded at any other time.

In April 1978, Bahraini warships conducted maneuvers close to the Hawar Islands, prompting Qatari authorities to detain Bahraini fishers in the area. In response, Bahrain held military exercises in the proximity. In 1982, Bahrain christened one of its new frigates "Hawar", to which Qatar formally protested, and Qatar accused Bahrain of navy exercises in Qatari waters. Both countries had used almost any non-coercive foreign policy tool available. Bahrain attempted mainly to create facts on the ground by building on the islands and developing tourism, while Qatar tried to change the status quo with more radical solutions (Lawson 1989, 133; cf. Wiegand 2012, 82–83).

At the height of the tensions, in 1986, this led to a confrontation by Qatar. Khalaf describes the "armed" clash between the two countries:

> The two mini-states expelled each other's citizens, cut all communications links with each other, including flights by jointly-owned Gulf Air, and blasted each other in their respective newspapers, radio and television. Ironically, one of the charges hurled between them was abuse of human rights. Both states put their military on maximum alert and "discovered" espionage networks aiding the enemy. On April 26, 1986, four Qatari air force helicopters landed on the uninhabited island of Fasht al-Dabal and arrested all 29 foreign workers surveying the area for a Dutch construction company contracted by Bahrain to build a coast guard base. The bizarre incident underlines the explosive nature of these disputes and the temptation to settle them by force. Bahrain's recent acquisition of new weapons systems may portend another, more serious round of hostilities.
>
> (Khalaf 1987)

The Bahrainis had been constructing a small base there and were transforming the island into a coast guard station. After the incident, they claimed the workers were building a GCC facility in agreement with a prior arrangement. Both parties called military alerts and reinforced their positions, Bahrain on Hawar and Qatar on the reef of Fasht al-Dibal, which formed part of the Hawar Islands (Cordesman 1997, 47).

In addition, Qatari helicopters attacked a Bahrain-based tugboat in the proximity with machine guns, to coerce it into leaving. Bahrain issued severe warnings and deployed its troops to the islands but did not attack or escalate in any way. During its occupation, Qatar dismantled the facilities that had been built there and began building a causeway linking the island to the Qatari mainland. Qatar justified its action by alleging Bahraini violations of a 1983 agreement (Wiegand 2012, 84). Despite the spike in the level of escalation, the situation was still far from an actual military clash. There were no casualties, and Bahrain did not reciprocate by occupying other territory; nor did they open fire on the helicopters.[8] Regional media emphasized the irregularity of the incident. Kuwaiti media referred to the event as a "temporary lapse in relations" and an "isolated incident" ("Isolated incident" occurs between Bahrain, Qatar 1986).

The 1986 incident was followed by a long period of tension (Zahlan 2002, 25), including an incident in June 1991, when the Qatari navy entered waters off Hawar Islands and Bahrain reacted by sending fighters into Qatari airspace. GCC mediation ended the spat and sent an observation team to the area, but tensions resumed after the First Gulf War (Cordesman 1997, 47). Nonetheless, despite the Qatari provocation, neither "another, more serious round of hostilities" nor "the temptation to settle them by force", as anticipated by Khalaf (1987), materialized.

Instead, it was evidently overcome by a desire to de-escalate. Both sides showed remarkable restraint, for the most part refraining from delegitimizing the other and engaging in rhetorical escalation. Although initial media reaction was alarmist and allegations of espionage were levied, there is little evidence of actual subversive acts of policies, indicating that 1986 formed an aberration in otherwise-restrained relations rather than the tip of an iceberg of hostility.

Following the clashes, Qatari official statements were firm but devoid of aggression or delegitimizing messages toward the counterpart. Instead, they emphasized the necessity to restore the perceived status quo ante instead of attempting to retaliate by force, as was the norm in many other conflicts in the Middle East:

> concerning the violation, the government of Qatar has been compelled to take action to stop the land reclamation and construction which Bahrain has carried out at Fasht al-Dibal, an action designed to restore the situation to what it was previously, which is what the principles of mediation and the rulings of the GCC Ministerial Council's resolution were directed at and to which Qatar had totally committed itself.
>
> (cited in: Wiegand 2012, 84)

After an agreement had been reached in May 1986, the workers were released. The following month, Qatar ended its occupation, and Bahrain agreed to destroy the facilities it had built on the island (Cordesman 1997, 47). Qatar stated regret for the disagreement. Both sides recognized that external mediation was necessary and in 1987 agreed to put the case jointly before the ICJ according to principles proposed by Saudi Arabia in 1983 (Wiegand 2012, 84).

Nonetheless, the 1986 altercations were serious enough that besides the (unilateral) Qatari decision to intervene with force, other measures to weaken the opponent's position were employed. Despite the official claims of the governments to have uncovered espionage networks by the other in both countries (Khalaf 1987), which would constitute subversion, the evidence for it was rather slim. Even if these networks existed, their main task seemed to be the collection of information, but not destabilizing the regime or even the individual rulers of Qatar and Bahrain (cf. Young 1997).

102 *When monarchies collide*

After the immediate tensions had been dissolved, the dispute continued. Apart from the question whether Zubarah should be included in possible settlement, the most important bone of contention was identifying an acceptable mediator. Bahrain insisted that it be a regional solution under the leadership of Saudi Arabia. Qatar was adamant that the ICJ would be a more objective and therefore acceptable mediator and arbitrator. In July 1991, Qatar unilaterally instituted proceedings to let the ICJ decide whether it had jurisdiction. Bahrain refused the jurisdiction of the court and insisted that they both agree to coordinate before involving the ICJ, which Qatar disrespected by its unilateral submission (Cordesman 1997, 47–48; Wiegand 2012, 85).

At the December 1990 summit of the GCC in Doha, Qatar brought up the dispute even before discussing the topical Iraqi invasion of Kuwait that had just taken place (cf. Al-Arayed 2003, 330). This indicated the seriousness of the issue, at least for Qatar, which was determined to go to great lengths to get the islands – although they mostly excluded violent measures. Indeed, in a confidential conversation with US diplomats, the advisor of Qatari Emir Khalifa bin Hamad Al Thani asserted in 1976 that if it were territory that the Bahrainis wanted, Qatar would build them "an artificial island to replace" Hawar and cover the cost for a causeway and many more benefits. In the same conversation, he relayed in flowery terms how he tried to impress on the mediating Saudi king, Khalid, and on Prince Saud that for Qatar it was "no rug merchanting operation but a serious matter" (Qatar-Bahrain Relations 1976). While this indicates the importance of the matter, it also clearly shows a great degree of willingness to compromise.

Following Qatar's unilateral submission of the case to the ICJ in July 1991, the atmosphere between Bahrain and Qatar grew more tense. In 1995, following an exchange of documents in 1993 and 1994, the ICJ ruled that it did have jurisdiction of the Hawar Islands dispute. As before, Bahrain rejected the court's involvement (Cordesman 1997, 48). In February 1995, a senior Bahraini government official reacted by dramatically proclaiming that in case of an ICJ ruling favorable for Qatar, features in question would be relinquished to the neighbor "over our dead bodies" (Schofield 2001, 219).

Although the islands and Zubarah were highly important to Bahrain and to Qatar, this is the most confrontational public statement issued in the whole dispute. At no point did the Bahraini or Qatari officials ever question the legitimacy or equality of their neighboring dynasty, only its stance on the territorial dispute. To the contrary, the dispute was more often than not deliberately downplayed while insisting on cooperation. Despite the importance of the issue for both sides, the issue was rarely couched in existential terms but was mostly presented as a clearly delimitated disagreement. The rhetorical escalation seemed to be as contained as the military one.

In addition, there were clear alliance ties between the two countries. Although there was no formal bilateral security alliance, the clearest and strongest sign of alignment and cooperation between Bahrain and Qatar was institutionalized in the Gulf Cooperation Council, the intragovernmental organization that unites all Arab Gulf monarchies. The founding of the council revealed a deepened shared

When monarchies collide 103

identity that was vividly formulated in the communiqué of the pre-meeting by the organization's foreign minister in Taif on February 4, 1981, regarding the reasons for its establishment:

> out of consideration of their *special relations and joint characteristics* stemming from their joint creed, *similarity of regimes*, unity of heritage, *similarity of their political, social and demographic structure*, and their cultural and historical affiliation.
>
> (cited in: Kechichian 2001, 281, emphasis added)

Since at least its second summit, the GCC was the forum where formal cooperation and defense arrangements were discussed and concluded rather than in bilateral. This is despite a lack of regional integration, obligations and interdependences via the GCC could not be easily reversed or abandoned as in ad hoc alliances, which illustrates the continually close ties of the states.

The alliance included other costly responsibilities and led to strong solidarity in times of need. During Operation Desert Storm in 1991, Bahrain and Qatar even shared military commitments when defending fellow monarchy and GCC member Kuwait, which marked the first major military engagement for either of them (Allison 2012, 122).

These alliances broadly followed the line of ingroup identity. During the escalation in 1986, Iranian Foreign Minister Ali Akbar Velayati offered Qatar support (Bahrain: Further Reportage 1986). However, Qatar chose to cooperate with Bahrain (and Saudi Arabia) to diffuse the bilateral tensions over the furtherance of its territorial interests by accepting the Iranian republic's offer.

Ingroup identification

The two states met the conditions for ingroup identification, being highly similar in all measured dimensions on many different levels. State building and the cementing of state borders enabled the acceptance of each other as separate but equal entities.

Group identification was catalyzed by a moderately high salience of monarchy. The salience was driven by the presence of a common threat by the anti-monarchic republics of Iraq and Iran (after 1979). In addition, there was no divisive hierarchic ideology between the two Gulf monarchies that could have obstructed ingroup identification. However, the salience was somewhat lowered because of the rise in the overall share of monarchies thanks to the simultaneous independence of the small Gulf monarchies. Although the wave of new independent monarchies in 1971 might have lessened monarchic salience, it also bound them together, having experienced similar historical trajectories and facing similar threats as *khaleeji*, Arab Gulf monarchies. Although they did not establish formal diplomatic relations, they cooperated on a personalized bilateral level as well as in international fora, especially the GCC. Right from the beginning, frequent bilateral visits and mediation meetings under Saudi aegis, as well as public and private

104 *When monarchies collide*

proclamations, emphasized the similarity and fraternity of the polities and rulers. Since 1981, the monarchy-only forum of the GCC indicates a quickly developing common bond. This process was accompanied by constant affirmations of similarity and fraternity.

Amid the intensive ingroup dynamics, a militarized altercation occurred only once. However, the April 1986 clash at the height of tensions was quickly diffused without casualties by a strong restraint from both sides, showing their preference for cooperation over conflict. Instead of direct retaliation, Bahrain reacted with restraint, thereby possibly precluding a crisis slide. Qatar quickly agreed to a compromise solution, issued statements of regret for past provocations and called for peaceful and diplomatic solutions. Although Qatar cooperated with Iran more than most other GCC members, it did not exploit the possibility of allying with a larger power against its "brother" and refrained from using Bahraini internal divisions to undermine the ruling family. Both countries preferred a compromise solution that bridged two seemingly incompatible demands – local mediation as preferred by Bahrain and international arbitration as preferred by Qatar. Both countries continuously cooperated and allied on a large scale, especially via the GCC. They also committed resources to the support of a fellow Gulf monarchy through their military cooperation during the Gulf War in 1991.

New leaders, new friendships (1995–2001)? Monarchic solidarity in the "Khaleeji club" of gulf monarchs

While Bahrain and Qatar retained most of their similarities, non-synchronized succession in both countries brought about some discordance due to the different worldviews and agendas of the leaders (although it affected restraint only on a non-military level). A period of deterioration in relations followed in the turn from 1995 to 1996 after Hamad bin Khalifa Al Thani became emir, having deposed his father in June 1995 in a bloodless palace coup (Cordesman 1997, 48). The rift was closed along with the generational gap after the succession of Hamad bin Isa Al Khalifa in Bahrain in 1999.

Structural similarities

Hamad reformed the institutions on the peninsula radically. He instigated a number of political and economic reforms, extending education, social services, and welfare to the broader citizenship population and introduced a constitution providing for basic civil rights and avenues of political participation (cf. Fromherz 2012, chapter 6; Kamrava 2009). He also reformed the decision-making process in foreign policy that was to a large extent centralized and patrimonial under his father. Emir Hamad, a Sandhurst graduate with broad international exposure, decentralized and diffused decision-making, already beginning while still crown prince (and minister of defense and commander-in-chief of the armed forces – the multiple simultaneous roles already indicating the highly centralized powers) (Wright 2012, 301).

Disagreement and rift over the general political worldview of the two rulers would resurface over the years, at least until the succession of Hamad bin Isa as emir (later as king) of Bahrain. The emir of Qatar had just overthrown his conservative father and opposed the politics of Bahraini Emir Isa bin Salman Al Khalifa for much the same reasons as he did his father's. In his view, Bahraini conservatism and lack of modernization caused the disruptive Shiite unrest in the country. The Al Khalifa, on the other hand, saw Qatari behavior as deliberately rude and provocative, careless about the "normal courtesies between Gulf ruling elites" and taking advantage of Bahrain's internal problems to further their agenda (Cordesman 1997, 49).

Qatar's disruptive influence in the GCC under Emir Hamad earned it the description of being the "gadfly" of the GCC by some observers (Teitelbaum 1999b, 600). Local scholars and observers emphasized that the disorderly succession by coup constituted a break with Gulf values and therefore ruptured the trust between the countries (Salama 2014), not dissimilar to the criticism it has faced since the eruption of the Qatar Crisis. It was not the palace coup per se that irked the conservative rulers of the Gulf. In fact, the now-overthrown Khalifa had come to power in exactly the same way in 1972, via a palace coup while his uncle and predecessor was abroad. The crucial difference was that the 1972 coup was supported by Qatari and Gulf (especially Saudi) elites (Commins 2012, 213), but the 1995 coup was not approved more broadly and therefore went against Gulf values of consultation and respect for tradition, authority, and seniority. While Qatar saw Bahrain as a Saudi tool, the distance to Saudi politics and ideology was even greater, and Hamad rejected the Saudi attempts to enforce their ultra-conservatism in its smaller neighbors in order to stabilize their own rule (Cordesman 1997, 225).

These rifts weakened the ingroup perception because the basis for similarity, institutions, and similar mindset and worldview among the rulers, which are the prime agents of ingroup identification, shifted. It was bridged once Bahrain "caught up" with Qatar on both fronts. In any case, even during the period of largest distance, the ingroup was never ruptured completely.

Salience: constraints and catalysts of ingroup identification

Between 1995 and 2001, there were no significant disruptions or transformations that affected monarchic salience. Since the threat level gradually decreased since the 1979 revolution and the 1990/1991 Gulf War, it could be said to have slightly lowered. Ingroup identification in this period could thus not have been driven by an especially heightened salience of the monarchic ingroup. This shifts the explanatory burden to the social processes in the second period. The second period in Bahraini-Qatari relations was not marked by a particularly high level of threat: with Baghdad severely weakened after two Gulf wars and a normalization of ties between (now less openly revolutionary) Iran and at least some of the Gulf monarchies, there was no direct threat against either monarchies in general or the GCC states in particular.

106   *When monarchies collide*

Despite the ongoing sectarianized unrest in Bahrain in the 1990s, the anti-Iranian stance was toned down by Saudi Arabia and Bahrain, and the latter even exchanged ambassadors with Iran in 1997, despite having formerly accused the Islamic Republic of backing the Shi'a unrest in the country (Teitelbaum 1999a, 294–296). Even relations with Iraq were on the upside, with both Qatar and Bahrain, along with the UAE and Oman, campaigning for a lifting of the embargo and sanctions and distancing from the official Arab League and GCC line led by Saudi Arabia and Kuwait (Maddy-Weitzman 1999a, 128).

No other significant competing identity overtook monarchism in salience either, as confessional and ethnic cleavages (Sunni–Shia/Arab–Persian) have declined for the same reasons.[9] Despite periods of stronger and weaker ideological fervor, there was no explicit ideology that could have divided the two countries, especially since the two rulers did not foster any such ideologies.

Social processes of ingroup identification

Despite the high tensions between the Gulf rulers, the periods of high tension were always temporary and confined, as no side was interested in a serious rupture. At the end of the 1990s, this finally translated into official diplomatic rapprochement. In 1997, the countries decided to establish embassies in the respective capitals, although the process of appointing ambassadors dragged on for several years. Qatar appointed Sa'd al-Rumaihi, who as head of Qatar television had broadcasted interviews with Bahraini opposition members, and Bahrain dragged its feet (Maddy-Weitzman 1999, 128; Teitelbaum 1999b, 298). The resolution of the dispute opened the way to establish full diplomatic relations.

The lack of embassies did at no time preclude direct contact between the emirs or foreign or prime ministers of the countries, which is why it should be interpreted not as a complete lack of mutual recognition but rather as a bargaining chip and signal of disagreement. The emirs and foreign ministers met frequently during the period, although cancelations and boycotts of meetings were also used strategically to protest. Despite some setbacks, the meetings resulted in significant steps to resolve the dispute and brought the countries closer together.

In June 1996, Hamad bin Jassim Al Thani, Qatar's foreign and prime minister, visited Bahrain to mend relations, and his nephew, the emir, proclaimed that "Qatar was keen to improve relations with Bahrain despite their dispute over the Hawar islands" (cited in: Wiegand 2012, 86). Bahrain agreed that there were more pressing matters, such as terrorism, Iraq, and Iran, but again pressed for Saudi mediation. After more declarations signaling the will to cooperate, the crown prince of Bahrain, Hamad bin Isa Al Khalifa, called for a summit to resolve the dispute in September 1996. In October, Bahrain submitted a petition to the ICJ, which Qatar welcomed, but it did not drop the call for Saudi mediation (Wiegand 2012, 86).

Bahrain still refused to attend the GCC meeting in Doha in 1996, in protest of Qatar's unilateral decision to put the dispute to the ICJ – despite royal intervention from Sultan Qaboos of Oman, Saudi Arabia, and King Hussein of Jordan (Hussain

When monarchies collide 107

1996a). It also boycotted further meetings in 1997 and a GCC air exercise in December (Teitelbaum 1999a, 298) and later declined to participate in the Organisation of Islamic Cooperation (OIC) meeting in 2000, which also took place in Doha (Wiegand 2012, 80).

Despite Bahrain's absence at the GCC summit in 1996, a ministerial committee tasked with mediating the dispute was installed at the summit and met several times in early 1997. In mid February, the Bahraini foreign minister and crown prince (later Emir Hamad bin Isa Al Khalifa) met with Qatari Foreign Minister Hamad bin Jassim bin Jabir Al Thani in London to discuss their relations (Teitelbaum 1999a, 297). In the following weeks, the foreign ministers of the states conducted official state visits to the respective neighbors and received a cordial reception. These meetings immediately preceded the decision to finally open embassies, thus normalizing relations (Teitelbaum 1999a, 298). The two emirs met again for separate talks during the following GCC summit in Kuwait in December 1997 (Maddy-Weitzman 1999, 128), and Qatar's emir visited Manama for the first time in December 1998. One of the results was an agreement to set up a joint committee encouraging cooperation, and a Qatari proposal to build a causeway linking the two states was welcomed by Bahrain. The commission was to be headed by the two crown princes (Wiegand 2012, 87, 93), one of whom, Hamad Al Khalifa, succeeded his father as emir of Bahrain in 1999 amid a period of internal tensions.

After his succession, another flurry of exchange visits followed, among which was Bahraini Crown Prince Salman bin Hamad Al Khalifa's visit to Doha (Teitelbaum 2001a, 196). While the exchange of ambassadors planned for 2000 failed, the rulers of the two countries once again met for talks to resolve the dispute (Peterson 2011, 32). In March 2000, Qatar Airways announced that it would begin daily flights between Doha and Manama (Wiegand 2012, 93).

These developments were a result of intense negotiations and mutual attempts at reconciliations but also, due to a feedback loop, itself an indicator of intensified international and transnational relations between the two countries. A new period of reconciliation was initiated after the coming to power of Emir Hamad bin Isa in Bahrain in 1999 and was stabilized by the ICJ ruling.

The successions in the two states, 1995 in Qatar and 1999 in Bahrain, brought a new generation of rulers, two namesake young reformer emirs, into power. They were closer in terms of outlook, worldview, and ruling ideology to each other and the generational gap that fired up the conflict between Bahrain and Qatar was closed. Before, Bahraini (and other Gulf) officials complained that the behavior of especially Hamad bin Khalifa and Hamad bin Jassim broke the norms that ruled the Gulf family with their disruptive modernization.

Not least due to their Western education – both monarchs were graduates of the British Royal Military Academy of Sandhurst, along with many other members of ruling families all over the world and especially in the Middle East, and the Bahraini emir is even the patron of the Sandhurst Trust, the Academy's alumni organization (Batty 2011; Watt 2016) – they shared many ideas about governance and what degree of liberalization and participation was appropriate. Their

108   *When monarchies collide*

worldview and ruling ideology differed in many ways from those of their fathers while resembling each other's. Another example where generational change among monarchs brought about closer relations is the Qatari-Jordanian relationship, where equally young and reformist King Abdallah succeeded his father in 1999 (Teitelbaum 2001b, 504).

During a visit of the Qatari emir to Bahrain in early 2001, he congratulated his counterpart on the successful referendum on the (new) National Action Charter, which ended a period of internal troubles in the island, and on the latter's efforts to modernize Bahrain via his social, political, and economic reforms (Al-Arayed 2003, 405). These reforms closed some of the gaps in institutional similarity caused by the Qatari emir's reforms.

Once the gulf between the Bahraini and Qatari rulers as the prime identification actors shrank with the consecutive successions, the shared norms of behavior again converged, and the dispute level shrank, leading not just to mutual restraint in times of conflict but even to a resolution of the conflict altogether.

Statements and interviews of the time paint a clear picture of a preference for cooperation over conflict, and one reason that was always given for it was the close familial ties of the two countries and their dynasties. These were reiterated incessantly via speeches, proclamations, and even rebukes of the other. The repeated and consistent invocation of the idea of "family" when speaking about a neighboring state is a strong indication of the presence of an ingroup identity among that "family", especially when there is a rhetorical differentiation between different "classes of states".

To Bahrain's prime minister, Khalifa bin Salman Al Khalifa, the family aspect was so important that he mentioned it twice in one sentence when he emphasized in February 1995 that "a *brotherly solution was best, particularly between brothers*, because it was one that would clear the atmosphere, unify positions, end the dispute and enable us to avoid the problems that resulted from border disputes" (Wiegand 2012, 92, emphasis added).

In September 1996, at the time still–Crown Prince of Bahrain Shaikh Hamad stressed the importance of family harmony (without forgetting economic benefits for Bahrain): "we reiterate our call because *our ultimate aim is a union with our brothers in Qatar.* . . . Qatar is considered one of the richest countries in the world, which is a plus in contributing toward this great union" (cited in: Wiegand 2012, 92, emphasis added).

A September 1996 interview with Qatar's foreign (and prime) minister, who decisively shaped the course of Qatari foreign policy in Emir Hamad's era, Hamad bin Jassim Al Thani, is highly instructive in that regard. While elaborating on the notion that it is important to have "good relations with everyone" for Qatar, Hamad bin Jassim distinguished between states with "better" or "good" relations and such with "normal relations" and referred to the latter as "neighbors", not family, or even "friends". An excerpt shows the outer layers outside the constructed ingroup:

Being a friend to everybody, I might note, is a very difficult mission, but we are on our way. We have military cooperation and friendship with the United

States and the European states. We have good relations with Iran. We have normal relation with Iraq. When people ask us 'Why do you help Iran and Iraq?' we reply, *"They are our neighbors."* We have to have an understanding with our neighbors that there will be no interference in our internal affairs. We cannot afford to have enemies. . . . I cannot tell you all the relations are alike; no, *there are different levels*. We cooperate militarily with the United States but not with Iraq or Iran. Still, we have good relations with the latter. I know where I should have better relations and where just normal relations. But even normal relations will spare me in a crisis.

(Pipes 1996, emphasis added)

Outside of the ingroup, the political system loses its relevance: answering a question about Iran and Iraq, Hamad bin Jassim replies, "The type of regime is not our business. We don't want them to interfere in our affairs and we stay out of theirs. Let the people there decide whom they want. . . . As long as they don't interfere in our affairs, they can have any kind of regime" (Pipes 1996). Here, the relations toward outgroup members are based not on a positively defined community but rather on the principle of quid pro quo of mutual noninterference.

Equally illuminating in this regard is the Bahraini decision to boycott the 1996 GCC summit in Doha and the justifications and accusations that accompanied it. Despite royal intervention from Sultan Qaboos of Oman, Saudi Arabia, and King Hussein of Jordan,[10] Bahrain decided to stick to its boycott decision (Hussain 1996a). Bahrain reaffirmed its decision but thanked "the brotherly countries who attempted to persuade Bahrain to attend" and wished success for the meeting (cited in: Hussain 1996b). Prime Minister Khalifa bin Salman Al Khalifa justified the decision on the basis that Qatar had "not favourably responded to calls and initiatives aimed at solving the outstanding issues between the *two brotherly states, in the spirit of the one Gulf family*", adding that this behavior threatened Bahraini national security (cited in: Young 1997, emphasis added).

The Qatari emir expressed regret, in his opening address during the summit, at Bahrain's absence without admonishing the Bahraini government and again unsparingly used familial rhetoric, both in abstract terms, referring to the state and in direct terms to the Bahraini ruler:

I would like to express our deep regret that the *sisterly State of Bahrain* has apologized that it would not be taking part in this summit meeting, and hence *my dear brother Sheikh Isa bin Salman al-Khalifa* could not come. . . . We hope that our future sessions will be complete with the valuable participation of His Highness in our deliberations.

(cited in: Hussain 1996b, emphasis added)

The fact that the graciousness was probably intended to signal Qatari generosity and Bahraini stubbornness (nor the fact that addressing Isa bin Salman as a "brother" despite Emir Hamad being of practically the same age as his son and heir was also probably a measured provocation) did not diminish the fact that "family" was a potent and resonating category to use and one that was used

110 *When monarchies collide*

frequently. Interestingly, when just before the meeting, Bahrain reiterated its reasons for the boycott and lashed out against Qatar listing all the wrongs it had committed against it, it used the same familial references, but in an accusatory fashion by expressing regret for the "*unfriendly and unbrotherly stance* of Qatar toward Bahrain, which has included threatening Bahrain's national security and stability" (cited in: Hussain 1996b, emphasis added). Clearly, from the Bahraini ruler's perspective, Doha had broken the family norms it was expected to upkeep, and this was infuriating, not just the behavior per se. The norms (of what constitutes "unfriendly" and especially "unbrotherly" behavior between the countries) and Bahraini expectations to its application were in place despite the Qatari non-adherence to them. This is also exactly what made Qatar's non-adherence so deplorable for Bahrain. Evidently, despite the conflict, both sides accepted that the similarities between the "brothers" vastly overshadowed the differences, an obvious indication of ingroup identification.

This was not restricted to the level of discourse but also extended toward symbolic politics and rituals signifying and signaling commonality. For example, despite the difficult relationship between the emirs of Qatar and Bahrain, after Isa bin Salman Al Khalifa's sudden death in March 1999, Qatar declared three days of mourning (Teitelbaum 2001b, 502). In April 1999, as soon as Emir Hamad succeeded his father in Bahrain, he renewed the call for cooperation on kinship grounds and "oneness":

> We are one country and one people and oneness in all fields with Qatar is a must, with the objective of achieving a real rapprochement . . . according to the wishes of the two brotherly peoples. . . . This is an invitation from me to the brothers in Qatar to fulfill everybody's hopes.
>
> (cited in: Teitelbaum 2001a, 196)

The invocation of "family" is formative for foreign policy behavior as it raises the stakes of conflict and the urgency of cooperation. Statements by Bahraini officials confirm this impression as when Prime Minister Khalifa bin Salman Al Khalifa said in 2000 that "this dispute threatens to cause deep friction in the *Gulf and Arab family links* and lead to tension in the region while exhausting our resources and obstructing the aspirations of our people" (cited in: Wiegand 2012, 81, emphasis added).

Both states accepted the decision of the ICJ in March 2001 and have fully enforced the ruling so that the dispute was settled in finality. Bahrain was more enthusiastic than Qatar in that it basically affirmed the status quo left by the British (Wiegand 2012, 87). The day after, the ruling was declared a national holiday to celebrate the resolution (Alter 2014, 176), further cementing the preference for cooperation between "brotherly people". Qatari Emir Hamad, although not completely happy with the ruling, insisted that it

> will enhance the security and stability of our Gulf states and contribute to strengthening the GCC. . . . I extend [to Bahrain] a hand that has always been full of fraternity and cordiality so that we can close that page and open a new

When monarchies collide 111

chapter where the two brotherly people take part in planning and deepening our future relations.

(cited in: Al-Arayed 2003, 404)

Bahrain's Emir Hamad bin Isa Al Khalifa also emphasized the bond between the countries and the finality of the settlement:

We salute the ICJ over its wise verdict and declare our complete acceptance of its ruling. We have given orders to take the necessary measures to ensure its implementation, taking into consideration that the outcome of the verdict is a joint gain for both the brotherly states of Qatar and Bahrain. We have jointly won the battle of the future and the time has come to open a brighter, new chapter in our relations and to accomplish the dreams and aspirations of generations of Bahrainis and Qataris.

(cited in: Al-Arayed 2003, 404)

Despite different sentiments toward the final ruling, both stressed the close bonds linking the two states (and their ruling houses) as *family*, not just neighbors or friends. It was therefore never questioned that this was an issue that needed to be *solved* – not an issue that needed to be *won*.

The familial references were so obvious and ubiquitous that they were adopted by external observers as well. Writing at a time of heightened tensions between Qatar and Bahrain after the latter's discovery of a spying network inside the country, Colin Young put his hope of "bringing the two feuding 'brothers' back into the family" on Saudi Arabia (Young 1997). According to analysts cited by Wiegand, "Bahrain's position was based on the necessity to solve the dispute in a brotherly and amicable way. The aim must be to *maintain the family ties and spirit of unity between the two nations*" (cited in: Wiegand 2012, 92, emphasis added).

Apart from family rhetoric, the ingroup identification of the Al Khalifa and Al Thani also found its expression in the role of the GCC. By institutionalizing Gulf links, it enhanced interdependence and mutual identification and led to a growing identification, even on the societal level (Barnett and Gause 1998, 162). This is even more true on the elite level. The GCC fostered the shared identification of Bahrain and Qatar and at the same time provided fora where relations could be personalized and interaction could become normalized and perpetuated.

The GCC is also important as an institution with explicit conflict-resolution mechanisms that enable cooperation between all members. Although it failed to solve the conflict, this failure does not imply a lacking ingroup identification. To the contrary, as Wiegand describes, the ICJ was more successful and ultimately preferable to the GCC not *despite* but *because* the latter had "close ties that interfered in the ability of the institution to work neutrally . . . the other GCC member states were considered too closely tied to Bahrain and Qatar as brotherly states" (Wiegand 2012, 88). Frauke Heard-Bey concurs:

As each one of the four non-disputant members of the GCC has some such deep emotional involvement with either Qatar or Bahrain or both, it was

112   *When monarchies collide*

difficult for the GCC as an organization to agree on one course of action vis à vis these two states.

(Heard-Bey 2006, 213)

In other words, not in spite of but exactly because of the strong intra-communal ties and perception of the council as a family, the GCC had difficulties in picking sides – which would not be a problem for an international court. Therefore, the ICJ ruling was welcomed by the GCC (Wiegand 2012, 89).

Regardless of the level of tension and hostility, at all times were the Bahraini and Qatari dynasties aware of their mutual bonds and openly emphasized them, even during criticism and rebuke of the other. If the norm of cooperative inter-family behavior were not already firmly in place, there would be no need to couch criticism in such terms, because blaming Qatar for contravening intragroup norms would have little force and effect. This is possibly the clearest indication that communal norms have developed between the two.

Foreign policy restraint

The ingroup identification established and indicated by the structural similarities and social processes of identification just summarized precluded another militarized interaction or, indeed, any sort of escalation. The conflict persisted until 2001, but it remained restricted to the rhetorical and symbolic level.

Even below the military level, escalation was rare, although there was enough explosive potential inherent in the dispute. The new Qatari emir, Hamad Al Thani, recognized the sensitivity of the quarrel, and in a 1995 interview, he acknowledged its potential for destabilization: "the thorny issue of border disputes between the Gulf countries is a time bomb that could threaten the stability and security of the whole region" (cited in: Wiegand 2012, 81). He also favored a more conciliatory approach to the matter (Peterson 2011, 31).

Nonetheless, he did his part in escalating the conflict: in protest of Saudi attempts to dominate the GCC (via the election for secretary general), Qatar walked out of a GCC meeting in December 1995, leaving the other members insulted and infuriated and setting off a spiral of provocations and counter-provocations (Cordesman 1997, 48). Observers described the countries at that time as "at the brink of a war" (Lotfian 2002, 119). In March 2010, Qatar repeatedly arrested Bahraini fishers who were allegedly in its maritime boundaries (107 altogether) (Toumi 2010), but there were no more irredentist claims for more territory than the ICJ ruling had granted by any of the parties. Nothing close to a war or any sort of bilateral violence occurred in the period before the settling of the conflict (or afterwards).

While military action remained beyond the pale, the heightened tensions in the second half of the 1990s saw other forms of confrontation. Some took the form of subversion attempts. They were, however, directed not at the regime but rather at the rulers and their immediate allies.

When monarchies collide 113

After the palace coup in Qatar by Hamad bin Khalifa Al Thani, Saudi Arabia, Bahrain, and the UAE began to court the deposed former emir who openly proclaimed his intentions to regain power, as if he were still in charge. Qatar retaliated by broadcasting calls for "democracy" by two Bahraini opposition members, Mansour al-Jamri and Shaikh Ali Salman, over its national television and reprinting them in their newspapers. The media in other Gulf states was in uproar and attacked the Qatari government, and Saudi and UAE newspapers launched targeted attacks against the new emir, Hamad bin Khalifa, and his uncle and minister of foreign affairs, Hamad bin Jassim Al Thani (Cordesman 1997, 48). There were even unsubstantiated rumors that Bahrain had struck a deal with the former emir, exchanging his reinstatement for his relinquishment of the Qatari claims on Hawar in 1997 (Young 1997).

The counter-coup attempt in February 1996 led Qatar to put heavy blame on its neighbors. According to the official Qatari version, forces of Qataris and 2000 Yemeni and other Arab mercenaries were organized by a French officer who had commanded Khalifa bin Hamad's personal guard. Qatar accused Bahrain, Saudi Arabia, and the UAE of allowing those forces to prepare inside Quatari borders. The accusations went as far as to allege readiness to provide air cover for the coup and of planned assassinations against Qatar's leaders. The Qatari government reacted strongly to the coup attempt, mobilizing the Emiri Guard on February 17 and arresting hundreds, including army and police officers and even members of the royal family, on February 20. The three countries denied all the accusations, and US intelligence did not report a buildup of forces, though senior US officials have stated that a coup attempt was being mobilized. Of the two remaining GCC members, Oman denounced the coup, whereas Kuwait did not react publicly (Cordesman 1997, 224).

With the abating of immediate tensions caused by a disagreement over the GCC secretary general, activism meant to hurt or weaken the opponent disappeared as well. Support for former emir Khalifa significantly declined in Bahrain, Saudi Arabia, and UAE. Instead, Saudi Arabia and Qatar announced that they were forming a joint commission to solve their own boundary dispute (Cordesman 1997, 225). The situation in Qatar itself had calmed down once an understanding between the former and the present emir had been reached and Khalifa Al Thani had been allowed to return in October 1996 as an elder politician (Pipes 1996).

Regardless of the actual level of Bahraini and GCC support for the former emir, it was indicative of attempts to undermine the new emir, Hamad, but not his regime or *the political system as a whole*, thus putting it outside the category of subversion that implies subversion of the regime, not just an individual ruler. Identification as equals on the basis of political system similarity implies that regimes are upheld and protected but does not say anything about personal likes or dislikes toward individuals. Even in the extreme case of the removal of an individual ruler in a palace coup by a rival member of the ruling family, the regime stays intact. The destabilization of a regime can, however, lead to its removal, which would also remove the basis of similarity and ingroup identification and

114 *When monarchies collide*

would contradict ingroup identification as a politically relevant phenomenon. In this case, however, there was no funding of revolutionary propaganda or groups that tried to change the regime as occurred often by and against republics during the high times of the Arab Cold War and that was still typical of Iranian subversion attempts of the Gulf monarchies.

Bahraini and Emirati ruling elites (who had provided political asylum to Emir Khalifa) found individual members of the ruling elite, namely mainly Hamad bin Khalifa and his uncle and Prime Minister and Foreign Minister Hamad bin Jassim, "objectionable" and "disruptive" (Foley 1999). They believed that these individual people were incompatible with Gulf politics, but at no point did they question the legitimacy of the dynastic system. In the same way, Qatari support for Bahraini opposition was confrontational and provocative but restricted and not destabilizing for the regime. Al-Jamri and Salman are known moderates who called for reform, but never for a change or downfall of the regime. Both were invited back into the country by Emir Hamad bin Isa after he came to power in 1999. Al-Jamri was even offered a cabinet position, which he rejected (Krauss 2011).

Another indication of tensions and contained subversion was the arrest of two Qatari citizens in Bahrain in the end of 1996 for spying (Peterson 2011, 32). On December 2, it was reported that the Qataris Fahad Hamad Abdulla Al Baker and Salwa Jassim Mohammed Fakhri had been arrested and admitted to having spied on Bahrain on behalf of the Qatari intelligence service to undermine Bahraini security. It was also reported that Bahraini security forces had uncovered a similar spying operation in 1987. Most probably, far from destabilizing the regime, they were simply collecting evidence that would help Qatar in the territorial dispute. Barely a month later, on January 1, 1997, First Lieutenant of Bahrain's air force (and member of the ruling family) Nasser Majid Nasser Al Khalifa defected in a highly public way, flying his military helicopter to Doha to request political asylum, which Qatar initially granted (Young 1997).

After the arrest of the alleged Qatari spies, the Bahraini media reaction was furious. In a tightly controlled autocracy like Bahrain, the national media reaction can be interpreted as the message that the government wanted to send but did not dare to articulate itself. The editorial of the Anglophone Gulf Daily News (GDN), headed "Wolf in sheep's clothing", consisted of vitriolic attacks on Qatar and included extracts like "no Gulf country ever lowered itself to the pathetic level you (Qatar) have now reached" and "We in Bahrain have always known that Qatar cannot be trusted" (Young 1997). It is an instance of a major rhetorical escalation, albeit an indirect one, via media, not any official outlet.

After the succession of Emir Hamad in Bahrain in 1999, a détente followed. Bahrain withdrew a diplomatic passport that it had issued to the Qatari emir's cousin, who was the prime suspect in the 1996 coup attempt in August. The following month, Qatar reciprocated by making the Bahraini defector Nasser Al Khalifa leave the country. Thus, both countries "made it clear . . . that battles within each other's royal family were not territory for intervention by the other" (Teitelbaum 2001a, 196), and the period of contained subversion stopped.

When monarchies collide   115

After the point of contention of the December 1995 GCC meeting, when the selection of the council's secretary general was resolved between Qatar, Bahrain, Saudi Arabia, and the UAE in the spring of 1996, relations ameliorated. Bahrain stated that it might accept ICJ jurisdiction. Still, relations were far from harmonious, and Emir Hamad continued to believe that Saudi Arabia and Bahrain actively supported the coup attempt by the former emir in February 1996. The final years of the 20th century proved tense because of a number of incidents that marred bilateral relations. Both parties attempted to create facts on the ground: Bahrain started building hotels and homes on the Hawar Islands, and Qatar included Zubarah in its municipal elections and withdrew 82 forged documents previously submitted to the ICJ after Bahraini protests and GCC intervention (Wiegand 2012, 87). In addition to the Qatari walkout, Bahrain also boycotted joint fora that could have enabled or eased cooperation to resolve the conflict (and, of course, other serious matters, such as the dealings with Iraq and Iran). It refused to attend the GCC meeting in Doha in 1996 in protest of Qatar's unilateral decision to put the dispute to the ICJ, and it declined to participate in the OIC meeting in 2000, which also took place in Doha (Wiegand 2012, 80).

Although all these activities suggest a high level of tensions, they are not indicative of a willingness to escalate or a preference against restraint, given that they were only mildly provocative and highly contained in their reach and ambition. There was no threat of violence and no sign of targeted action or even delegitimization attempts aimed at the overthrow of the regime or the change of the political system.

There was still no formal alliance between the two countries, but the settling of the conflict by the ICJ opened the door for broad cooperation. Joint projects further linking Bahrain and Qatar with each other and other GCC states were established, some of which had been stalled for years.

In January 2000, a "new spirit of cooperation" was expressed, and the plans for a connecting causeway progressed.[11] The two Hamads expressed their intent "to go ahead with cooperation and integration steps", including speeding up the opening of embassies. Later that month, the two countries established a committee promoting joint trade and economic projects. In a meeting on the causeway in February 2000, it was decided to allow citizens of the two states to use only identity cards for entry. For the first time, Manama and Doha exchanged ambassadors, and Qatar Airways announced that it would begin daily flights between Doha and Bahrain in March 2000 (Wiegand 2012, 93). Still, full cooperation could not be achieved as long as the dispute was pending, and Bahraini officials announced that "contemplation of such projects should start after reaching a final decision on the border dispute between the two fraternal countries, on Zubara, and other issues under review at present by the International Court of Justice" (Wiegand 2012, 93).

The official statements by the heads of states on the ICJ ruling were conciliatory, although especially Qatar was not euphoric about the compromise but refrained from revisionism. Qatar's Emir Hamad's statements reflect the higher value attributed to conflict resolution instead of winning: "we realize that our sacrifice

116 *When monarchies collide*

will not be in vain since it lays the foundation for closer and broader unblemished relations between Qatar and Bahrain" (cited in: Wiegand 2012, 93–94).

The resolution of the conflict paved the way for similar settlements in that it proved the possibility of peaceful and mutually satisfactory outcomes in territorial conflicts within the "family". Immediately following the ICJ ruling, oil and gas exploitation resumed, and just a few days after the ICJ ruling, Qatar and Saudi Arabia declared the ending of their own border dispute of 35 years (Wiegand 2012, 89). Prince Saud told reporters after the ceremony that "With the signing of this agreement, all border conflicts between countries of the Gulf Cooperation Council (GCC) are settled", and his Qatari counterpart declared that following the settlement of the conflict with Bahrain, "we are proud of our relations with Saudi Arabia" (Saudi and Qatar End 35-Year Border Dispute, Sign Accord 2001).

These developments indicate a deepening level of cooperation, further enhancing and cementing the ties already institutionalized by the GCC.

Ingroup identification

Bahrain and Qatar enjoyed the benefits of enduring ingroup identification in the second period as well, especially in the final years before (and even more so after) the ICJ ruling that settled their territorial conflict. Most indicators have remained stable, but leadership changes and the clash of the differing political worldviews and ruling ideologies first widened (after the succession in Qatar) and then narrowed (after the succession in Bahrain) the gulf between the emirs of Qatar and Bahrain. The hostility level and escalation potential rose and fell following these disruptions. Still, there was never any militarized threat or altercation.

The change was not driven by monarchic salience per se, which was low in that period due to a lacking common threat and no change in the overall distribution of monarchies. Instead, two different elements of the causal model underwent a significant change. The first was an institutional change on level of the regime/political system. The institutional changes brought about by the liberalization and reform projects of the emir of Qatar somewhat lowered the (structural) similarity of the political systems. The second was located on the level of the political leader: the worldview, ruling ideology, and socialization of the new generation that ruled Qatari (including its Emir) weakened the personalization of the elite-level relations. This incongruence disappeared with a similar changing of the guard in Bahrain. Since the remainder of the analyzed period after the second succession in Bahrain is only two years, the timeframe might be too short to draw any meaningful conclusions. Nonetheless, the fact that most instances that most instances of hostility and provocation occurred during the period of incongruence between the political elites might be interpreted as indication of the validity of the theorized mechanism.

Ultimately, the strong and consistent ties, which were affirmed and reaffirmed even at the height of political confrontations, led not only to foreign policy restraint in conflict but to the resolution of the conflict altogether, a process ushered in by the ICJ ruling and its mutual acceptance in 2001.

When monarchies collide 117

Bahrain and Qatar: synthesis and findings

As the summary in Table 4.1 shows, the Al Thani and the Al Khalifa are prime candidates for a peace based on ingroup identification. Their political and economic systems are similar and have been especially after the state and institution building progressed, not least thanks to the influence of oil wealth and British (and later US) support. The two dynasties share the same worldview, especially among corresponding generations.

Table 4.1 The Hawar Islands Dispute

Indicators			*Period I*	*Period II*
1. Structural similarities	1.1	Shared language, culture, history, and religion	++	++
	1.2	Similar political system	++ with somewhat uneven development at the beginning	+ Initial reforms by Qatar's emir created an institutional gap that was later bridged by the new Bahraini emir
	1.3	Similar economic system	++	++
2. Salience	2.1	Low/decreasing share	+/ – Minority, growing in 1971, shrinking in 1979	– No change
	2.2	Common threat	+ Iran and Iraq, directed against monarchies	+ Iran and Iraq, directed against monarchies
	2.3	Absence of divisive ideology	+ Irredentism abandoned before statehood	
	3.1	Mutual recognition	+ But no diplomatic ties	+ Diplomatic relation development since 1997
	3.2	Personalization of bonds between ruling elites	++	+/ – Rift between 1995 and 1999

(*Continued*)

118 *When monarchies collide*

Table 4.1 (Continued)

Indicators		Period I	Period II
3 Social processes of ingroup identification	3.2.1 *Frequent high-level state visits*	+	+/ – Sometimes boycott as signal of disagreement
	3.2.2 *Kinship, intermarriage and friendship bonds*	+ Shared Najdi Anaza tribal heritage	+ (same as period 1)
	3.2.3 *Shared socialization*	+ Traditional education and British institutions, "clannish democracy"	+/ – Broader socialization and worldview gap with new Qatari emir, later closed with new Bahraini emir (both Sandhurst graduates and reformers)
	3.3 Affirmation of commonality	++	++
	3.3.1 Kinship and family references	+ Fraternal over othering rhetoric	+ Fraternal over othering rhetoric
	3.3.2 Emphasis on similarity	+	+
	3.3.3 References to shared historical narratives	+ Shared (Sunni) conservative worldview, pro-British outlook, Western alliance	+ Shared (Sunni) conservative worldview, pro-British outlook, Western alliance
	3.3.4 Common ceremonies/shared institutions	+ GCC, mourning periods for other khaleeji royals	+ Monarchic protocol (e.g. funerals, condolence rituals), GCC
4 Foreign policy restraint	4.1 Military restraint	– 1 MID in 1986 but quickly diffused without casualties	+
	4.2 Non-military restraint	+	+
	4.2.1 *Refraining from delegitimization*		+ Except some press reactions
	4.2.2 *Refraining from subversion*	+ But espionage allegations	+/ – Espionage, some opposition support

Indicators		Period I	Period II
	4.2.3 *Rhetorical restraint*	+ differences framed in terms of disagreements, not incompatibility	+ Indirectly by media during short period in mid 1990s
4.3	Alliance and solidarity	+ GCC, Gulf War 1991 coalition	+ GCC, growing interdependence

They see themselves (and in extension their populations) as a large family with disputes to be resolved, not prolonged or escalated. Once the states had consolidated and once the Al Khalifa ceased to see themselves as suzerains over the Al Thani, a stronger basis for equality between the rulers could be achieved.[12] Shared tradition, history, and socialization, both based on traditional sources, local customs, and British influence, shaped the institutions and mindsets of the rulers in significant ways, leading the ruling families to perceive themselves as part of an ingroup.

This perception was expressed in numerous ways, by public and less public proclamations, by de-escalatory policies, and by refraining from a retaliation spiral. The royal families engaged in frequent direct visits, and constantly valued cooperation over confrontation and similarity over difference. When differences were expressed, except for rare cases such as the GDN uproar, they were couched as differences of opinion, not more-existential and unbridgeable differences of identity and incompatibility. Throughout the conflict, statements of the involved parties emphasized the inherent desirability of cooperation over conflict, especially "among brotherly states", a phrase deployed as something more meaningful than standard rhetoric. That fraternal basis was not only an oft-cited reason for the need to cooperate. Even when relations were tense, instead of expelling the opponent from the ingroup, the shared community and values were emphasized. The opponent's behavior was criticized because it did not conform to intergroup norms, which continued to be accepted and expected of ingroup members.

Once the ingroup had developed, there was no need for a common threat to bind the two sides together. This indicates that the degree of monarchic salience might be more relevant for the early stages of ingroup development.

The most important evidence for the validity of the proposed mechanism can be found in constant affirmations of ingroup identity in times of severe conflict. While family rhetoric might be expected in conflict-free times, the ongoing use of metaphors of shared belonging (instead of othering and delegitimization) is especially surprising at the height of tensions. This indicates that the shared sense of identity went beyond the level of symbolic regime legitimacy but had an actual

120 *When monarchies collide*

effect on foreign policy. Policy decisions and political attacks were justified by the expectations derived from family membership. Qatar needed to be rebuked for its "unbrotherly behavior" because brothers should behave differently toward each other. Had Qatar not been seen as a brother, the prioritization of policy choices might have been different.

But family and similarity-affirming discourse are not the only pieces of evidence of the ingroup identification processes at play. The rhetoric of solidarity was matched by numerous indicators of close bonds like high-level state visits, economic cooperation projects, and the acceptance of an unpopular territorial settlement. While the level of public discourse points to normative expectations of behavior, the sometimes-costly foreign policy decisions by the two countries clearly transcended the level of "cheap talk".

The case study also shows the intricate balance between the individual and the regime level in shaping an ingroup identity. This insight lends additional support to the idea of situating the SPSP identification processes on the regime level. The logic of SPSP assumes that ingroup identification takes place on the level of the regime type and political system, as perceived by the individual decision makers, the ruler being one of them. Therefore, both levels are decisive for the formation and changes in ingroup perception. The incongruence on the leadership level between the two successions of the Hamads could not destroy the ingroup that had already formed because the ingroup was based on the regime level. Mere incongruences on the level of political leadership like the successions could not undermine the sense of ingroup identification on the level of regime. Nonetheless, this incongruence in terms of worldview rapidly led to less restraint than usual. This insight underlines not only the idea that the SPSP goes beyond institutions alone but also the idea that perception of the other is key.

The GCC represented an important element in shaping and affirming commonality: the joint political forum provided a ready-made club, prescribed behavioral norms, and reified the community based on regular meetings and ritualized procedures. While the GCC is far from a full-blown security community comparable to the European Union, it represents the most successful regional organization in the Arab world, especially on the level of leadership cooperation (cf. Çetinoğlu 2010; Partrick 2011). This is possible due to a common identity present that provides the basis for GCC solidarity – including the possibility of establishing a shared front against outgroup members.

However, this sense of shared identity goes beyond monarchies; it is also "*khaleeji*", pointing to a certain caveat against overestimating the relevance of the political system element in the SPSP. After all, the GCC is more than a monarchic club; it is a "*khaleeji* club", based on a shared political system (the monarchic core). But it also encompasses a shared sense of history and belonging specific to the Arabian Peninsula that transcends monarchism.

It might be important to consider to what extent similarity is based on the *multiple* ties of culture, history, and kinship instead of the regime type alone. To separate the effect of political system from other cultural and historical dimensions,

When monarchies collide 121

the following case study analyzes monarchies that are from different subregions. Jordan is not *khaleeji*, but if similar processes can be identified, it would affirm the argument that regime type is relevant or even decisive in ingroup identification.

The Bahraini-Qatari case also shows how ingroup perception relates to other factors that contribute (or obstruct) conflict management, here notably oil wealth. Solving a dispute via the ICJ among autocracies, and especially among Arab states, was unprecedented. Wiegand explains the success of this avenue with the failure of regional mediation, incentives for oil and gas exploitation, and finally incentives for cooperation between the countries since 1980 (2012). Although these elements were undoubtedly important, similar contexts have failed to bring about the same results in other territorial disputes in the region, including between Iran and Iraq or between Iraq and Kuwait. Apparently, these incentives mattered more in a pre-established ingroup.[13]

4.2 The Al Saud and the Hashemites: from rivals to equals

The Saudi-Hashemite rivalry shows the slow emergence of ingroup identification between two rivaling dynasties initially divided by hierarchic ideologies. After the abandonment of the ideology and rivaling dynastic claims, and catalyzed by the threat by socialist pan-Arabist revolutionary republics, they extended recognition to each other. Slowly, a shared group identity as monarchies formed, showing that a similar political system has a unifying effect even in the absence of an otherwise-close connection as between *khaleeji* monarchies.

The rivalry between the two dynasties can be traced to a time before either of the states that bear their names (or have in the past), the Kingdom of Saudi Arabia and the Hashemite Kingdoms of Jordan and Iraq, had been established.

The following case study proceeds by first elaborating on the role of the scope condition of state building by setting up the pre-independence context before going through the process indicators from ingroup development toward peacefulness.

The struggle over the Hijaz (1917–1926): state building as a scope condition

At the beginning of the 20th century, the relations between the Hashemites, who ruled over the Hijaz, and the Al Saud, whose power base was centered on the Najd region, were respectful and even cooperative. There was no sign of a grand expansionary design during the First World War, when Hashemite ruler Hussein bin Ali, Sharif and Amir of Mecca, asked Ibn Saud (also known as Abd al-Aziz Al Saud, the founder of the Saudi Kingdom) to join the Arab Revolt in July 1916 and the latter agreed. Although no direct collaboration followed, the war bolstered Ibn Saud's importance. In November 1916, Hussein's son Abdallah described Ibn Saud with respect and called him "Chief of Arabs" (Kostiner 1995, 48).

But this honeymoon was not too last, and soon after, relations deteriorated on both sides. An example of the deep enmity that developed is Ibn Saud's remark to John Philby, the political resident in the Gulf's secretary, that although he would

122 *When monarchies collide*

marry an Englishwoman or eat meat slain by Christians, he would never marry a daughter of the *sharif* or eat meat slain by the Sharifian *mushrikun* (polytheists, ergo no true Muslims) (Teitelbaum 1995, 83, fn 23). This shows not only that there was no ingroup identification at the beginning but also that the difference was emphasized and maximized, resulting in othering even on the basis of qualities that should have been unifying rather than divisive, namely their shared adherence to conservative Sunni Islam.

But at this point, it is hard to describe the two dynasties as full-blown monarchies that should "naturally" develop a sense of community, because they were still long way from the modern monarchies examined here. Thinking of power in categories of clearly delineated territory was then not the established norm on the Arabian Peninsula, and even the urban Hashemites at that time based their rule on tribal law and de-emphasized state building. Tribal politics entailed a "perennial struggle over undemarcated territories" (Kostiner 1995, 49). John Philby was instrumental in British policy on the Peninsula at that time. Although he was a supporter of Ibn Saud, he attempted to separate the two dynastic spheres of influence and turn their expansionary drives in different directions. The British introduced a system of division of power based on demarcated territorial lines, as opposed to the earlier hegemonic custom of tribal allegiance, into the region. It was accepted by the Najdis and Hijazis alike (Kostiner 1995, 57).

Amid growing Hashemite expansionism and territorial uncertainty, Ibn Saud capitalized on the wariness of local rulers. At that time, the British supported both dynasties in their respective geographical areas and promised protection of Saudi territories in Najd, although with a mere 5000 pounds per month, Ibn Saud only received a 25th of the amount Hussein commanded (Kostiner 1995, 53, 55).[14]

The difference was not restricted to the level of British support: Ibn Saud's legitimacy was based not on descent from the prophet, as was the Hashemites', but on his appeal to Wahhabi revivalism, which gained a growing following, even among Hashemite chieftaincies (Kostiner 1995, 53).

The Khurma incident was the first major disruption in their relations and was triggered when Hussein attempted to consolidate his control over the strategically important town, affiliated with both Wahhabis and Hashemites in political, economic, and tribal terms. Khurma's local governor, Amir Khalid, called for Saudi help to balance Hashemite pressure (Kostiner 1995, 53). Before Ibn Saud could arrive, Amir Khalid surprisingly attacked Abdallah's camp at Turaba independently, along with a following of *Ikhwan* fighters, the Wahhabi tribal warriors infamous for their fanaticism. The attack decimated most of the Hijazi forces; the rest, including Abdallah, fled. This marked a turning point in military balance between the continually shifting rivaling fronts (Kostiner 1995, 60).

Hussein's standing among the British and the Muslim world deteriorated not least due to his mismanagement of the annual *hajj*, while Wahhabi influence grew stronger. By 1923, a Wahhabi invasion of the Hijaz was probably in its preparatory stages. In 1924, Egyptian King Fu'ad received a congratulatory letter on the opening of the first Egyptian parliament from Ibn Saud, who clearly tried to capitalize on the Egyptian-Hashemite rivalry. When, in his ever-growing

When monarchies collide 123

self-aggrandizement, Hussein proclaimed himself caliph in early March 1924, after the collapse of the Ottoman Caliphate, he was met with rejection (Teitelbaum 1995, 75–77). Ibn Saud's actions affirmed that he did not accept the status change either give that he moved to attack later that year after the British had withdrawn their subsidies (Al-Rasheed 2010, 43).

When the Hashemites refused to grant the Najdis access to the *hajj* that year, Ibn Saud's *ulama'* declared it a casus belli. On September 5, 1924, the occupation of Ta'if marked the beginning of the Hijaz invasion. By mid October, Mecca was occupied by the *Ikhwan*, and Hussein had left for Aqaba. His eldest son, Ali, who was put in charge, retreated to Jidda, which he surrendered in December 1925 (Teitelbaum 1995, 77–79).

As the sole reason for invading the Hijaz, Ibn Saud gave the aim to "guarantee the liberty of pilgrimage and to settle the destiny of the Holy Land in a manner satisfactory to the Islamic world" (cited in: Al-Rasheed 2010, 44). Acknowledging the finality of the Hashemite loss, Ali had agreed to recognize King Fu'ad of Egypt as caliph and an Egyptian protectorate over the Hijaz some weeks previously, to no avail (Teitelbaum 1995, 81). This desperate attempt shows the lengths to which the Hashemites were willing to go to prevent the upstart Saudis from consolidating their rule, having failed militarily.

The Wahhabi *Ikhwan* forces of Ibn Saud eventually conquered most of the Arabian Peninsula with tacit British support. Hussein fled into exile in Cyprus, where he died in 1931, while his sons, Abdallah and Faisal bin Hussein Al Hashemi, went on to claim the thrones of Transjordan, Iraq, and briefly Syria (Teitelbaum 2001c, 282). Faisal proclaimed himself king of Syria in 1918 and was recognized by an all-Arab congress in July 1919 as king of a united Syria, Lebanon, Palestine, and Transjordan before being evicted from his throne by the French in summer 1920. To make up for the loss, the British accorded him the Iraqi throne, to which he formally ascended in October 1921. His brother Abdallah claimed Transjordan in passing by Amman on his way to confront the French. To get him to relinquish this ambition, the British recognized his rule in Transjordan in 1922 (Weinberger 1986, 244–245).

This marks the beginning of the statehood period of Saudi-Hashemite relations, characterized by Hashemite irredentism (and weakening Wahhabi expansionism) and state building in both dynastic realms that only just began to crystallize into nation-states. It is in this time that the first signs of ingroup identification occurred, having been notably absent in the pre-state period.

A precursor to official mutual recognition is the symbolic equalization expressed in chosen styles and titles at that time. Due to their high symbolic importance, there was a certain amount of competition for styles conveying sovereignty and superiority. It was around the time when Hussein became cognizant of the Saudi rise that he demanded a new title from the British, to reflect his superordinate position in December 1917, explicitly also vis-à-vis Ibn Saud (Kostiner 1995, 53). He had already declared himself "king of the Hijaz" and "king of the Arab Lands" (*malik bilad al-'arab*), thereby becoming the first modern Arab monarch to claim that title (Lewis 2000, 19). However, the latter title, that implied a wider

124 *When monarchies collide*

sovereignty over all territory occupied by Arabs, was not widely recognized, including by Ibn Saud (Kostiner 1995, 54). His self-elevation to caliph in early March 1924, after the collapse of the Ottoman Caliphate, was met with near universal rejection (Teitelbaum 1995, 77)

Previously known as an *amir* (prince) and *imam* (since 1902), Ibn Saud adopted the title of sultan of Najd after Faisal's ascent to the Iraqi throne as king of Iraq. The British confirmed the title in August 1921. In contrast to the former two, the latter title was not claimed by other local rulers in central Arabia (Al-Rasheed 2010, 60–61), which thus gave Ibn Saud a competitive edge on the peninsula. Still, one step remained to elevate him to the formal level of the Hashemites; after the conquest of the holy cities, Ibn Saud declared himself "king of Hijaz" in December 1925 with the local notables pledging allegiance and proclaiming him "king of Hijaz and sultan of Najd and its dependencies" on January 8, 1926, thus finally elevating him and his dynasty to long-sought royal status (Al-Rasheed 2010, 44).[15]

This symbolic equality would provide the basis for an acceptance of equal status by other monarchs in later periods. The two domains were merged into one in 1932, when the Kingdom of Saudi Arabia was proclaimed (Podeh 1995, 86). Hashemite Iraq, a kingdom since 1921, declared its independence a short time afterward, while Transjordan remained an emirate until May 1946, when Abdallah crowned himself king (Milton-Edwards and Hinchcliffe 2009, 28).

State consolidation and state competition in Arabia and the Levant (1926–1953): the limits of ingroup identification

The first period of interstate relations began in earnest after the final expulsion of the Hashemite from Arabia, followed by the formation and entrenchment of two Hashemite dynasties in (Trans)Jordan and Iraq and the consolidation of the Saudi Kingdom. As long as rivaling claims to the same land and title (king of Hijaz) formed the center of a vaguely defined territory – much more a realm than a demarcated state – no ingroup identification could arise. Since both could not take the title at the same time, the dynasties were incompatible and an existential threat to each other, precluding any recognition of equal status, which would mark a first step toward ingroup identification. Once state borders and institutions hardened and the states recognized each other, the preconditions for ingroup identification were met and developed slowly. State building and the solidification of borders also dampened the effect of divisive ideology driven by irredentism.

Structural similarities

Although both powers shared similarities – being religiously legitimized, expansionary, tribally supported Sunni Arab dynasties hailing from the Arabian Peninsula and both being at some point supported by the British – these similarities were superficial.

When monarchies collide   125

While the Hashemites derived their legitimacy from their status as *ashraf* (plural of *sharif*), i.e. descendants of the Prophet, the Al Saud based their religious legitimacy on its bond with the Al Shaikh, the descendants of Muhammad bin Abd al-Wahhab, the founder of the *muwahhidun*, or the Wahhabi movement, and their adherence to Wahhabi doctrine.[16] Although Hashemites were long-established urban elites in a culturally diverse region with a strong economic focus on the extraction of *hajj* taxes and rents, the Al Saud were basically tribal warriors who hailed from the much more conservative and homogeneous rural region of central Arabia. The structural and institutional similarities thus provided a weak basis for ingroup identification to emerge in the first period of the case study.

Salience: constraints and catalysts to ingroup identification

As long as Sharif Hussein and especially Ibn Saud and other tribal chieftains were two among a plethora of pre-eminent shaikhs whose manner of succession always entailed a hereditary element but one that was not yet understood in the terms of a full-fledged monarchic state, the salience of the monarchy divide was low – especially since monarchy was then the norm rather than an exception. Before the regime change in Egypt, there were seven independent monarchies in the Middle East (Libya, Egypt, Saudi Arabia, Yemen, Jordan, Iraq, and Iran), in contrast to four republics – half of which were non-Arab (Syria, Lebanon, Israel, and Turkey). Thus, Arab identity and Muslim identity were more salient to most rulers.

The more elaborate the state apparatuses and institutional and organizational rules as well as state ceremonies were established and entrenched, the more the distinction of a specific "monarchic" element became present. The same developments also decreased the role of irredentism, the major divisive ideology between the Hashemites and the Al Saud, by cementing state borders and therefore also enabled a slow rise in the salience of monarchism.

A salient threat was posed by the Jewish national movement: since 1948, the newly formed Israel was seen as a challenge for the Arab or Islamic community but was irrelevant for any autocratic regime type distinction. Of far greater importance for the salience of the monarchy –republic distinction was the potential threat posed by the expansion of republican Arab nationalist ideology, which jumped to the forefront with the regime change in Egypt in 1952.

Its effects were therefore highly limited at first, restricted to bringing the Hashemite kingdoms closer together. This became possible only because their threat conception was shared: as of joint threats and not threats toward each other, collective defense rather than collective security. However, their "collective" was still rather small and did not yet extend toward other monarchies, least of all Saudi Arabia, the main regional rival.

The main candidate for an ideology sowing division and distrust between the potentially similar systems was irredentism, especially from the Hashemites. Wahhabi expansionism, a major source of conflict in early Saudi-Hashemite relations, was mostly pacified after the dismantlement of the *Ikhwan* (Al-Rasheed 2010, 63–67).

126 *When monarchies collide*

Hashemite irredentism was shaped by two main regional projects by the two Hashemite monarchies: "Greater Syria", a cornerstone of Abdallah's regional ambitions, and Iraqi Prime Minister Nuri al-Said's Britain-coordinated policies enshrined in the Fertile Crescent Plan, effectively claiming the same territory alongside Iraq – both shaping Hashemite foreign policy in the 1940s and 1950s. These conceptions were divisive in that they presumed Hashemite leadership over other domains instead of an egalitarian club of monarchies. Neither of these plans ever gained a popular following. Rulers of other states, including monarchic Egypt, were wary of Hashemite ambitions (Weinberger 1986, 244–245).

Despite the Hashemite's common roots in their expulsion from the Hijaz, the Hashemite position on the Al Saud dynasty was all but monolithic, influencing the relationship to Saudi Arabia in different ways for Iraq and Jordan. Faisal I and his successors in Iraq hoped for the reunification of the territory under Hashemite sovereignty after the demise of its founder and were therefore willing to tentatively recognize its legitimacy (cf. Podeh 1995, 86). Abdallah, on the other hand, clung to Hashemite irredentism, focusing on the Hijaz longer than his brother did in Iraq. His Greater Syria Plan, presented to Britain in 1942, included political change in the Hijaz (Podeh 1995, 87). Like his father, Abdallah harbored expansionist pan-Arab leadership aspirations and wanted to unify "Greater Syria" under his rule and, when that failed, Mandatory Palestine. This was to be added to his artificially carved out territory as amir of Transjordan – later as king of Transjordan after independence in 1946. The name was changed to Kingdom of Jordan in 1949 after the annexation of the West Bank of the Jordan river – a move not recognized by any Arab state except fellow Hashemite Iraq. However, the expansion and grounding of the Hashemite state in the Levant that the control over Jerusalem signified also helped disentangle Jordan from the Arabian Peninsula (Partrick 2013, 3).

Despite the obstacles to monarchic ingroup identification that Hashemite irredentism brought with it, it was firmly tied to monarchism. During 1941–1947, when Abdallah's attempts to form a greater union including Syria reached an apex, one of the reasons for the policy's failure was the Syrian government's adamant insistence on retaining its republican state form rather than the idea of incorporation or unity itself. Under the Syrian nationalist president Shukri al-Quwatli, the burden of change was even reversed: he called on Transjordan to "let her people join the mother country [Syria] as a free republic" (cited in: Simon 1974, 317).

The Fertile Crescent Plan of Iraqi Prime Minister Nuri al-Said went even further than Abdallah's Syrian unity agenda in that it sought to unite Syria, Lebanon, and Palestine and Transjordan. These countries would then compose the Arab League along with Iraq, headed by a permanent council nominated by member states and presided over by their rulers chosen in a manner acceptable to the states concerned. It is no accident that this plan was designed by commoner al-Said rather than a member of the Hashemite family. The key difference was that al-Said's plan prioritized Arab unity over dynastic Hashemite union and even left the question of the form of government open (Simon 1974, 317–318). His proposal to the Saudi Kingdom in early 1943 was, however, more agreeable for the Saudis,

When monarchies collide 127

because it incorporated "Greater Syria" but no Hijazi territory (Podeh 1995, 86). In turn, Abd al-Ilah, the regent of Iraq and son of Abdallah's brother Ali (the successor of their father Sharif Hussein), attempted to convince Syrian politicians of Iraqi-Syrian unity until the plan collapsed with the establishment of the Syrian-Egyptian United Arab Republic (UAR) (Simon 1974, 318), but frequent changes of government through the then almost annual coups in Syria precluded a final agreement in the previous years as well (cf. Simon 1974, 319).

Social processes of ingroup identification

While Emir Abdallah, the son of the former Hashemite ruler over the Hijaz, Sharif Hussein, refused to recognize the Saudi Kingdom, Iraqi and Saudi representatives had already signed an agreement of mutual recognition of the independence of the two countries in February 1930. It dealt mainly with border issues. This marked the first step toward the consolidation of ingroup identification. It was followed by another symbolic concession. In 1936, Ghazi, son of Faisal I, signed the Arab Entente Cordiale among the monarchies of Iraq, Saudi Arabia, and Yemen, an essential hallmark in Iraqi-Saudi relations in that it implied a withdrawal of all Iraqi Hashemite claims on the Hijaz (Podeh 1995, 87).

Faisal I and his successors in Iraq believed the Saudi regime to be a flash in the pan and hoped for reunification of the territory under Hashemite sovereignty after the demise of its founder. They were therefore willing to tentatively recognize its legitimacy. His brother Abdallah, who vividly remembered his humiliating half-dressed flight from the Saudi victory at Turaba, denied its right to existence (cf. Podeh 1995, 86). The first signs of convergence were prompted by the losses of the First Arab-Israeli War of 1948/1949. As the threat from each other lessened while another loomed larger, cooperation could begin to merge into a common identity. The first step – the recognition as equals – was taken at this meeting: "One important aspect of the meeting was Ibn Saud's recognition of King Abdallah as an independent monarch, and his agreement to exchange diplomatic representatives" (Al-Rasheed 2001, 244)

Relations remained strained between the Iraqi Hashemites and the Saudi regime as well, but these steps later led to mutual recognition because "like polities" that were not present before borders were clearly delineated and because state building took a back seat to – often-shifting – tribal allegiances.

Although relations between the Hashemites and the Al Saud were distanced, first signs of rapprochement were shown in first visits. That the personalization of relations via visits is important for the forging of community is shown by changed attitudes of the elites after such visits, later leading to a rapprochement. Long-standing British efforts to reconcile the two dynasties led to first successes in the background of the Arab-Israeli War, when both monarchs began to see the advantages of cooperation for a common goal – avoiding imminent military defeat – and Ibn Saud and Abdallah met for a tentative rapprochement, eased by the shrunken military capabilities and entanglement of the Arab Legion. Some 16 years after the kingdom's formation, Ibn Saud relented and received Abdallah

128 *When monarchies collide*

in Riyadh from 27 to 30 June 1948, without letting his son Faisal know. A Hijazi dissident described the visit as the opportunity to "end any separatist tendencies between the Hijaz and Nejd and would allow the country to develop on a proper basis of unity" (cited in: Al-Rasheed 2001, 243). It was not a warm affair from the beginning, and King Abdallah consciously omitted the Hijaz, his homeland, from his itinerary (Maddy-Weitzman 1990, 69–70).

Nevertheless, while Abdallah previously openly voiced his hostility toward the Al Saud, his meeting with Ibn Saud (and his heir, Saud bin Abd al-Aziz) apparently influenced his stance toward him, as he described the Saudi ruler as a "pleasant companion" (*hulwu l-ma'ashshar*) in his memoirs, toward whom he felt "heartfelt respect" (*ihtiram qalbi*) and was similarly inclined toward the crown prince (Abdallah I King of Jordan 1951, 66–67, 1954, 57–58).[17]

The difference in the personalization of bonds between monarchies and republics is well illustrated by the example of Syria. Meaningful personal relationships at the regime level could hardly be upheld with almost annual coups, furthermore, there were few similarities between the political systems that evoked familiarity and trust and the revolutionary rhetoric accompanying the coups was explicitly directed against the monarchies. Lacking any durable bonds, no options were off-limits per se: to circumvent Damascus's opposition to unification plans with Iraq, Baghdad even drafted an invasion plan in the early 1950s, known as Plan X (Simon 1974, 320) – which also indicates that monarchies are not necessarily less aggressive than are republics, per se.

During the reign of the sons of Sharif Hussein, there is no particular recognition of being part of larger "family" or even "club" with Saudi Arabia. There are, however, signs that Abdallah more regularly used fraternal addresses toward monarchs than he did toward Arab presidents, despite his claim to the vanguard of Arabism, which should not differentiate between different political systems.

His memoirs, where he relates official visits and communications to other heads of states, are instructive in this regard. In a letter reprinted there, he addresses King Faruq of Egypt as his brother (which the latter reciprocates in his answer letter), but not Syrian President Shukri al-Quwatli or the Palestinian leader Amin al-Husseini. In addition, he also fraternally addresses non-Arabs, like the Berber Riffian anticolonial leader Abd al-Karim al-Khattab (while referencing Morocco as a "Hashimite state", due to the Alaoui dynasty's shared descent from the prophet) and the Persian shah of the "sister Muslim country" of Iran (Abdallah I King of Jordan 1954, 44, 47, 53, 57, 62–65). Even without trusting the memoirs at face value, the overlap of the friendship category overlap with monarchism is conspicuous.

Another major instance of centripetalism among monarchies are the royal unification attempts at the time that attempted to institutionalize community. While no broader union (including Saudi Arabia and Kuwait) came about, both were approached and engaged in negotiations. More prominently, we see the beginning of the formation of the Arab Union (or Arab Federation, AFU), which united the Hashemite sister kingdoms shortly before the downfall of the Iraqi monarchy. In

When monarchies collide 129

April 1947, Iraq and Transjordan signed the Treaty of Brotherhood and Alliance, emphasizing the close bonds in its name (Maddy-Weitzman 1990, 66).

A few months before his assassination, Abdallah floated the idea of a confederation between the two Hashemite states on the basis of the broad autonomy of the states but a single foreign policy, mutual defense responsibilities, and a single flag, "the first Hashemite flag of the Hijaz" (Maddy-Weitzman 1990, 66–67) – a jab at the Al Saud but a further reification of the Hashemite bond. Iraqi politicians took over the initiative after Abdallah's death (Gelber 2004, 225).

Foreign policy restraint

The abating of previously frequent raids and skirmishes indicate that constraints toward the use of force in the inter-dynastic relationships were in the process of being established. State consolidation increasingly restricted hostile interactions. Irredentist aspirations persisted on both sides, and military measures were common and normalized at least into the late 1920s and early 1930s, as the frequent Saudi raids into Transjordanian territory demonstrate. Nonetheless, border solidification was in process, exemplified by the (albeit begrudging) Saudi acquiescence to Abdallah's incorporation of two provinces into his dominions after his victory over a Saudi Wahhabi raid by Bani Sakhr tribespeople into Transjordan in 1925. The southern borders remained in most parts unchanged in the future (Milton-Edwards and Hinchcliffe 2009, 20).

Of special importance is role of state building in the crushing of the *Ikhwan* rebellion of 1927–1930. Ibn Saud recognized the importance of reigning in the *Ikhwan*, who were challenging him on a number of grounds (including the political system) and whose raids into Jordanian, Iraqi, or Kuwait territory brought about interstate conflicts (Al-Rasheed 2010, 63–7). By crushing them (with British assistance), he strengthened the state monopoly on violence and implicitly declared his abandonment of an imperial expansionary logic for the benefit of a nation-state logic of fixed borders, the prerequisite of ingroup identification.

Despite balancing alliances of the Saudis against the Hashemites, especially marked during the First Arab-Israeli War and Hashemite attempts to, in Emir Abdallah's words, weaken "a dangerous Saudi-Syrian-Lebanese understanding" (Abdallah I King of Jordan 1950, 250), there was no active attempt to change the regime, no "Plan X" as toward Damascus. Still, mistrust defined the relationship at the time, witnessed by mutual attempts to delegitimize and weaken the other.

For Abdallah, the Saudi Kingdom was illegitimate. When his brother officially recognized it, he accused him of "treason to the Hashemite family" (Podeh 1995, 87). In his memoirs a few years later, he condemned the Saudis as a corrupt sect and responsible for Arab discord while denying their right to Arab leadership. In a "review of the present position of the Arab countries", written in 1943–1944, Abdallah condemns the Al Saud as "the fanatic minority which now rules the Hejaz" and which "has done nothing for Islam, neither of old nor in modern times" (Abdallah I King of Jordan 1950, 250). Even when appearing conciliatory, as in a letter to Sir Harold McMichael, the high commissioner of Transjordan in April 1944, he uses

130 *When monarchies collide*

his position as a "Hashimite [*sic*] Prince" to intervene in the matter of gold and petrol exploitation in the Hijaz, not under Hashemite control since two decades. While he grudgingly accepts Ibn Saud as the custodian of the two mosques, he also disparages him as ignorant because he is "new to his position" and as callous toward the sacred places that he claimed to protect: "Even if King Ibn Sa'ud has conquered and occupied this area, he has no right to disturb its sacred character, and to change its rites" (Abdallah I King of Jordan 1950, 258–259). The othering is pronounced at this point. The attempts at *takfir* (excommunication from the Muslim faith) of the Saudis mirror those of Ibn Saud in previous years.

Saudi Arabia reciprocated and refused to establish diplomatic relations with Transjordan while continuing to rival and sabotage Abdallah's policies. Delegitimization was the rule rather than the exception. As so often before and since, Syria formed a main battleground. The Saudis rejected and countered attempts at establishing a Hashemite monarchy in Syria, fearing that it would bolster the basis for Hashemite irredentism. It is in opposition to the Hashemites that fervent Saudi support for independent Syria is best explained in the early period of the republic. Before the establishment of the Arab League, Ibn Saud opposed any plans to attach Syria, Lebanon, or Palestine to Egypt or Iraq and supported the League only after it became clear that Egypt did not harbor greater ambition to Arab unity but also saw the Hashemites as the primary threat, which formed the basis of a short-lived axis between King Ibn Saud, King Faruq of Egypt, and President Shukri al-Quwatli of Syria (Podeh 1995, 87).

There is no evidence of any Jordanian Hashemite-Saudi alliance or even mutual support in this period, although there are hints of growing Iraqi-Saudi ties. On the other hand, there is close cooperation, up to the Treaty of Brotherhood and Alliance between the two sister Hashemite kingdoms of Jordan and Iraq, later leading to the institutionalization of alliance in the AFU.

Once his unification plans with Syria had failed, Abdallah turned his focus back on Iraq after failing to expand his control over Syria, within the framework of his "Greater Syria" scheme. In April 1947, he and his nephew Abd al-Ilah, the regent of Iraq and son of Sharif Hussein's heir and Abdallah's brother Ali, signed the Treaty of Brotherhood and Alliance. The treaty provided for consultation on defense measures against a third-party aggressor and permitted military intervention by one party to suppress disorders or a rebellion in the other. Abd al-Ilah took over the leadership of the alliance and Hashemite ambitions after Abdallah's death (Simon 1974, 317).

The cooperation of the two Hashemite dynasties became more evident during the Arab-Israeli War with Abdallah's appointment as supreme commander of the Arab Forces, with Iraqi Mahmud as his deputy (and ALA commander Qawuqji, also an Iraqi). After the war, the Iraqi prime minister acknowledged Transjordanian support for Iraqi's military and economic strategies but blamed the other Arab states for rejecting them (cf. Tripp 2001, 135–136, 139).

Saudi relations with Iraq were not quite as abysmal. The text of the inter-Hashemite Alliance and Brotherhood treaty followed a similar one of 1936 signed by Saudi Arabia and Iraq (Maddy-Weitzman 1990, 66).

Ingroup identification

The period of early state building in Jordan, Iraq, and Saudi Arabia shows a core ingroup of the Hashemite twin monarchies but only limited first signs of expanding this "monarchic club" toward Saudi Arabia. After all, the conditions for ingroup development were lacking in that both structural similarity and monarchic salience were low. Consequently, isolated raids and skirmishes indicate the absence of any nonviolence norm. Over the years, the solidification of borders and state institutions and the increasing personal interaction between the monarchs amid the backdrop of the looming threat of pan-Arab republicanism planted the seeds for monarchic cooperation and community.

In Abdallah's later years, he muted his (personal) opposition to the Saud dynasty. His visit to Saudi Arabia in the summer of 1948 made a partial rapprochement seem within reach. Still, it took his death in 1951 to remove the prime obstacle to reconciliation. Neither his son, the short-lived King Talal, nor his grandson Hussein raised any irredentist claims. The Saudi-Jordanian border finally solidified. Iraq had begun making overtures even earlier and the acknowledgment of mutual recognition softened relations with Saudi Arabia in the 1930s. While this growing closeness did not preclude rivalries and intrigues, the relationship of the dynasties was marked by a growing trust level that others, like the Syrian leadership, did not enjoy.

From rivalry to rapprochement (1953–1958): how common enemies forge a family

With the aggravation of the immediate threat by radical republicanism led by Nasser's Egypt, rapprochement between Jordan and Iraq resulted in the formation of the AFU and the rapprochement with other monarchies, including Saudi Arabia.

Structural similarities

Although the intricacies of the political systems have not changed in a major way since the states' independence, the consolidation of the state and its borders have contributed to an increased similarity as Saudi Arabia, Iraq, and Jordan became full-fledged states on the basis of a defined territory, population, and monopoly of violence rather than tribal fiefdoms on the basis of allegiance rather than territory. And set against the rising threat by communism, both the Hashemite and Saudi kingdoms were firmly based on capitalist economic principles, leading to further structural convergence.

Salience: constraints and catalysts for ingroup identification

The share of republics in the system became a majority by the early 1960s. Adding to the decreasing share of monarchies was the dramatically surging republican

132 *When monarchies collide*

threat, and divisive ideology among monarchies declined significantly. With the demise of King Abdallah of Jordan and with the imminent common threat toward monarchies, Hashemite irredentism waned significantly. While Saudi Arabia had long accepted extant Jordanian borders to the south, Hashemite claims to the Hijaz also waned, never to return. This meant that all relevant conditions heightened the salience of monarchy that supported the emergence of an ingroup.

The coup revolutions of 1952 and 1958 were followed by those in Yemen in 1962 and in Libya in 1969, which all gave birth to revolutionary anti-monarchical and anti-Western regimes, emphasizing the fragility and anachronism of the monarchy as a viable political system. The Egyptian revolution caused the remaining monarchies to change their priorities regarding unity: "Henceforth, the goal of the monarchs was to preserve their Hashemite thrones and their conservative regimes against pressure from the radical Arab governments" (Simon 1974, 321).

The revolution also strengthened the individual monarchic identity of the states, which led to greater identification with other "similar" systems. Saudi Arabia's "close and cordial relations with Egypt over a considerable period inevitably produced at first a reaction of sympathy and concern for the fallen dynasty and its leading personalities, who had all been actively associated with the king and his government" (Philby 1955, 354).

Despite the new catalytic threat by Gamal Abd al-Nasser's pan-Arab republicanism, the formation of a concept of monarchic identity was slow. The establishing of the Baghdad Pact in 1955 did not stifle King Saud's fears of Hashemite domination ambitions and led to an intense period of Saudi-Egyptian cooperation, culminating in their joint effort to prevent Jordan from joining the pact despite British and Iraqi pressure (Podeh 1995, 89). Despite this new Saudi-Egyptian friendship, the kingdom could not help but recognize the adverse effects of Egyptian antiroyalist propaganda and Nasser's turn away from the West to the Soviet Union. Egyptian bids at leadership resonated increasingly among other Arab republics and the populace in the monarchies and formed a major domestic threat to the existence of the monarchic regimes. As early as in 1955, the Saudis uncovered their own "Free Officers" movement, which plotted a coup *à la égyptienne*, having been educated in Egypt or trained by Egyptians. A movement of "Saudiyyun al-Ahrar" ("the Free Saudis") agitated in the country, called for strikes and trade unions, and railed against the American presence in the kingdom (Patai 2015, 60).

The announcement of the Eisenhower Doctrine in January 1957, which provided for a possible military reaction of the United States to any "armed aggression from any nation controlled by international communism" served as convenient grounds to form a royalist coalition. Nuri al-Said recognized that removing Saudi Arabia from the Egyptian sphere of influence was crucial to the survival of the Iraqi regime that was heavily damaged by its links to the United Kingdom. British Ambassador Wright succinctly summed up the situation and the common threat perception that aligned worldviews and aims and led to a stronger perception of similarity:

> Among the motives of the Iraq government in making this sustained effort were the appreciation that the Royal Families of Iraq, Jordan and Saudi

When monarchies collide 133

Arabia have a common interest in opposing Communist subversion in the Middle East, an interest so strong as to require the composition of past differences between the Hashemite Family and the Rulers of Saudi Arabia; the desire flowing from this, to open the eyes of Saud to the reality and danger of co-operation between Nasser and Communist Russia, not least in terms of the situation in Syria, and to try and detach Sa'ud from Nasser, and the hope of securing at least the benevolent acquiescence of Sa'ud in Iraq's membership [in] the Baghdad Pact, thereby diminishing the relative isolation of Iraq in the Arab World.

(cited in: Podeh 97–98)

The 1958 revolution and the elimination of the Hashemite Kingdom of Iraq served as a further unifying driver for Saudi Arabia, the remaining Hashemite Kingdom of Jordan.

Social processes of ingroup identification

In contrast to the previous period, the second was marked by mutual recognition and increasing interaction between royals and other high-ranking representatives of the three countries. Between the Hashemite kingdoms, kinship bonds led to a more pronounced shared identification.

Once Abdallah was out of the way, Jordan could directly recognize Saudi Arabia, which de facto happened with Talal's royal visit to Saudi Arabia in November 1951 – his first. He made up for his father's 1948 omission by visiting the Hijaz, symbolically recognizing the legitimacy of Saudi rule (Gelber 2004, 223; Maddy-Weitzman 1990, 69–70). Reciprocity and reconciliation were achieved in June 1954 by Ibn Saud's son and successor King Saud's first royal visit to King Hussein of Jordan, the grandson of his father's greatest rival. Although the conflict with (Trans)Jordan was personal and easily mended with King Abdallah's demise, the successions in Saudi Arabia and Iraq did not serve as clear-cut occasions for rapprochement, though they eased the personal rivalry as a basis for tensions. King Saud attempted to step out of the larger-than-life shadow of his father. In Iraq, Faisal's inexperienced and young son Ghazi came to power for a short time, followed by the even younger Faisal II, who took over the reins from his uncle Abd al-Ilah when he came of age in 1953 – although he could not escape the elder's influence. Abd al-Ilah, who was the son of Ali, the eldest son of Sharif Hussein (and the one pushed out of the Hijaz by Ibn Saud), still harbored vaguely Greater Syrian designs for both Damascus and the Hijaz (Podeh 1995, 88).

Nevertheless, stronger engagement with each other followed. After Nasser's nationalization of the Suez Canal in 1956, Baghdad saw an opportunity to drive a wedge between Riyadh and Cairo by moving the former into its own orbit. Nuri al-Said dispatched Amir Zaid, Iraqi ambassador to the United Kingdom and the last surviving son of Sharif Hussein, to Riyadh, to usher in a new era between the two dynasties. He arrived there on August 26, 1956 (Podeh 1995, 92–93). The meeting was successful, and King Saud even voiced some guarded approval of the Baghdad Pact. A meeting of the two monarchs was prepared for September 20,

134 *When monarchies collide*

1956, in Dammam. Abdallah al-Damluji, a former advisor of Ibn Saud and later Iraqi foreign minister, was sent to Riyadh. It proved productive: King Saud promised not to impose an oil boycott and to refrain from other anti-Western actions (Podeh 1995, 94).

Although figures close to King Saud remained staunchly pro-Egyptian, such as Crown Prince Faisal and the king's two senior advisors, the meeting proved a turning point in Saudi-Iraqi relations. The two leaders revived their earlier mutual recognition. The next day after the meeting, Saud reluctantly received the Egyptian and Syrian presidents to offset the Iraqi offensive. In response, Nuri al-Said informed Saud of Iraq's intentions to send troops to Jordan in case of an Israeli attack and floated the idea of a meeting of the three kings during Saud's scheduled visit to Amman in November 1956 that would symbolize the new "conservative-royalist axis in the Arab world". This failed to come to fruition, because of the outbreak of the Suez War in October (Podeh 1995, 96). The war temporarily obstructed the development of a monarchic community and alliance because it boosted Nasser's prestige and raised the importance of the Arab-Israeli conflict. King Saud was left with no choice but to cut diplomatic relations with Britain and France. Iraq had cut relations with France but refused to do the same with Britain. But the development of monarchic identification and solidarity had just begun. Saudi-Iraqi meetings in Washington initiated a new stage in the rapprochement and marked the termination of the conflict. The relationship between Jordan and Saudi Arabia was also ameliorating and even resulted in military cooperation (Shlaim 2009, 127).

The first official Saudi royal visit Saudi-Iraqi to Hashemite Iraq was conducted by King Saud on May 11, 1957, who had concluded that Nasser was a greater threat than the Hashemites from the Suez conflict the previous year (Shlaim 2009, 136–137). A series of visits by King Saud to Jordan and King Hussein to Iraq followed in June 1957 (Podeh 1995, 99–100).

Personal relations were of prime importance in the diffusion of the rivalry of the kingdoms. In many ways, the rapprochement in Jordanian-Saudi relations was a monarchic and a (royal) family affair: Queen Mother Zain, a Hashemite, seeing the threat for the conservative monarchies from Arab nationalism, arranged a meeting in Medina in mid January 1957 between her son, King Hussein, and King Saud, who offered financial support (Shlaim 2009, 127). Despite the opportunity, Jordan was not yet ready to join the royalist coalition, due to its pro-Egyptian government at that time. That obstacle was removed after an alleged coup attempt by the army's chief of staff, Ali Abu Nuwar, who fled to Damascus. In reaction and after cabinet actions challenging the royal prerogative, King Hussein in April 1957 dismissed the country's first democratically elected government (Shlaim 2009, 132–133).

Especially the two sister Hashemite monarchies were linked via kinship and friendship ties, particularly between the cousins Hussein and Faisal. Avi Shlaim describes their close relationship: "Hussein and Faisal had been the best of friends: they were born the same year, and were at Harrow together; their fathers were first cousins and best friends; their grandmothers were sisters; and they became kings on the same day" (Shlaim 2009, 165). Faisal was also a witness at Hussein's wedding (Shlaim 2009, 92). It is therefore not surprising that Faisal's killing by the coup leaders in July 1958 was "one of the heaviest blows" (H. King of Jordan 1962, 197) for King Hussein, as he relays in his memoirs:

> Throughout our short lives we had been so close, united in many ways. Our grandfathers had also been closely bound. On my side was King Abdullah; on his, Abdullah's brother, the first King Feisal, who played a major role in the Arab Revolt and on whose side Lawrence of Arabia had served. As boys we had played together – hadn't Feisal given me my first bicycle? – and later at Harrow, we had discussed so often the problems which would one day face us. Now that he is lost, I believe many, many Iraqis, for or against the monarchy, feel a deep sense of guilt for the brutal assassination.
>
> (H. King of Jordan 1962, 198)

The deep, personal bonds between the monarchs gave the fate of the Iraqi monarchy a personal meaning for Hussein, making him identify with the Iraqi monarch more than he would have with another "friendly" regime and shaping his persona as a monarch and head of state.

Such a deep connection was not yet present between Saudi Arabia and the Hashemite monarchies, which differed in their institutions and intensity of connection to Britain – although the Saud also started sending their sons to Sandhurst and elsewhere (Hurewitz 1969, 251). But both shared a pro-Western outlook and an anti-communist and conservative stance. The basis for a community had slowly formed between the independent monarchies and was now strengthened, articulated and reified by rituals and ceremonies more openly.

By the 1950s, the Saudi-Hashemite relationship had transformed from an enmity that would have rather seen the other disappear to a rivalry that still aimed to weaken, but not destroy, the other, because their fates were linked. Even during Ibn Saud's anti-Hashemite agitation in 1951, Ibn Saud also made his hope clear that the British (and Americans) would protect the rights of Abdallah's heirs, indicating that he was aware that the fall of one monarchy might spell doom for his as well (Maddy-Weitzman 1990, 69–70).

Coronation ceremonies marked significant occasions for the affirmation of shared monarchism. At the beginning of the second period, however, they were an ambivalent sign. Then–Crown Prince Saud was coolly received at Iraqi King Faisal's coronation in 1953, and the Iraqi representatives were notably absent from the funeral of Ibn Saud and the coronation of his son (Podeh 1995, 88). On the one hand, these are indications of tense relations between Saudi Arabia and Iraq. On the other hand, absence could be seen as an affront only if royal presence were expected and an existing protocol were in place. This means that certain monarchic rules of engagement and behavior had already been established among the monarchies. Also, especially the coronations were specifically monarchic rituals that they shared, thus cementing a shared belonging and an equality of royal status despite conflict while excluding republics from these ceremonies.

136 *When monarchies collide*

Increasingly, the belonging to a joint "club" became apparent and was voiced more openly by the royals themselves. In a meeting between Iraq and Saudi Arabia in late 1956, King Saud, in clear recognition of the common club membership of the royal regimes, asserted that he rejected supporting "dictators and presidents" and would rather cooperate "with the fellow monarchy of Iraq" (Podeh 1995, 94). This meeting was so successful that it brought about the idea of another, this time including three kings (Saud, Faisal, Hussein), during Saud's scheduled visit to Amman in November 1956. The constellation was not an accident but rather a conscious inclusion of fellow monarchies meaning to symbolize the new "conservative-royalist axis in the Arab world" (Podeh 1995, 96).

Foreign policy restraint

The salience of monarchism has helped tone down some of the most hostile interactions in the second period. Only one MID (display of force) is recorded for the Saudi Arabia–Jordan dyad (there are no recorded MIDs for the Saudi–Iraq dyad), in 1956. This is the highest point of escalation and the only militarized dispute of the dyad after World War II, and it falls well short of military action ("display of force", hostility level 2 out of 5). Military restraint prevailed in this period.

1956 was a disruptive period in Jordanian history with massive popular unrest caused by the Baghdad Pact, and protesters in the southern city of Ma'an called for annexation to Saudi Arabia. In other parts of Jordan were calls for Syrian annexation (Patai 2015, 60). Amid the unrest, a Saudi force of 1500–2000 troops moved toward the border. British Prime Minister Anthony Eden warned the Saudi government against aggression and the force withdrew (Shlaim 2009, 89). While British disapproval was clearly important, it is unclear whether the Saudis would have advanced in the face of a British acquiescence. In any case, the confrontation was short-lived and quickly de-escalated, and there was no actual clash.[18]

Alliance patterns changed abruptly with the rising threat from Nasserism. During the Suez War, just a few months after the border saber rattling, Saudi Arabia even dispatched an army contingent to Jordan as a sign of solidarity and support. A meeting in Cairo on February 25, 1957, marked the formation of Saudi Arabia–Jordan axis against an Egyptian–Syrian one vis-à-vis the Eisenhower Doctrine (Shlaim 2009, 127).

The second period rarely witnessed attempts to subvert or delegitimate the royal opponent, although these methods were extensively used against republics (as detailed in Chapter 3). There was little rhetorical or political escalation, and disagreements were voiced not in terms of general incompatibility but as differences of opinion.

King Saud initially supported the anti-government protests in Jordan, cozying up to Nasser, mainly to prevent Hashemite closeness at his expense. However, the alliance crumbled as the threat of republicanism hit ever closer to home, with the coup attempt a particularly visible marker of Egyptian subversion. It was after Nasser's September 1956 visit to Saudi Arabia to promote a union between Egypt,

When monarchies collide 137

Syria, and Saudi Arabia that Saud realized the differences were unsurmountable. The short-lived friendship dissipated completely after the establishment of the UAR and after Saud's attempt to arrange Nasser's assassination in March 1958 came to light, forcing him to cede his position to his brother Faisal (Al-Rasheed 2010, 111–112).

The tamed rivalry between the three kingdoms stood in sharp contrast to the existential conflict between the monarchic and the republican camp. Reciprocal subversion attempts, including coups and assassinations, indicate a hostile relationship beyond mere disagreements and show the difference in scale between intra-monarchic conflict and conflict between monarchies and revolutionary republics. Evidently, Baghdad's disagreement with Riyadh over the Baghdad Pact never took an as shrill and polemic a tone as that between Baghdad and Cairo; to the contrary, there was an informal understanding to cease the propaganda war, though it was later breached. The US ambassador supported the two monarchies' rapprochement attempts that were in US interests in balancing against the Soviet Union and Nasser (Podeh 1995, 90).

While a clash of Jordan and Saudi Arabia was prevented in early 1956, in March 1958, Jordanian and Syrian troops clashed along the border, while al-Said plotted to topple the republic in Syria and replace it with a monarchy (headed by Abd al-Ilah). He tried to get the British and Americans on board as well (Shlaim 2009, 157). In the 1950s, Iraqi Regent Abd al-Ilah actively tried to undermine the Syrian republic (Seale 1965, 136–141).

Saud's support base in the royal family had been crumbling for a while, leading his brother and Crown Prince Faisal to assume the premiership. Faisal's pro-Egyptian stance, however, did not lead to a withdrawal from the monarchic coalition, and the revolution in Iraq a few months later forced Jordan and Saudi Arabia even closer together (Podeh 1995, 85–108).

In contrast to the first period, the second saw not only a cold peace and restraint against military campaigns against the royal neighbor but also first signs of mutual support and solidarity by virtue of belonging to the same community of fate. The Saudis and the Hashemites sat in the same boat in a storm fired up by revolutionary ideology.

Although the forming alignment was not as obvious as the one between the Hashemite sister kingdoms that was about to be institutionalized in the AFU, the monarchic club began extending toward Saudi Arabia as well. During the Suez War, Saudi Arabia had dispatched an army contingent to Jordan as a sign of solidarity and support, mere months after the near-clash at the border. To counteract Nasser, King Saud also offered his support in form of two brigades put at Jordanian disposal and a subsidy of £5 million in May 1957 (Shlaim 2009, 127, 136–137). This shows a commitment toward the other that affirms the verbal rapprochement was not merely rhetorical. The new alignment that took shape in the mid and late 1950s now included Saudi Arabia, Iraq, and Jordan but also Lebanon and to a lesser degree Morocco, Libya (both monarchies at that time), Tunisia, and Sudan. The key decision makers of these countries frequently visited each other (Podeh 1995, 99–100).

138 *When monarchies collide*

This liaison went beyond a mere convergence of interests, although the aim of weakening the revolutionary republican bloc initially brought them together. Charles Johnston, the British ambassador in Amman, describes the visit by Saud to Jordan in 1957 as a union based on shared interests (anti-communism, anti-Nasserism) as well as shared institutions and values:

> further step towards the new alignment in the Arab world by which Jordan is linked with Saudi Arabia, and less strictly with Iraq and the Lebanon, in opposition to Egypt and Syria. The new 'Arab caravan' is a much more homogeneous collection of animals than the group which came together with such enthusiasm last January and February and disintegrated so spectacularly in April and May. More narrowly, King Hussein and King Sa'ud have in common their crowns, their anti-communism, and their distrust of Colonel Nasser, and for the time being these factors are more than strong enough to lay that antique Middle Eastern ghost, the traditional rivalry between the Hashemite and Saudi dynasties. I hope that the new association will continue, and I see no reason why it should not.
>
> (cited in: Podeh 1995, 100–101)

With the backing of its royal friends, the Jordanian government felt emboldened to openly accuse Egypt and Syria of plotting the overthrow of all the Arab Kings – of Jordan, Saudi Arabia, Iraq, and Libya – and of recruitment attempts of Jordanians to assassinate royal family members by the Egyptian military attaché in Amman (Patai 2015, 71).

The emerging community did not spell the end to intra-royal conflict and mistrust. King Hussein hoped to include Saudi Arabia and other conservative countries in this plan of an Arab Union, after uniting the two Hashemite dynasties. Early contacts between Jordan, Iraq, and Saudi Arabia had already been made in November 1957, but Saud was wary of financial entanglement and association with the controversial Baghdad Pact and preferred to remain in an arbiter position, although with a "tilt to the monarchist side" (Podeh 1995, 101; Shlaim 2009, 154). Saudi ambivalence was not completely distinguished, meaning that the AFU would not expand to include more monarchies than the two Hashemite ones. Nuri al-Said tried to pressure Kuwait into participating but failed. King Saud made clear that Saudi Arabia also had no intention to join in the near future on the occasion of a visit by the two states' foreign ministers at the end of February, but congratulated them on the union. Saud, a mediator rather than proactive leader, was still concerned with his perceived neutrality in the Arab World, feeling that noninterference in inter-Arab conflicts would best serve the country's territorial integrity. The strong pro-Egyptian sentiments in his own administration were another constraint (Shlaim 2009, 157).

Iraq's King Faisal arrived in Amman on February 11, 1958, to discuss the union, and it was established three days later, on February 14, among the two Hashemite states as the Arab Federation (or Arab Union, *al-ittihad al-arabi*), 13 days after the announcement of the UAR, the opposing United Arab Republic between Syria

When monarchies collide 139

and Egypt, on February 1, 1958. The third attempt at Hashemite unification, it had jurisdiction over foreign and defense affairs, the establishment and management of the armed forces, diplomatic representation abroad, customs, currency, educational policy and curricula, and transportation and communication. Unlike the 1951 attempt, it was not supposed to merge the two crowns and was therefore more successful as a loose confederation of two sovereign monarchies (Maddy-Weitzman 1990, 72).

The key difference between the two mergers (the UAR and the AFU), especially concerning the conception of the AFU as a "royal club" were clear to observers. It was ultimately detrimental for regime stability, as Simon notes: "Regarded as the union of two monarchs rather than true Arab unity, this last attempt by 'Abdul-Ilah at regional unity was to be a major contributory factor in the revolution which occurred in Iraq in July of the same year" (Simon 1974, 321). This bolsters the view that monarchic identification rather than cold, rational cost–benefit calculations were driving the institutionalization of alliance.

Even without Saudi participation, the AFU marked a peak in monarchic cooperation, the importance of which was underlined by the 1958 revolution. Alliance commitments were tested soon after the formation of the federation. After the coup attempt against pro-Western President Camille Chamoun in Lebanon, King Hussein of Jordan asked Iraq for troops for help, and an Iraqi brigade was to be sent to its sister monarchy on 13 July, the day before the coup in Iraq by Brigadier Abd al-Karim Qasim and Colonel Abd al-Salam Arif took place. On hearing the news of the coup at 7:00 a.m. the next day, Hussein ordered an expeditionary force to Baghdad and took over the presidency of the Arab Union, in a doomed attempt to restore the monarchy (Shlaim 2009, 159–161).

The consequences of the revolution would reverberate throughout the monarchic club and further push them together in later years. Initially, however, it also showed that the monarchic club was not yet fully formed and that other monarchies were reluctant to take big risks for others that seemed doomed to collapse. While the British and Americans immediately reacted to King Hussein's call for support and Israel facilitated their actions, Saudi Arabia initially refused overflight rights for critical oil shipments to the US after an initial agreement, citing inter-family discord (Shlaim 2009, 157–164).

King Hussein's memoirs give an inkling into the sense of personal betrayal he felt from the Saudis when he talks about the "cowardice of our Arab brethren" and the disdainful references to "our Arab friends".[19] But the actual explanation to him is clear: Saudi Arabia had meekly given up on Jordan, whose fall seemed imminent (H. King of Jordan 1962, 203).

The implications of ingroup identification mean first and foremost nonviolence inside the group. Stronger and more-demanding norms of intergroup solidarity call for a stronger bond. The monarchic club, still in its developing period, was not consolidated enough to deliver it.

The Saudis thus preferred to cut a doomed Jordan loose, in a time that was marked by a sense of monarchic ephemerality. It is embodied by King Hussein's comment on his cousin's murder: "They were kings in an age of republicanism;

140   *When monarchies collide*

Arabs in a century of Arab impotence; Anglophiles in the last days of British supremacy; Moslems among agnostics; traditionalists amid constant change" who described his family history as a "caravan of martyrs" (quoted in: Shlaim 2009, 168). Especially Jordan's demise seemed imminent and probable to most foreign observers and Jordanians themselves (Shlaim 2009, 168).

After the immediate threat had subsided and it had become clear that Jordan would not collapse, Saudi-Jordanian relations began to heal again and were fortified during the Arab Cold War. During the civil war in Yemen, sparked by the coup in 1962, as the republics of Iraq, Syria and Lebanon recognized Yemeni revolutionaries and Egypt started to provide financial and military support to them, Saudi Arabia and Jordan jointly supported the royalists, as Malcolm Kerr states, "out of dynastic solidarity" (Kerr 1971, 40–41). The strong Saudi-Jordanian relationship persists without major disruptions (the aforementioned Gulf Crisis 1990–1991 as the only exception) to this day (cf. Partrick 2013).

Ingroup identification

The final period of the rivalry is marked by the slow formation of an ingroup identification, ushered in by the deaths of the rivals Abdallah in 1951 and Ibn Saud in 1953. A sense of monarchic solidarity was catalyzed in the years 1956–1958, when the Iraqi Hashemites were overthrown and their Jordanian brothers almost followed their path. Following the 1958 coup in Iraq, the rivalry between the two remaining rivals finally dissipated completely (Podeh 1995, 85). A monarchic club had emerged, even if it was still far from transformation into a more formal arrangement, indicated for instance by the Saudi reluctance to join the AFU or to support Jordan in the wake of the coup in Iraq in 1958.

Although the balance of power between the two countries was always unequal and tensions at the regime level were frequent, the

> maintenance of monarchical systems of government in an area dominated by radical regimes is one of the chief factors which has cemented Jordanian – Saudi Arabian relations together for so long. In particular this relationship is often only explicable by the common thread of monarchy pushing otherwise natural rivals together in a region of populist nationalist regimes.
>
> (Milton-Edwards and Hinchcliffe 2009, 105)

The Hashemite and Saudi dynasties: synthesis and findings

The rivalry of the two dynasties from the Arabian Peninsula was laid to rest by the abandonment of irredentist claims toward the territory and dominion of the other. This critical juncture enabled the development of joint identification, based on a heightened sense of structural similarity. This shift was set in motion by the transformation of the two dynasties into three clearly demarcated and geographically separate kingdoms with fixed borders, with its leaders now sovereigns of modernizing nation-states – which came to recognize a shared threat to them as monarchs.

When monarchies collide 141

While the early Saudi-Hashemite confrontation resembled "a struggle between competing tribal chieftaincies for the loyalty of certain tribes" (Teitelbaum 2001c, 249) between two competing "confederacies" (Teitelbaum 2001c, 282), the demise of those opponents who had a personal memory of the dynastic conflict paved the way to reconciliation. The recentering of Hashemite religious identity away from the two holy places (the *haramain* in Mecca and Medina) toward the "third haram", the *haram ash-sharif*, or "noble sanctuary" in Jerusalem, occupied by Jordan in 1948, together with the West Bank in 1948, also helped to disentangle mutually exclusive territorial and legitimation claims.

Although it took the immediate external threat of revolutionary republicanism to forge a monarchic sense of community (beyond immediate kinship bonds as existed between the two Hashemite kingdoms), this ingroup did not fall apart once the external threat subsided. The persistence of this alignment indicates that a stable alliance had formed that transcended a mere ad hoc coalition. A monarchic club, a "more homogeneous collection of animals", as described by the British ambassador to Jordan (cited in: Podeh 1995, 100–101), was able to build durable political bonds.

Although markedly different from the case of Bahraini-Qatari relations, the two cases converge on the indicators that trace the theorized causal mechanism. Despite being larger military powers that fought republics such as Israel and Syria, Jordan, Iraq, and Saudi Arabia allied with each other instead of clashing, just as the small and oil-rich Gulf monarchies had. At the same time, the stronger alliance between the Hashemite rulers of Jordan and Iraq indicates that, similar to the previous case, stronger similarities result in a stronger effect of ingroup identity.

As shown in Table 4.2, the contrast between the two periods is marked. During the first period, a low monarchic salience resulted in little personalized ties and no recognition of a shared identity. Consequently, there was no barrier against potential escalation (although military altercations stopped after the 1930s). Overall, the structural similarity was not pronounced, hinging mostly on the monarchic regime type.

The analysis just presented shows the validity of the scope conditions specified by the causal model. The lack of stable statehood and clearly demarcated borders turn any rivalry into an existential danger, thereby precluding any process of ingroup identification due to existential insecurity. Without the development of nation-states (or at least clearly separate political entities), there is no basis for ingroup identification and thus no restraint in confrontation.

Furthermore, the divisive and incompatible ideologies of Wahhabism and Abdallah's Arab nationalism were linked to modern statehood. Abdallah's "specific brand of Arab nationalism" entailed a double primacy: the primacy of the Arabs in Islam and the primacy of the Hashemites among the Arabs (Teitelbaum 2001c, 286). As this necessitates a hierarchy and calls for a single ruler (in this case, Abdallah), it represents a strong hindrance against ingroup recognition, similar to the divisive effect of the Ba'th ideology on Arab socialist states (Walt 1985, 21–23). With the consolidation of nation-states, territorial boundaries became more stable and irredentism was gradually discredited. The establishment

142 *When monarchies collide*

Table 4.2 The Saudi-Hashemite Conflict

Indicators			Period I	Period II
1. Structural similarities	1.1	Shared language, culture, history, and religion	+	+
	1.2	Similar political system	+/ – Monarchies, but differing institutions especially at beginning of state building	+ But differing institutions
	1.3	Similar economic system	+	+
2 Salience	2.1	Low/decreasing share	– Majority	+ Decrease from majority status via revolutions, beginning with Egypt 1952
	2.2	Common threat	– But rising republicanism	+ (spike in 1952 & 1958) Radical pan-Arab republicanism
	2.3	Absence of divisive ideology	– But decreasing Hashemite irredentism/ Wahhabi expansionism reigned in	
	3.1	Mutual recognition	KSA & Iraq: + KSA & Jordan: – (first steps in 1948 meeting)	+
	3.2	Personalization of bonds between ruling elites	– Weak (but very high between sister Hashemite monarchies)	+ increasing
	3.2.1	Frequent high-level state visits	– /+ Few, some first meetings	+ intensification

Indicators		Period I	Period II
	3.2.2 Kinship, intermarriage and friendship bonds		– /+ Via emissaries (Damluji, Amir Zaid), close personal bonds
	3.2.3 Shared socialization	– But British alliance connection	– Tight family bonds among Hashemites and common socialization of Hussein and Faisal at Harrow School), slowly developing between Hashemite and Saudis
3.3 Affirmation of commonality		+/ –	+
	3.3.1 Kinship and family references	– Strong among the Hashemite monarchies	–
	3.3.2 Emphasis on similarity	– /+ (not toward KSA)	– /+ (not toward KSA)
	3.3.3 References to shared historical narratives	– Shared alliance with British, contested (opposing) historical narrative on the Hijaz	+ Forming shared narrative by shared threat, traditionalism, Western alliance
	3.3.4 Common ceremonies/shared institutions	+/ – Attempts at formal alliance between Hashemites	+ Some, coronation ceremonies and royal weddings & funerals Hashemites: AFU
4.1 Military restraint		– 1+/– Mostly: some altercations, but strong preference for diplomacy especially since neutralization of *Ikhwan*	+
4.2 Non-military restraint		+/ –	+ Especially in contrast to anti-republican activities

3 Social processes of ingroup identification

4 Foreign policy restraint

(*Continued*)

144　*When monarchies collide*

Table 4.2 (Continued)

Indicators		*Period I*	*Period II*
	4.2.1 *Refraining from delegitimization*	– Takfiri tendencies on both sides	+
	4.2.2 *Refraining from subversion*	– Mostly via Syria	+
	4.2.3 *Rhetorical restraint*	–	+
4.3	Alliance and solidarity	+/ – Some signs, but mostly between Hashemite monarchies	+ Military support by KSA in 1956/1957, AFU between Hashemites

of clear territorial borders contributed to a sense of equality: symbolically, this was achieved in 1932, when Ibn Saud was made king, but it took longer for the perception to develop among the ruling elites of the kingdoms.

This disentanglement of the two dynasties enabled joint recognition and legitimization as the basis of mutual support that continues to this day. State consolidation also made the states more similar to each other. While at the starting point of their relationship, their differences overshadowed the similarities, the tables turned once the point of comparison shifted toward vastly different presidential republics shaped by revolution and coup.

Monarchic salience catalyzed that process. During the initial phase of the rivalry, almost all states in the region were monarchies. By 1948, Syria and Lebanon were the only independent Arab republics. The declining proportion of monarchies in the regional system went hand in hand with the wave of revolutions that replaced them with "progressive" republics, starting with the Egyptian Revolution in 1952. By 1962, the revolution in North Yemen and Algerian independence shifted the ratio toward a republican majority.

The second period witnessed a marked rise in the salience of monarchic identity. Consequently, the countries developed stronger interpersonal bonds and increasingly affirmed their shared path and "club membership", ultimately establishing strong and mostly supportive relations without military confrontation. The integration attempt of the two Hashemite monarchies shows their even stronger sense of shared identity. Once the dynastic question was off the table, the level of conflict between the dynasties never reached militarization, not even during the rift caused by Jordanian ambivalence toward Saddam Hussein during the Gulf Crisis (Partrick 2013, 4).

This case of the Hashemite sister kingdoms and particularly their unification attempts also support a key finding of the previous case: more formalized forms of alliance formation require a higher level of similarity beyond the political system. This finding of a Hashemite peace in addition to the previously established *khaleeji* peace confirms the assumption that similarity is better captured as a multidimensional concept. As SPSP is not monarchy-specific, there is no contradiction in stating that the unification attempts of the Hashemite monarchies were not due to "any intrinsic affinity between monarchical regimes" (Walt 1990, 213). They were guided by the perception of the ruling elites as members of the same "club" or community of fate, forged by crisis situations but not dependent on a common threat for their continuation.

Indeed, the monarchic alliance between Saudi Arabia and Jordan has not ceased with the end of the Arab Cold War but instead persisted for decades, frequently based on a close personal basis. Despite the rivalry and misgivings because of Jordan's role in the Kuwait Crisis in 1990, Saudi King (then–Crown Prince) Abdallah visited Jordan's King Hussein in the last months of his life and brought him sacred Zamzam water from Mecca in a gesture of friendship (Abdallah II King of Jordan 2011, 146).

Notes

1 And there were numerous: as of 1984, 21 territorial disputes (either settled or not) were counted in the Persian Gulf region (Martin 1984, 33).
2 So much indeed that, e.g., David Commins, who discusses each Gulf state in a separate section, summarizes Bahrain and Qatar in one section (Commins 2012, 197–199).
3 The term "*khaleeji*" will be used henceforth to denote the monarchies on the Arabian Peninsula. It is preferred to similar but more-widespread terms like "(Arab/Persian) Gulf" because it explicitly excludes Iran and usually also non-monarchic Iraq.
4 At the beginning of the Arab Spring protest diffusion, Bahrain was the only monarchy that was seriously destabilized by huge mass protests engulfing about one-sixth of the whole citizen population and the government reprisals. Qatar was on the other end of the scale and – along with the UAE – the only Gulf country without any protests whatsoever. In the UAE, however, a few Emirati intellectuals signed a petition demanding greater participation, which was sometimes counted as protest (Barany 2013).
5 For example, in 1972, Iran was among the first countries to recognize Emir Khalifa after he had deposed the previous emir in 1972 (Crystal 1990, 166).
6 While emphasizing similarity in times of *conflict* relates more to the fourth indicator set of the outcome of political restraint, the parading and signaling of commonality in less-tense times shows the creation and solidification of bonds that ultimately lead to more restraint. There is an evident feedback loop that, albeit not made explicit by the theoretical framework, should be kept in mind. As in all processes involving identifications and social constructions of reality, there are multiple feedback effects instead of a straightforward linear causal path.
7 One of the major participants in the attempted coup aimed at restoring Khalifa Al Thani as emir in 1996, not to be confused with the one-time prime and foreign minister of Qatar of the same name.
8 The MID data set codes the incident with a hostility level of 4, i.e. "use of force", just below "war", the highest action in dispute being the occupation of territory ("hiact = 14") by Qatar, while Bahrain is coded as not having reciprocated (hostility level 1, i.e. no militarized action) (Ghosn, Palmer, and Bremer 2004).
9 Especially the Sunna–Shia cleavage was and continues to be crucial to Bahrain, which suffered a period of severe internal crisis in the 1990s. However, this barely reverberated in other Arab monarchies and remained an isolating instead of a unifying issue for the GCC members and, mutatis mutandis, for Bahrain and Qatar.

146 *When monarchies collide*

10 This supports the view of a monarchic community where monarchies are prime attachment references for each other.
11 Despite countless proclamations and commitments, the causeway (also aptly named Friendship Bridge) was quietly abandoned and replaced by a ferry service, which has also been rendered moot since 2017, due to the blockade.
12 The transformation of the Bahraini emirate into a kingdom did not disrupt this equality, because its symbolism was directed mostly inside Bahrain.
13 While the ability to finally drill for oil was important in settling the ownership of Hawar, in the case of Zubarah, Bahrain had waived all rights to oil if it was ever found there (which was unlikely anyway) (Belgrave 1972, 153). Although compromising with a "sisterly" country could be forgiven and mutual cooperation was valued higher than confrontation, this is not automatically true in case of a "foreign" or threatening regime. Also, although both monarchies are also rentier states with an expansive welfare economy, the much richer Qatar was the revisionist actor, disproving the "saturated status quo power" explanation discussed as an alternative that explains the peace among monarchies.
14 The ambiguous British position can be explained by the split between the officials in Cairo clearly preferring the "less-fanatic" Hashemites over the Saudis and trying to safeguard their role in the Arab revolt and the India Office officials who were reluctant to support the revolt because of its revolutionary character (Kostiner 1995, 55).
15 Religious sensitivities of the Najdi *ulama'* also played a role in delaying the transformation of Ibn Saud's realm into a kingdom (cf. Al-Rasheed 2010, 61). The fact that he did not attempt to repeat Sharif Hussein's mistake by claiming the title of caliph for himself indicates that it was about status and competition with the Hashemites, not about hegemony or supremacy per se.
16 Although its adherents regard the term as pejorative, "Wahhabi" is used here as a neutral description, conforming to its usual usage in Western literature.
17 The memoirs were written with a political agenda in mind and should therefore be taken with a grain of salt. However, Abdallah had no qualms with voicing open and public opposition and hostility to Ibn Saud before, making even purely rhetorical deviations indications of a rapprochement.
18 The most confrontational action taken during the dispute was "show of force", stage 7 out of 21 possible escalation levels (Ghosn, Palmer, and Bremer 2004).
19 After King Saud excused this decision with a supposed final government decision in a personal phone call to the fellow Jordanian monarch, the latter quipped the following to his chief of Diwan: "This is probably the first time in history that any government has ever taken any decision in Saudi Arabia, or for that matter, even met!" (H. King of Jordan 1962, 204)

References

'Abd al-Hakim al-Wa'ili. 2002a. "'anaza." *Mawsu'a qaba'il al-'arab* 4.
———. 2002b. "'utub." *Mawsu'a qaba'il al-'arab* 3.
Al-Arayed, Jawad Salim. 2003. *A Line in the Sea: The Qatar v. Bahrain Border Dispute in the World Court*. Berkeley, CA: North Atlantic Books.
Alkim, Hassan Hamdan al-. 1989. *The Foreign Policy of the United Arab Emirates*. London: Saqi.
Allison, William Thomas. 2012. *The Gulf War, 1990–91*. Basingstoke, Hampshire [England]; New York: Palgrave Macmillan.
Al-Musfir, Muhammed Saleh. 2001. "The GCC States: Internal Dynamics and Foreign Policies." In *Iran, Iraq and the Arab Gulf States*, ed. Joseph A. Kechichian. New York: Palgrave, 313–24.

Al-Rasheed, Madawi. 2001. "Saudi Arabia and the 1948 Palestine War: Beyond Official History." In *The War for Palestine: Rewriting the History of 1948*, eds. Eugene L. Rogan and Avi Shlaim. Cambridge: Cambridge University Press, 228–47.

———. 2010. *A History of Saudi Arabia.* 2nd edition. Cambridge: Cambridge University Press.

AlShehabi, Omar Hesham. 2017. "Contested Modernity: Divided Rule and the Birth of Sectarianism, Nationalism, and Absolutism in Bahrain." *British Journal of Middle Eastern Studies* 44(3): 333–55.

Alter, Karen J. 2014. *The New Terrain of International Law.* Princeton University Press. http://faculty.wcas.northwestern.edu/~kal438/NewTerrainFromDepot/docs/Bahrain-vQatarTerritorialDispute.pdf (February 23, 2017).

Assiri, Abdul-Reda. 1990. *Kuwait's Foreign Policy. City-State in World Politics.* Boulder; London: Westview Press.

Ayubi, Nazih N. 1995. *Over-Stating the Arab State: Politics and Society in the Middle East.* London: I.B. Tauris.

"Bahrain: Further Reportage, Comment on Dispute with Qatar." 1986. *al-Watan.*

Bahry, Louay. 1999. "Elections in Qatar: A Window of Democracy Opens in the Gulf." *Middle East Policy* 6(4): 118–27.

Barany, Zoltan. 2013. "Unrest and State Response in Arab Monarchies." *Mediterranean Quarterly* 24(2): 5–38.

Barnett, Michael, and F. Gregory Gause III. 1998. "Caravans in Opposite Directions: Society, State, and the Development of Community in the Gulf Cooperation Council." In *Security Communities*, eds. Emanuel Adler and Michael Barnett. Cambridge: Cambridge University Press, 161–97.

Batty, David. 2011. "Worries About Sandhurst Links After Bahrain Protest Crackdown." *The Guardian.* www.theguardian.com/world/2011/feb/18/sandhurst-bahrain-protest (February 21, 2017).

Belgrave, Charles. 1972. *Personal Column.* 2nd edition. Beirut, Lebanon: Librairie du Liban.

Boghardt, L.P. 2006. *Kuwait Amid War, Peace and Revolution.* New York: Palgrave Macmillan.

Cable: Qatar-Bahrain Median Line. 1976. Bahrain Manama: US Embassy Manama Bahrain. Wikileaks Public Library of US Diplomacy. https://wikileaks.org/plusd/cables/1976MANAMA00444_b.html (February 19, 2017).

Cable: Qatar-Bahrain Relations: Hwar Island Dispute. 1976. Qatar Doha. Wikileaks Public Library of US Diplomacy. https://wikileaks.org/plusd/cables/1976DOHA00401_b.html (February 22, 2017).

Cable: Qatari Police Chief on Qatar Police. 1978. Qatar Doha: US Embassy Doha Qatar. Wikileaks Public Library of US Diplomacy. https://wikileaks.org/plusd/cables/1978DOHA00988_d.html (February 19, 2017).

Calvert, Peter, and Antony Alcock, eds. 2004. *Border and Territorial Disputes of the World.* 4th edition. London: John Harper.

Çetinoğlu, Nur. 2010. "The Gulf Cooperation Council (GCC) After US Led Invasion of Iraq: Toward a Security Community." *Review of International Law and Politics* 6(24): 91–114.

Chubin, Shahram, and Charles Tripp. 2014. *Iran-Saudi Arabia Relations and Regional Order.* London; New York: Routledge.

Commins, David Dean. 2012. *The Gulf States: A Modern History.* London: Tauris.

"Consultations in Progress on Meeting of Tripartite Committee." 1986. *Gulf States Newsletter* 293: 4.

148 *When monarchies collide*

Cooke, Miriam. 2014. *Tribal Modern: Branding New Nations in the Arab Gulf*. Berkeley: University of California Press.

Cordesman, Anthony H. 1997. *Bahrain, Oman, Qatar, and the UAE: Challenges of Security*. Boulder, CO: Westview Press.

Crystal, Jill. 1990. *Oil and Politics in the Gulf: Rulers and Merchants in Kuwait and Qatar*. Cambridge: Cambridge University Press.

Diwan, Kristin Smith. 2016. "National Identity and National Projects in the Arab Gulf States." *Arab Gulf States Institute in Washington*. www.agsiw.org/national-identity-and-national-projects-in-the-arab-gulf-states/ (June 16, 2016).

Erskine-Loftus, Pamela, Mariam Ibrahim Al-Mulla, and Victoria Hightower. 2016. *Representing the Nation: Heritage, Museums, National Narratives, and Identity in the Arab Gulf States*. London; New York: Routledge.

Foley, Sean. 1999. "The UAE: Political Issues and Security Dilemmas." *Middle East Review of International Affairs* 3(1).

Fromherz, Allen J. 2012. *Qatar: A Modern History*. London: Tauris.

Gelber, Yoav. 2004. *Israeli-Jordanian Dialogue, 1948–1953: Cooperation, Conspiracy, or Collusion?* Brighton Portland: Sussex Academic Press.

Ghosn, Faten, Glenn Palmer, and Stuart Bremer. 2004. "The MID3 Data Set, 1993–2001: Procedures, Coding Rules, and Description." *Conflict Management and Peace Science* 21: 133–54.

Heard-Bey, Frauke. 2006. "Conflict Resolution and Regional Co-Operation: The Role of the Gulf Co-Operation Council 1970–2002." *Middle Eastern Studies* 42(2): 199–222.

Hurewitz, J.C., Council on Foreign Relations. 1969. *Middle East Politics: The Military Dimension*. Westport: Frederick A. Praeger.

Hussain, Thomas. 1996a. "Bahrain Charges 2 with Spying for Qatar." *UPI*. www.upi.com/Archives/1996/12/02/Bahrain-charges-2-with-spying-for-Qatar/3814849502800/ (February 23, 2017).

———. 1996b. "Dispute Overshadows Gulf Arabs Meeting." *UPI*. www.upi.com/Archives/1996/12/07/Dispute-overshadows-Gulf-Arabs-meeting/2182849934800/ (February 23, 2017).

"'Isolated Incident' Occurs Between Bahrain, Qatar." 1986. *KUNA*.

Joyce, Miriam. 1998. *Kuwait, 1945–1996: An Anglo-American Perspective*. London; Portland, OR: Frank Cass.

Kamrava, Mehran. 2009. "Royal Factionalism and Political Liberalization in Qatar." *The Middle East Journal* 63(3): 401–20.

Kechichian, Joseph A. 2001. "Unity on the Arabian Peninsula." In *Iran, Iraq and the Arab Gulf States*, ed. Joseph A. Kechichian. New York: Palgrave, 281–302.

Kerr, Malcolm H. 1971. *The Arab Cold War. Gamal 'Abd al-Nasir and His Rivals, 1958–1970*. 3rd edition. London: Oxford University Press.

Khalaf, Abd al-Hadi. 1987. "The Elusive Quest for Gulf Security." *MERIP Reports* 148(17). www.merip.org/mer/mer148/elusive-quest-gulf-security?ip_login_no_cache=373d5fd0abcead5f1e000abe64d5dbe3 (December 26, 2016).

King of Jordan, Abdallah I. 1950. *Memoirs of King Abdullah of Transjordan*. ed. Philip Graves. London: Jonathan Cape.

———. 1951. *Al-takmilah min mudhakkirat hadrat sahib al-jalalah al-hashimiyyah al-malik Abdallah bin Husayn*. Jerusalem: Matba'ah tijariyyah.

———. 1954. *My Memoirs Completed (al-Takmilah)*. Washington: American Council of Learned Societies.

King of Jordan, Abdallah II. 2011. *Our Last Best Chance: The Pursuit of Peace in a Time of Peril*. New York: Viking.

King of Jordan, Hussein. 1962. *Uneasy Lies the Head: The Autobiography of His Majesty King Hussein I of the Hashemite Kingdom of Jordan*. First Printing edition. New York: Bernard Geis Associates.

Kostiner, Joseph. 1995. "Prologue of Hashemite Downfall and Saudi Ascendancy: A New Look at the Khurma Dispute, 1917–1919." In *The Hashemites in the Modern Arab World: Essays in Honour of the Late Professor Uriel Dann*, eds. Asher Susser, Aryeh Shmuelevitz, and Uriel Dann. London: Frank Cass & Co. Ltd., 47–64.

———. 2009. *Conflict and Cooperation in the Gulf Region*. Wiesbaden: VS Verlag für Sozialwissenschaften. http://site.ebrary.com/id/10274811.

Krauss, Clifford. 2011. "Editor of Independent Bahrain Newspaper Silenced." *The New York Times*. www.nytimes.com/2011/04/09/world/middleeast/09bahrain.html (February 23, 2017).

Lafraie, Najibullah. 2009. *Revolutionary Ideology and Islamic Militancy: The Iranian Revolution and Interpretations of the Quran*. London: I.B. Tauris.

Lawson, Fred Haley. 1989. *Bahrain: The Modernization of Autocracy*. Boulder: Westview Press.

Lewis, Bernard. 2000. "Monarchy in the Middle East." In *Middle East Monarchies. The Challenge of Modernity*, ed. Joseph Kostiner. Boulder, CO: Lynne Rienner Publishers, 15–22.

Lotfian, Saideh. 2002. "A Regional Security System in the Persian Gulf." In *Security in the Persian Gulf*, eds. Lawrence G. Potter and Gary G. Sick. London: Palgrave Macmillan US, 109–34.

Maddy-Weitzman, Bruce. 1990. "Jordan and Iraq: Efforts at Intra-Hashimite Unity." *Middle Eastern Studies* 26(1): 65–75.

———, ed. 1999. *Middle East Contemporary Survey*. Tel Aviv: The Moshe Dayan Center.

Martin, Lenore G. 1984. *The Unstable Gulf: Threats from Within*. Lexington, MA: Lexington Books.

Milton-Edwards, Beverley, and Peter Hinchcliffe. 2009. *Jordan. A Hashemite Legacy*. 2nd edition. London; New York: Routledge.

Partrick, Neil. 2011. *The GCC: Gulf State Integration or Leadership Cooperation?* LSE. http://eprints.lse.ac.uk/55660/ (September 27, 2016).

———. 2013. "Saudi Arabia and Jordan: Friends in Adversity." http://eprints.lse.ac.uk/55661/ (November 17, 2016).

Patai, Raphael. 2015. *Kingdom of Jordan*. Princeton: Princeton University Press.

Peterson, J.E. 2011. "Sovereignty and Boundaries in the Gulf States. Settling the Peripheries." In *International Politics of the Persian Gulf*, ed. Mehran Kamrava. Syracuse: Syracuse University Press, 21–49.

Philby, Harry Saint John Bridger. 1955. *Sa'udi Arabia*. London: Ernest Benn.

Pipes, Daniel. 1996. "Interview with Hamad Bin Jasim Bin Jabr Al-Thani." *Middle East Quarterly* 3(4): 71–8.

Podeh, Elie. 1995. "Ending an Age-Old Rivalry: The Rapprochement Between the Hashemites and the Saudis, 1956–1958." In *The Hashemites in the Modern Arab World: Essays in Honour of the Late Professor Uriel Dann*, eds. Asher Susser, Aryeh Shmuelevitz, and Uriel Dann. London: Frank Cass & Co. Ltd., 85–110.

Rugh, Andrea B. 2007. *The Political Culture of Leadership in the United Arab Emirates*. New York: Palgrave Macmillan.

150 *When monarchies collide*

Sadik, Muhammad, and William Snavely. 1972. *Bahrain, Qatar, and the United Arab Emirates: Colonial Past, Present Problems, and Future Prospects*. Lexington, MA: Heath.

Salama, Samir. 2014. "Qatar's History of Turbulent Relations with UAE." *GulfNews*. http://gulfnews.com/news/uae/government/qatar-s-history-of-turbulent-relations-with-uae-1.1312739 (February 19, 2017).

"Saudi and Qatar End 35-Year Border Dispute, Sign Accord." 2001. *Al Bawaba*. www.albawaba.com/news/saudi-and-qatar-end-35-year-border-dispute-sign-accord (February 14, 2017).

Schofield. 2001. "Down to the Usual Suspects: Border and Territorial Disputes in the Arabian Peninsula and Persian Gulf at the Millenium." In *Iran, Iraq and the Arab Gulf States*, ed. Joseph A. Kechichian. New York: Palgrave, 213–36.

Seale, Patrick. 1965. *The Struggle for Syria: A Study of Post-War Arab Politics 1945–1958*. 2nd edition. London: Oxford University Press.

Shlaim, Avi. 2009. *Lion of Jordan: The Life of King Hussein in War and Peace*. New York: Vintage.

Simon, Reeva S. 1974. "The Hashemite 'Conspiracy': Hashemite Unity Attempts, 1921–1958." *International Journal of Middle East Studies* 5(3): 314–27.

Teitelbaum, Joshua. 1995. "Pilgrimage Politics: The Hajj and Saudi-Hashemite Rivalry, 1916–1925." In *The Hashemites in the Modern Arab World: Essays in Honour of the Late Professor Uriel Dann*, eds. Asher Susser, Aryeh Shmuelevitz, and Uriel Dann. London: Frank Cass & Co. Ltd., 65–84.

———. 1999a. "Bahrain." In *Middle East Contemporary Survey*, ed. Bruce Maddy-Weitzman. Tel Aviv: The Moshe Dayan Center, 294–300.

———. 1999b. "Qatar." In *Middle East Contemporary Survey*, ed. Bruce Maddy-Weitzman. Tel Aviv: The Moshe Dayan Center, 600–8.

———. 2001a. "Bahrain." In *Middle East Contemporary Survey*, ed. Bruce Maddy-Weitzman. Tel Aviv: The Moshe Dayan Center, 192–200.

———. 2001b. "Qatar." In *Middle East Contemporary Survey*, ed. Bruce Maddy-Weitzman. Tel Aviv: The Moshe Dayan Center, 497–506.

———. 2001c. *The Rise and Fall of the Hashimite Kingdom of Arabia*. London: Hurst.

Toumi, Habib. 2010. "Bahrain Calls for the Repatriation of 107 Fishermen Held by Qatar." *GulfNews*. http://gulfnews.com/news/gulf/bahrain/bahrain-calls-for-the-repatriation-of-107-fishermen-held-by-qatar-1.631059 (February 23, 2017).

Tripp, Charles. 2001. "Iraq and the 1948 War: Mirror of Iraq's Disorder." In *The War for Palestine: Rewriting the History of 1948*, eds. Eugene L. Rogan and Avi Shlaim. Cambridge: Cambridge University Press, 125–49.

Ulrichsen, Kristian Coates. 2014. "Qatar and the Arab Spring: Policy Drivers and Regional Implications." *Carnegie Endowment for International Peace*. http://carnegieendowment.org/2014/09/24/qatar-and-arab-spring-policy-drivers-and-regional-implications (January 19, 2015).

Walt, Stephen M. 1985. "Alliance Formation and the Balance of World Power." *International security* 9(4): 3–43.

———. 1990. *The Origins of Alliances*. Ithaca: Cornell University Press.

Watt, Nicholas. 2016. "'Sandhurst Sheikhs': Calls to Stop Training Cadets from Gulf States with Bad Rights Records." *The Guardian*. www.theguardian.com/uk-news/2016/jan/22/sandhurst-sheikhs-calls-to-stop-training-cadets-from-gulf-states-with-bad-rights-records (February 21, 2017).

Weinberger, Naomi Joy. 1986. *Syrian Intervention in Lebanon: The 1975–76 Civil War*. New York: Oxford University Press.

Wiegand, Krista E. 2012. "Bahrain, Qatar, and the Hawar Islands: Resolution of a Gulf Territorial Dispute." *The Middle East Journal* 66(1): 78–95.

Wright, Steven. 2012. "Foreign Policies with International Reach: The Case of Qatar." In *The Transformation of the Gulf: Politics, Economics and the Global Order*, eds. David Held and Kristian Ulrichsen. New York: Routledge, 1–25.

Young, Colin. 1997. "Bahrain–Qatar Relations at Lowest Ebb." *The UK Defence Forum. Grey Papers*. www.ukdf.org.uk/assets/downloads/rs13.htm (February 19, 2017).

Zahlan, Rosemarie Said. 2002. *The Making of Modern Gulf States: Kuwait Bahrain Qatar, The United Arab Emirates and Oman*. Reading: Ithaca Press.

5 From monarchy to republic – from peace to war?

"Quasi-experiments" of collapsed monarchic couples

The case studies presented so far in this book do not reject the possibility that monarchies might have special characteristics that make them amenable to de-escalation, which has nothing to with whether they face monarchies or republics. To make sure, we need to compare two mostly identical cases differing only regarding *joint* monarchy. In contrast to scientists and engineers, social scientists are not able to conduct large-scale controlled experiments inside a lab. The closest approximation, however, would be a "quasi-experiment" that aims to keep other variables as constant as possible while changing only one – in this case, the monarchic political system. The following two case studies investigate pairs of monarchies where one experiences revolution that changes the political system while other factors (size, capabilities, geostrategic location, oil revenues, etc.) stay mostly the same. In reality, of course, a revolution or coup results in the change of other parameters as well. However, by identifying the continuities and changes, we can try to distill the effect of joint monarchism through third factors as clearly as possible.

The following two cases cover different countries and combinations of countries with vastly different trajectories. In both cases, interstate conflicts did not just arise after revolutions but were present and salient in jointly monarchic periods as well. Still, following the regime changes, their bilateral relationship became significantly more antagonistic, in the case of Iraq and Kuwait even leading to war.

5.1 Iraq and Kuwait: from "sister people" to the conquest of the "19th province"

The relationship of Iraq and Kuwait is an ambivalent one with many ups and downs. The territorial dispute between them goes back to a claim based on the boundaries of the Ottoman Empire and has been raised since the beginning of the statehood of Iraq and later Kuwait. In 1958, Iraq changed its political system to a republic after the overthrow of the Hashemite monarchy. While the Iraqi monarchy never attempted to take the territory by force, republican Iraq tried so twice, in 1961 and in 1990.

There are caveats to the conclusions to be drawn from the case, particular connected to Kuwait's relatively late formation and independence. The context

From monarchy to republic   153

in the two time periods to be compared is not exactly the same, because Kuwait was not yet independent at the period of the Iraqi Hashemite monarchy. Also, since state building there was a more recent process than it was in Iraq, its nation-state character was not consolidated during the monarchic period. We have established independence (and state consolidation) as a scope condition, implying that the theorized effect is less likely to be observed without it. Yet we do observe a clear effect consistent with the theory that might even strengthen the theory, given that it seems to work even in less-than-ideal circumstances. If Kuwait had become independent and had been more consolidated as a state while the Iraqi monarchy was still intact, the effect might have been even stronger.

Peace among kings (1945–1956): royal brothers and royal borders under British influence

Kuwait had been a British "protected state" since 1899. Kuwait's autonomy and especially the demarcation of its borders and its identity as a separate state are quite recent in that tribal (semi-)nomadic lifestyle was the rule rather than the exception until well into the 20th century. The first delineation of its borders was conducted in the Anglo-Ottoman Convention signed on July 29, 1913, but never ratified (Khadduri and Ghareeb 2001, 14). Saudi-Iraqi and Saudi-Kuwaiti borders were drawn at a conference in 'Uqayr in Saudi Arabia in November 1922, attended by a Saudi, Iraqi, and Kuwaiti delegation (the last one represented by a British agent). Two-thirds of, at the time, Kuwaiti territory was reassigned to Ibn Saud; the borders were drawn onto a map with a red pencil (Khadduri and Ghareeb 2001, 27–28; Zahlan 2002, 24–25).

Iraq became a Hashemite monarchy in 1921 under Faisal, but it continued to be under British protection as a Mandate (decided in April 1920 at the San Remo Conference) until 1932, when it declared independence. Notwithstanding, British influence remained crucial until the end of the monarchy, in 1958. Iraq reconfirmed the border with Kuwait for the third time (after 1913 and 1923), and it was informally delineated (but not demarcated) by Britain in 1932. However, as there was no formal agreement, claims to Kuwaiti sovereignty or territory were raised often over the decades. The main issues of contention between the two countries were territorial – the establishment of an Iraqi port aside from Basra and claim to the islands of Warba and Bubiyan – but also disputes over water and ownership of date gardens (Joyce 1998, 94).

Structural similarities

Especially at the beginning of bilateral relations, the two countries were highly dissimilar in institutional framework, political culture, and historical trajectory. The Iraqi monarchy covered a large territory and population, and its state institutions were comparably consolidated. Its system was, like the Egyptian, "of a more modern type, whose leaders tried to assimilate not just the royal title but also some

154 *From monarchy to republic*

of the other institutions of the European example", i.e. constitutionalism and parliamentarianism (Ayalon 2000, 24).

Kuwait, on the other hand, was a traditional dynastic shaikhdom and practically a city-state where the family (the Al Sabah) remains the ruling institution that practically monopolizes the state apparatus to this day – although since 1963 it has also had a parliament, the National Assembly, the most active and powerful legislative in the Gulf (Herb 1999, 2002, 41–45).

This uneven state development influenced not only Iraq's feelings of superiority but also the Kuwaiti self-image. Before the advent of oil, the Kuwaiti populace was not disinclined to unify with Iraq. Kuwaiti merchants visiting Iraq frequently saw its oil-financed social and economic development as a role model for the nepotistic shaikhdom then ruled by Ahmad Al Sabah (Khadduri and Ghareeb 2001, 5, 34–36).

Nonetheless, both shared cultural and cross-border tribal and family ties and both dynasties were Arab and Sunni Muslim ruling over a more heterogeneous population in terms of ethnicity and religious composition (more so in Iraq than in Kuwait). Both were also oil-exporting rentier states, though Kuwait was wealthier due to its smaller population but for the same reason also significantly weaker militarily. They also shared historically close ties with the British, who had a profound influence on the creation and development of the political entities and their ruling families (cf. Sunik 2015).

Salience: constraints and catalysts for ingroup identification

The salience of monarchy started to grow in the 1950s, mostly due to the rising republican threat. In the 1950s, the monarchies still constituted the majority of all states in the Middle East. At this time, monarchy was still the "default" category and therefore not a distinguishing feature of the states in the region.

Especially since the Egyptian Revolution in 1952, radical republicanism was identified as a common threat to monarchies (a fear proven true by the Iraqi Revolution in 1958). As it was still early in the period of the Arab Cold War when that dynamic became most pronounced, the common threat did not always come to the fore. After Nuri al-Sa'id's visit to Kuwait in June 1958, just three weeks before the revolution that toppled the Iraqi monarchy, the British Foreign Office dispatched a note to the shaikh of Kuwait warning that the "spread of radical republican nationalism will engulf *hereditary regimes one after the other*. Whether the ruler likes it or not, the fact is that if Nasir [*sic*] triumphs it will be the *end of the ruling family* of Kuwait" (Khadduri and Ghareeb 2001, 61, original emphasis). The phrasing of the latter sentence ("whether he likes it or not") also shows that the Kuwaiti ruler did not always perceive the threat clearly. While the shaikh shared most concerns of the British and other Middle Eastern monarchs, he also allowed civil society more room to maneuver than many of his monarchic neighbors did, in part because of concerns for domestic stability. A confidential report from the Political Agency in Kuwait of January 9, 1957, speaks of a "noticeably greater anti-British and pro-Egyptian feeling in Kuwait than in Iraq and Lebanon" (cited in: Assiri

From monarchy to republic   155

1990, 8). Despite the perpetuation of territorial claims, there was no explicit hierarchic ideology that could have divided the countries or monarchies in general.

The only exception is found beyond the analyzed time period, under the rule of King Ghazi in the 1930s. Ghazi was a fervent proponent of pan-Arabism who succeeded his father Faisal to the throne at the age of 21. He adhered to the aim of Arab unity consisting of the "unification" or incorporation of countries – via military force, if need be. Because this presupposes Iraqi leadership as the incorporating entity, it hinders the formation of an ingroup identity, even though both regimes were monarchic. Notably, King Ghazi's rule was also the period of greatest tensions between the two countries (cf. Finnie 1992, 110–113; Khadduri and Ghareeb 2001, 40–45). This once again proves that it is not monarchy per se but rather joint identification as equals that fosters peaceful intergroup behavior.

Social processes of ingroup identification

When Kuwait became independent in 1961, the Iraqi monarchy had already vanished, and full formal diplomatic recognition could thus not be established. Nonetheless, political and cultural relations between the two countries existed early on.

There was, however, some question on the mutual recognition and acceptance as equals as especially the Kuwaiti state and nation had only just started developing before World War II, which was compounded by Kuwait's non-independence. Given the brevity of the states' existence, the artificiality of the recently formed state institutions and the dependence as a British protected state of Kuwait, it was no surprise that Iraqi rulers looked down on its small neighbor.[1] The novelty of Kuwait was not just a matter of *alter* perception as the emirate had not even developed its own national identity yet. The legitimation of the Al Sabah depended largely on their coalition with the merchant class and not on any "traditional" authority.

However, the situation was slowly changing, helped along by British preference for the establishment of monarchic systems "in its image" in the region. The first steps to the elevation of the status of the Kuwaiti ruler consisted in promoting the shaikh from "His Excellency" to "His Highness" in 1937. British alliance with the Al Sabah, to the exclusion of all other societal groups, made the Al Sabah "more royal" than their predecessors, who were *primi inter pares* rather than monarchs (Finnie 1992, 89, 95). It was still a long way to matching "His Majesty", the king of Iraq.

The slow growth of acceptance of Kuwait as an independent entity was matched by the intensification of personal relations. Formal visits were infrequent before the 1950s, but they intensified in that period.[2] Personalized links via shared socialization also increased due to the shared British connection. In 1952, Shaikh Abdallah al-Salim Al Sabah (Abdallah III), who had taken over from his cousin Ahmad in 1950, became the first Kuwaiti ruler to visit Iraq, after Nuri al-Said had visited Kuwait the year before. A second visit followed in 1956 (Joyce 1998, 99). These visits contributed to the normalization of relations and the reification of joint recognition as separate and equal entities.

156 *From monarchy to republic*

The British monarchic connection was also important for the ties and socialization that it provided, because many among the royals in the protected territories and the mandates went to Britain for their education and visited Harrow School (like Iraqi King Faisal II) (Seale 1965, 228) or the Royal Military Academy of Sandhurst (like Fahad al-Ahmad Al Sabah, the brother of future Kuwaiti Emir Jabir al-Ahmad Al Sabah, who died in the Gulf War) (Batty 2011; Teller 2014).

In the early phase of state building in Kuwait before the Second World War, the identification as family existed mostly on the level of the populace, not the rulers (this as well was especially pronounced in the period of King Ghazi, who sympathized with the opposition more than with the regime): the family reference was reserved for the "sister *people* of Kuwait" instead of the brotherly shaikh or his allies (cited in Khadduri and Ghareeb 2001, 37), as we have seen was the case for Bahrain and Qatar. This slowly changed by the 1950s, when an ingroup developed on the regime level that was strengthened by both sides.

Over time, the relationship transformed. Ceremonies served to enhance the self-identification as royals and the state as a monarchy, especially in Kuwait. This would later form the basis for ingroup identification between the two monarchies. A letter from the British ambassador to the residency in Bahrain in February 1960 describes Shaikh Abdallah Salim's impressions of the British monarchy, conveying both the self-identification as a monarch (and not a tribal shaikh) even before independence and the strong link between monarchism and regime stability:

> I shall not forget his almost ecstatic descriptions of the scene he had witnessed in Westminster Abbey as we drove back from the Coronation in 1953 and his exclamations of wonder at the manifest affection felt for Her Majesty by the huge crowds on that pouring wet afternoon. The words he chose with which to greet The Queen at the State Banquet which he attended were "I congratulate Your Majesty on the love of your people" and *as a monarch* he would dearly love to discover the secret of the stability of the British throne.
>
> (cited in: Joyce 1998, 71, emphasis added)

Foreign policy restraint

There were no military confrontations in the monarchic period. The only episode of acute hostility that might have resulted in military action is during the reign of King Ghazi before World War II. Ghazi's reign was seen as an aberration by contemporary observers and historians. The king did not see the Al Sabah as his equivalent counterparts and did not deeply identify with monarchism, instead propagating pan-Arabist ideology. There was thus no ingroup identification, although other Iraqi regime members acknowledged the monarchic character of Kuwait and its value as an ally and thus tried to prevent confrontation. Like in the case of Bahrain and Qatar, this shows the complicated relationship of regime and individual ruler-level identification.

In the late 1930s, tensions inside Kuwait and rising ideological calls for Arab unity led to an acute crisis that pitted King Ghazi against Shaikh Ahmad of Kuwait

From monarchy to republic   157

and even against his own members of government. Despite the joint efforts of Iraqi prime ministers Jamil al-Midfa'i and Nuri al-Said to stop it, King Ghazi continued to disseminate propaganda against Shaikh Ahmad via his own radio station. The Kuwaiti opposition grew increasingly vocal and even openly called for the overthrow of the regime, requesting Iraqi annexation, and Ghazi chimed in. At some point, the king responded to the demands by promising the Kuwaiti merchants to intervene militarily. Although the opposition could be silenced, the idea of unity with Iraq remained throughout the 1930s and 1940s (Khadduri and Ghareeb 2001, 37–41). He amassed troops on the shared border but stopped short of using them (Musallam 1996, 90).

Naji Shawkat, minister of interior and acting prime minister in Nuri al-Said's absence, relates the séance with King Ghazi on February 19, 1939, in his memoirs. When the king asks him what he had done "about the occupation of Kuwait", Shawkat advises the young king to refrain from such action and reminds him of what Britain, Iran, and Saudi Arabia would think of such behavior. He asked whether the king would be "prepared to go to war against three states at the same time".[3] Following this exchange, Ghazi relented and decided to wait for Nuri's return. When asked about Iraqi plans by the British ambassador, Shawkat felt confident enough to state that "nothing of this sort [the occupation of Kuwait] will ever happen" (Khadduri and Ghareeb 2001, 41–42).

Although deterrence by British reaction and the authority of more-senior members of state and government rather than monarchic solidarity have dissuaded Ghazi from putting his fiery radio rhetoric into action, it was unclear whether Ghazi's intention to annex Kuwait was genuine. Of a meeting with King Ghazi on March 8, 1939, British Ambassador Peterson reported to London, "His Majesty's rather incoherent explanations were to the effect that he had no intention of attacking Koweit [sic], but wished only to egg on its ruler to concede liberal institutions" (cited in: Finnie 1992, 110). Gerald de Gaury, the political agent in Kuwait, later described Ghazi's propaganda against the Kuwaiti regime as exhibiting "bizarre irregularities of behavior" (Finnie 1992, 112). Ultimately, military action against a country protected by the British was an impossibility for Iraq, despite its ruler's beliefs. At that time, however, the perception of the Iraqi ruler toward the Al Sabah, influenced by pan-Arabist ideology instead of by monarchic socialization, was far from equality.

The king was seen as an embarrassment and a loose cannon by the British as well as the Iraqi royal family and state apparatus. Neither his successors nor his father Faisal I shared his ideological inklings and disregard toward the legitimacy of the Kuwaiti rulers (cf. Finnie 1992, 106–113). Other members of the ruling family, such as Taha al-Hashemi, the defense minister, harbored no intentions of military incorporation of Kuwait and were sidelined by Ghazi in order to avoid interference (cf. Khadduri and Ghareeb 2001, 41).

Nuri al-Said, along with the British, saw Ghazi as unfit for the royal position anyway, and the king's obsession over Kuwait has been described as "the most crucial part in his failure to cope with his royal responsibilities" (Finnie 1992, 113). At the time, the development of a joint monarchic ingroup between

158 *From monarchy to republic*

the Kuwaiti and Iraqi ruling elites were hampered by Kuwait's lack of sovereignty and Ghazi's personality. While Prime Minister Nuri al-Sa'id and the British were discussing possible candidates for King Ghazi's replacements as he became increasingly untenable, he died in a car crash in 1939 at the age of 27. His cousin Abd al-Ilah succeeded him as regent until his son Faisal II came of age in 1953 (Khadduri and Ghareeb 2001, 45–53).

Although claims to Kuwaiti territory and frontier renegotiations did not disappear, there were no more calls for annexation or incorporation. Military means were taken off the table. Infrequent minor clashes serve as proof of a different behavior by Iraq under Abd al-Ilah and, later, Faisal II (Joyce 1998, 96).[4]

The 1940s and 1950s were also not characterized by delegitimization or subversion attempts of the monarchy or the ruling families. In fact, the border conflict was of so little consequence to Iraqi politics under the Hashemites that one of the staples on Iraqi history before the revolution, "Independent Iraq. 1932–1958" by Majid Khadduri, mentions Kuwait only once – when discussing King Ghazi's legacy (1960, 141).

Although monarchic Iraq did not attempt to occupy Kuwait before or after Ghazi, it was not out of general monarchic pacifism. During the height of inter-Arab conflict in 1958, the Iraqi government considered invading Syria to prevent Egyptian takeover but failed to secure Western backing for it. The military restraint did apparently not apply to all states equally; instead, it exposed a monarchic preference that even led to monarchic solidarity. When Qasim's revolutionary officers took control of Baghdad and launched their coup d'état, they were supposed to be on their way to Jordan, acting on the Iraqi government's orders to buttress the Jordanians against the immediate threat by the United Arab Republic (UAR) (Eppel 2004, 146–147).

At the height of the Arab Cold War in the 1950s, Kuwait and Iraq moved closer together, as did the rest of the monarchies. There were attempts at formalizing their alliance, although they did not come to fruition before the fall of the Hashemite monarchy in Iraq. Demarcation negotiations dragged on until a British-sponsored draft agreement was almost agreed on in 1955. The nationalization of the Suez channel and the strong pan-Arab current sweeping the region led to the establishment of the UAR in 1958. Jordan and Iraq, reacting to the threat of militant pan-Arabism, formed the Arab Federal Union (AFU, see Chapter 4, especially section 4.2) to which they also invited Kuwait, which they perceived as sharing the Hashemites' pro-Western outlook (Khadduri and Ghareeb 2001, 48–54).

Shaikh Abdallah III was ceremonially invited to Baghdad to participate in a dinner with the two Hashemite kings. Kuwait was hesitant to join, and British reaction was disapproving because Kuwait was not yet fully independent. Earlier, Nuri al-Said had also unsuccessfully tried to integrate Kuwait into the ill-fated Baghdad Pact (Finnie 1992, 123–124).

Despite all obstacles, an ingroup that did not exist before was about to be constituted. Suwaidi, who was now the foreign minister of the AFU, drafted a memorandum for the British stating that should Kuwait choose not to join the AFU, the

From monarchy to republic   159

question of territory would be solved by a treaty of friendship and *bon voisinage*, a stark contrast to calls for military annexation in other periods and an indication of respect for Kuwaiti sovereignty (Khadduri and Ghareeb 2001, 60). After, Nuri al-Sa'id also promised to guarantee Kuwaiti territorial integrity in May if Kuwait joined (Joyce 1998, 100). Abdallah decided against joining any of the unions, instead choosing neutrality. The July revolution shook him profoundly, and his policy was abandoned by late 1960 (Assiri 1990, 8–9; Joyce 1998, 100).

Although the July revolution was one of the clearest instances of monarchic solidarity, the AFU lacked the capability to shield the monarchs against revolution and was quickly dismantled by the new republican regime. The revolution, as Khadduri and Ghareeb lament, "had virtually deprived Iraq of perhaps the most prospective attempt to settle peacefully the longstanding disputes between Iraq and Kuwait" (2001, 62).

Ingroup identification in the monarchic period

Although many differences and a slow pace of state building set the two monarchies of Iraq and Kuwait apart, they slowly developed an ingroup identity based on structural similarities and a shared threat by radical republicanism, especially from Egyptian and Syrian-led Arab nationalist movements.

Although Kuwait was not yet formally independent, it came to be accepted as a partner instead of as a subject or a subordinate by Iraq, as shown by frequent official visits and attempts to forge formal alliances and common socialization frequently through the British connection. This led to their mutual reliance on diplomacy and friendly ties, refraining from military action.

The only exception to the generally friendly relations was the period of King Ghazi's rule in Iraq. This period might best be characterized as a short-lived aberration under an exceptionally ideological ruler, regarded as "unfit" for the throne and its responsibilities by contemporary Arab elites and the British alike. This exception to the rule provides an important qualification for the causal model: monarchic institutions are not sufficient for the establishment of a monarchic ingroup identity. Instead, this identification relies on a multidimensional similarity as *perceived* by the ruler himself and other political elites.

When revolution leads to war (1958–1991): monarchic solidarity in the gulf war

Along with Iraq's institutions and regime, its approach to Kuwait also changed dramatically after the revolution. In sharp contrast to the monarchic period, invasion and occupation attempts (and actual invasion and occupation) were made under at least two different rulers, with a delegitimizing policy toward the Al Sabah as a continuity among the often-changing regimes and rulers of republican Iraq. While King Ghazi's period might be seen as an exception, the anti-Sabah continuity in the republican period must be seen rather as the rule, belying a depiction as a mere "Saddam effect".

160 *From monarchy to republic*

After coming to power in 1958, Brigadier General Abd al-Karim Qasim attempted to reverse the monarchy's domestic and foreign policies, especially regarding its alliance with Western powers and opposition to Arab nationalist forces. This led him to attempt to invade his neighbor in 1961, which was precluded by a broad British and Arab coalition. In 1990, Saddam Hussein invaded Kuwait and was pushed out by a broad US-led Western and Arab coalition.

Structural similarities

Apart from continuing tribal and family ties that spanned across borders and the continuing Arab identity of the rulers, almost everything that linked the two countries and especially its rulers and regimes was ruptured by the coup in 1958. The new regime was a military dictatorship, secular instead of the traditional monarchy's reliance on Islamic values and guidance, socialist instead of capitalist (or quasi-feudal), and staunchly anti-Western and anti-imperialist, resulting in the deterioration and even cessation of relations with Western countries and a pivot into the sphere of influence of the USSR. Even the link via Arab identity was turned into a divide between the traditionally but not politically Arabist Kuwaiti elite and the fervently pan-Arab Free Officers inspired by the Egyptian model that had removed the monarchy.

Salience: constraints and catalysts of ingroup identification

After the breakdown of the monarchic dyad, the categories of salience can relate only to the smaller potential ingroup of the two states but not to broader alternative categories. In the Iraq–Kuwait case, no clear larger alternative group membership can be identified. Pan-Arabism contained at least as many divisive elements directed against Kuwait's monarchism as it contained legitimation for unity and could thus not serve as an alternative "club". Shared ethnicity/language or religion could theoretically crystallize into an ingroup. But if we look at the indicators for salience – overall share of states with a shared trait, common threat, and divisive ideology – we find that it has not in the given case. While Pan-Islamism has in later years started to erode Iraq's staunch secularism, it was too broad: there are about 50 Muslim-majority countries, and they are too heterogeneous. One main driver of Pan-Islamist ideology was Iran, which formed a threat to both Iraq and Kuwait. In addition, the impact of joint threats as well as divisive ideologies hampered joint identification even between the smaller possible ingroup of just the two states.

Until 1979, there was thus hardly any external danger to bind the Kuwait and republican Iraq together. Israel was conceived of as a non-Arab, non-Muslim "other" by both sides, but despite a strong pro-Palestinian current and activism in Kuwait, it was not seen as a direct threat to Kuwait specifically. While Iraq had been involved in numerous wars against Israel, Kuwait had mostly stayed out of them, sending only nominal support (Tucker and Roberts 2008, 596).

From monarchy to republic 161

Iran emerged as a hostile power toward both after the revolution in 1979. However, even after 1979, the threat from Iran did not lead to a clear anti-Iranian front. Despite strong Kuwaiti support for Iraq during the Iran–Iraq War, Kuwait was also one of the first Gulf states to re-establish relations with Iran after the war, in September 1988 (Karsh 2002, 87).

The threat *from* Iraq *to* Kuwait, however, rose significantly. Given that there is no shared political system, there can be no ideology inside the "club" that is inherently divisive and hierarchic. There was, however, a strong ideology that divided Kuwait and Iraq specifically, namely revolutionary pan-Arabism.

The freshly post-revolutionary regime led by Qasim used fiery rhetoric to match its ideology. However, this did not mean a complete rupture or about-face in all respects. One aspect that remained was Iraqi irredentism, now clad in a pan-Arabist vesture instead of a dynastic Hashemite robe. Qasim revived the Greater Syrian Fertile Crescent idea of the Hashemites in 1959 but gave a different justification for it to justify republicanism:

> this project was an imperialistic project when Iraq was a strong imperialist base but now that Iraq has become a free, liberated, fully sovereign and independent country, this project does not constitute a danger. . . . Also the Syrian people had the right to decide their destiny.
>
> (Tonini 2003, 242).

Iraqi discourse on Arab unity and unification were highly ambivalent and reached their apex with the invasion and subsequent annexation of Kuwait in 1990. Saddam Hussein justified these actions by Arab unity (*wahda arabiyya*) before and after the invasion. That this overrode all other issues, be they national or even familial, was exemplified by a quote by Saddam Hussein in 1990 that "Brotherhood [*ukhuwwa*] is always the most important step – [but] *wahda* remains the nation's aim" (cited in: Bengio 1998, 47, italics in original).

Part of the preparation for the incorporation of Kuwait into Iraqi territory were attempts to control and rewrite history. Books with titles such as *Kuwait is Iraqi* and *Iraq's Kuwait* were published that supported Iraq's territorial claim and bolstered the continuity of Iraqi leaders' attempts at "reclaiming" Kuwait through King Ghazi, Nuri al-Said, and Qasim (Bengio 1998, 171). This resonated among the Iraqi populace, who already believed that Kuwait was "an artificial, colonial creation" (Kamrava 2011, 182).

In Saddam's reading, Arab unity was the goal overriding all other separate and national interests, and this unity could be achieved only by unification instead of by federation or solidarity, thus necessitating a leader – the hallmarks of a divisive ideology that impedes ingroup identification. Saddam Hussein's divisive transnational *pan-Arabism* was not the inevitable outcome of identification with the Arab cause, as the contrast to Egypt's *Arab nationalism* demonstrates. Egypt's take on the conflict was decidedly different despite adherence to the Arab cause, and its officials continued to emphasize the principles of nonviolence in inter-Arab

162 *From monarchy to republic*

conflicts, nonintervention in the domestic politics of Arab countries, and the need for Arab solutions to Arab problems throughout the conflict (cf. Lesch 1991, 38). This sentiment against Iraq's invasion was shared even by Islamist opposition and leftist opposition alike, who were aghast at an inter-Arab war (Lesch 1991, 39–40).

Social processes of ingroup identification

When Kuwait declared its independence in 1961, Qasim not only did not recognize it but also threatened military invasion. After he was overthrown in 1963, the new regime under President Abd al-Salam Arif and Prime Minister Ahmad Hassan al-Bakr seemed prepared to extend recognition and resume diplomatic relations.

Kuwait tried to seize this opportunity and sent a delegation headed by Kuwaiti Foreign Minister Sabah al-Ahmad to Baghdad soon after the coup. Sabah's Iraqi counterpart, Talib Shibib, de facto extended recognition and agreed to remove objections to Kuwait's applications to the Arab League and the UN under the single condition of ending British protection. However, the next day, he withdrew his statements. He had been instructed by the National Revolutionary Command Council (NRCC), the prime decision-making institution in the new regime, that the relations between the two countries must be conducted in the framework of "unity" – that is, with the goal of incorporation into Iraq. The NRCC officials confirmed that the removal of Qasim did not imply a rejection of his policy toward Kuwait's annexation. Although the Iraqi minister of economy disagreed with the decree, the meeting ended coolly (Khadduri and Ghareeb 2001, 68–69). In contrast to the Ghazi period, this was the decision not of just one individual but of the regime as a whole.

The frequent change of personnel and responsibility in the republic made the development of durable personal bonds on which mutual trust could be based difficult, if not impossible. Although rapprochement was often signaled by a heightened frequency of visits, these meetings did not generally translate into a greater acceptance of the other or a more intense friendship, because there was little personal continuity.

After Qasim's invasion attempt, the sudden opening of the Iraqi border to Kuwait on February 18, 1963, signaled détente (Joyce 1998, 113, 128). A few months later, members of the Iraqi cabinet visited Kuwait on an informal basis to talk mostly about economic issues but also about bilateral political relations (Khadduri and Ghareeb 2001, 69–70). However, by mid 1963, the political resident in Bahrain, Sir William Luce, would state that he considered the current government potentially more dangerous than Qasim's (Joyce 1998, 131). His concerns were somewhat borne out. On a visit to Baghdad in October 4 to discuss the border issue, the Kuwaiti delegation presented Iraq with a ready-made agreement that included Iraqi recognition of "the independence and complete sovereignty" of Kuwait and the agreed-on borders of 1932. Kuwait insisted on it being accepted without changes, and the Iraqi officials

From monarchy to republic 163

accepted the agreement, but only after the Iraqi defense minister reassured them by whispering that they had already come "to an understanding with several Kuwaiti army officers that, within a year or two, they would stage an uprising as a signal to the Iraqi army to occupy Kuwait!" (cited in: Khadduri and Ghareeb 2001, 70).

Apparently, the flowery rhetoric was not backed by a new acceptance of the Kuwaiti monarchy by the Iraqi leadership. However, a month later, the Iraqi officials involved were dropped from power, and President Arif, who never ratified the agreement, died under three years later, while the Kuwaiti emirate endured. With the following president, the former president's brother, Abd al-Rahman Arif, negotiations dragged on (Khadduri and Ghareeb 2001, 71). On April 20, the SC unanimously recommended Kuwait's acceptance into the UN, which was achieved in May, when Kuwait became the 111th UN member state. Although the October 4 agreement was never ratified, a tenuous understanding was reached, and Iraq received an $80 million interest-free loan in return (Assiri 1990, 24).

Since the republic replaced the monarchy in Iraq, invocations of fraternity by referring to "sister countries" or "brotherly nations" were common, but they referred to the level of the populace, not the regime. While Kuwait attempted to emphasize the remaining connection and the Arab and Islamic bond between the two countries, Iraqi rulers were more circumspect about it.

Following the 1958 revolution, Qasim at first tried to attract Kuwait and distance it from imperialist Britain. Shortly before its independence, he declared that there were no "frontiers between us and the Kuwaiti people", who were "Arab brothers" to Iraq (cited in Khadduri and Ghareeb 2001, 64); however, at that time, the family reference was not detached from the regime completely, in that he also discouraged activities directed against the Kuwaiti government (Joyce 1998, 102). This lasted only until the opportunity to invade presented itself with Kuwaiti independence and continued British links.

After Qasim was removed from office, not least because of his failed attempt to incorporate Kuwait, another possibility for rapprochement emerged. Kuwait attempted to inscribe the familial relationship into official documents, but Iraq resisted. The agreement, Kuwait insisted, should be adopted by Iraq without changes. A visit by a Kuwaiti delegation to Baghdad on October 4, 1963, mentioned in the previous section, emphasized the "fraternal relations" between "sister countries, inspired by their national duty, common interest, and aspiration to a complete Arab unity". The Iraqi officials present accepted the agreement after the Iraqi defense minister reassured them that a coup and the opportunity to invade were imminent (Khadduri and Ghareeb 2001, 70).

The breakdown of commonality was especially pronounced before and during the invasion of Kuwait by Saddam Hussein, although the August 2 attack took Kuwait utterly by surprise. Just a day prior, after a meeting of the two conflict parties in Jeddah, the Kuwaiti negotiator and Crown Prince Sa'ad bin Abdallah Al Sabah issued optimistic statements of further upcoming negotiations between the two "brotherly nations" (cited in: Heard-Bey 2006, 205).

164 *From monarchy to republic*

Foreign policy restraint – and escalation

In contrast to the monarchic period, militarized clashes were a frequent occurrence in the relations between Kuwait and republican Iraq. Apart from the escalation peaks in 1961 and in 1990, there were 14 other MIDs in the republican period before and after the attempted and actual war, the vast majority of which (ten out of 14) reached the highest possible escalation level before full-out war ("use of force", hostility level 4), and most were recorded as at least "attacks" or "clashes", many resulting in fatalities (Ghosn, Palmer, and Bremer 2004).[5]

After the Kuwaiti declaration of independence, Qasim reacted with hostility and raised territorial claims in a press conference on June 25, 1961. The British Foreign Office was informed about rumors of troop concentration in the Basra area, only 40 miles away from Kuwait, and warned that Qasim might plan to attack Kuwait to coincide with the third anniversary of the Iraqi revolution on 14 July and launched Operation Vantage to deter Iraq's attack. It was later replaced by an Arab force, consisting mainly of Saudi, Jordanian, and UAR troops (Bismarck 2009, 80).

The resultant embarrassment and marginalization in the Arab world proved taxing for Qasim's reign and contributed to the eventual toppling of his regime in February 1963 (Tonini 2003, 249–250). The last of the 3300 troops that arrived from Arab states departed on February 19, 1963 (Assiri 1990, 22–23; Khadduri and Ghareeb 2001, 66).

The coup in Iraq did not usher in a significant change in relations. After having "temporarily" stationed Iraqi troops south of Umm Qasr in Kuwaiti territory because of mounting tensions between Iran and Iraq in 1969, Iraq reinforced a garrison on the Kuwaiti side of the border in 1973. On March 20, 1973, Iraqi troops occupied Al-Samita, a Kuwaiti police post. When apprehended, the responsible commander opened fire on the poorly armed Kuwaiti police gendarmes who tried to stop the Iraqi construction. Two Kuwaiti soldiers and one Iraqi soldier were killed in the process, and two Kuwaiti soldiers were missing. Kuwait declared a state of emergency, and tensions flared up again (Assiri 1990, 54).

Further Iraqi action was precluded by external intervention, by the British in 1961 and by pressure from Iraq's Soviet ally in 1973. Kuwait's immediate neighbors were reluctant to move beyond diplomatic support. After settling the Shatt al-Arab dispute in 1975, Iraq attempted to appear moderate and thus withdrew troops in 1977 (Assiri 1990, 54). In 1978, however, Kuwaiti oil provoked another Iraqi military posturing at the border (Tétreault 2000, 69). Kuwait tried to settle the conflict numerous times over the years, but Iraqi proposals entailed concessions that it was not willing to make, afraid it might whet Iraqi appetite for more Kuwaiti territory (Khadduri and Ghareeb 2001, 75), clearly an indication that mistrust was still ingrained in the bilateral relations.

In 1990, after a period of rising tensions and citing anti-imperialist arguments based on pan-Arabist tenets, Saddam Hussein annexed Kuwait on August 2, 1990, and a week later declared Kuwait the "19th province" of Iraq (Hassan 1999, 157). The attack took Kuwait and most of its neighbors by surprise. This blatant

From monarchy to republic 165

transgression of international and inter-Arab norms instigated the intervention of a broad-based coalition of Western and Arab states led by the US, later known there as the First Gulf War.[6] By October 1990, 220,000 coalition troops stood against nearly 400,000 Iraqi forces (Allison 2012, 78). An air campaign was launched on January 17, and with operations Desert Shield and Desert Storm, a large international coalition of 34 countries led by the US eventually forced the Iraqi army out of its neighbor's territory by February 28, 1991; four days (or – deliberately – exactly 100 hours) after the launch of the ground initiative (Allison 2012, 139).

A "final" agreement followed the UN Boundary Demarcation Commission decision in 1993 (Hassouna 2001, 237), but hostilities have reappeared from time to time, showing the conflict as a rule rather than an aberration. In October 1994, Iraq staged maneuvers near the shared border, acting in a way that was seen as similar to those preceding the 1990 invasion (Al-Nahyan 2013, 99). In 1997, shooting incidents followed Kuwaiti drilling operations near Umm al-Qasr (Okruhlik and Conge 1999, 243).

The lack of restraint from escalation runs through the whole range of Iraqi policy, even apart from military action. Iraq employed a broad range of instruments to discredit, delegitimize, and destabilize the Kuwaiti regime. Vocal propaganda campaigns not only demonized the Kuwaiti regime but also at times eliminated the Kuwaiti state altogether, presenting Kuwait as an "integral part" of Iraq. Subversion was an oft-used element against the monarchy. There was no ingroup identification with the regime that could have precluded rhetorical and eventually military escalation. Rather, escalation and attack were often precluded by fear of external (super)power intervention. When this deterrent failed, Iraq attacked and annexed Kuwait in 1990.

This has been a constant driver in all Iraqi regimes since the revolution and until Saddam Hussein. Despite previous attempts at rapprochement by the new post-revolutionary regime, the cancelation of the British protection agreement, and its recognition of Kuwaiti independence in 1961 opened a window of opportunity that could not be resisted. As Joyce put it, "as soon as Kuwait declared independence it was clear that General Qasim's intention was domination rather than cooperation" (Joyce 1998, 104).

Instead of the expected congratulations by Iraq to their neighbor's independence, Qasim held a press conference on June 25, 1961, in which he laid irredentist claims on the whole territory of Kuwait (Assiri 1990, 19). He announced publicly that Kuwait had always been "an integral part" of Iraq given its historical connection – that is, it was part of the Ottoman province of Basra before being severed illegally by the British – and Iraq had decided to "protect the Iraqi people in Kuwait" from imperialism by subjecting it under Iraqi authority (cited in Khadduri and Ghareeb 2001, 65). He stated that "the Iraqi republic will never cede a single inch of this land" (cited in: Tonini 2003, 248). Qasim escalated his rhetoric further, depicting the Kuwaiti rulers who made contracts with Britain and signed the independence treaty as "irresponsible people who are under the sway of imperialism" (Assiri 1990, 19). He then brought to mind the futility of peace with imperialists and threatened to kindle an "internecine war" (Assiri 1990, 19–20).

166   *From monarchy to republic*

Not only were these utterances evidence of high hostility, but they also delegitimized the Kuwaiti leadership entirely, who were portrayed as having no agency or legitimacy. They also delegitimized the Kuwaiti state as an independent entity, all according to the will of "the Iraqi people" (since there was no Kuwait, there could be no "Kuwaiti people"). This goes beyond a contained territorial dispute and a difference of opinion and shows a high willingness to escalate.

The day after the British mobilization in Operation Vantage, the UN SC session on July 2 provided the diplomatic battlefield to match the military one. The Kuwaiti representative presented a letter objecting to the Iraqi aggression and Qasim's statement "to protect the Iraqi people in Kuwait and to demand all the territory belonging to the Qadha of Kuwait in the Liwa of Basrah" and the Iraqi announcement to appoint the "present Ruler of Kuwait as Qaimaqam of Kuwait", who would be considered a rebel and receive severe punishment if he "were to misbehave" (UN Security Council 1961, 5).

The Iraqi representative, for his part, launched a tirade denigrating Kuwaiti statehood:

> Kuwait is not more than a small coastal town on the Gulf. There is not and has never been a country or a national entity called Kuwait, never in history. It is only a town surrounded by barren desert which is inhabited by nomads who roam the deserts stretching from the Euphrates in south central Iraq to Nejd in the heart of the Arabian peninsula [*sic*]. It has a population of 206,473, according to the 1957 census, of whom more than three-quarters reside in the town of Kuwait. Of these, the sheikhs considered only 30,000 as citizens of Kuwait. So here we have a situation whereby a small town with none of the historical and legal prerequisites of statehood is composed, according to its <u>de facto</u> ruler, of 85 per cent foreigners and only 15 per cent citizens, and we are now called upon to elevate that town to the dignity of national statehood.
> (UN Security Council 1961, 11, underlined in original text)

The whole passage completely dismisses any legitimate statehood appeal that Kuwait might have and, especially combined with the "Qaimaqam" announcement, denigrates the Kuwaiti leader – now emir and independent monarch of an independent state – to a mere subordinate position as a regional governor. This sentiment was not confined to the leadership. Dr. Abdallah al-Hussain, Iraq's acting director-general of political affairs and lecturer at Baghdad University, stated that Kuwait is an anachronism, "a family rather than a state" (quoted in: Joyce 1998, 93). These snippets make clear that there was no hint of mutual recognition, at least on the part of Iraq.

Although the new government after Qasim accepted Kuwait's independence and its boundaries, the agreement remained unratified, and annexation plans would resurface over the next years. After the coming to power of the Ba'th party in 1968, ideological conflict increased. Iraq supported Popular Front for the Liberation of the Occupied Arabian Gulf (PFLOAG) activities that were directed against the monarchies of the Arabian Peninsula (Ahmadi 2008, 112).

From monarchy to republic 167

In the 1970s, Iraq also again laid claim to two Kuwaiti islands, Bubiyan and Warba, "replacing" that claim for the claim on Kuwait proper, thus minimizing the conflict issue, although larger claims tended to reappear from time to time. In interviews with as-Sayyad and al-Nahar, Iraqi Foreign Minister Murtada Abd al-Baqi stated that Iraq needed the islands because it should be a Gulf state and declared in an interview that "the whole of Kuwait is a disputed area. There is a document saying that Kuwait is Iraqi territory. There is no document which says it is not Iraqi territory" (cited in: Assiri 1990, 54). Troops were mobilized at the border. During an official visit of heir apparent Jabir al-Ahmad Al Sabah, the claim was transformed into a bid for a lease of the islands, which Kuwait did not grant (Hassan 1999, 157).

In the prelude to the invasion in 1990, claims and threats intensified again. Baghdad demanded a moratorium on its loans accumulated during the Iran–Iraq War, when it was strongly supported by Kuwait and Saudi Arabia (and the US) and by additional funds. Saddam Hussein directly and openly threatened the Gulf monarchies when he said, for example, that "if they will not give this money to me, I will know how to get it", relaying this message via King Hussein of Jordan (cited in: Karsh 2002, 90). Economic pressure on Iraq was also constituted by the Gulf monarchies' refusal to abide by the oil production quota agreed on by OPEC in early 1990. When these demands were not met, Saddam Hussein's rhetoric grew more and more histrionic. He demanded "an Arab plan similar to the Marshall Plan to compensate Iraq for some of the losses during the war" and accused Kuwait of conspiring with "world imperialism and Zionism" – reminiscent of the most menacing of Arab Cold War times (both quotes in: Karsh 2002, 91).

Kuwait rejected the allegations and demands, feeding Hussein's image of Kuwait as a rich parasite that had to be forced to contribute to the cause. Kuwait and the UAE had agreed to curb production in June 1990, but it was already too little too late for Iraq. By July 19, Iraqi troops were stationed on the border to Kuwait, their number reaching 100,000 by the end of the month. On August 8, annexed Kuwait was announced by Saddam Hussein as the 19th province of the Republic of Iraq (Allison 2012, 41, 50).

Saddam Hussein also used every trick in the book to discredit, delegitimize, and demonize the Kuwaiti leadership and later the US-led alliance. Saddam Hussein's rationalizations for the war were numerous, often presenting it as the will of the people, as Qasim had done before him (Long 2004, 27).

Rhetorical escalation was the norm, often combined with intense othering rhetoric, which even expanded toward traits that Iraq and Kuwait and their elites shared, such as religion. Despite (secular) pan-Arabist rhetoric and institutions, Ba'thist Iraq started to use Islamic frames of reference, even calling the coalition the "imperialist camp of the infidel" (Long 2004, 82). This linking of Arabism to Islam had been employed in the prelude to the invasion for many months (Long 2004, 81–138). The Iraqi regime also delegitimized the Saudi regime by referring to the country as the "lands of Hijaz and Najd" and thus disconnected from the Al Saud as the official name of the kingdom demanded. This appellation also served as a necessary step before the invocation of Hussein's alleged Sharifian ancestry,

168 *From monarchy to republic*

which he pointed out neither the Al Saud nor Mubarak possessed (Bengio 1998, 79–80; Long 2004, 106–107).[7]

Saddam Hussein clearly directed his mélange of pan-Arabist and Islamic calls to arms against a broader front, as when he exclaims in his infamous "jihad speech" on August 10, the day of the annexation: "Until the voice of right rises up in the Arab world, hit their interests wherever they are and rescue holy Mecca and the grave of the prophet Mohammed in Medina" (Long 2004, 85). Before the launch of the air campaign on January 17 that would result in the liberation of Kuwait, Saddam Hussein prepared his people and his attackers for a fight that he called "the mother of [all] battles" (*umm al-ma'arik*). In a public speech on January 20, Hussein invoked religious identity and sacrifice by casting the attackers as "infidels" and the Iraqis as supported by God ("all the means and potential that God has given us"), calling them (and all Arabs) to jihad and delegitimized the coalition members as "infidels, the Zionists, and the treacherous, shameful rulers, such as the traitor [King] Fahd", repeatedly linking the conflict to Palestine (Allison 2012, 106).

Kuwait also employed Arabist and Islamic frames of reference. Both identities could have been used to appeal to unity and friendship with Iraq, which was also Arab and increasingly emphasized Islamic identity as well. Instead, as Iraq, they were employed to "other" the opponent and rally possible supporters to their cause. Thus, the last appeal of Kuwaiti radio on the day of the invasion was "In the Name of God, the Compassionate, the Merciful. This is Kuwait. O Arabs, o brothers, O beloved brothers, O Muslims, your brothers in Kuwait are appealing to you. Hurry to their aid" (quoted by: Long 2004, 81). The Islamic frame was a desperate last-minute attempt in that Kuwait had drawn heavily on pan-Arabist tropes before. Apart from mobilizing support, it was used to delegitimize Iraq. Kuwait railed against the "Tatars" who came to invade their land, as Saddam Hussein has done before in relation to Iran and has done since in relation to the US coalition forces (Long 2004, 82). At the height of the conflict, the affiliation with Iraq as an Arab neighborly state broke down. While Kuwait appeals to Arab (and Muslim) "brothers", it simultaneously excludes the Iraqis from that appellation, who become foreign "Tatars".

There is a plethora of explanations for Saddam Hussein's actions, as there was for Qasim's. Psychological approaches were exceptionally popular in explanations of Saddam Hussein's behavior, whose belligerent foreign (and domestic) policy lends itself to psychological profiling and personalization (see e.g. Post 2003; Renshon 1993), and indeed, some features of his personality – paranoid inklings and a drive for power and prestige – seem to suggest idiosyncrasies.[8] An Iraqi opposition member contended that it was the former obsession with making history (quoted by: Bengio 1998, 243, fn 18). Another consequence of Saddam's psychology was the miscalculation of the reaction of both superpowers – erroneously hoping for the crumbling Soviet Union's support (Allison 2012, 71) and US acquiescence (Karsh 2002, 91, 92).[9]

However, these and other factors, like economic and hegemonic explanations, cannot explain the timing of the attack, because they were present at other times when Iraq refrained from aggression. The timing of this particular attack can be

From monarchy to republic 169

explained instead via a combination of an increased perception of threat and the open possibility to "strike at the foreign sources of domestic problems" to explain war initiation (Gause 2002, 51–53). But this in turn does not explain the continued and persistent Iraqi hostility up to military action throughout the over three decades before as well. This and other attacks and destabilization campaigns were enabled by the breakdown of the monarchic system.

Kuwaiti-Iraqi cooperation was mostly opportunistic and ad hoc and therefore easily turned into hostility on numerous occasions. It was not a persistent alliance that continued during periods of diverging interests and aims.

During the Iran–Iraq War, Kuwait moved ever closer toward Iraq and became the main economic supporter, along with Saudi Arabia. Iran had to mostly rely on aid from outside the region (except for Libyan, Syrian, and Israeli support) (Karsh 2002, 44–45). Compared to the revolutionary Shia regime in Tehran, Saddam Hussein appeared a pragmatic choice. Being more clearly delimitated and restricted, shared Arab identity proved more powerful than pan-Islamic identity did, despite Iranian attempts to threaten Kuwait into neutrality (cf. Khadduri and Ghareeb 2001, 71–74). Although Kuwait (along with Saudi Arabia) was the biggest supporter of Iraq during the war, the bond did not outlast the divergence of interest and can therefore not be considered an informal alliance. Saddam Hussein's tone and foreign policy behavior changed in early 1990 and were accompanied by an increasingly hostile stance toward the GCC states, which ended in the confrontation described earlier (Gause 2002, 57–58).

But solidarity and alliance in periods of Iraqi aggression toward Kuwait exists – among monarchies. The actions of Arab monarchies during the Gulf Crises of 1961 and 1990 demonstrate monarchic solidarity and will thus be shortly addressed in this section, which is otherwise reserved for Iraqi-Kuwaiti cooperation.

Kuwait appealed for British (and Arab) protection after Qasim's speech. Saudi Arabia vocally proclaimed its support, in which King Saud reassured Emir Abdallah Salim in a telegram on June 28 that "We are with you through thick and thin and shall be faithful to our undertakings" (quoted by: Joyce 1998, 105). Saud also expressed dismay at the Iraqi ruler behaving like a "maniac" (Joyce 1998, 105). British troops and subsequently Saudi Arabian-led Arab League troops came to Kuwait's rescue and prevented Iraqi intervention (Bismarck 2009; Metz 1994). Britain launched Operation Vantage, the largest mobilization of forces in the Middle East since the Suez Crisis (Bismarck 2009, 75), which were subsequently replaced by Arab troops (Joyce 1998, 108). Saudi Arabia and Jordan, the two largest monarchies, were major contributors, and their forces were the last to leave, in 1963. The year before, Kuwaiti soldiers were sent to Jordan for training. When the kings of Jordan and Saudi Arabia eventually withdrew their troops, it was not because of disagreement with the Al Sabah but because of the unfriendly atmosphere among the population in the country, evoking an atmosphere of imminent revolutionary takeover (Joyce 1998, 111–112). The episode reverberated among the Gulf monarchies and shaped a community of fate among them. Following Abdallah Salim's death in 1965, they all sent condolence telegrams (except for Muscat-Oman) (Joyce 1998, 140).[10]

170 *From monarchy to republic*

The invasion by Saddam Hussein had an even greater impact on the monarchic club. It polarized the Arab world. Most of the Arab governments condemned the invasion and annexation, and only Jordan and the PLO remained as Iraq's allies (although King Hussein would criticize the invasion as well). The populaces were similarly divided. Arab states provided two-thirds of the funding for the coalition that ultimately pushed out Iraq (Allison 2012, 102).

This attempted erasure of a dynasty by invasion prompted a show of broad monarchic solidarity. All monarchies of the region at the time participated in the efforts to reinstate it, even Jordan, which refused to join the military coalition against Iraq and attempted to mediate the conflict. It was the first war experience for some of them: Kuwait, Oman, Qatar, and the UAE had never been active (interstate) war participants before.

The fates of the monarchies were connected, which made solidarity more pronounced. Anti-Kuwaiti propaganda was also directed against other reactionary and "parasitic" monarchies and shaikhdoms. Saudi Arabia feared not only for the Al Sabah but also for its own territorial integrity. Saddam Hussein ordered Scud missiles which directly attacked the country. King Fahd and the Kuwaiti Emir supported the coalition with $15 billion, and Saudi Arabia provided crucial flyover access. In an attempt to drag the coalition into a ground war, Iraqi forces thrust into Ras al-Khafji, a small town 10 miles inside Saudi Arabia. Apart from US troops, Saudi and Qatari military played a major role in pushing them out, losing 19 soldiers in the process (Allison 2012, 67, 117, 120–122). The UAE was among the first Arab countries to send ground forces to Kuwait and repeated the feat in October 1994, when Iraqi troops moved toward the Kuwaiti border (Hellyer 2001, 169). Following the emergency Arab League summit two days after the Iraqi annexation of Kuwait on August 10, Egypt, Morocco, and Syria sent troops to Saudi Arabia, while Somalia and Djibouti provided staging areas for international forces (Lesch 1991, 37). In a later meeting in Jiddah on August 22, the defense ministers of the GCC would lament the aggression by "an Arab brother", but their weak military capabilities did not allow them to act on their own. Still, each GCC state contributed to the international coalition (Heard-Bey 2006, 205).

The Iraqi aggression prompted wide outrage among most of the Arab world, and important supporters – like Egypt or Syria – were republican. However, the unified reaction and commitment by countries that – unlike Egypt or Syria – had no combat and war experience is remarkable. Saudi Arabia, Bahrain, Qatar, the UAE, Oman, and (to a lesser extent) Morocco, objected not only out of respect for the international norm of territorial integrity but also because the victim was "one of them".

The only seeming exception to monarchic solidarity was the policy of Jordan, which did not take part in the anti-Iraq coalition. This is even more puzzling in light of the fact that more "radical" Syria did take part, a constellation that would be reversed in the Second Gulf War of 2003, when the sons of Hussein and Hafiz al-Asad took the opposite position from their fathers in the First Gulf War (cf. Hinnebusch and Quilliam 2006) and that Jordan had been hostile toward Iraq since the 1958 revolution well into the 1980s (Lynch 1998, 354–355).

From monarchy to republic 171

Nevertheless, while Jordan was a monarchic outlier, it was not a complete contradiction. Although King Hussein preferred to abstain from military efforts against Iraq, he fulfilled a mediating role rather than full alliance, which would imply support for Iraqi aggression. To the contrary, he always made his support for the Al Sabah and their legitimacy evident.

King Hussein claimed that Saddam Hussein gave him Saddam's personal assurance that Iraq would not use military force against Kuwait (Allison 2012, 45). As were the rest of the Arabs, he was taken by surprise and woke up to the startling news of invasion by a call by King Fahd at 5:50 a.m. on August 2. Because of his strong ties to Saddam (he was described as a "personal friend" of the Iraqi president) and his chairpersonship of the Arab Cooperation Council (ACC), a short-lived organization of which Iraq, Egypt, and North Yemen were also members, it was a particular sharp blow (Shlaim 2009, 486). In addition, the closeness of the relationship heightened distrust against Jordan among its Arab neighbors; Kuwaitis suspected Jordan of being an accessory; and the Saudis even feared that Hussein intended to renew Hashemite irredentism and join Iraqi forces to reclaim the Hijaz. This suspicion was aggravated by Hussein's defiant behavior and his public request in front of the Jordanian parliament to call him "sharif" (Shlaim 2009, 488–489). For the next few weeks, he also started wearing Hashemite garb and grew a beard, increasingly resembling his namesake great-grandfather (Shlaim 2009, 489, 503).

The day after the invasion, King Hussein flew to Baghdad and attempted to broker a peaceful solution without relinquishing his support for his Iraqi neighbor, but he was ultimately unsuccessful (Allison 2012, 72–73). Although Jordan abstained from the anti-Iraq front as the only monarchy, its stance was not one of unequivocal support of Saddam Hussein's action. In contrast, King Hussein stated his disapproval of annexation and his belief that the Al Sabah continued to be the legitimate rulers of Kuwait (Lesch 1991, 45). He also tried numerous diplomatic endeavors, pleading with the Iraqi president to pull back to avoid war and foreign intervention (cf. Shlaim 2009, 500–501).

Inside Jordan's regime, the policy was highly controversial, and his intention to restore Jordanian-Iraqi ties to pre-1958 closeness caused a severe row between him and his brother Hassan. As King Hussein's popularity at home soared to unseen heights, he was talking privately about abdicating. In the aftermath of the conflict, it was so essential for Jordan to appear "neutral" in the conflict that it prompted the government to release a white paper containing the official stance on the crisis and 15 official documents (Shlaim 2009, 485, 491–493).[11]

Still, the Jordanian behavior had long-lasting repercussions for Kuwaiti-Jordanian relations. It led Kuwait to refuse normalization with it up to the late 1990s, after all other Arab states had already done so, despite King Hussein's support for Iraqi opposition aiming at regime change in Iraq since 1995 (Maddy-Weitzman 1999, 129–130).

Besides important domestic and economic factors, it could be argued that ideational factors that competed with monarchic ingroup solidarity might explain King Hussein's deviation.[12] Marc Lynch argues that the crucial factor was in fact

172 *From monarchy to republic*

common identity with Iraq, albeit on the societal instead of elite level: the "networks of community of identity and interests" between the two states, which are not easily replaced, made Jordan put normative values before material ones (cf. Lynch 1998, 363). Lynch claims that it was not the existence of a threat per se but the construction of a community of fate of sorts where a threat to Iraq was seen as a threat to Jordan (Lynch 1998, 361). If that were indeed the case, it would compete on the same identity-based level with monarchic solidarity and might explain, along with economic and geopolitical reasons, why Jordan did not conform completely to the policy of the "royal club".

Ingroup identification after regime change

In contrast to the monarchic period, republican Iraq and monarchic Kuwait do not have many unifying similarities, resulting in a high level of hostility throughout the period. Iraq's republican period is characterized by a lack of joint identification. Shared categories (Arab, Muslim) are used just as much to "other" Kuwait as to affirm commonality. Few structural similarities remained between the two states. Instead, representatives of Iraq's republican ideology frequently called for the abolishment of the "reactionary" system still in place in Kuwait.

Building personal relations also became more difficult: Iraq's republican elites had been socialized in different education facilities (especially the military) and upheld a different and highly divisive ideology. In addition, no long-term interpersonal relations on the political level could be forged, because of the frequent coups and regime changes in Iraq. Overall, there was thus no sense of community that could be affirmed and reified.

Therefore, there was no established norm of respect for national sovereignty between the two states. From Qasim to Arif to Saddam Hussein, Iraqi rulers heavily criticized the Kuwaiti regime and the Gulf monarchies in general. The brotherly spirit of former times was nowhere to be found. Since Iraq did not recognize Kuwait as an equal and legitimate partner, military escalation was not precluded by bilateral interstate bonds. When hostility built up, it was usually de-escalated by external deterrence not by a preference for cooperation over conflict. Once that deterrence failed (as in the Glaspie episode in the wake of the First Gulf War), there was nothing to stop an Iraqi attack. Restraint based on deterrence is naturally weaker than restraint based on community bonds. Not wanting to *risk* war with someone is a less stable condition than not wanting war *at all*.

The hostility between Iraq and Kuwait not only stands out in comparison to the jointly monarchic period. Iraq's expansionist foreign policy contrasts starkly with the behavior of other monarchies once their fellow dynasty in Kuwait came under attack, based on a strong sense of monarchic identification with the victim. In 1961, Saudi Arabia and Jordan supported Kuwait diplomatically, financially, and ultimately militarily. In 1990/1991, all monarchies except Jordan joined in a military coalition against Iraq, even if they had never fought a major war before. Even Jordan, while under heavy political and economic pressure to support Iraq, stood by the affirmation of the legitimacy of the Kuwaiti regime that Iraq denied.

From monarchy to republic 173

While some republics also participated in the joint effort to liberate Kuwait, only Egypt and Syria provided troops. Their participation, however, was less surprising given their size and important role in Middle East relations and their ample military experience. While small republics like Lebanon and Tunisia did not participate, small monarchies like Qatar and the UAE all united in support of Kuwait. While the "Arab club" was divided by Iraqi irredentism and Arab nationalism, the "monarchic club" rallied around one of its own.

Iraq and Kuwait: synthesis and findings

As summarized in Table 5.1, with the breakdown of Iraq's monarchy, the ingroup identification between Iraq and Kuwait also fell apart, resulting in significantly and persistently more hostile relations.

Table 5.1 Deterioration of Iraqi-Kuwaiti Relations

Indicators			*Period I*	*Period II*
1. Structural similarities	1.1	Shared language, culture, history, and religion	+	+
	1.2	Similar political system	+ But asymmetric development	−
2 Salience	1.3	Similar economic system	+	− Socialist vs. capitalist
	1		− /+	Not applicable
	2		Majority, but falling	
	2.1	Low/decreasing share	since 1952	
	2.2	Common threat	+ increase since 1952	− (later Iran)
	2.3	Absence of divisive ideology	+ (Except Ghazi's period before WWII)	−
	3.1	Mutual recognition	+ quasi-recognition before independence	+
	3.2	Personalization of bonds between ruling elites	+	− decrease

(*Continued*)

174   *From monarchy to republic*

Table 5.1 (Continued)

Indicators			Period I	Period II
3 Social processes of ingroup identification		3.2.1 Frequent high-level state visits	+ Yes, esp. since 1950	+ Yes, esp. since 1950
		3.2.2 Kinship, intermarriage and friendship bonds	+ Closer bonds since Abd al-Ilah and King Faisal II	– decrease
		3.2.3 Shared socialization	+ shared socialization via British institutions and royal identity	– Separate socialization after Iraq cut ties with Britain
	3.3 Affirmation of commonality		+ Stronger with developing institutions and monarchic identity in Kuwait	–
		3.3.1 Kinship and family references	–	– used mostly in ref. to population
		3.3.2 Emphasis on similarity	+	– Strong othering discourse
		3.3.3 References to shared historical narratives	+	– Anti-colonialist/-imperial narrative fostered by Ba'thist Iraq, contradicting pro-Western outlook of Kuwait
		3.3.4 Common ceremonies/shared institutions	+ Prelude to AFU establishment	– Less-common ceremonies (mostly restricted to Arab League protocol)
4 Foreign policy restraint	4.1 Military restraint		+	– Invasion attempt 1961, invasion 1990
	4.2 Non-military restraint		+ (except in Ghazi's period)	–
		4.2.1 *Refraining from delegitimization*	+	– Delegitimization of dynasty, system, and even state itself

Indicators	Period I	Period II
4.2.2 Refraining from subversion	+	– Frequent subversion attempts
4.2.3 Rhetorical restraint	+	– Claim to Kuwait whole instead of negotiable parts ("19th province")
4.3 Alliance and solidarity	+ Prelude to AFU	– Cooperation: Iran–Iraq War, but outpouring of monarchic solidarity at attack of fellow monarchy

The massive escalations in 1961 and 1990 are not sufficiently explained by irredentism and aspirations for regional hegemony or great power–small power relations alone. Saudi Arabia also had territorial and hegemonic ambitions vis-à-vis Kuwait but reacted in a completely different way to the declaration of Kuwait's independence. Rather than delegitimizing the new state, the Saudis welcomed it into the monarchic club. The Saudi ambassador was the first to present his credentials to the Kuwaiti authorities, even preceding the British (Joyce 1998, 121). For the Saudis, a new monarchy was an asset and an ally, while for Iraq, it was an illegitimate "reactionary" regime that was fair game.

This adversarial perception of Kuwait was not mere an elite affair. That Kuwait "rightfully" belonged to Iraq was the "prevailing view on the streets of Baghdad and elsewhere within Iraq" (Schofield 2001, 228). This irredentist vision was deeply ingrained in society at least since the monarchical period and had even been formally taught in schoolbooks all over the country since Iraqi independence in 1932 (Finnie 1992, 126). Still, Iraq's regime raised the level of hostility toward Kuwait only once they encountered one another as *different* types of states.

Divisive ideology played a major role in the deepening rift. By framing the conflict in pan-Arabist terms (of "Arab unity"), Qasim and (later) Saddam delegitimized the norm of territorial integrity, the Kuwaiti political elite, and even the overall existence of Kuwait. This process was facilitated by the different political systems: Iraq's was revolutionary republican and thus intrinsically opposed to traditionalist monarchic rule. Had Iraq been a monarchy, the lack of ideological rigor would probably have precluded a war between the two countries.

This interpretation is supported by the exception of Ghazi's reign. Although also a proponent of pan-Arab unity and incorporation of Kuwait, Ghazi's ideology was restricted to his convictions and was not shared by other regime members. Consequently, the impact of his ideological inklings remained limited, and he could successfully be deterred from acting on his convictions without major costs.

176 *From monarchy to republic*

In contrast, the strict ideological line of the Iraqi Ba'thists (especially after the 1968 coup) entrapped them in a conflict that they were unable to de-escalate. The longue-durée view therefore shows that Iraqi belligerence toward Kuwait is an effect of the republican system under different Iraqi regimes that cannot be reduced to a "Saddam effect", as suggested by psychological explanations of his idiosyncratic psyche and his behavioral patterns.

The recognition as a viable, autonomous, and "real" state is a precondition of the development of an ingroup identification. Because Iraq's republican leaders rejected the legitimacy of Kuwait as a state, they were unencumbered by any sense of moral wrongdoing.

This sentiment when facing "illegitimate states" is prevalent in many cases of bilateral relations between Middle Eastern states, many of which have artificial borders and developed state institutions only under (generally) British control or protection. Some extent of condescension by older states with a history of independence toward younger, "more-artificial" states can be found even between monarchies. Similar sentiments were prevalent among the Saudi rulers, although they allied with Kuwait: as Joyce notes of Saudi perception toward newly independent Kuwait, "the only acceptable alternative to independence for the smaller states of the Arabian peninsula was inclusion in Saudi Arabia" (Joyce 1998, 104). Even during the Hashemite period in Iraq, British authorities recommended caution in dealing with Iraq to the Kuwaitis, because there were "numerous issues which led to friction, including boundaries, water and ownership of date gardens" (cited in: Joyce 94). These frictions persisted throughout the whole period of Iraqi independence, as a quote in 1959 by political agent Halford illustrates:

> So long as Iraq was a backward province of the Ottoman Empire or even the unsteady nursling of the British mandate, the question of her relations with Kuwait remained academic. Since the attainment of independence in 1930, however, every Iraqi Government has had its eye on Kuwait and no Iraqi Government has ever made the suicidal political mistake of committing itself to formal recognition of Kuwait's independent status.

> (quoted in: Joyce 101)

Nevertheless, both monarchical Saudi Arabia and monarchical Iraq refrained from acting on their sentiments of superiority toward Kuwait. Republican Iraq did not.

5.2 Iran and the UAE: from dynastic friendship to "seas of blood" – the Tunb islands dispute

After the increasing destabilization of the Middle East in the 2010s, the polarization between Iran and Saudi Arabia and their respective allies has reached unprecedented heights. The two Gulf states are portrayed as regional rivals engaged in a cold war with "proxy wars" across the Middle East: in Iraq, Bahrain, and especially in Syria and Yemen. The UAE and especially Abu Dhabi share much of their larger neighbor's hostile relationship with Iran, as their involvement in major Saudi-backed initiatives like the Yemen War and the stabilization of the Bahraini regime show. But mere two generations away, Emirati-Iranian relations were marked by cooperation and closeness – before the revolution that replaced the Iranian kingdom with a republic in 1979.

The most defining feature of Iranian-Emirati relations was the dispute about three islands claimed by both countries, Abu Musa and the Greater and Lesser Tunb, once described as the "most intractable Gulf territorial issue" (Calvert and Alcock 2004, 466). The islands issue therefore formed a major stumbling block between the two countries even while they shared a monarchical system – but re-erupted with a vigor after the revolution. This case study therefore centers on the islands disputes, which have "served as indicators of Iranian policy and motivation for much of the twentieth century" (Caldwell 1996, 57).

Both Abu Musa and the Tunbs are located at strategic choking points but are of little intrinsic value. Iran has larger military bases on the islands of Qeshem, Hengam, and Larak, which are all closer to the Strait of Hormuz (Kostiner 2009, 199). British sources estimated a population of 150 Arab inhabitants for the Greater Tunb in 1970. Lesser Tunb is waterless and uninhabited. Abu Musa is the largest of the three with about 8 square kilometers and was estimated to house a seasonally varying population of about 800 people (both Arab and Iranian) just before British withdrawal (Mobley 2003, 628).

In contrast to Kuwaiti-Iraqi relations, the republican period did not witness a military conflict between the two countries, but relations were significantly more distrustful, confrontational, and distant than before – with much more escalation potential in times of conflict. Despite the antagonistic action of Iran, the seizure of the islands on the eve of UAE independence in 1971, the shah was mostly accepted as the protector and "police officer of the Gulf", while the theocratic clerics and presidents after 1979 were viewed as threatening, even during periods when Iraq was a more direct military threat to the Gulf monarchies.

While the dispute was a constant factor in relations, the handling of the conflict during periods of shared and distinct political systems was decisively distinct. The bilateral relationship between Iran and the UAE and their legal predecessor (the Trucial states) was ridden with conflict.

Two points make this case a particularly "strong test" for the SPSP theory, in that it is a "least-likely case", i.e. the conditions for the theory to work are far from ideal. If it still has explanatory power under these conditions, it is even likelier to hold true in more-applicable ones. This makes it a suitable case to explore the limits of monarchic ingroup identification as a conflict diffuser. What makes the context problematic for an SPSP? First, the countries, even in jointly monarchic periods, are highly dissimilar. Second, the available time for an ingroup identification to occur is especially short – the period between the UAE's independence and the Iranian revolution spans only eight years (1971–1979), meaning that an ingroup would just be in its developing stages, similarly to the Iraqi-Kuwaiti case. In contrast to it, there was no war in the second period, meaning that the implications from this case are more limited.

178 *From monarchy to republic*

The case begins with a contextualization of the conflict in the pre-independence period under British influence. This period culminated in an Iranian occupation of the three disputed islands, one with the permission and participation of the contestant Emirati ruler of Sharjah (Abu Musa) and two against the explicit resistance of the shaikh of Ras al-Khaimah (the Tunbs). Preceding UAE statehood and independence by just two days, it constitutes clear military action, though of limited scope (seven police officers and soldiers died, in total).[13]

The first period under analysis traces the monarchic (and jointly independent) period 1971–1979, when a common identity develops slowly and the most intense cooperation is seen – though the dispute remains unresolved. The second period traces the deterioration of relations after the Islamic Revolution in 1979 until the rapprochement in the late 1990s that heralds a period of renewed tension and hostilities, with immediate revisionism toward the islands issue leading to a new height of confrontations in 1992. The dispute has not been settled to this day.

General dynamics and pre-independence period

General developments in the 1960s pointed to an Arab-Persian convergence and harmonization with the Arab Gulf monarchic entities before British withdrawal, although border issues elicited tensions. Especially in the early statehood years, border delimitation was not just a problem of interstate Gulf relations but also a major issue inside the UAE when each emirate had a border dispute of some kind with another emirate or a neighbor, such as Oman. Although these disputes rarely escalated to violence, they influenced intra-UAE relations and therefore also the federation's foreign policy. With state consolidation came the consolidation of foreign policy. Following independence, the UAE foreign ministry took over the dispute from the emirate of Sharjah (Gargash 1996, 152).

The federal nature of the UAE compounded the difficulties of forging a national foreign policy, as the individual emirates had wide autonomy. Iranian ties were of different intensity and a different nature to different emirates: the closest ties and the best working relationship were traditionally with the second-largest emirate of the federation, Dubai. Historically, a substantial proportion of Dubai's population is of Iranian origin, so the trade with Iran is intensive and the personal relationship between Shah Reza Pahlavi and Shaikh Rashid of Dubai was especially close (Alkim 1989, 149–150). Mainly because of Iran–Dubai ties, Iran and the UAE were each other's largest trading partner until 2009 (Al-Nahyan 2013, 67).

Regional dynamics mattered especially because of the politics on the Arabian Peninsula, but also in the broader Gulf, and were shaped by the asymmetry of power, size, military capabilities, and historical development. The larger states – Iran, Saudi Arabia, and Iraq – would often use or pressure the smaller emirates to achieve their ambitions. Iran used veiled military threats but especially economic pressure on the Trucial Coast states and would remind them of its opposition to the idea of federation as long as the territorial claims were not settled. When the British announced their withdrawal, Iran saw the opportunity to expand its influence at the expense of the smaller not-yet-independent states and reaffirmed its claim to Bahrain and then to the three islands ruled by the emirates Sharjah and

Ras al-Khaimah. Independent larger neighbor Saudi Arabia triggered a different approach of cooperation and coordination. The starting point of a closer relationship between the two monarchies was launched with a state visit by the shah in 1968 to Saudi Arabia, which ultimately resulted in his abolishment of the claim to Bahrain (Alkim 1989, 138).

The claim to Bahrain initially had priority (Sirriyeh 1984, 74–75), but good relations with the conservative monarchies in the Gulf were vital for the shah, so he eventually relented. When redrawing provincial boundaries in 1957, Iran designated Bahrain as the 14th province, but with Saudi-Iranian rapprochement, it lost its importance. In 1965, Iran announced it had no intention of using force to resolve the dispute, and the shah considered Bahrain not essential strategically, economically, or politically. It was small, its oil reserves were modest, and it was far from the Strait of Hormuz, the shah's primary geostrategic locus of interest. Also, an invasion would trigger violence and civil conflict (Alvandi 2010, 162). In contrast to the islands dispute, the Bahrain affair was eventually settled agreeably in 1970, followed by reciprocal state visits by the prime minister of Bahrain on May 24, 1975, and the Iranian prime minister, Amir Abbas Hoveida, on November 29, 1975. Hoveida used to opportunity to express that there were no difficulties in relations between Iran and Bahrain and that cooperation between them was being fostered by a joint ministerial commission (Calvert and Alcock 2004, 452).

In contrast, the shah refused to budge on the issue of the smaller islands. While initially in favor of a united Arab federation to include the emirates, but possibly also Bahrain and Qatar, he would later block and threaten such a creation before the island dispute was not resolved. He began to publicly threaten to take the islands, emboldened by the upcoming British withdrawal announced in 1968 (Mobley 2003, 630). Alvandi cites popular opinion as the main reason for the shah's initial reluctance to give up the claim to Bahrain, having once confided that he feared going down "in history as the man who lightly abandoned his country's '14th province'" (Alvandi 2010 164, 171). A popular interpretation of the contrast to the islands claim is therefore compensation: the shah occupied the islands to save face because of Bahrain (Alkim 1989, 141).[14]

Although the claim to the Tunbs and Abu Musa was not withdrawn, cooperation between Tehran and Riyadh did not cease but instead expanded to Saudi Arabia's neighbors. In 1968, the shah invited UAE rulers for a state visit and the shaikh of Ras al-Khaimah came for ten days in August, a major success for Iran and perceived as rapprochement between the two monarchies. Over the years, eventually all of the Gulf rulers paid a visit to Iran, even Bahrain after the outstanding territorial claim was abandoned (Alkim 1989, 139–140).

The islands were claimed by two emirates: Abu Musa by Sharjah under Shaikh Khalid bin Muhammad Al Qasimi and the two Tunbs by Ras al-Khaimah under the leadership of Shaikh Saqr bin Muhammad Al Qasimi. The British supported Arab ownership of the islands and were optimistic that this would be the result of an independent legal review, but the shah claimed the islands for Iran and refused to submit the dispute to international arbitration (Mobley 2003, 629). The shah achieved an agreement with the shaikh of Sharjah, but not with the ruler of Ras al-Khaimah.

180 *From monarchy to republic*

However, he did not initially intend to use violence. One British proposal included awarding the Sirri island to Iran while enabling a purchase of the Tunbs. Abu Musa would remain with Sharjah. The shah was open to the possibility of purchase, but possible Arab opposition hindered the progression of the plan, although the Emirati shaikhs entertained the possibility. In an August 1968 meeting between Shaikh Saqr Al Qasimi and Iranian Prime Minister Hoveida and Foreign Minister Ardeshir Zahedi, the Iranian representatives offered "compensation" and access to any mineral wealth discovered or the establishment of an Iranian naval base in exchange for anything that the Ras al-Khaimah leader wanted in return. He in turn offered the renting out of the islands while retaining sovereignty, a suggestion that the Iranian representatives refused. By July 1970, Iran had updated its position. It would not abolish its sovereignty claim over the islands but would not demand its recognition by the Arabs; it would garrison the islands, and mineral rights would be shared between Iran and Sharjah. Neither Iran, Sharjah, nor Ras al-Khaimah were ready to relinquish the sovereignty claim to the islands, and Iran resorted to open threats of occupation if diplomatic means came to naught. In 1971, it anchored warships in the vicinity of the Tunbs. Libya offered to send troops for protection, but the emirates refused the offer (Mobley 2003, 634–636).

Proposals and counter-proposals followed. On November 24, Foreign Secretary Alec Douglas-Home forwarded a letter with a memorandum of understanding (MoU) by Shaikh Khalid to Iran's Abbas Ali Khalatbari that stated that while neither side would abandon its sovereignty claim, the matter would proceed with the arrival of Iranian troops on Abu Musa that would occupy the areas previously assigned. On this area, Iran would have jurisdiction, fly the Iranian flag, and have the right to station troops (Alkim 1989, 142; Mobley 2003, 642). Sharjah would retain its sovereignty on the rest of the territory; its police post would fly the Sharjah flag; the oil revenues would be split equally between the two; and nationals of both countries would have equal fishing rights (Mobley 2003, 643). Also, an assistance agreement would be signed providing up to £1.5 million per year from Iran to Sharjah until the emirate's annual receipts from oil reached 3 million. Both Iran and Sharjah would also recognize a 12-mile limit of territorial waters around the island (Alkim 1989, 142).

Khalatbari accepted the terms of the letter but added that Iranian freedom of action to safeguard the security of the island or Iranian forces would not be restricted (which later served as the reference point for Iran in the 1992 escalation). Khalid announced the final accord on November 29 (Mobley 2003, 643).

The monarchic alliance (1971–1979): monarchic solutions to territorial conflicts and the limits of the monarchic peace

Perhaps the most concise description of the particularities of the short but memorable monarchic period is provided by Ahmadi:

> This period began with the Iranian government moderating its policy and seeking rapprochement with other Gulf states from early 1972. Strengthening

From monarchy to republic 181

this approach between 1974 and 1979, Iran succeeded in systematically mending fences with conservative Gulf states. It supported Kuwait during its periods of tension with Iraq, enhanced cooperation with Bahrain, provided aid to the United Arab Emirates, and Dubai in particular, gave military support to Oman in suppressing the Dhofar rebellion, helped North Yemen replace its Soviet arms and furnished arms to Somalia. Iran also signed an agreement with Oman in December 1977 providing for joint patrol of the Strait of Hormuz (the key channels of which are in Omani waters).

(Ahmadi 2008, 111)

Great inequalities of size, power, history, and culture hampered the development of a fully developed ingroup identification or a "West Asian community" (Adib-Moghaddam 2006, 129), but numerous scholars acknowledge the unifying force of political system similarity. Hellyer explains the comparatively weak ties with Iraq vis-à-vis other Gulf states with "the radically different nature of the Iraqi political system" (Hellyer 2001, 168). Ahmadi draws attention to the relatively harmonic monarchic period:

the Arab Persian Gulf sheikhs and monarchs continued to feel more comfortable with Iran throughout the 1970s. They regarded Iran as a conservative, status quo-oriented power, and preferred it over Iraq's revolutionary and ideological regime.

(Ahmadi 2008, 110)

Structural similarities

Apart from major conflicts of interests, the differences between the two countries were vast and the basis for ingroup identification therefore especially weak. Iran was an ethnically Persian and denominationally Shiite state, whereas the territories of the Trucial Coast were Arab and mostly Sunni. Their political systems, albeit monarchic, also differed significantly – Iran's more-than-bimillennial history of statehood and empire, its elaborate bureaucracy, and its political institutions stood in sharp contrast to the tribally based federation of seven distinct tiny emirates that started to develop modern state institutions only after the British arrival and consolidated them with income from oil exports that did not arrive until well into the 20th century (although both were rentier states, albeit to various degrees). Whereas Iran is a classic linchpin monarchy where the monarch is the pivotal point of the system balancing different institutions and societal groups (Lucas 2004), the UAE is a typical dynastic monarchy where not the monarch alone but rather the family forms the main focal group and ruling institution of the state (Herb 1999).[15]

Salience: constraints and catalysts to ingroup identification

The salience of monarchism before the 1979 revolution was high due to threats from external powers, coups and revolutions, and the minority status of monarchies, although it did not reach the peaks of the period of the Arab Cold War.

182 *From monarchy to republic*

Although the Gulf states' independence bolstered the numbers of monarchies, they remained a (large) minority, with nine (the Gulf monarchies, Jordan, Morocco, and Iran) out of 19, i.e. 47%, in contrast to the previous five (Jordan, Morocco, Iran, Saudi Arabia, and Kuwait) out of 15, i.e. 33%. The Iranian Revolution in 1979 was the last time a monarchy in the Middle East was overthrown and replaced by a republic. Four such regime changes had already taken place in the region before (1952, 1958, 1962, and 1969), the last one just two years before the small Gulf monarchies' independence.

During the rule of Shah Reza Pahlavi, Iranian interests and worldviews largely overlapped with its monarchic Arab neighbors because they were conservative status quo powers. They were all threatened by and opposed to radical Arab nationalism, especially by Iraq abroad and internally by opposition actors. They all favored an intimate relationship with Western powers, especially the United States, and opposed Soviet influence; they were all interested in oil price and transport security and tried not to get too involved in the Arab-Israeli conflict. Combined with Washington's Twin Pillars policy that relied on Iran and Saudi Arabia as the two guarantors of regional stability, many expected the emergence of joint Gulf security in the 1970s.

The relationships between the hereditary rulers of the Gulf were boosted by past changes in the monarchic community: before the revolution of 1979, another monarchic breakdown profoundly shaped the regional dynamics, the coup of 1958, whose effects are poignantly described by Halliday:

> Prior to the Iraqi revolution of 1958, Iran and Iraq, as two monarchies formed after World War I, enjoyed reasonably co-operative relations, even if there remained the issue of the territorial dispute between them, concerning the division of the Shatt al-Arab. . . . At that time a combination of *shared monarchical political system and British influence in Iraq* kept conflict under control. The Iraqi revolution of July 1958 destroyed all that: the two countries then found themselves involved in competitive interference in each other's internal affairs.
>
> (Halliday 2011, 179, emphasis added)

1958 was the first turning point that altered Iranian threat perception via the fall of a fellow conservative monarchic regime and the institution of a revolutionary and pan-Arab republic. The ranks of the radicals swelled, and the shah saw a clear anti-monarchical threat in the rising Arabism. Iran felt the immediate repercussions after its de facto recognition of Israel on July 24, 1960, which drew the ire of revolutionary republics. Egypt attacked Iran's territorial integrity by claiming the province of Khuzestan (which the revolutionary Arab states called "Arabistan") for the Arab nation. Two days after the recognition, the United Arab Republic broke off diplomatic relations with Iran, and following another two days, President Nasser denounced the shah in a speech. On August 8, the Arab League declared a boycott against Iran (cf. Ahmadi 2008, 76–77).

From monarchy to republic 183

Although the peak of republic–monarchy tensions abated with the fading of the Arab Cold War, they did not cease completely. The radical republican threat was still active in Iraq, which contributed to forging a zone of peace crossing Arab-Persian boundaries during the era of the shah: "between 1972 and 1978, Iraq's support of various radical movements in the Gulf led Saudi Arabia and Iran to co-operate in supporting the growth and stability of the UAE" (Cordesman 1984, 419).

Inside the "club of monarchies", there was no full-fledged divisive ideology per se, but some currents within the larger members' outlook, and especially Iran, induced tensions. Iranian dominance often proved problematic and divisive given that "Iran–UAE relations largely follow the pattern of relations between a large regional power and a smaller neighbor" (Gargash 1996, 151). At the time, the region was dominated by Iran. The shah followed a dual strategy of carrots and sticks. He threatened the small emirates to deter them from allying with another power and extended support to develop special relationships with some rulers of the emirates such as Shaikh Rashid of Dubai (Alkim 1989, 138). The shah's hegemonic aims were bolstered by notions of Persian supremacy, down to the renaming of the country from Persia to Iran, relinking it to its "Aryan" heritage. Adib-Moghaddam emphasized this as a main stumbling block for the formation of community in the Gulf:

> The brand of Iranian nationalism espoused by the shah, and more specifically, the reification of the insidious, metaphysical mendacity of racially coded Iranian supremacy, not only widened the gulf between the state elites of the region, it inhibited the formal translation of communitarian norms into a functioning security architecture.
>
> (Adib-Moghaddam 2006, 18)[16]

Saudi Arabia's behavior toward its smaller Arab neighbors was often similar, but without an equivalent for Persian supremacism. Among the open territorial claims to almost every single one of its neighbors' territory was also a territorial dispute with the UAE regarding the Buraimi oasis. Even while trying to claim territory from the Trucial Coast states, it supported regional stability and federation formation (of a broader federation that included Bahrain and Qatar as well as the seven emirates that would make up the UAE) before their independence and yet withheld recognition once the federation was announced (Alkim 1989, 115–116). Although the kingdom's policies could be interpreted as hegemonic or domineering, they were not inherently ideological. The dispute was declared resolved in 1975.

Social processes of ingroup identification

As Ahmadi notes, the bond between the Arab and Iranian monarchies was due to mutual interest and a shared worldview and joint identification:

> While the opposition of the Arab radicals to the Pahlavi regime was categorical, the Arab moderates and conservatives identified themselves with imperial

184 *From monarchy to republic*

> Iran's general game plan, executive strategies and strategic outlook, although they were never fully convinced of the innocence of the shah's regional aims.
>
> (Ahmadi 2008, 133)

Despite earlier repeated threats to withhold recognition, Iran recognized the UAE two days after its declaration of independence (four days after the islands' occupation), although the establishment of diplomatic relations took almost another year. Relations were cool in the beginning, with the strongest partners being Dubai and Sharjah, but bilateral contacts slowly intensified. President of the Federation Zayed Al Nahyan visited the shah in 1975, signaling the normalizing of relations (Alkim 1989, 140; Gargash 1996, 150). Strong personal relations with rulers of the shaikhdoms of the Arabian Peninsula were generally essential for the shah, who frequently invited them for vacations and hunting trips (Alvandi 2010, 161). They continued in the 1970s, despite the islands dispute.

While reciprocal recognition is usually the first necessary step toward joint identification, in this case it is doubtful that the threat of withholding was directed against the institutions of the emirs or a federal monarchy per se. To the contrary, the shah's vision entailed stable conservative monarchical entities. Even before the recognition, he emphasized that he favored independence for the Trucial Coast. The point of contention was the shape of the polity, not its existence. He saw the emirates as disparate and inexperienced, making them unstable and prone to revolution or coups. For him, an alternative solution consisted in independent statehood for the larger and more viable emirates, such as Abu Dhabi, Bahrain, Dubai, and Qatar and Omani protection for the rest of the territory (Agwani 1978, 114; Alkim 1989, 139). The initial Iranian rejection of UAE sovereignty thus lay in the weakness and instability of their entity, making it unlikely to be stable enough to become a strong monarchy worthy of recognition – not in hostility or power rivalry.

Although Iran was usually considered too "foreign"[17] to be seen as a brother,[18] the Gulf monarchies saw it as a friendly state. Apart from references to a shared monarchic-conservative worldview, ceremonies involving monarchic protocol were notable occasions to forge and signal royal bonds.

Notable examples that emphasized the monarchical element were the festivities in Persepolis in October 1971, marking the 2500th anniversary of the founding of the Persian monarchy by Cyrus the Great. At the festivities, mere weeks before the Trucial states' independence, the heads of states of many countries were invited and present. Especially royals – European, Asian, and African – were abundantly present, including an emperor of Ethiopia (Haile Selassie), nine kings, three ruling princes, two crown princes, two sultans, and ten sheiks (including the four amirs of the Western Gulf – of Bahrain, Kuwait, Qatar, and Zayed Al Nahyan of the Trucial states). Although republics were already the vast majority of political systems at the time, there were "only" three prime ministers, 12 presidents, two vice presidents, and a cardinal present (Stevenson 2008, 22).

Royalty were further distinguished from other guests by the protocol that gave them priority of entrance and seating, due to their permanence, resulting in two

From monarchy to republic 185

queues at the welcoming procedure: one for the monarchs and one for "lesser mortals" (i.e. presidents and prime ministers) in the words of the attending Iranian diplomat Bijan Dolatabadi (Amini 2016). Particularly visible were Middle Eastern monarchs and their relatives. King Hussein of Jordan arrived with his wife and his younger sister; the emirs of Oman, Kuwait, and Bahrain and Prince Abdul Vali Khan, the uncle of the king of Afghanistan, were also present. King Hassan II of Morocco sent his brother (Royal Events 2002).

The Persepolis celebrations offered a unique opportunity for the leaders of the world and especially the monarchs to come together in a less than formal atmosphere. Outside of the regular program, they could visit each other in their respective tents, which fostered personal networks of mutual trust. At least some monarchs seized the opportunity: Sultan Qaboos of Oman met King Hussein of Jordan and Prince Nawaf bin Abdalaziz of Saudi Arabia there for the first time and had his first discussions with the shah, with whom he arrived at a consensus on numerous regional issues (including negative opinions on Abu Dhabi, the Iraqis, and the Palestinians). The Iranian and Jordanian kings offered assistance to Qaboos, and he accepted an offer of "three good officers" from Jordan, pledging $2 million in return (Takriti 2016, 226). The Persepolis celebrations thus served to reify monarchic bonds by distinguishing royals from other rulers and providing opportunities for personal contact and relations, which in some cases transformed into tangible support and solidarity.

The shah prioritized regional stability and was thus keen on settling the islands issue peacefully, so he attempted to frame the conflict as a confrontation with colonial Britain, not one with the emerging UAE. During the rule of the shah, Iran adhered to its agreement with Sharjah on Abu Musa and began violating provisions only after the revolution and especially during the Iran–Iraq War.

Foreign policy restraint

Although strictly speaking the occupation of the islands is outside the time scope, because the UAE was not yet independent, it is recounted here because of its impact on future relations between Iran and the UAE. No MID has been recorded between the dyad (or any other Iran–Arab monarchy dyad) in this period (Ghosn, Palmer, and Bremer 2004).

On November 30, 1971, the day before the British withdrawal from the Gulf and two days before the announcement of the UAE's independence, Iran occupied the islands (Mobley 2003, 627). While Iranian troops arrived in Abu Musa with Sharjah's cooperation and were accompanied by a representative of Sharjah, the shaikh's brother and heir apparent,[19] their arrival on Greater Tunb was met with resistance (Alvandi 2010, 176). A skirmish led to seven deaths – four Ras al-Khaimah police officers and three Iranian soldiers (Alkim 1989, 143). This was probably unintended given that the occupying Iranians were instructed not to open fire and first shots came from Arab resistance, which killed the three Iranian marines and injured another (Metz 1994). All inhabitants were evacuated to Ras al-Khaimah, and rioting in both affected emirates ensued despite Shaikh Khalid of Sharjah's acquiescence to the agreement (Mobley 2003, 643).

186 *From monarchy to republic*

Despite Iran's territorial claims, the handling of the conflict was remarkably civil, with little to no escalation and provocations. Since the UAE's independence, there has been no significant delegitimization attempts and no subversion between Iran and the UAE and the Arab Gulf states in general. The *khaleeji* reaction to Iranian occupation was highly restrained.

Fourteen months of British mediation attempts under the deadline of their withdrawal had brought successful conflict resolution between Iran and Sharjah between the shah and Shaikh Khalid regarding Abu Musa. In the case regarding the Tunbs, it failed because Ras al-Khaimah's ruler Shaikh Saqr was less amenable to an agreement with Iran (Mobley 2003, 627).

UAE declared independence on December 2, 1971, after Bahrain and Qatar had already done so in September. Both the Arab League and the UN addressed the islands question (Mobley 2003, 643), but the shah's abandonment of his claim on Bahrain muted reaction in the Arab world. Only Arab nationalist Iraq severed relations (Alvandi 2010, 177). An Arab League emissary concluded that local rulers were in favor of diplomatic solutions. Despite the tensions, Ras al-Khaimah was still open about the possibility of leasing the islands to Iran, but Tehran had lost interest. In a December 9 session of the UN Security Council, delegates of the republican states of South Yemen, Libya, Iraq, and Algeria declared that the invasion violated the UN Charter and that the agreement between Sharjah and Iran over Abu Musa must be annulled, because it was concluded under duress. No resolution was adopted (Mobley 2003, 643–644).

A joint Arab letter was signed on July 18, 1972, and sent to the UN to protest against the occupation and declare the islands Arab. Not every Arab country signed, however, and the monarchies were split. Morocco, Bahrain, Kuwait, Oman, and the UAE signed, along with the radical states, but Jordan, Qatar, and Saudi Arabia (along with non-Arab North Korea and Somalia) abstained. Although hardly a united effort, the letter was to be the last joint Arab action before the revolution (Ahmadi 2008, 102–103).

Despite the immense impediments in Arab-Iranian relations, the monarchies cooperated with one another even on the eve of occupation. Saudi Arabia only reluctantly criticized the hostile Iranian action. At first, it merely expressed sorrow but refrained from condemning it, instead expressing surprise and regret at the incident. Ahmadi describes it thus: "Saudi Arabia, as a conservative and pro-Western state, indicated only its dissatisfaction with the Iranian move and did not even directly urge an Iranian pullout" (Ahmadi 2008, 110). Saudi Arabia also did not participate at the Arab League crisis council on December 6 and did not request participation at the UN SC session three days later (Sirriyeh 1984, 85). Kuwait enjoyed friendly relations with the shah, who was also seen as a bulwark against Iraq, which had in the past often threatened the statelet militarily and was thus reluctant to criticize the occupation (Assiri 1990, 64).

The UAE itself was slow to reply. On December 5, President Zayed bin Sultan Al Nahyan condemned "the aggression by a neighbouring and friendly state" – eschewing family rhetoric but affirming friendship – and stated that "we are awaiting the Arab states' concrete support to assist us in regaining our rights", but it was

From monarchy to republic 187

not followed by more-concrete actions (Alkim 1989, 144). And even this appeal for support seemed more rhetorical than sincere, given the UAE's rejection of Libya's "concrete support" offer to send troops (Ahmadi 2008, 102). This was hardly surprising given the vastly differing viewpoints and approaches among the emirates themselves.

The lone exception amid the tepid Arab Gulf reaction was Ras al-Khaimah, the last emirate to join the union in 1972, for reasons mainly connected to the Iranian question. Initially, Ras al-Khaimah refused to join the UAE, in protest of its passivity in light of the occupation (Gause 2010, 24), but its later application was rejected, in part because of its more radical stance on Iran (and its ambitions vis-à-vis its future position and power in the federation) (cf. Ahmadi 2008, 95–96). The emirate agreed to join theunion in December 10 if, among others, the UAE would "liberate the three islands from Iranian occupation by armed force" (cited in: Alkim 1989, 47).

This stance was rooted in the actual occupation as much as in personal traits of the ruling Shaikh Saqr, who was sometimes also jestingly referred to as "the Napoleon of the Gulf" or "Bonaparte of the Trucial Coast". Saqr had a reputation of contrarianism besides the islands issue. Among the most notable disagreements with other Emirati shaikhs were his informal claims to neighboring Sharjah, legitimized by it being a part of a larger Qawasim state;[20] his reluctant support for the UAE before the 1979 revolution; and his unilateral decision to invite Soviet military technicians to Ras al-Khaimah (Ahmadi 2008, 97).

Saqr's foreign policy decisions did not show any acceptance for sovereignty or territorial integrity norms among states, regardless of the closeness of relations. He laid claim not only to the Tunbs and Sharjah but also to Omani territory and offshore rights, which in November 1977 resulted into an armed confrontation between the two countries "that ended like 'a comic opera' when the large number of Omanis in Shaikh Saqr's forces refused to fight Oman's forces" (Ahmadi 2008, 98). This attempt to seize part of Oman won Ras al-Khaimah' the Soviet Union's support (Foley 1999). To add insult to injury, UAE president and emir of Abu Dhabi Zayed Al Nahyan backed Oman in the dispute, which exposed the UAE's vulnerability to pressure from Oman and led to continued tension between Shaikh Saqr and other members of the UAE (Ahmadi 2008, 98).

Ras al-Khaimah's practically sole close supporter was republican Iraq, whose relations to Iran had deteriorated massively after the revolution in 1958. Early on, Iraq pushed the UAE to press the matter of returning the islands to their Arab owners, but with little effect (Alkim 1989, 53).

In the case of the Iranian move on the islands, both monarchies and republics flocked with birds of the same feather, and ideology rooted in the different political systems trumped geographic proximity and personal concernedness. The delegitimization and subversion of Iran and the UAE came mainly from republics, not each other. The "radical" Arab countries reacted much more vigorously, despite their greater distance, first by calling for immediate Iranian withdrawal, then with more robust calls and actions. Libya offered military support and prepared troops to move to the Gulf, while Iraq deported about 120,000 purported "Iranians" over the turn of the year 1971/1972 (Ahmadi 2008, 102).

188   *From monarchy to republic*

Iraq was also the only country to continuously put the islands issue on the public agenda (at least until the Algiers Accord of 1975). This was not done out of solidarity with a politically and militarily weak UAE; to the contrary, Iraq even pressured the Emirates into a more confrontational stance while withholding formal recognition of the new state (Ahmadi 2008, 107). Iraq also began equating "Persian nationalism" with Zionism and imperialism, two mortal enemies of the Arab nation in its worldview (Ahmadi 2008, 102).

After a coup attempt in Sharjah in 1972 that killed the compliant Shaikh Khalid, who had agreed to the MoU on Abu Musa, the emirate accused Iraq of support and providing an arms shipment. Khalid was replaced by his brother Sultan bin Muhammad, who affirmed his adherence to the MoU but stated his intention to come to a new understanding with the shah. Somewhat ironically, the crisis led Iraq to heighten its pressure on Kuwait to cede the islands of Warba and Bubiyan to Iraq, which had already risen in the late 1960s, due to its tensions with Iran. In April 1973, Iraq's foreign minister stated that without these islands, Iraq could not become a Gulf power, and its cession was therefore necessary for a border delimitation. Riyadh and Tehran together pressured and appeased Baghdad, and Kuwait offered large payments (Ahmadi 2008, 108, 110).

In the 1970s, Iran moved closer to other Arab states and especially monarchies and even provided protection, as if the islands dispute never existed. Despite strong ingroup solidarity, the divisions between Iran and the Arab Gulf monarchies were too strong to successfully institutionalize the alignment in the Iran-led Gulf Security Pact. Nevertheless, mutual support was strong: security guarantees, pressure, and financial incentives from both the Arab states and Iran are said to have deterred Iraq from attacking Kuwait in 1973 (Adib-Moghaddam 2006, 15; Ahmadi 2008, 110).

Because revolutionary Iraq was the more immediate threat, the other Arab monarchies gave only token support to Ras al-Khaimah in its dispute with Iran in late 1971. Abu Dhabi, the largest and most influential emirate in the federation, wanted to counterbalance the Saudis, with whom it had a territorial dispute until 1974, via good relations with Iran and Oman and thus opposed Shaikh Saqr's adventures. Sharjah, the other affected emirate, had already settled for part of Abu Musa and was keen to not jeopardize the oil rent and Iranian financial assistance. At the opposite end of the spectrum of necessary means in the islands question across Ras al-Khaimah was pro-Iranian Dubai, with its intensive trade and historical relations with Iran. The ties were so resilient that Dubai sided with Iran even in the border dispute. In 1976, Iran and the UAE signed an agreement of economic cooperation 1976, of which Dubai was the prime beneficiary (Alkim 1989, 53, 152–154).

The commercial sector was a main driver of cooperation between the two states, but bilateral relations expanded in general in the 1970s, despite the invasion (Hellyer 2001, 170). The UAE in general preferred good relations with Iran, despite the seizing of the islands, because of its vulnerability toward Saudi Arabia (the border issue between Abu Dhabi and the kingdom had not yet been settled) and because of the power vacuum left by the British withdrawal, especially given the

From monarchy to republic 189

ongoing Dhofar rebellion and the Marxist regime in South Yemen. This made the shah suitable as protector of the "conservative status quo" (cf. Gargash 1996, 149).

In January 1975, Iran extended its naval presence in Oman under an agreement for joint naval operations in the crucial Strait of Hormuz. According to the Iranian foreign ministry, 3000 troops were deployed to Oman to help against the Dhofar insurgency, and the Omani military announced that Iran had guaranteed air support against foreign intrusion into Oman's airspace on February 2, 1975, as requested. The Omani minister of state for foreign affairs, Qais Abd al-Moneim al-Zawawi, said that Iran would have the major responsibility for implementing the agreement, which was aimed at keeping the waters on both sides of the strait "secure and free". He denied that the operations were a threat to Iraq. This bolsters the interpretation that the Iranian military buildup at the time was perceived as a relief more than a threat by the littoral states (Ahmadi 2008, 112), indicating a high degree of trust. Following the revolution, Iranian troops and military guarantees to Oman were removed (Halliday 1980, 13).

Ingroup identification led the shah to believe the time was a ripe for a joint regional security cooperation framework, and he proposed the Gulf Security Pact, which he tried to make palatable to the Gulf states. The pact would have posed an alternative to the later GCC and would have included Iran (while excluding republican Iraq). Although it ultimately failed, there was some level of support among the smaller Gulf states for a joint security arrangement. Apart from Iraq, the most critical Gulf state was Saudi Arabia as it ran counter to its own ambitions of regional hegemony over the smaller states – although its level of support and opposition varied (cf. Gause 2010, 39).

The pact was officially directed "against outside interference" but in reality most likely against internal threats, combining the monarchies in a framework based on their shared threat of regime overthrow and coup d'état that forged their identity and worldview (Halliday 1980, 10). On the shah's first visit to Saudi Arabia in March 1957, he proposed his vision for a bilateral defense pact but was rebuffed because Saudi Arabia feared entrapment into the controversial Baghdad Pact that ultimately was put to rest by the breakdown of the Iraqi monarchy. After the Six-Day War in 1967 dealt a heavy blow to radical Arab nationalism, King Faisal proclaimed during visit to Tehran in December that "now is the time for more cooperation and coordination between the two countries". One result was the Organization of Islamic Cooperation, founded in 1969. The shah reiterated his proposal of a Gulf collective security pact after his visit to the desert kingdom after Faisal's death in April 1975. The Saudis signaled interest but stayed noncommittal (Ansari 1999, 857–859).

During November 25–26, 1976, all littoral states met for the first time on the foreign-ministerial level at the Muscat conference. The proposals presented there included Iranian-style cooperation projects and Iraqi-inspired denials of any necessity for collective projects (Ansari 1999, 859). Iran proposed a unified military under joint command. The Muscat conferences' failure to reach a conclusion was a setback for the shah, and Iranian press blamed Iraq and foreign powers for it – but not the monarchies (Parveen 2006, 114, 53). Despite the setbacks, the

190   *From monarchy to republic*

shah did not abandon his idea and instead kept bringing it up on various occasions and official visits to the Arab monarchies. In May and June 1978, talks were held between Iraq, Iran, and Saudi Arabia, but any possible consensus was undercut by the revolution in Iran in February 1979, which put an end to all of these efforts (Ansari 1999, 860).

The pact failed in part because the small Arab monarchies were still distrustful of the shah and his hegemonic ambitions in the Gulf, despite his insistence that Iranian policy did not constitute a "big brother attitude" (Parveen 2006, 54). However, the smaller Gulf states' lukewarm reactions extended equally to similar Saudi proposals for unity and thus cannot be reduced to mistrust of Persian Iran alone. After he succeeded his half-brother Faisal after the latter's assassination in March 1975, King Khalid became the first Saudi monarch to visit the Gulf states during March–April 1976 and used the occasion to advertise a Saudi alternative, which consisted of numerous bilateral agreements on internal security cooperation. Kuwait and Oman "politely demurred" from the proposal in fall 1976, to form an organization for internal security cooperation that would consist exclusively of Arab monarchies, thereby excluding republican Iraq and Persian Iran, both special allies of the two small monarchies (Gause 2010, 39–40). After the Saudi-Emirati border issue was settled in 1974, the UAE also reacted more coolly to Iranian advances regarding the security pact (Gargash 1996, 150).

Certainly, at that time, the obstacles were too great for a full-fledged security community to form: the small Gulf states had just begun to develop into nation-states with their own national identity (let alone a cross-national joint identity), and the regional system was still adapting to the entries and exits of previous years and decades. It remained a "rump international society" (Adib-Moghaddam 2006, 15). Nonetheless, the long process of negotiations showed the first signs of the transformation of cooperation and coordination out of a short-term convergence of interest into a longer-term identification with common goals and each other.

Ingroup identification in the monarchic period

The developments in this period show that despite the salience of the Arab-Persian cleavage, in critical situations, regime type trumped ethnicity. In both countries, the political leadership identified more with conservative monarchic interests than with Arab or Persian nationalist causes and ideas. Iran and the UAE shared many similarities, although not as many as, for example, Iraq and Kuwait in the previous case. In addition, while not a full-fledged ideology, Iran's "Persian supremacy" and dominating role in the Gulf had a divisive effect on the group, making it harder for ingroup identification to arise. Consequently, there are fewer (albeit still notable) indications for the development and affirmation of such a sense of monarchic solidarity. The resulting sense of proximity was fostered by the shared threat from revolutionary republicanism, resulting in a remarkable level of restraint even during conflict periods.

Despite the military and political superiority position of Iran (especially after the departure of the British), Tehran attempted to pursue negotiations instead of

From monarchy to republic 191

a policy of confrontation. This resulted in a diplomatic agreement in the case of Abu Musa and, more importantly, in the abandonment of Iran's territorial claim to Bahrain. As a consequence, the capture of the Greater and Lesser Tunb did not result in a major escalation. Because the UAE was not yet an independent state, it was not an "equal" and was more likely to be perceived as "fair game", which contributed to a more muted reaction.[21] However, the first signs of recognition and symbolic "club membership" association were already present throughout this period, including frequent visits by high-ranking officials; festivals celebrating joint club membership, such as the Persepolis festivities; and the quick recognition of independence of the UAE.

This short period between the British withdrawal from the Persian Gulf, the Trucial Coast states' independence in late 1971, and the fall of the Iranian monarchy in early 1979 was "the most stable in the recent history of the Gulf" (Gause 2010, 42). Interstate disputes over the domestic bases of political legitimacy among the regional states were muted at first and nonexistent later on in this period. Instead, the monarchies shared a core interest that ensured regional peace: regime stability. Overall, there was a high level of agreement over the domestic legitimacy base, because it was essentially the same – monarchic, threatened by the republican current sweeping the region. As long as there was a shah in power in Iran and not a president (or a "Supreme Leader"), there was a strong sense of monarchic solidarity despite the divisive power of Arab and Persian nationalism (cf. Adib-Moghaddam 2006, 18–21).

This dynamic turned completely in the post-revolutionary period. Although material capabilities and regional hegemonic ambition remained largely constant, it was the perception of similarity that had changed: "The shah's power was not a threat to regime stability in the Arab monarchies; it provided support" (Gause 2010, 43).

Down with monarchism, down with peace (1979–2003): counterbalancing for the advanced – the UAE and the coalition against Iran

Following the revolution, relations deteriorated significantly and persistently, leading to a breakdown of ingroup identification and multiple episodes of provocations, crisis escalation, and militarized altercations. This describes not only Iranian behavior; especially after the crisis in 1992, UAE policy on the islands issue also became increasingly proactive and assertive (Hellyer 2001, 171).

Structural similarities

The Islamic Revolution in 1979 resulted in a new kind of system, completely foreign to the remaining Gulf monarchies. A pan-Islamist driving ideology was added to Iranian expansionism, the linchpin monarch replaced by a two-headed (initially even three-headed[22]) executive, and foreign policy prerogatives divided among the president and the supreme Spiritual Leader on the top brought about a theocracy that was institutionally and ideologically unlike both monarchies and republics in the region (cf. Ehteshami 2014, 269–271).

192 *From monarchy to republic*

System dissimilarity is more than a curiosity, in that it influences perception and behavior toward the other: as Anwar Gargash emphasizes, the nature and foreignness of the inscrutable and idiosyncratic *velayet-e faqih* system introduced distrust via uncertainty to the relationship. The decision-making process became highly untransparent, and the identification of the actual decision makers became more complicated than in monarchical times. Thus, the Arab Gulf monarchies could not always correctly interpret abrupt changes in Iranian behavior and accord the benefit of the doubt. An example was a crisis in 1993, when Iranian media sharply attacked Kuwait for its support of the UAE after having talked of a rapprochement in the wake of Foreign Minister Ali Akbar Velayati's visit there just five months prior (Gargash 1996, 157). The implication is that difficulty to identify the prime decision makers and their motivation raises the difficulty to identify *with* the decision makers.

Further widening the rift was the changing role of oil. While Iran remained dependent on oil income, the new regime attempted to lower its dependence on it and on the West, thereby curtailing capital flows and trade and stifling its economic development (Ehteshami 2014, 267).

Salience: constraints and catalysts to ingroup identification

Iraq, which attacked Iran shortly after the revolution, leading to almost a decade of war, and later attacked Kuwait, was a major threat to both Iran and the UAE. However, as in the previous case of Iraqi-Kuwaiti relations, since Iran was also perceived as a threat by Gulf states, Iraq and Iran alternated in cooperating with the UAE and the other Gulf monarchies. Iran and Iraq remained mutual threats to each other throughout the Ba'thist period in Iraq.

Since the revolution brought radical anti-monarchists to power, the impact of the divisive ideology was strong, especially in the first years after the revolution. While the pan-Islamic ideology did not inherently assume a leader (although the Iranian version naturally favored Iran as a vanguard), it delegitimized other forms of government, especially monarchies. Before Iraq posed the major threat against conservative monarchies (see Chapter 3.2), Iranian opposition was at least just as vitriolic. Khomeini himself had railed persistently against monarchies, which he considered to be incompatible with Islam (Khomeini quoted by Rajaee 2010, 122), "wrong and invalid", and even an "evil form of government" (Moghadam 2011, 50–51). Pan-Islamic mission was a dual threat, internal and external: it underlined Iranian aggressive intentions and gave support to opposition actors eager to undermine or overthrow the monarchic regimes inside the countries.

Public reaction in the Gulf states was completely opposite to elite reaction and supportive of the revolution (Assiri 1990, 65). There were large demonstrations in the UAE after the fall of the monarchy (Abdullah 1980, 19). This explains the strongly perceived ideational threat that was different from mere power concerns, as described by al Nahyan:

> Arab unease was focused less on Iran as a military threat, but instead gave primacy to the potential spread of Iranian revolutionary ideology, its

'political and ideational leverage', and these concerns were only intensified yet further when Ayatollah Khomeini announced that Islam was not compatible with monarchy, the prevailing system of government in the region. The pronouncement was accompanied by fiery speeches by Iranian officials denouncing all political systems in the Gulf, and accusing them of being tools of American colonization.

(Al-Nahyan 2013, 88–89)

The cutting of the unifying ties of monarchism led to a greater perceived proximity among the Arab states of the Gulf, with Iraq now sensing an opportunity for inclusion and hegemony over the smaller Arab states. Iran, on the other hand, now had no unifying ties whatsoever except for historical memory, and as Iraq attempted to tie the Arab monarchies closer to itself, Iran enhanced anti-monarchic and anti-secular propaganda, widening the rift even more. The monarchies reciprocated (Khalaf 1987). Sectarianism also proved divisive but became the main catalyst for inter-Gulf conflict only after the transformation of the regional system set in motion by the Arab Uprisings.

Social processes of ingroup identification

The Arab rulers' official reactions to the revolutionary turmoil were mixed and recognition not immediately extended. Saudi Arabia affirmed their support for the shah. On November 21, 1978, Foreign Minister Saud al-Faisal insisted that "the Shah must stay . . . his achievements are remarkable", and King Khalid himself proclaimed in January 1979 that "the Shah's regime is legitimate and Saudi Arabia supports it" even after he announced his intention to leave (both quotes in: Alkim 1989, 126). Omani and Kuwaiti officials also openly proclaimed their support for the shah. Kuwait had turned down Khomeini at their doorstep (Alkim 1989, 152; Assiri 1990, 64).

The UAE eventually supported the "people's choice", albeit reluctantly. Because opposition figures during the monarchic era had frequently raised the issue of renegotiating the islands situation, there was some hope of a blessing in disguise, but it was soon crushed because the new regime turned out to be more hostile toward the monarchies than its predecessor was (Gargash 1996, 150). The statements by UAE officials were guarded but concerned amid the turmoil of the revolution and became more favorable only after it had become clear that the new regime was a fait accompli. Despite the grudging acceptance, official relations were not established until 1982 (Alkim 1989, 61, cf. 156).

PERSONALIZATION OF BONDS BETWEEN RULING ELITES

Regularized personal interaction settled down only by the late 1980s and under heavy criticism, especially inside Iran. Short periods of rapprochements were followed by backtracking and by boycotts and cancelations of joint meetings.

Between September and October 1989, Iranian foreign ministry officials paid at least three visits to the small Gulf monarchies. Iranian hardliners, however,

194 *From monarchy to republic*

opposed this rapprochement, especially regarding Saudi Arabia, and the daily news outlet *Kayhan* railed against the "mirage" pursued by the government. Nevertheless, Ali Akbar Hashemi Rafsanjani, elected into presidency in 1989, prevailed, enabling Iran to upgrade relations with Kuwait and Bahrain and starting negotiations with Saudi Arabia to improve their relations by the middle of September 1989, over a decade after the regime change. After the Iraqi invasion in Kuwait, Iranian Foreign Minister Velayati visited the UAE, Oman, Bahrain, Qatar, and Syria and met with the Kuwaiti foreign minister, all the while explicitly proclaiming Iran as a balancing power to Iraq (Ahmadi 2008, 146).

The GCC summit in Doha in December 1990 provided the opportunity for the Gulf states to pay back Rafsanjanis advances, and many GCC representatives called for an inclusion of Iran into a post-liberation Gulf security arrangement, including Sultan Qaboos of Oman, traditionally one of the closest Gulf states to Iran; Shaikh Nasser Mohammed al-Sabah, the minister of state for foreign affairs of Kuwait; and Mubarak al-Khater, the Qatari foreign minister and summit spokesperson. For the first time since the creation of the GCC, its members' foreign ministers and its secretary-general, Abdallah Bishara, met with Velayati in New York. The closing statement of the summit in Doha included a paragraph on Iran welcoming the recent conciliatory gestures and emphasizing the mutual intention to solve differences (Ahmadi 2008, 147). Nonetheless, the usual and often exaggerated friendliness and familial references present in such declarations are lacking: except for a minor reference to religious and historical linkage, the text is dry and neutral.[23]

As expected of a conjunction based on interest convergence rather than a long-term alliance, once the imminent threat posed by expansionary Iraq subsided, the commitment to cooperate between the GCC states and Iran waned and was not followed by the growth of an ingroup. Attempts to relaunch negotiations after the 1992 clashes came to naught, and meetings have been derailed or canceled frequently. Accusations of stalling and hindering resolution were widespread on both sides (Calvert and Alcock 2004, 469).

On May 23, 1993, UAE Minister of State for Foreign Affairs Shaikh Hamdan bin Zayed al Nahyan met Velayati in Abu Dhabi to discuss the matter and both expressed "their willingness to hold further talks". A reciprocal visit should have followed on June 6, but on September 10, 1993, Shaikh Hamdan canceled his scheduled visit, blaming Iranian intransigence (Ahmadi 2008, 170; Al-Nahyan 2013, 53–54).

In mid November 1995, Qatar, under the aegis of its minister of foreign affairs, Shaikh Hamad bin Jassim bin Jabir Al-Thani, attempted to mediate another round of bilateral negotiations. Because the UAE proposed effectively the same agenda as in December 1992, Iran refused, and talks broke down again. Although both parties again reiterated their willingness for further negotiation, the head of the UAE delegation and later ambassador to Iran, Khalifa Shaheen al-Mirri, expressed strong doubts about the Iranian commitment and painted the Iranian behavior as an affront to Qatari efforts (Al-Nahyan 2013, 55–56). The same pattern was repeated in the following years and hardly changed even in the new millennium.

From monarchy to republic 195

Although the visit by Iranian Foreign Minister Kamal Kharrazi in Abu Dhabi in May 1998 was cordial and both he and the UAE president spoke of reconciliation, no new proposals resulted. A month later, Iran named three naval vessels after the islands, leading the UAE to protest at the United Nations. Kharrazi visited twice more and invited Zayed to the conference of the OIC in Tehran, but no talks ensued (Al-Nahyan 2013, 60–61). In 2007, the first Iranian head of government visited the UAE. A visit by the Iranian president to sign an MoU (unrelated to the islands dispute) in January 2009 was marred but not precluded by mutual recrimination over the UAE decision to fingerprint Iranian visitors to UAE (Al-Nahyan 2013, 100, 67–68).

The 1979 revolution opened a rift between the Arab monarchies and Iran. The victory of the Islamists who had railed against the pro-Western conservative monarchies for years could not bode well. Some lip service was paid to the unifying similarities of Islam and common interests, but mostly, relations were cold, even in "friendly" periods. In terms of reference, Iran was demoted from the "friend" in times of the shah to mere "neighbor", sometimes with the attribute of "friendly relations". In less-friendly periods, consistent othering became the norm.

Khomeini had derided the religiosity of ruling families in the Gulf who practiced what he termed "American Islam" or "Golden Islam" (Assiri 1990, 65). He dismissed the Gulf rulers as "mini shahs", equating them with the regime that he had just overthrown (Boghardt 2006, 29) and delegitimized the monarchic system in general, stating that "Islam proclaims monarchy and hereditary succession wrong and invalid" (Khomeini quoted by Rajaee 2010, 122). There was no love lost across the Gulf, and the Arab monarchs denounced Khomeini for advocating "wrong subversive ideologies" (Korany 1984, 252).

Initial signs of a friendly approach toward its smaller neighbors were implicit in Tehran's inclusive pan-Islamic rhetoric and the recall of all territorial ambitions in the Gulf in October 1979, but that policy was soon reversed (Alkim 1989, 61). The new Iranian leadership was split on the issue of the Gulf states question. Some officials affirmed the necessity of good neighborly relations, whereas others railed against their support for imperialist Western powers. That official relations were not established until 1982 serves as an indication of the factional struggles inside the newly formed republic. Pressure from Iran forced the UAE into a "friendly" relationship, and they walked a tightrope between Saudi Arabia, Iraq, and Iran. After the head of Islamic Revolutionary Court Sadegh Khalkali's state visit to the UAE in mid 1979, alcohol bans and other Islamic-inspired laws were enforced (mostly on a temporary basis) in the UAE.[24] In 1980, some Iranian officials proclaimed Iran would not export their revolutions to their societies (Alkim 1989, cf. 156–158, 205).

Other officials, including Iranian president Abdul Hasan Bani Sadr, were more critical and confrontational, openly delegitimizing the Gulf monarchies (Alkim 1989, 159). In an interview shortly after the revolution, Bani Sadr affirmed Iran's ownership of the islands and stated that the Arab Gulf states (including Abu Dhabi, Qatar, Oman, Dubai, Kuwait, and Saudi Arabia) were not independent states (quoted in: Ahmadi 2008, 126). In June 1979, Foreign Minister Ibrahim

196 *From monarchy to republic*

Yazdi denied that Iran would give the islands back, and relations soured amid an extradition request by Iran. The UAE failed to comply, and Iran halted efforts to improve relations (Alkim 1989, 159).

The reemergence of the islands issue took place in the context of the rising influence of the US in the Gulf and the strengthening of the conservative alliance since the Gulf War (cf. Ahmadi 144). Rafsanjani used the Iraqi aggression to normalize relations with the Gulf monarchies and promised a respite from the hostile relationship since the revolution. Even in his period, the relations were based on a shared interest to cooperate, not on similarity or ingroup identification, and therefore did not last. While running for office, he announced a policy "based on the expansion of relations and good neighbourliness" (Ahmadi 2008, 145).

In the communiqué in Kuwait City in the wake of the liberation on May 5, 1991, mention of Iran is conspicuously lacking and security assistance and agreements are sought with foreign, mostly Western powers, but not Iran. It was the very outcome the Iranian rapprochement sought to prevent by establishing the country as an alternative protector in the Gulf – like in the times of the monarchy (cf. Ahmadi 2008, 148).

This is evidence that common threat alone cannot explain prolonged alliances and is not sufficient to develop a common identity. The attitude of the UAE, but also GCC states in general, is well encompassed in an interview statement by the director of the department of GCC and Gulf state affairs in the UAE Foreign Ministry, Khalifa Shaheen al-Mirri:

> We cannot have a regional security arrangement because of Iran. To have [a] reliable security arrangement, the first thing you need is trust. That's why we see the solving of the islands dispute with Iran, as well as boundary problems within the GCC, as a pre-requisite. Since 1991, we [have] detected some intention by Iran to establish itself as the regional power after Iraq's defeat. . . . This is where the gap between Iran and the UAE lies.
>
> (cited in Ahmadi 148)

The difference in the monarchic period is once again striking when the "islands dispute . . . as well as boundary problems within the GCC" were no obstacle to an informal regional security arrangement with Iran at the helm. Trust was present then because Iranian actions were perceived to be (mostly) for the good of the group and a bulwark against threats against it, which were generally republican in nature. However, no such identification with the goals and fears of the group could be discerned at that time: any common group that included the GCC states and Iran had disappeared.

The director-general of the Persian Gulf Department of the Iranian Foreign Ministry, Hossein Sadeghi, voiced Iranian disappointment and bitterness at this rebuff:

> In the meetings at the UN in September 1990, we offered them our help in solving the Crisis and in securing the region, but after Kuwait was freed we

From monarchy to republic 197

saw that they did not want our support. Kuwait, Saudi Arabia and the others in the meeting said they would help us reconstruct our economy, but after Kuwait was liberated they forgot.

(cited in Ahmadi 148/149)

Although the Arab monarchies attempted to avoid antagonizing Iran, this was far from a cooperative relationship. The Saudi foreign minister added that the eight Arab states were "keen to develop cordial relations with Iran" and called for a dialogue "with Islamic countries, including Iran" (Ahmadi 2008, 150). Economic rapprochement with Israel also served to focus Gulf states' fears on Iran and Iraq and oppose Iran for its rejection of the peace process (Ahmadi 2008, 150–151). While Iran at times attempted to include the Arab monarchies by using Islamic references that could apply to them together or fraternal references in terms of a family of Islamic nations, the Gulf monarchies did not reciprocate.

Iranian Foreign Ministry spokesperson Mortaza Sarmadi blamed the Arab side for not taking the olive branch after Iranian withdrawal and proclaimed that Arab residents on Abu Musa could live in harmony with their "Iranian brothers and sisters on the island"[25] and excoriated the GCC communiqué as "a blatant violation of the good neighborly relations". He also outlined the Iranian reaction underlining that Iran "would not allow any country to interfere in its internal affairs or violate its national sovereignty". In a statement from September 12, 1992, Iran's Supreme National Security Council (SNSC) criticized the recent "unjustified" positions and propaganda campaigns of its neighbors on the islands issue and reiterated Iran's "fraternity and good-neighborliness" with the Muslim states of the region (cited in: Ahmadi 2008, 172). It denied Iran had any expansionary objectives and attempted to reframe the dispute as a minor border issue by parallelizing it with the ongoing dispute between Qatar and Saudi Arabia, although it failed to achieve that effect (cf. Al-Nahyan 2013, 52). In mid September, Velayati told his Syrian counterpart Farouq al-Sharaa in Tehran that Iran wanted friendly ties with the UAE but would insist on its claims to the islands, while Iraq kept claiming that it was the only regional power able to offer protection against Iranian expansionism (Caldwell 1996, 52).

Following the failed Doha talks, President Zayed used the occasion of the 24th National Day of the UAE to signal the UAE's commitment and implicitly criticize Iran, in a friendly but cool speech. The careful wording eschews any familial mention:

For our side, we have shown our good will towards Iran on more than one occasion, sufficiently so for them to decide upon their own options, based upon our historic links, our friendly relations, good neighbourliness and common interests.

(cited in: Al-Nahyan 2013, 56–57)

Iranian assertiveness led to hardening of the UAE position that spilled into the larger GCC framework. In the GCC Summit documents of December 1993 and in

198 *From monarchy to republic*

a statement by its secretary-general in October 1994, he said that the foundations for the establishment of good relations with Iran "are non-existent because of the issue of the islands" (Ansari 1999, 865).

A fleeting and inconclusive attempt to readopt the old idea of the Gulf Security Pact of the shah by the Khatami government serves as another reminder of the difference between the two periods. During a five-day visit of Saudi Defense Minister Prince Sultan ibn Abdel Aziz to Tehran, President Khatami proposed the creation of a joint Muslim defense force with Saudi Arabia. In contrast to the long-winded negotiations and presentations in the 1970s, this proposal was dead in the water. Khatami, in an interview to the Arab News on February 22, 1998, optimistically opined that his "visit will be the beginning of a new chapter to expand and strengthen cooperation". Al Hayat reported Crown Prince Abdallah's remark that "Iran is a dear and friendly country" on May 11, 1999 (Ansari 1999, 871). Notwithstanding, Sultan was dismissive and was quoted by the official Saudi Press Agency as saying that "the question of military cooperation between the two countries is not an easy one and that any cooperation should start with economic, social, and cultural subjects" (Recknagel 1999).

Foreign policy restraint and escalation

Iranian inhibition toward attacking its Arab neighbors has been significantly lowered by the revolution, not only against the UAE – leading to numerous clashes, most notably in 1992.

MID data shows no disputes whatsoever between the monarchy of Iran and any monarchy of the Arabian Peninsula before 1979 but five MIDs between Iran and the UAE (all between 1984 and 1992) and an additional 14 with other Gulf monarchies after the new regime came to power until 2001 – most during the Iran–Iraq War (Ghosn, Palmer, and Bremer 2004). Most reach the hostility level of "use of force", directly below "war". Iran's inhibition threshold toward hostile and aggressive actions against the UAE has been significantly lowered since 1979. On November 12, 1980, Iranian aircraft launched the first direct attack on a Kuwaiti border post in Abdali (Assiri 1990, 69). The confrontational stance spilled over to the islands dispute. From 1983 on, Tehran made repeated patrols into the southern part of Abu Musa, administered by Sharjah, in violation of the 1971 MoU (Calvert 468).

Despite the continued power imbalance, even the Arab monarchies contemplated, prepared, and sometimes conducted military action. Saudi Prince Nayef labeled Iran "the terrorist of the Gulf", and in June 1984, the Saudi Air Force attacked Iran militarily for the first time, by shooting down an Iranian F-4 fighter over Saudi waters (Ulrichsen 2013, 115).

At the beginning of the 1980s, Emirati reaction was mostly low-key and waxed and waned with Iraqi strength and possibility of protection. Although the UAE attempted to avoid aggressively antagonizing Iran, a clear tilt toward Iraq and away from Iran was recognizable, leading to the rising importance of Arabism in the Gulf and ameliorating Saudi-Iraqi relations (Ahmadi 2008, 115–118). A few

From monarchy to republic   199

altercations with Iran strained relations, and Iranian troop movement to the islands to counteract a coup in Sharjah in 1987 temporarily terrified the Gulf states, especially because Iran did not withdraw the troops once Shaikh Sultan was reinstated. This marked the first escalation peak with Iranian forces, lowering the Sharjah flag for a short time after the attempted coup (Al Roken 2001, 195).

The UAE did not react then but was all the swifter during the next Iranian transgression in 1992, which marked the nadir of Iran–UAE relations. The escalation caused a departure from the cautious Emirati approach. The Emirates' growing linkage to the West and especially the US fed Iranian suspicions, which had already led to a more assertive stance toward the islands issue (Ahmadi 2008, 165). In January 1992, Iranian distrust of UAE policies led it to ask Sharjah for permission to issue security passes to non-UAE nationals visiting from the UAE in January 1992. Iran considered these actions to be well within the agreement on Abu Musa with Shaikh Khalid of Sharjah. The UAE declined, leading to the April confrontations (Ahmadi 2008, 167; Calvert and Alcock 2004, 468).

In March, Iran had refused to negotiate with Abu Dhabi because it claimed that the agreement was made with Sharjah, before the establishment of the UAE (Okruhlik and Conge 1999, 240). Both sides accused each other of demographic engineering. Iran suspected that the UAE attempted to shift the demographic balance by offering large salaries to Arab families to settle on Abu Musa and reacted by refusing entry to certain non-UAE nationals to the southern part of the island in April that year (Calvert and Alcock 2004, 468). In early April, Iranian forces seized control of the rest of the island, including the local school, police station, and desalination plant, and expelled hundreds of the circa 2000 UAE and other nationals of the Abu Musa population. Iran dismissed all protests, insisting that it did not violate any agreements with the UAE or change the status quo, instead dismissing the issue as "US-concocted" (Kostiner 2009, 133). Iran further justified the action by claiming that it was not receiving its proper share of oil and gas revenues from offshore production near the island. Further threat gestures and displays of military power followed. Iranian military exercises were conducted from April 25 until May 4 – involving 45 ships, 150 small boats, air force planes, on about 10,000 square miles of ocean. The exercise was designed to practice closing the Straits of Hormuz to an outside invader.

Initially, the UAE reacted with appeasement. It offered to lease the entire island to Iran and increase the Iranian share of oil and gas revenues. When Iran rejected this offer, the UAE asserted its authority over the two Tunbs and enlisted the assistance of the GCC and the Arab League to negotiate with Iran (Kostiner 2009, 199). In August, the UAE sent the *Khatir*, a passenger ship with 104 island residents (including the governor that Sharjah appointed, but mostly expatriate workers), to Abu Musa. Tehran felt provoked, refused permission to disembark, and sent the ship back to Sharjah on August 24, 1992. This move led to an explosion of international attention in Arab and Western media (Ahmadi 2008, 167; Al-Nahyan 2013, 50).

Initial claims that UAE nationals were expelled or the whole island had been annexed proved unfounded later, but the reaction was severe. In "a

200   *From monarchy to republic*

striking departure from that of the successive UAE governments of the preceding 20 years", the Emirati reaction turned strongly critical and non-complacent to the status quo (Ahmadi 2008, 168). Although Iran allowed the governor and 20 other UAE nationals to return on September 3, it still refused entry to the others (Al-Nahyan 2013, 50).

The issue was accorded an unprecedentedly high priority: the communiqué issued by the 44th session of the Ministerial Council of the GCC in Jeddah during September 8–9, 1992, ranked the issue as the second-most important on its agenda, after the crisis between Iraq and Kuwait but before the Palestinian question. The UAE raised the issue at regional and international fora, the GCC, the Arab League, and the UN; put forth preconditions for negotiations; and issued ultimatums (Ahmadi 2008, 168–171). In bilateral negotiations, the UAE demanded the end of the occupation and presented a catalogue of demands, but Iran refused, because no agreement could be reached even regarding the agenda, so talks broke down (Calvert and Alcock 2004, 468). The two countries were on the brink of war. On September 21, 1992, Iranian Air Force Commander General Mansur Satari announced on Tehran radio that Iran was prepared to shoot down any aircraft violating its airspace, that his aircrafts were stepping up their watch over the three islands, and that his pilots were ready to repulse any intrusion by "mischievous foreigners" (Ahmadi 2008, 173).

From 1992 onward, the UAE followed a policy of protesting against any, even minor, civilian activities by Iran on the three islands (Ahmadi 2008, 143). The Iranians blamed the UAE's insistence to include the Tunbs in the negotiations for their breaking down and accused the GCC states of conspiring with the US while also attempting some conciliatory steps that were mostly ignored by the UAE and other Arab states (Ahmadi 2008, 171; Kostiner 2009, 199). Arab governments and media continued a confrontational policy of admonishing Iran, while it kept insisting that it adhered to the 1971 MoU (Calvert and Alcock 2004, 468).

Possible explanations for Iran's escalation in 1992 abound: it was interpreted as a probe of the Arab states or the US; as an exploitation of the weakness of the Gulf states or a signal of Iranian assertiveness; and as a military or strategic necessity or a result of domestic infighting (cf. Chubin and Tripp 2014, 29). Schofield attributes the "clumsy reactivation" of the issue by Tehran to Iranian frustration at its regional isolation and its exclusion from regional security frameworks after the Gulf War (Schofield 2001, 224), whereas Ahmadi points to the new alignment patterns with the West having turned against Iran and the camp of the moderate/conservative states emboldened to pursue a more assertive foreign policy (2008, 174). He nevertheless considered a further escalation by the UAE unlikely, for several reasons, including the federation's economic interdependence with Iran and the disaccord on the issue inside it; the weakness of the UAE vis-à-vis Iran; and the lack of commitment on the part of Arab allies who did not care deeply about the issue except for a period in Saddam's politics (Ahmadi 2008, 177). However, Foley also sees the absence of war as the outcome of a fragile interdependence and short distances, predicting that "This vulnerability in large part explains why the dispute over Abu Musa and the Tunbs has, and likely will remain, largely a war of

From monarchy to republic 201

words" (Foley 1999). Thus, regional and global security constellations precluded a further escalation between the two Gulf states but do not explain the differences between the treatment of the issue before and after the Iranian revolution.

On November 11, 1992, Iran facilitated the reopening of schools in the Arab quarter of Abu Musa and the return of the teachers and their families (Ahmadi 2008, 172), but Iranian isolation was complete by late 1993: the GCC and 21 members of the Arab League, including the usually Iranian-friendly Syria, sided with the UAE, although Syria attempted mediating the dispute through 1993 and 1994 (Caldwell 1996, 52–54). Meanwhile, the status of affairs on the islands itself returned to normal by 1993, leaving only tougher Iranian procedures and patrols and the open question of the security passes as remnants, but the hostility between the two states persisted (Calvert and Alcock 2004, 468).

In October 1994, while Saddam Hussein made threatening military moves toward Kuwait, US intelligence noted Iranian military buildups near Abu Musa and the Tunbs (Caldwell 1996, 52–54). Saudi Foreign Minister Saud al-Faisal expressed "great concern [for] the continued occupation" and called for a referral of the case to the ICJ, speaking on behalf of the GCC at a UN GA address in October 1994 (UN General Assembly 1994, 16). The UAE kept pressing for a redressing of the issue and called for its submission to the ICJ in November 1994 as a way out of "Iranian intransigence", but Iran refused (Calvert and Alcock 2004, 468). On December 19, Shaikh Hamdan expressed the UAE's concern over the arms buildup on the islands (Al-Nahyan 2013, 54).

The UAE's call was part of its successful strategy of the internationalization and Arabization of the dispute, and the GCC and Arab League became more vociferous on the UAE side (cf. Schofield 2001, 216). While in the 1970s, the UAE was pressured in a confrontational stance, now it attempted to set the agenda itself. From 1992 onward, all GCC summits reiterated support for the UAE and called for the resolving of the issue until at least 2010, and the UAE spoke yearly at the UN, to keep the issue on the agenda (Al-Nahyan 2013, 58–59, 65).

Although immediate tensions abated, the dispute not only remains unresolved but instead continues to be a major source of provocation and conflict. For the most part of post-revolutionary Iran–UAE relations, there was little restraint from escalation, military or non-military. Subversion and delegitimization attempts by both sides undermined the opponent's regimes, and there was few attempts to minimize the conflict issues. Instead, disagreements often led to rhetorical escalations and threats of violence.

The atmosphere first exploded with the Iraqi military offensive on Iran in September 22, 1980, initiating the Iran–Iraq War. Saddam Hussein's conditions for a ceasefire included the return of the three Arab islands occupied by the shah in 1971 and "non-interference in the affairs of other states". Saddam's political flirtations with the smaller Gulf states included ending his subversion campaign against the monarchies and closing down the information offices of the Gulf opposition groups that had operated out of Baghdad. Iran, for its part, intensified its denunciations of "the stooges of the Great Satan" and renewed calls for the peoples of the Gulf to rise up in defense of "true Islam" (Khalaf 1987).

202 *From monarchy to republic*

The Iran–Iraq War showed the profound change in alliance patterns in the Gulf (and in the broader Middle East) that followed the change of regime in Iran. Radical anti-Iranian sentiment grew on the monarchic side. King Khalid declared that Saudi Arabia stood "with Iraq in its pan-Arab battle and its conflict with the Persians, the enemies of the Arab nation". Jordan's King Hussein convened a meeting in Amman that put out a statement calling for Arab cooperation in full support of "fraternal Iraq" (cited in: Goodarzi 2006, 34), a state that he had been in constant strife with since the 1958 coup that killed his cousin King Faisal (Lynch 1998, 347) – a stark contrast to the fraternal relations that he cultivated with the shah, whom he had considered his mentor (Goode 2014, 449). Kuwait was increasingly leaning toward Iraq, but Iran threatened the statelet, to coerce it to remain neutral in the late 1980s. Nevertheless, internal polarization with Shiites tilting toward Iran and fears of destabilization made Saddam seem like a "pragmatist", and Arab identity then trumped Islamic identity (cf. Assiri 1990, 71, 74).

The rhetoric of the Gulf monarchies has become nearly indistinguishable from the vocal republics like Egypt, but especially Iraq, which threatened to "cut off the criminal hands" that challenged Arab sovereignty territorial integrity in July 1979 (Kostiner 2009, 48) or that railed against the "Persification" of the Arab Gulf (Ahmadi 2008, 126–127, 137). Iran had not suddenly become "more Persian" (in fact, it might even be less explicitly Persian after the revolution); rather, the new perception after the revolution suddenly defined Iran as an "other" in a way that it did not before.

The UAE remained officially silent on the Iran–Iraq War (as did Qatar), because the federation was divided: Abu Dhabi and Ras al-Khaimah were strongly pan-Arabist and pro-Iraq and had loaned the neighbor $1.3 billion by 1981. Sharjah and Dubai, not least due to their trade links with Iran and their large communities of Iranian origin, continued to trade with Iran during the war. Sharjah had the added incentive of the Abu Musa agreement that provided for joint oil access of the Mubarak oilfield. This neutrality initially belied Iraqi efforts to paint the conflict in ethno-sectarian terms (Gargash 1996, 151), but the federation soon tilted toward Iraq (Alkim 1989, 205).

This time, it was the other way around, and the "radicals" (except, of course, Iraq) were wary of war. The distinction between friend and enemy appeared more relevant than any intrinsic belligerence of revolutionary republics: "Qadhafi and Arafat plead to both capitals for an end of the war and Syria was also inclined to side with Iran, but at least put a stop to the war" (Goodarzi 2006, 34).

After Iran had begun its counteroffensive in the Iran–Iraq War, the mood tilted irretrievably. GCC states grew more anxious and openly declared their support for Iraq on the third summit of the Council in Bahrain in November 1982. Because the conservative monarchic frame was not available anymore, the Arab conceptional frame took over, thus excluding Iran. Declarations spoke of "dire consequences . . . on the safety and security of the Arab homeland". Only by November 1985, on the sixth summit of the GCC, did the support declarations for

From monarchy to republic   203

Iraq subside (Khalaf 1987). All in all, Saudi Arabia, the biggest supporter, sent $25 billion to Iraq. Kuwait followed suit, and Abu Dhabi and Qatar also contributed (Ulrichsen 2013, 115).

The Iraqi invasion of Kuwait has brought along only a short-term rapprochement with Iran. By late 1992, Sharjah and Iran had reaffirmed the 1971 agreement regarding Abu Musa, but Ras al-Khaimah had not reached a settlement with Iran concerning the Tunbs. While the outcome initially resembled the situation in 1971, the handling of the crisis afterwards was now markedly more hostile. In late December, Iran deployed additional Islamic Revolutionary Guards Corps troops to the islands. Several media outlets in Iran called for a reassertion of Iran's claim to Bahrain that the shah had abolished to bolster his claim to the three smaller islands (Caldwell 1996, 52–55). Instead of restraint and restriction on the conflict issue, these calls intended to expand it.

The rhetoric had not even reached its boiling point. In December 1992 after a meeting in Abu Dhabi, the GCC called on Iran to "abolish measures taken on Abu Musa island and to terminate the occupation of the Greater and Lesser Tunb islands". This prompted an infamous vitriolic reaction by Iranian President Rafsanjani, who otherwise continued to downplay the dimension of the dispute: "Iran is surely stronger than the likes of you . . . to reach these islands one has to cross a sea of blood. . . . We consider this claim as totally invalid" (both quoted in: Calvert and Alcock 2004, 468). Whether or not the show of hostility was for domestic consumption (Schofield 2001, 216), the fact remains that no pronouncement by the shah or his officials after UAE's independence ever came close to that level of antagonism.

At the Friday prayers of December 25, two days after the GCC proclamation, Rafsanjani warned the GCC countries to "not repeat the same mistakes as Saddam", who tried to "transform Iran's Arvand-Roud river into the Shatt al-Arab and Kuwait into an Iraqi province". He continued stating that "Iran is stronger than you" and accused the GCC states of having chosen "Satan's path" (all quoted in: Ahmadi 2008, 173).

US Acting Secretary of State Lawrence Eagleburger gave an estimation of the graveness of the situation saying on September 12, 1992: "I don't think there is any question that the issue could become very serious if the Iranians were to decide to resort to force" (Ahmadi 2008, 174). The mobilization was not merely rhetorical: Iran also increased its military presence on Abu Musa and Greater Tunb, effectively turning the islands into military bases (Kostiner 2009, 199). Even before the 1992 escalation, Iranian activity and subversive policy in the region often undermined Gulf security: the 1981 coup attempt in Bahrain, a series of bombings in Kuwait in early 1980s, the attempted assassination of the Kuwaiti Emir in 1985, and ongoing problems during the *hajj* were proof enough of Iranian ill-intent for the Arab Gulf states (Gargash 1996, 143).

The founding of the GCC in Abu Dhabi on May 25, 1981, was linked to the heightened threat by Iran and Iraq, but at the time, it was clear where the main danger came from. Abdallah Bishara, the first secretary-general of the GCC,

204 *From monarchy to republic*

declared Iranian ambitions for hegemony in the region to be the prime threat to Gulf stability (Ulrichsen 2013, 114), reversing the pattern of the monarchic period.

There are even indications that the Gulf monarchies were also ready to support all means available against Iran, including subversion: Anthony Cordesman refers to covert efforts to recover the islands in the wake of an Iraqi attack on Iran and claims that Oman, the UAE, and Bahrain were initially supportive of Iraqi invasion plans (1984, 61, 397). Clearly, the rules against nonviolence were not in place anymore.

The Arabism that served to exclude Iran had a minor influence on Arab monarchies during the rule of the shah but was now adopted enthusiastically. While Iraq again emerged as a prime sponsor of the islands claim, this time the UAE and other small Gulf monarchies took a more active role as well. Especially during the brief period from August 1980 to March 1981, the UAE came forward with some initiatives, in part due to the window of opportunity opened by the revolution and Iraqi ambitions and aggression toward Iran, in part acting on pressure from Iraq. The activities included two letters to the secretary general of the UN. The first UAE actor to bring up the issue publicly was the most aggravated, Shaikh Saqr of Ras al-Khaimah, who had voiced cautious optimism that the new regime would return the islands in an interview in April 3, 1980. It was followed by a letter to the UN SG in August 8, 1980, by Rashid Abdullah, the UAE minister of state for foreign affairs, who reacted to an Iranian letter to the same address. Another letter reprimanded Iranian president Bani Sadr for his assertion that the shah had paid Emirati shaikhs off in return for their silence on the issue, saying "we believe that such statements are detrimental to the reputation of the Government of the United Arab Emirates and to harmonious brotherly relations between the Arab and Iranian Muslim peoples" and reiterating UAE claims on December 1, 1980 (Ahmadi 2008, 138–140).

More robust action was precluded by intra-Emirate discord: in 1980, Ras al-Khaimah requested that Iraq base a fighter squadron there. But Zayed intervened and sent the planes home so that the UAE would not be drawn directly into the war (Foley 1999). Diplomatic initiatives continued. In January 1981, the UAE minister of state for foreign affairs stated that the Emirates "still have rights to these islands and we are still calling for the return of the Islands". Saqr continued his fight for the islands. On March 28, 1982, he stated that "The three islands are an Arab right about which there can be no discussion. Iran's rulers know this better than others; however, no contact on this issue has been made between them and us" (cited in: Ahmadi 2008, 140).

Despite multiple rapprochement attempts by both sides, there was no period of durable cooperation patterns, and the polarization following the upheavals after 2011 suggests that this will not change in the foreseeable future. After President Ahmadinejad's visit to Abu Musa in 2012, the UAE withdrew its ambassador to Iran. The UAE foreign minister described the visit as a "flagrant violation" of his country's sovereignty, and Ahmadinejad used to opportunity to raise the issue of the naming dispute of the "Persian Gulf" vs. "Arab Gulf" (CNN Wire Staff 2012).

From monarchy to republic 205

The GCC and the Arab states at the UN panned the visit as "against good neighborly policy" (Al-Nahyan 2013, 67).

The cooperation between Iran and the Arab Gulf monarchies remained on an ad hoc basis, and even the more immediate threat by Iraq during the Gulf War never resulted in a long-term alliance. Periods of rapprochement were patchy and frequently interrupted. Cooperative periods in the early 1980s and late 1990s were marred by mixed signals and haphazard attempts at settlement. Attempts at minimizing the conflict to a difference of opinion were often followed by provocations and aggressive posturing that could hardly be differentiated from the hostile periods analyzed in the previous section.

Following the revolution, the new authorities turned out to be just as interested in regional ambitions as the shah was but were less circumspect about it. Other territorial claims were soon revived again, such as the claim to Bahrain: instead of the containment and minimizing of the conflict issue, it was broadened. In June 1979, Ayatollah Sadeq Ruhani called for Bahraini annexation and announced in September 1979 that Bahrain was "an integral part of Iran", using much the same words as the shah did some two decades prior. The claim was strongly rejected by Bahrain and denounced by other Arab states (Ahmadi 2008, 117; Calvert and Alcock 2004, 452). Although Iranian authorities, including Deputy Prime Minister Sadeq Tabataba'i and Iran's ambassador to Kuwait, were quick to emphasize that the remarks were Rouhani's personal opinion and that Iran harbored no territorial ambitions on Bahrain, the damage was done (Ahmadi 2008, 117). Similarly, in the period of beginning cooperation at the end of the 1990s, heralded by the election of the moderate Mohammad Khatami as president of Iran in 1997. Shaikh Saqr of Ras al-Khaimah was quick to congratulate Khatami on his victory on May 26, but within days, Khatami reiterated that the islands belonged to Iran (Al-Nahyan 2013, 59–60).

The Tripartite committee for mediation set up by the GCC and including Bahrain, Oman, and Saudi Arabia in 1999 was dissolved in January 2001 because of Iranian refusal to cooperate. Bahrain's Foreign Minister Shaikh Mohammed bin Mubarak Al Khalifa's final statement in regard to the committee was a laconic: "it is finished" (Osman and Farook 2001). Whereas Iran dismissed the committee as biased (Calvert and Alcock 2004, 470), pro-Arab authors such as Al Roken attribute the failings of all negotiation rounds in 1992, 1995, and 1999 to Iranian intransigence, which contrasts with the moderate approach of the UAE (Al Roken 2001, 196).

On the other hand, and like in the previous examined case, the revolution resulted in stronger intra-monarchic relations. It brought Saudi Arabia and the UAE, as well as Dubai and Abu Dhabi, closer together: the president of the UAE and the king of Saudi Arabia met more than 16 times between 1979–1983 (Alkim 1989, cf. 130, 235, endnote 173).

While Iraq clearly saw a window of opportunity to bolster its influence on the other Gulf states, and the revolutionary republican regimes used the issue to showcase ideological commitment, this time it was not just the radical and revolutionary regimes but the monarchies as well that began blowing in that horn. In 1980,

206 *From monarchy to republic*

Saudi Arabia declared "full support for the UAE in its demand for the recovery of sovereignty over the islands", which stood in sharp contrast to previous lukewarm proclamations during the Pahlavi era (Alkim 1989, 132).

While the moderate reaction to the seizure in 1971 was openly criticized by republics only, this stronger show of support was now deemed insufficient by the UAE. In May 1999, Shaikh Zayed did not attend a GCC heads of states meeting in Jeddah and in June threatened to leave the GCC unless the other states tied in progress with Iran with a resolution of the dispute. During the monarchic period, the UAE was reluctant to do anything about the islands while it now agitated for more multilateral action. There were disagreements on the handling of the issue between the federal government and the emirate of Sharjah. On the 29th anniversary of the UAE, founding the conflict was an important point of reference, with Shaikh Zayed stating that Iran's "continued occupation" marred Arab-Iranian relations, which Iran rebuked as baseless. Iran rejected another attempt to put the dispute to the ICJ in December 2000 and its Foreign Ministry's spokesperson reiterated that "Our position is clear. The Gulf islands are an integral part of Iran's territory. . . . It is not a court matter" (Calvert and Alcock 2004, 469). This stands in contrast to the conflict management between Bahrain and Qatar but also between the UAE and the Iranian monarchy under 30 years prior.

Ingroup identification after regime change II

No time period after the Iranian revolution yielded the same extent of cooperation between Iran and the UAE (or Arab Gulf monarchies in general) as the period between the independence of the small Gulf monarchies and the downfall of the shah. While interstate relations did not deteriorate into open war, militarized confrontations increased markedly, and subversion attempts by both sides were common, including tacit and open support of Iraq's invasion of Iran. The clashes on the contested island of Abu Musa 1992 also saw a renewal of territorial claims and an escalating rhetoric, including open military threats voiced by Iran.

Since the Islamic Revolution, the UAE started gravitating more toward Saudi Arabia. Saudi hegemonic ambitions as well as the disparity in size and capability had not changed, but confronted with the choice between a potentially threatening familiar monarchy and an also potentially threatening but in addition strange and dissimilar republic, the choice was clear.

While the basis for ingroup identification was not stable to begin with, given the ethnic and confessional outsider status of Iran, this similarity perception disappeared completely, taking with it any basis for political and military restraint.

The islands conflict: synthesis and findings

Iran's Islamic Revolution of 1979 has rightfully been described as "a pivot of modern Middle Eastern history" (Gause 2010, 43). It changed regional dynamics profoundly. Iran became uniquely isolated in the region and started to develop hostile relationships with most of its neighbors. In addition, the Iranian regime

From monarchy to republic 207

was vehemently opposed by the West that had tacitly supported (or at least not opposed) Iranian policy toward the contested islands in the 1970s. Tehran's new friends were the shah's old enemies, "radical" Arab states like Syria and Libya. When this radical axis weakened, the conservative-moderate bloc of the monarchies and their allies used the opportunity to bring the territorial dispute back on the agenda.

However, power shifts alone cannot explain the rapid deterioration of interstate relations. The change in regional alliance patterns was a clear consequence of the revolution, which abolished the monarchy and installed an extremely dissimilar system, legitimized by an ideology vehemently opposed to monarchism.

In comparison, the contrast is obvious: in 1971, the occupation of the Tunb islands was met with only weak reactions. Two decades later, the mere assertion of broader Iranian sovereignty on an already-shared island was met with a much more vigorous response. What had changed? From an Emirati point of view, it was finally *possible* to stand up to Iran, knowing that Western and Arab allies would be by the UAE's side, unlike in 1971. However, a major change was that it had also almost become *desirable*. Iran had long ceased to be an ally and had transformed into a major threat. Iran's clerics called for the overthrow of monarchism, and its presidents were dismissive of the smaller neighbors' issues. Once Iran turned into a theocratic republic, it turned its back on the "monarchic club" that now symbolized everything the Islamic Revolution claimed to struggle against. As long as Iran had been a monarchy, the sense of similarity and shared monarchic fate had succeeded in overcoming the regional security dilemma. Thus, there was good reason to restrict and oppose the shah – but not to undermine him. But republican Iran was different: it remained Persian and Shia and remained a large rentier state, but now it became republican and theocratic. As all remaining links were severed, undermining the new Islamic revolutionary regime in Tehran promised benefits for regime security and interstate violence returned as a legitimate mode of foreign policy, resulting in numerous militarized confrontations.

Although the closeness of the larger Arab-Persian monarchic ingroup was not as pronounced as between Arab monarchies in general between the GCC member states in particular, in retrospect, it seems remarkable that for almost a decade, monarchic ingroup identity trumped both geopolitics on one hand and ethnic and sectarian tensions on another, which are known to generally supersede competing identities (cf. Saideman 2002). With no political system similarity to foster connection, ethnicity trumped historical alliances, so the quest for regional hegemony could now be pursued unencumbered.

Iranian revisionism did not derive from a change in the balance of power; rather, the country had always been the region's dominant power. In 1971, the International Institute for Strategic Studies (IISS) concluded that Iran's air force and navy could match the forces of all the Persian Gulf Arab littoral states combined (Ahmadi 2008, 78). Although a powerful Iranian monarchy was relatively friendly toward its fellow monarchies, a powerful Iranian Islamic Republic was not.

After the change of the regime in Iran, the interstate norm of peaceful conflict settlement had been greatly weakened, evidenced by MID data. The change of

208 *From monarchy to republic*

Table 5.2 Deterioration of Iranian-UAE Relations

Indicators			Period I	Period II
1. Structural similarities	1.1	Shared language, culture, history, and religion	–	–
	1.2	Similar political system	+ but highly dissimilar institutions	–
	1.3	Similar economic system	+	– /+ Rentier states, but reorientation of new Iranian regime inapplicable
2 Salience	2.1	Low/decreasing share	– /+ Minority, increase in 1971	
	2.2	Common threat	+ Iraq, radical republicanism	– /+ Iraq, but not consistently
	2.3	Absence of divisive ideology	– /+ Persian and Arab nationalisms, but no full-fledged ideologies	–
	3.1	Mutual recognition	+	+ official relations only since 1982
	3.2	Personalization of bonds between ruling elites	+	–
	3.2.1	Frequent high-level state visits	– /+ Few, some first meetings	– /+ beginning in late 1980s, frequency of state visits rose in times of rapprochement around Gulf War, but also frequent cancelations and boycotts
	3.2.2	Kinship, intermarriage and friendship bonds	– Little between Iran and UAE, but some between Iran and larger linchpin monarchies (Jordan, Egypt, Oman)	– Frequent change of official staff in Iran precluded longer-lasting bonds

Indicators			Period I	Period II
		3.2.3 Shared socialization	– Shah Swiss educational background, Arab Gulf British	– Separate socialization after cut with West
	3.3	Affirmation of commonality	+	–
		3.3.1 Kinship and family references	–	– Often "neighbor", rarely "friend"
		3.3.2 Emphasis on similarity	+ although ethnic difference remained pronounced	– Persian and Shia fault line stronger than before, though initially some attempts at uniting via pan-Islamism
		3.3.3 References to shared historical narratives	+ Shared conservative outlook	– Common ceremonies only in broad international for a (OIC, UN, etc.)
		3.3.4 Common ceremonies/shared institutions	+ Persepolis, OIC	– Less-common ceremonies (mostly restricted to Arab League protocol)
	4.1	Military restraint	– /+ *However, the seizure of the islands dates before independence and was largely settled by negotiation*	– 5 MIDs between 1984 and 1992
	4.2	Non-military restraint	+	–
		4.2.1 *Refraining from delegitimization*	+	– Delegitimization of regime, discrediting Islamic credentials
		4.2.2 *Refraining from subversion*	+	– Frequent subversion attempts

3 Social processes of ingroup identification

4 Foreign policy restraint

(*Continued*)

210 *From monarchy to republic*

Table 5.2 (Continued)

Indicators		*Period I*	*Period II*
	4.2.3 *Rhetorical restraint*	+	– Rhetorical escalation, threat of violence
4.3	Alliance and solidarity	+ No formal alliance, but strong de facto alignment, solidarity (e.g. support of Kuwait); institutionalization failed	– Ad hoc cooperation, no alliance (But monarchic solidarity with UAE)

the political system lowered the similarity to the Gulf monarchies but made Iran more similar to "radical" Arab republics. Given the unique nature of the Islamic Republic, this shift did not result in a clear-cut ingroup of revolutionary republics. Nonetheless, Iran was able to establish new alliance patterns of coordination and cooperation in the region. Clearly, this reorganization of Iran's regional alliances can be traced back to the overall regime change.

Of course, other important factors should not be ignored. There can be no doubt that the nature of the political system, traditional decision-making process, and smallness of the UAE shaped its foreign policy independently of any possible identification as a member of a larger monarchic community. In the same way, the personality of the long-time ruler for most of the analyzed period, Shaikh Zayed Al Nahyan, heavily influenced UAE foreign policy behavior (Al-Nahyan 2013, 72–73) toward a policy of systematic war avoidance. Although these and similar caveats (power asymmetry, oil wealth, transnational identities, etc.) explain specific elements of the UAE's foreign policy, they fail to capture the radical change of Iranian-UAE relations that occurred after the downfall of the shah.

The conditions for the development of a shared identity were problematic. The states coexisted as monarchies only for a limited time period (1971–1979). Apart from the political system, they shared little else. Thus, the ingroup was still weak: although interstate relations were highly cooperative and peaceful, Iran *did* act aggressively by seizing the Greater and Lesser Tunb, although it officially preferred a diplomatic solution like the one reached for Abu Musa. The seizure took place at a time when the UAE could not be seen as an independent actor or as a "real" monarchy, but the conflict over the contested islands still shows that monarchic ingroup identification is not automatic and can be overshadowed by other factors. Despite all complications regarding the development of a monarchic ingroup identity, a monarchic peace prevailed while no such stable peace was found in the mixed-dyad period.

Notes

1 In many ways, the relationship was a mirror image of the future one. This was most pronounced in the 1930s but later dissipated. An illustration is again found in King Ghazi's reign: an April 1938 article in the pan-Arab Iraqi paper al-Istiqlal calling for Kuwaiti-Iraqi unity wrote the following: "It pains Iraq to behold on her borders an Arab territory with an excellent geographical position and yet in a backward state, lacking modern systems of education, health, and economic organizations". It then goes on to embrace the ideas and demands of their "sister people of Kuwait" (cited in Khadduri and Ghareeb 2001, 37).

2 Here again we see the match between mutual ingroup perception and de-escalative behavior. King Ghazi, who came close to taking over Kuwait by force, only had a weak personal relationship with the Kuwaiti political elite. Shaikh Ahmad of Kuwait visited Ghazi on two occasions, in 1935 and in 1936, but a counter-visit was prevented by Ahmad's advisors, who feared that it might be counterproductive to Kuwaiti interests. An opportunity to foster closer relations that might have instilled a shared identity in both rulers was missed (cf. Khadduri and Ghareeb 2001, 35).

3 All referenced actors that were apparently vital for Iraqi decision-making and seemingly prepared to stop an invasion of Kuwait by force, if need be – Britain, Iran, and Saudi Arabia – were monarchies.

4 For instance, in a border incident in January 1952, two Iraqi police officers on camels had entered Kuwaiti territory, and one fired his rifle. He was disarmed by Kuwaiti guards, and no casualties ensued. Iraqi authorities insisted that the police officers had trespassed unintentionally (Joyce 1998, 96).

5 The recording of Kuwait's MIDs starts with its official independence in 1961, which is why a direct comparison is not possible with the data. It is still safe to say that no similar level of hostility can be discerned in the monarchic period, including the 1930s.

6 Internationally, the 1990/1991 war is better known as the Second Gulf War (the first being the Iran–Iraq War). This chapter follows the (US) naming conventions of the CoW data set, the main source for quantitative data on wars in the region used here.

7 This was an ironic twist, given the fact that the overthrown Hashemite monarchy derived its legitimacy from its Sharifian heritage. It was overthrown in a bloody coup d'état supported by a popular uprising that catapulted the Iraqi republic to power, paving the way for the Ba'th party's rise.

8 David Winter found an above-average score for affiliation motivation, which he attributed to Hussein's need to be in cooperative and warm relationships,

> but *only* with people they perceive as similar to themselves and *only* when they feel safe. Under threat, they are often quite "prickly and defensive". The president had exhibited this type of behavior when he surrounded himself "with his own like-minded people . . . and fusing his affiliative concerns with his power motives in a messianic message of "brotherhood" directed . . . to the wider Arab community.
> (Winter 2003, 373, emphasis in original)

These are the classical descriptions of ingroup identification and outgroup hostility. In addition, Margaret Hermann finds above-average scores for nationalism (that might entrench an us-vs.-them mentality) and mistrust of others (2003, 376–378).

9 This theory is based on the by-now-infamous meeting on July 25 with US Ambassador to Iraq April Glaspie, who stated that the US did not have an opinion on inter-Arab conflicts. One week later, the Iraqi army crossed the shared border with Kuwait. However, the meeting with Glaspie could not have been decisive for Iraqi action because it had been decided months before (Gause 2002, 62).

10 The value of perceived similarity as a driver of solidarity and support was not lost on Kuwait in other areas either. Kuwait attempted to foster the similarity with the US that

212 *From monarchy to republic*

it was denied with Iraq. To attract US attention and support, a 15-page advertisement in *The New York Times* on June 2, 1963, extolled Kuwait's democratic values, proclaiming that "Kuwait is a democracy" (Kuwait is a democracy 1963).

11 It was alleged that the last-minute decision to change the line of succession from King Hussein's brother Hassan to his son Abdallah was driven by the Jordanian desire to be welcomed back into the fold of the Gulf monarchies, as Abdallah was unblemished by the Gulf Crisis decisions (interview with former Jordanian ambassador, September 9, 2015, Amman).

12 A detailed explanation of Jordanian foreign policy during the Gulf War is beyond the scope of this chapter, but see (Brand 1995; Lynch 1998; Reed 1990) for extensive analysis.

13 Although technically outside the analyzed period, the confrontation is included because of the short duration before independence and its major effect on future Iran–UAE relations.

14 Incidentally, popular opinion also led the hardening of the bargaining position of the Arab shaikhs: in later meetings with the British mediator and special envoy Sir William Luce, both shaikhs admitted that internal opposition would not allow them to sell the islands. Saqr said that it would be better if Iran seized the islands but paid nothing. Khalid voiced a similar opinion, saying it would be far better for him if the shah or Britain just took the islands for Iran. On September 18, Shaikh Khalid told Luce that he would be willing to let Iranian forces on a designated area in Abu Musa and allow them jurisdiction; both sides would stay silent on the sovereignty issue; and Iran would have to rent the area under command (Mobley 2003, 640).

15 A succinct description of the formative aspects of the UAE political system is provided by Peter Hellyer:

> the UAE seeks to avoid rushed or impulsive decisions. . . . Action for the sake of being seen to act, or statements for the sake of mere public effect, is disdained. . . . the basic elements of this approach, which are also visible in domestic policy, can be traced back to the nature of the country itself. . . . Tribal society in the Arabian Peninsula, heavily influenced by Islam, is essentially communal, requiring consultation and consensus in order to be able to survive.
>
> (Hellyer 2001, 164)

16 The author goes as far as to identify the ethnic groups as the defining ingroups – in the case of Iran, the "'positive distinction' of the (Iranian-Aryan) 'in-group' vis-à-vis the (Arab-Semitic) 'out-group'" (Adib-Moghaddam 2006, 18). Because ingroups are malleable and overlapping, this does not negate the simultaneous existence of a monarchic ingroup, but it shows the potential for ideological divisions inside it.

17 Dubai and Oman had the closest relationship with monarchic Iran leading up to fraternal ties, whereas other Arab Gulf monarchies had a less-trusting relationship. When Iran intervened to support Oman in its Dhofar war, the commander-in-chief of Qatar's armed forces, Shaikh Hamad bin Khalifa al-Thani, complained about Oman's dependence on "foreigners", i.e. non-Arab Iranians (Goode 2014, 458).

18 However, such a perception was pronounced in monarchic crisis such as during the Arab Cold War (see section 3.2.1) or among monarchies that shared more similarities with Iran such as linchpins Jordan and Oman.

19 This cooperation (and its manifestation in form of the photograph of him shaking hands with the head of the Iranian troops) probably cost Saqr bin Muhammad, the namesake of the Ras al-Khaimah shaikh, his right to rule (Peterson 2011, 27).

20 Sharjah and Ras al-Khaimah are both ruled by different branches of the larger Qasim family.

21 The non-independence certainly provided the opportunity to redraw borders before the formation of a state that could claim the right of territorial integrity, as codified by the UN Charter (United Nations 1945).

22 The premiership was abandoned by the republic in 1989.

From monarchy to republic 213

23
> The GCC Higher Council welcomes the desire of the Islamic Republic of Iran to improve and promote its relations with all GCC countries. The GCC Higher Council underlines the importance of serious and realistic action to settle the outstanding differences between Iran and the GCC Member States so that the countries of the region can proceed to achieve their cherished goals and exploit their resources for comprehensive economic development. The GCC Higher Council stresses its desire to establish distinguished relations with Iran on the basis of good-neighborliness, non-interference in domestic affairs and respect for sovereignty, independence and peaceful coexistence deriving from the bonds of religion and heritage that link the countries of the region.
>
> (cited in: Ahmadi 2008, 147)

24 In a conciliatory twist on the naming conflict over the Persian/Arab Gulf, Khalkhali declared it should be called the "Islamic Gulf" (Goodarzi 2006, 297).
25 Here, the fraternal reference is applied to the societal level on the islands, not to the regimes or even the countries as a whole.

References

Abdullah, A. 1980. "The Revolution in Iran Stimulated the Existing Contradictions in the United Arab Emirates." *MERIP Reports* (85): 19–25.

Adib-Moghaddam, Arshin. 2006. *The International Politics of the Persian Gulf: A Cultural Genealogy*. London; New York: Routledge.

Agwani, Mohammed Shafi. 1978. *Politics in the Gulf*. Noida: Vikas Publishing House.

Ahmadi, Kourosh. 2008. *Islands and International Politics in the Persian Gulf: Abu Musa and Tunbs in Strategic Perspective*. London; New York: Routledge.

Al Roken, Mohamed Abdullah. 2001. "Dimensions of the UAE-Iran Dispute Over Three Islands." In *United Arab Emirates: A New Perspective*, eds. Ibrahim Abed and Peter Hellyer. Capetown: Trident Press Ltd, 179–201.

Alkim, Hassan Hamdan al-. 1989. *The Foreign Policy of the United Arab Emirates*. London: Saqi.

Allison, William Thomas. 2012. *The Gulf War, 1990–91*. Basingstoke, Hampshire [England]; New York: Palgrave Macmillan.

Al Nahyan, Khalid. 2013. *The Three Islands. Mapping the UAE-Iran Dispute*. RUSI. https://rusi.org/sites/default/files/201312_bk_the_three_islands_2.pdf (January 4, 2017).

Alvandi, Roham. 2010. "Muhammad Reza Pahlavi and the Bahrain Question, 1968–1970." *British Journal of Middle Eastern Studies* 37(2): 159–77.

Amini, Hassan. 2016. *Decadence and Downfall: The Shah of Iran's Ultimate Party*. BBC Documentary, London.

Ansari, M.H. 1999. "Security in the Persian Gulf: The Evolution of a Concept." *Strategic Analysis* 23(6): 857–71.

Assiri, Abdul-Reda. 1990. *Kuwait's Foreign Policy. City-State in World Politics*. Boulder, CO; London: Westview Press.

Ayalon, Ami. 2000. "Post-Ottoman Arab Monarchies: Old Bottles, New Labels?" In *Middle East Monarchies. The Challenge of Modernity*, ed. Joseph Kostiner. Boulder, CO: Lynne Rienner Publishers, 23–36.

Batty, David. 2011. "Worries About Sandhurst Links After Bahrain Protest Crackdown." *The Guardian*. www.theguardian.com/world/2011/feb/18/sandhurst-bahrain-protest (February 21, 2017).

214 *From monarchy to republic*

Bengio, Ofra. 1998. *Saddam's Word: The Political Discourse in Iraq*. New York; Oxford: Oxford University Press, USA.

Bismarck, Helene von. 2009. "The Kuwait Crisis 1961 and Its Consequences for Great Britain's Persian Gulf Policy." *British Scholar Journal* 2(1): 75–96.

Boghardt, L.P. 2006. *Kuwait Amid War, Peace and Revolution*. New York: Palgrave Macmillan.

Brand, Laurie. 1995. *Jordan's Inter-Arab Relations. The Political Economy of Alliance Making*. New York: Columbia University Press.

Caldwell, Dan. 1996. "Flashpoints in the Gulf: Abu Musa and the Tunb Islands." *Middle East Policy* 4(3): 50–7.

Calvert, Peter, and Antony Alcock, eds. 2004. *Border and Territorial Disputes of the World*. 4th edition. London: John Harper.

Chubin, Shahram, and Charles Tripp. 2014. *Iran-Saudi Arabia Relations and Regional Order*. London; New York: Routledge.

CNN Wire Staff. 2012. "Ahmadinejad's Visit to Island Prompts UAE to Recall Iran Ambassador – CNN.Com." *CNN*. www.cnn.com/2012/04/12/world/meast/uae-iran-ambassador-recall/index.html (December 15, 2016).

Cordesman, Anthony H. 1984. *The Gulf and the Search for Strategic Stability: Saudi Arabia, the Military Balance in the Gulf, and Trends in the Arab-Israeli Military Balance*. Boulder: Westview Press.

Ehteshami, Anoushiravan. 2014. "The Foreign Policy of Iran." In *The Foreign Policies of Middle East States*, eds. Raymond A. Hinnebusch and Anoushiravan Ehteshami. Boulder: Lynne Rienner Publishers, 261–88.

Eppel, Michael. 2004. *Iraq from Monarchy to Tyranny: From the Hashemites to the Rise of Saddam*. Gainesville: University Press of Florida.

Finnie, David H. 1992. *Shifting Lines in the Sand: Kuwait's Elusive Frontier with Iraq*. London: I.B. Tauris.

Foley, Sean. 1999. "The UAE: Political Issues and Security Dilemmas." *Middle East Review of International Affairs* 3(1).

Gargash, Anwar. 1996. "Iran, the GCC States, and the UAE: Prospects and Challenges in the Coming Decade." In *Iran and the Gulf: A Search for Stability*, ed. Jamal S. Suwaidi. Abu Dhabi, UAE: The Emirates Center for Strategic Studies and Research, 136–57.

Gause, F. Gregory, III. 2002. "Iraq's Decisions to Go to War, 1980 and 1990." *Middle East Journal* 56(1): 47–70.

———. 2010. *The International Relations of the Persian Gulf*. Cambridge: Cambridge University Press.

Ghosn, Faten, Glenn Palmer, and Stuart Bremer. 2004. "The MID3 Data Set, 1993–2001: Procedures, Coding Rules, and Description." *Conflict Management and Peace Science* 21: 133–54.

Goodarzi, Jubin M. 2006. *Syria and Iran: Diplomatic Alliance and Power Politics in the Middle East*. London; New York: Tauris Academic Studies.

Goode, James F. 2014. "Assisting Our Brothers, Defending Ourselves: The Iranian Intervention in Oman, 1972–75." *Iranian Studies* 47(3): 441–62.

Halliday, Fred. 1980. "The Gulf Between Two Revolutions: 1958–1979." *MERIP Reports* (85): 6–15.

———. 2011. *The Middle East in International Relations: Power, Politics and Ideology*. New edition. Cambridge University Press.

Hassan, Hamdi A. 1999. *The Iraqi Invasion of Kuwait: Religion, Identity, and Otherness in the Analysis of War and Conflict*. London: Pluto Press.

From monarchy to republic 215

Hassouna, Hussein. 2001. "The Kuwait-Iraq Border Problem." In *Iran, Iraq and the Arab Gulf States*, ed. Joseph A. Kechichian. New York: Palgrave, 237–61.

Heard-Bey, Frauke. 2006. "Conflict Resolution and Regional Co-Operation: The Role of the Gulf Co-Operation Council 1970–2002." *Middle Eastern Studies* 42(2): 199–222.

Hellyer, Peter. 2001. "Evolution of UAE Foreign Policy." In *United Arab Emirates: A New Perspective*, eds. Ibrahim Abed and Peter Hellyer. Cape Town: Trident Press Ltd, 161–78.

Herb, Michael. 1999. *All in the Family: Absolutism, Revolution, and Democracy in the Middle Eastern Monarchies*. Albany: State University of New York Press.

———. 2002. "Emirs and Parliaments in the Gulf." *Journal of Democracy* 13(4): 41–7.

Hermann, Margaret G. 2003. "Saddam Hussein's Leadership Style." In *The Psychological Assessment of Political Leaders: With Profiles of Saddam Hussein and Bill Clinton*, ed. Jerrold M. Post. Ann Arbor: University of Michigan Press, 375–86.

Hinnebusch, Raymond A., and Neil Quilliam. 2006. "Contrary Siblings: Syria, Jordan and the Iraq War." *Cambridge Review of International Affairs* 19(3): 513–28.

Joyce, Miriam. 1998. *Kuwait, 1945–1996: An Anglo-American Perspective*. London; Portland, OR: Frank Cass.

Kamrava, Mehran. 2011. *The Modern Middle East: A Political History since the First World War*. 2nd edition. Berkeley: University of California Press.

Karsh, Efraim. 2002. *The Iran–Iraq War, 1980–1988*. Oxford: Osprey Publishing.

Khadduri, Majid. 1960. *Independent Iraq, 1932–1958: A Study in Iraqi Politics*. Oxford: Oxford University Press.

Khadduri, Majid, and Edmund Ghareeb. 2001. *War in the Gulf, 1990–91: The Iraq-Kuwait Conflict and Its Implications*. Oxford: Oxford University Press.

Khalaf, Abd al-Hadi. 1987. "The Elusive Quest for Gulf Security." *MERIP Reports* 148(17). www.merip.org/mer/mer148/elusive-quest-gulf-security?ip_login_no_cache= 373d5fd0abcead5f1e000abe64d5dbe3 (December 26, 2016).

Korany, Bahgat. 1984. *The Foreign Policies of Arab States*. 1st edition. Cairo: American University in Cairo Press.

Kostiner, Joseph. 2009. *Conflict and Cooperation in the Gulf Region*. Wiesbaden: VS Verlag für Sozialwissenschaften. http://site.ebrary.com/id/10274811.

"Kuwait Is a Democracy." 1963. *New York Times*: 12.

Lesch, Ann Mosely. 1991. "Contrasting Reactions to the Persian Gulf Crisis: Egypt, Syria, Jordan, and the Palestinians." *Middle East Journal* 45(1): 30–50.

Long, Jerry M. 2004. *Saddam's War of Words: Politics, Religion, and the Iraqi Invasion of Kuwait*. 1st edition. Austin: University of Texas Press.

Lucas, Russell E. 2004. "Monarchical Authoritarianism: Survival and Political Liberalization in a Middle Eastern Regime Type." *International Journal of Middle East Studies* 36(1): 103–19.

Lynch, Marc. 1998. "Abandoning Iraq: Jordan's Alliances and the Politics of State Identity." *Security Studies* 8(2–3): 347–88.

Maddy-Weitzman, Bruce, ed. 1999. *Middle East Contemporary Survey*. Tel Aviv: The Moshe Dayan Center.

Metz, Helen Chapin, ed. 1994. *Persian Gulf States: Country Studies*. 3rd edition. Washington, DC: Federal Research Division, Library of Congress.

Mobley, Richard A. 2003. "The Tunbs and Abu Musa Islands: Britain's Perspective." *Middle East Journal* 57(4): 627–45.

Moghadam, Assaf. 2011. *Militancy and Political Violence in Shiism: Trends and Patterns*. London; New York: Routledge.

Musallam, Musallam Ali. 1996. *The Iraqi Invasion of Kuwait: Saddam Hussein, His State and International Power Politics*. London: British Academic Press.

216 *From monarchy to republic*

Okruhlik, Gwenn, and Patrick J. Conge. 1999. "The Politics of Border Disputes on the Arabian Peninsula." *International Journal* 54(2): 230–48.

Osman, Mohammed, and Latheef Farook. 2001. "UAE Wins GCC Backing Over Islands Dispute with Iran." *Gulf News*. http://gulfnews.com/news/uae/general/uae-wins-gcc-backing-over-islands-dispute-with-iran-1.407047 (January 4, 2017).

Parveen, Talat. 2006. *Iran's Policy Towards the Gulf*. New Delhi: Concept Publishing Company.

Peterson, J.E. 2011. "Sovereignty and Boundaries in the Gulf States. Settling the Peripheries." In *International Politics of the Persian Gulf*, ed. Mehran Kamrava. Syracuse: Syracuse University Press, 21–49.

Post, Jerrold M., ed. 2003. *The Psychological Assessment of Political Leaders: With Profiles of Saddam Hussein and Bill Clinton*. Ann Arbor: University of Michigan Press.

Rajaee, Farhang. 2010. *Islamism and Modernism: The Changing Discourse in Iran*. Austin: University of Texas Press.

Recknagel, Charles. 1999. "Iran: Gulf Security Proposal Unlikely to Be Realized." *RadioFreeEurope/RadioLiberty*. www.rferl.org/a/1091243.html (December 26, 2016).

Reed, Stanley. 1990. "Jordan and the Gulf Crisis." *Foreign Affairs* 69: 21–35.

Renshon, Stanley A., ed. 1993. *The Political Psychology of the Gulf War: Leaders, Publics, and the Process of Conflict*. Pittsburgh: University of Pittsburgh Press.

Royal Events. 2002. "The Persepolis Cebrations. The World Gathers in Persepolis." *From Tehran to Persepolis*. www.angelfire.com/empire/imperialiran/guests.html (February 6, 2017).

Saideman, Stephen. 2002. "Conclusion: Thinking Theoretically About Identity and Foreign Policy." In *Identity and Foreign Policy in the Middle East*, eds. Shibley Telhami and Michael Barnett. Ithaca: Cornell University Press, 169–200.

Schofield. 2001. "Down to the Usual Suspects: Border and Territorial Disputes in the Arabian Peninsula and Persian Gulf at the Millenium." In *Iran, Iraq and the Arab Gulf States*, ed. Joseph A. Kechichian. New York: Palgrave, 213–36.

Seale, Patrick. 1965. *The Struggle for Syria: A Study of Post-War Arab Politics 1945–1958*. 2nd edition. London: Oxford University Press.

Shlaim, Avi. 2009. *Lion of Jordan: The Life of King Hussein in War and Peace*. New York: Vintage.

Sirriyeh, Hussein. 1984. "Conflict Over the Gulf Islands of Abu Musa and the Tunbs, 1968–1971." *Journal of South Asian and Middle Eastern Studies* 8(2): 73–86.

Stevenson, Michael. 2008. *Celebration at Persepolis*. Arnolfini. http://corner-college.com/udb/cpro1N2bVIPersepolis.pdf (January 2, 2017).

Sunik, Anna. 2015. "The Royal Special Relationship. Großbritannien und die arabischen Monarchien." In *Sonderbeziehungen als Nexus zwischen Außenpolitik und internationalen Beziehungen*, Außenpolitik und Internationale Ordnung, eds. Sebastian Harnisch, Klaus Brummer, and Kai Oppermann. Baden-Baden: Nomos, 55–80.

Takriti, Abdel Razzaq. 2016. *Monsoon Revolution: Republicans, Sultans, and Empires in Oman, 1965–1976*. Oxford: Oxford University Press.

Teller, Matthew. 2014. "Sandhurst's Sheikhs: Why Do so Many Gulf Royals Receive Military Training in the UK?" *BBC*. www.bbc.com/news/magazine-28896860 (October 3, 2014).

Tétreault, Mary Ann. 2000. "Kuwait's Unhappy Anniversary." *Middle East Policy* 7(3): 67–77.

Tonini, Alberto. 2003. "Propaganda Versus Pragmatism: Iraqi Foreign Policy in Qasim's Years, 1958–63." *Review of International Affairs* 3(2): 232–53.

From monarchy to republic 217

Tucker, Spencer C., and Priscilla Roberts. 2008. *The Encyclopedia of the Arab-Israeli Conflict: A Political, Social, and Military History [4 Volumes]: A Political, Social, and Military History*. Santa Barbara: ABC-CLIO.

Ulrichsen, Kristian Coates. 2013. "The Gulf States and Iran–Iraq War. Cooperation and Confusion." In *The Iran–Iraq War: New International Perspectives*, ed. Nigel John Ashton. London; New York: Routledge, 107–24.

UN General Assembly. 1994. "17th Meeting. 49th GA Session. A/49/PV.17." www.un.org/ga/search/view_doc.asp?symbol=A/49/PV.17 (November 28, 2016).

UN Security Council. 1961. "Official Records. 16th Year. 957th Meeting." http://repository.un.org/bitstream/handle/11176/82133/S_PV.957-EN.pdf?sequence=2&isAllowed=y (January 6, 2017).

United Nations. 1945. "Chapter I, Article 2." www.un.org/en/sections/un-charter/chapter-i/index.html (May 1, 2017).

Winter, David G. 2003. "Motivations and Mediation of Self-Other Relationships." In *The Psychological Assessment of Political Leaders: With Profiles of Saddam Hussein and Bill Clinton*, ed. Jerrold M. Post. Ann Arbor: University of Michigan Press, 370–4.

Zahlan, Rosemarie Said. 2002. *The Making of Modern Gulf States: Kuwait Bahrain Qatar, The United Arab Emirates and Oman*. Reading: Ithaca Press.

6 The limits of SPSP
Deviant cases?

The different case studies all illuminate different aspects of the SPSP and present evidence of the effect of a monarchic peace. However, there are two episodes of intra-monarchic conflicts that merit an examination because both seem to pose challenges to the concept: the Saudi–Yemeni War of 1934, the only case of war among MENA monarchies in the 20th century, and the Qatar Crisis, ongoing since 2017. However, as the following chapter shows, instead of falsifying the theoretical framework, they instead confirm it and illuminate the validity of the scope conditions under which it operates. The war between Saudi Arabia and Yemen shows that a peace between monarchies can arise only if monarchy is a salient characteristic of states, because a "royal club" can develop only in that case. The Qatar Crisis on the other hand shows that although an existing monarchic ingroup does not eliminate conflict; ingroup-specific conflict-solving mechanisms keep it from escalating into war even during heated quarrels and a volatile regional climate.

6.1 The Saudi–Yemeni War 1934

The war between Yemen and Saudi Arabia was fought between two states with monarchic political systems. On first glance, this seems a prime example to disprove the SPSP theory. However, SPSP works only under the scope conditions of independent nation-state monarchies, which became true for most Middle Eastern monarchies only well after World War II. Although both countries were formally independent, they were not yet consolidated nation-states. Furthermore, an ingroup of monarchies can develop only once monarchy becomes a salient category for the self-identification of regimes. At that time, in between the world wars, monarchic salience was nonexistent, because all independent states in the region then were monarchies. One of the three conditioning factors for monarchic salience is whether monarchy is a minority of states or a decreasing share. Furthermore, not just the regional system but also the states were not yet consolidated, and imperial logic, instead of the logic of nation-states with their different handling of territory and borders, was entrenched. Saudi Arabia had just been declared two years prior, having had massively expanded its territory by raids, warfare, and tribal allegiance. The Yemeni imamate had a centuries-old history but was far from a modern nation-state monarchy. In fact, it was barely a state; rather, it operated on tribal allegiance basis instead of territorial demarcation. Its remote location and isolationist policies of the imam meant that it was behind the modernization that had just started in other Arab countries.[1] The prewar negotiations illustrate this different logic in respect to borders: the Yemeni negotiator insisted that there was no need for territorial demarcation, because "the two countries were like one body" and "everything under God's hand was one".[2] The Saudis were not impressed by that reasoning, and war soon broke out ('Uqāb 2011, 56–57).

The scope conditions for SPSP were clearly not met. It is thus hardly surprising that the imam and the king did not recognize each other as equals. The probably apocryphal quote of Imam Yahya regarding Ibn Saud best illustrates the deep asymmetry and lack of mutual recognition between the two war parties: "Who is this Bedouin coming to challenge my family's 900-year-long rule?" (quoted in: Orkaby 2015).

After the war, however, when territorial demarcation had been mostly accepted and the salience of monarchy rose with the rising republicanism, the two monarchies extended mutual recognition. When they consequently developed strong albeit wary relations, it was directly "attributed to the fact that both political systems were traditional and monarchical" (Zabarah 2001, 266). In support of this view, Zabarah cites the Saudi scholar Saeed Badeeb, who repeats the main assumptions of the SPSP framework almost verbatim:

> The political system of a country is undoubtedly a major determinant in its foreign policy behavior. Accordingly, the more closely one country's political system resembles that of another, the greater the degree of mutual understanding which can be expected between them. Conversely, as the differences between the political systems widen, so do their chances for misunderstanding.
> (Badeeb 1986, quoted in: Zabarah 2001, 266)

When that political system was threatened for the first time by a coup attempt in 1948, Ibn Saud began supporting Imam Ahmad, whom he had strongly disliked and undermined before (Gause 1990, 58–59). The relations grew so close that Saudi Arabia even represented Yemen, where the latter had no diplomatic missions (Zabarah 2001, 266). Three decades after their war, Saudi Arabia intervened in the Yemeni Civil War on behalf of the Royalists. A monarchic ingroup identification had developed by then to an extent that instead of going to war against each other, Saudi Arabia went to war *for* the Imamate.

Although it was the common threat facing the ruler of a similar political system that drove the two together, the alliance before the civil war prevailed even in the face of strong differences and diverging interests. Yemen, a highly isolated monarchy on the periphery of the Arab world and the Middle East, initially played an ambivalent role in the bipolar confrontation, and Imam Ahmad had initially supported the UAR in 1958 – as he explained to King Saud, to avoid becoming a target of Nasser's ire. However, once he started criticizing Nasser's economic

220 *The limits of SPSP*

policies as un-Islamic, this weak coalition broke down (Rogan and Aclimandos 2012, 156). The founding values inherent in Middle East monarchies proved incompatible with republicanism, and their differences in institutions and ideology developed to differences of opinion and, ultimately, opposition.

The war does not disprove the monarchic peace; instead, it emphasizes the important nuance that institutional commonality is no automatism for common identity. Perception of similarity is key, and this is predicated on the recognition of equality, as the Saudi-Hashemite case also showed.

6.2 The Qatar Crisis since 2017: resilience of family identification in a hostile conflict

The Qatar Crisis broke out recently and is still ongoing at the time of writing (January 2020), with little scholarly literature on it. Therefore, it cannot be included as a comprehensive case study like the four in Chapters 4 and 5. However, since it is a case of severe intra-monarchic conflict analogous to the case studies analyzed in Chapter 4, it will shortly be examined in the following section.

On first glance, the Qatar Crisis seems to challenge the monarchic peace hypothesis. Since the clash between Qatar on the one hand and (primarily) Saudi Arabia and the UAE on the other broke out in 2017, the level of tension was not limited to rhetorical signaling of determination, as is often found in conflict periods. Instead, in a surprising move, almost all relations between the blockading states and Qatar were cut. There were accusations of spying and sabotage and even veiled threats of military action. It is certainly one of the most serious crises, if not *the* most serious crisis, among the "royal club" members and the GCC in history.

And yet how the conflict played out instead confirms most theoretical expectations and not just because there are already possible first signs of reconciliation (Ulrichsen 2019). Although the conflict is severe, there is no sight of a military escalation. More importantly, frequent references to family and intragroup norms continue, in a similar way as during the Hawar Islands crisis. This all supports the conclusion that the crisis is temporary and the divide reversible – a spat in the family.

Background

Qatar's relationship with (at least some of) its GCC neighbors was not always harmonic, as evidenced by the Hawar Island dispute. In recent years, tensions have risen again in particular between Qatar on the one hand and an alliance of Saudi Arabia, the UAE, and Bahrain on the other. A first outburst of the conflict erupted in 2014, when the latter countries withdrew their diplomats from Doha in protest of Qatari foreign policy. They were returned a few months later, after the Riyadh agreements, the details of which were not disclosed to the public.

Relations seemingly normalized for the next three years. However, in June 2017, Saudi Arabia, the UAE, Bahrain, and Egypt broke off diplomatic and economic relations with Qatar and imposed a sea, air, and land blockade after the expiration of an ultimatum. The four blockading countries labeled themselves the Anti-Terror Quartet and initiated a severe campaign of accusations and sanctions against Qatar. They were joined and supported to various degrees by other (mostly Arab) states, including Jordan. The main driver behind the campaign is the leadership of Saudi Arabia and the UAE, with the economically and politically dependent Bahrain and Egypt in tow. Especially the aspiring future rulers, Muhammad bin Salman and Muhammad bin Zayed, also known as MBS and MBZ, were identified by many observers as the main architects of the Qatar-critical policy (Bianco and Stansfield 2018; Sunik 2017). Although the conflict has often been portrayed as one of the GCC against Qatar, Oman and Kuwait have so far remained on the fence and conducted mediation efforts to solve the crisis without joining the blockade. Oman's foreign minister even visited Emir Tamim in Doha the day of the crisis outbreak (Bianco and Stansfield 2018). The other monarchies are also not convinced: Morocco has also offered to mediate the crisis (al-Jazeera 2017), and Jordan merely downgraded its ties to Qatar but refrained from cutting them off entirely.

The blockade has several precursors, with some developments in 2017 having served as potential triggers (Bianco and Stansfield 2018, 614–615). After a group of falcon hunters from Qatar, including royals and other members of the elite, were captured by militias in Iraq and held for 16 months, Qatar allegedly paid more than US$700 million to Shia militias supported by Iran and jihadists groups to free them in April 2017, which outraged Saudi Arabia and the UAE. The Riyadh Summit a month later marked a turning point, as President Trump seemingly aligned with Saudi Arabia's (and the UAE's) policies at the expense of discordant allies like Qatar. This could have been seen as an encouragement by the two monarchies to push hard against detractors. Shortly after, Qatar News Agency (QNA) published remarks by the Qatari emir expressing support for Iran and Israel as well as Hamas and Hezbollah. Qatar denied the statements and alleged that the website was hacked. An FBI investigation was conducted, and US intelligence agencies later claimed that the UAE was responsible for the hacking as part of a large-scale cyberwar among the monarchies. High-ranking UAE government representatives had been discussing the plan the previous day (DeYoung and Nakashima 2017). In May 2017, the emails of the UAE's ambassador to the US, Yousef al-Otaiba, were hacked, which raised accusations of Qatari involvement (cf. Kirkpatrick and Frenkel 2017).

Among other things, the Anti-Terror Quartet demanded that Qatar terminate support for the Muslim Brotherhood, to shut down Al Jazeera and other media seen as connected to Qatar like Middle East Eye, and to sever or downgrade relations with Iran and Turkey respectively. Qatar condemned this as an illegitimate infringement on its national sovereignty. Consequently, the blockade of the heavily import-dependent country has continued since. While the quartet has portrayed its actions as part of a fight against international terrorism and interference, it is more likely that it is meant to bring Qatar in line with Saudi and Emirati policies against Iran (cf. Bianco and Stansfield 2018; Ulrichsen 2018).

222 *The limits of SPSP*

The campaign has so far failed to achieve any of its goals: the Qatari economy has diversified and lost some of its import dependence while intensifying trade with new partners – Turkey and Iran but also East Asian states and even other Gulf partners such as Oman. The crisis sparked the development of a Qatari national identity and a wave of unprecedented solidarity for the policies of Qatar's leadership that has so far cushioned domestic pressure (Gengler and Al-Khelaifi 2019).

Even in terms of consolidating the Sunni bloc against Iran, it has backfired by destabilizing the GCC and by pushing Qatar closer toward Iran and Turkey. To prioritize liquid natural gas (LNG) production and non-oil revenues but also to signal its detachment from its neighbors, Qatar declared its withdrawal from OPEC in 2019. Since the beginning of the conflict, Qatar has ceased to be a member of the Yemeni intervention coalition, in which all GCC states except Oman participated from the outset. Qatar has also restored full diplomatic relations with Iran as a reaction to the blockade in August 2017, although the closeness of the relationship is limited by fundamental strategical and geopolitical disagreements between the countries (Cafiero and Paraskevopoulos 2019).

The crisis is exacerbated by the inconsistent position of the United States, the main ally of the Gulf states. While Secretary of Defense James Mattis and then Secretary of State Rex Tillerson tried to mediate and emphasized the importance of US-Qatari ties, President Trump clearly sided with Saudi Arabia. However, this position was thwarted only a few months later, when the United States and Qatar signed an anti-terror cooperation agreement in July 2017 (Katzman 2019). Other accounts cite the US role as a deterrent to military escalation (Gengler and Al-Khelaifi 2019).

Foreign policy restraint?

Despite the enormous political and economic costs, a military escalation of the conflict is unlikely in the near future – conflict measures were so far limited to media campaigns and economic sanctions, although as mentioned earlier, there was some speculation that a military invasion was planned but averted due to US and Turkish deterrence. At this point, it is unclear how serious this threat was. Publicly, Tillerson affirmed that "throughout the dispute, all parties have explicitly committed to not resort to violence or military action" (Emmons 2018). Given that the US was split on the Qatar question, with the president being (initially) firmly on the side of the quartet, the US role as a deterrent would be in serious doubt. It is therefore unlikely that such plans, if they existed, were designed to be actionable at all. Since it never occurred, it is also unclear what intensity it would have taken. A war was always extremely unlikely: it is more realistic that the planned military action would not have been more serious than the 1992 Saudi-Qatari confrontation that resulted in an MID.

Other than that, the most aggressive measure has been Saudi Arabia's announcement that it intends to build a canal on the Saudi Arabia–Qatar border, thereby turning the peninsula into an island (Perper 2018). Despite numerous announcements and the initiation of a bidding process, there seems to have

The limits of SPSP   223

been no movement in this area. Other provocations that have so far not translated into actions include the veiled threat in a TV segment on Saudi-linked Al Arabiya simulating the shooting down of a plane bearing the logo of Qatar Airways (O'Connor 2017).

Apart from threats of escalation and potential violence, other steps include delegitimation and even subversion. For example, the quartet has pushed several Qatari royals as alternative rulers to Emir Tamim, like Abdallah bin Ali Al Thani and Sultan bin Suhaym Al Thani, both close relatives to former emirs. These attempts have led nowhere, because the Qatari public rallied around its ruler and because at least one of the candidates seemed to be coerced into acting, along with Saudi Arabia and Abu Dhabi (Gengler and Al-Khelaifi 2019, 402–403).

The conflict is rarely referred to in existential terms, a level of hostility that seems to be reserved for actual enemies, such as Iran, which is often demonized.[3] Instead, the blockading countries seem to see the blockade as a disciplinary measure for Qatar – not an opportunity to ostracize or destroy it. This is also reflected in statements by the UAE, which announced that they would lift the blockade should the World Cup be withdrawn from Qatar, because the country would then have suffered enough (Gambrell 2017b).

Without question, these provocations are serious. But they seem far from "unique", as some observers claim, despite seemingly being more public than previous were spats (Bianco and Stansfield 2018). Nonetheless, even the highly emotionalized media wars – with Qatari-aligned media maligning every UAE and Saudi policy misstep and putting the spotlight on their problems, like the Khashoggi killing (Mekhennet and Miller 2018), and vice versa – recall the intense episode of the Hawar conflict with its walkouts, public disagreements, espionage, and subversion accusations. All of these methods closely mirror those used by the conflicting sides in the historical Bahrain–Qatar conflict illustrated earlier, up to the cutting of ties and buildup of alternative leadership. However, then and now, they stopped short of calls for regime change (instead of leadership change), framing the conflict in terms of incompatibility and retaining the family rhetoric.

Ingroup identification since 2017

Ingroup identification can help de-escalate problems, as the case studies in this book have shown. But does the ingroup identification still exist between Qatar and its fellow monarchies? The institutional context factors have mostly remained the same: Qatar and the other Gulf states have not changed their political or economic systems to such an extent as to weaken their *institutional similarity* – although Muhammad bin Salman's domestic reforms have led to a certain "presidentialization" of the Saudi monarchy, which might be a step toward greater dissimilarity (cf. Sunik 2019).

The *salience* of monarchic identity has declined in recent years, because the common threat posed by anti-regime uprisings has mostly evaporated. Other factors affecting salience have remained constant: there is no significant divisive

224 *The limits of SPSP*

ideology shared by members of the group, apart from quotidian geopolitical power balancing and the fac that the number of monarchies in the system has not changed. Thus, we would expect a naturally lowered salience, meaning a lowered perception of similarity – but not a change significant enough to rupture the bonds that have so far precluded violent conflict.

As salience is lowered, we must look to the *social processes of ingroup identification* for significant developments. We can observe several changes in key indicators. The blockade and disruption of relations means that there are less-personalized bonds from visits and shared summits, at least between the Anti-Terror Quartet and Qatar. On the other hand, the personalization due to marriage, kinship, and shared socialization has remained. Indeed, personalized relations continue to play an important role in de-escalating and mediating the conflict. One example is the Saudi concession to allow Qataris access to the hajj pilgrimage following a meeting of Qatari royal Abdullah Al Thani (one of the rival rulers the quartet attempted to support) with Muhammad bin Salman and later with Saudi King Salman himself, who at the time was vacationing in fellow monarchy Morocco (Gambrell 2017a).

Historical narratives do not appear to have changed, although the interpretation of the current situation differs significantly for the conflict actors. Othering attempts are balanced by appeals to similarity and brotherhood. Of particular note is the continued family rhetoric by external observers as well as by GCC representatives, similar to the Hawar dispute period. There are constant references to the idea of a "Gulf family" (see e.g. Al-Haida 2019). Kuwait's ruler and foreign minister emphasized the "brotherly relations" (*"al-'alaqat al-akhawiya"*) and described the GCC members as "siblings" (*"ashiqqa"*) while mediating the conflict (BBC Arabic 2017). Qatar's Foreign Minister Mohammad Al Thani also referred to "talks with the brothers in Saudi Arabia" after the kingdom had invited Qatar's ruler to attend the GCC summit in Riyadh in December 2019 (Hamid 2019).

Although some othering attempts were also employed by both sides, a main point of contention of the other GCC states toward Qatar is its seeming detachment from Gulf values and community. Qatar's belonging to the GCC club is not questioned. However, in order to belong, it is expected to act in a certain way. This point could be seen in the Hawar crisis but also in the more recent disagreements concerning Qatari foreign policy in 2013–2014. As an Emirati expert explained, "what strains their relations is not rivalry or competition. It is the extent of commitment to the legacy of Gulf values and traditions", while another Emirati analyst emphasized that "neither Turkey nor the Muslim Brotherhood would do any good to Doha" and that "only sisterly Gulf countries are the real supporters of Qatar at good and bad times" (both quotes in Salama 2014).

In addition, the blocs are not as clear-cut as they appear. It is not a conflict between Qatar and the rest of the GCC: Kuwait and Oman refrained from taking sides, and the stance of Bahrain and even Dubai is to a large extent influenced by their larger and richer neighbors. It is even much less a conflict between Qatar and the rest of the monarchies: Morocco joined Kuwait and Oman in attempting

The limits of SPSP   225

to mediate, and Jordan downgraded its ties with Qatar under pressure but stopped short of cutting them off completely and restored formal diplomatic relations in summer 2019 (Rubin 2019).

What does that mean for the SPSP? Is the conflict serious enough to disrupt ingroup identification among Middle Eastern monarchies? Although predictions are difficult, especially about the future, as the old adage goes, the answer so far seems to be that it is unlikely.

First of all, the mechanism relates first and foremost to war, which did not occur, and despite rumors to the contrary, it is unlikely that it was ever a realistic option. So far, most provocations that might have resulted in irreversible damage (shooting down planes, eliminating Qatar's only land border, and advocating leadership change) have not been followed through on.

Of the social processes in play, the forces that lead to othering and escalation are countered by those emphasizing commonality and family belonging. The end of this conflict will be reached when that balance tips onto one side or the other. Given our theoretical expectations in the case of intact ingroup identification, the likelihood of eventual rapprochement is higher than rupture is. It is likely that even if the rift continues for the following years, Qatar will eventually rejoin the fold of the Gulf monarchies. The fact is that Qatar left OPEC but did not leave the GCC – nor were there serious demands to expel it. In addition, the continued family rhetoric both support this interpretation of a long-term view of history by the participants. This conclusion is, however, not set in stone.

How the "royal club" might break apart

There are some developments that could have a centrifugal effect, making the drift away from the cozy royal club irreversible. A main factor is Qatar's developing national identity, catalyzed by the crisis. While structural similarities remain constant, a strong separate national identity based on subsistence and self-reliance on the level of citizenry and ruling elite could weaken inter-regime identification. A possible tipping point may be the future relation to regime security. The SPSP mechanism hinges on the link to regime survival because similar systems recognize that their fates are linked and that they better hang together or hang separately. This might be one reason why the blockade states were so far not too concerned with regime (instead of leadership) change, as that would threaten them with a domino effect. Even the attempts to parade around Al Thani contenders to the throne against Emir Tamim substantiates this interpretation: while the emir is vilified, his replacement should come from his own family, i.e. the monarchic system with its *khaleeji* dynasty linchpin would be preserved, and thus, system similarity would not suffer.

However, Qatar is the monarchy whose regime is least threatened: it is a much more homogeneous state (at least in relation to the citizenry), with hardly any domestic cleavage like the Sunni–Shia division in Saudi Arabia or Bahrain; no domestic rival for power like Muslim Brotherhood–aligned factions in the UAE; no significant economic problems and class gaps like in most other GCC states;

226 *The limits of SPSP*

and no looming succession challenges like it seemed to be in Oman before the quick succession of the new sultan in 2020. Along with the UAE, Qatar has been the Arab country least affected by protests in the past. This means that the incentive for Qatar to preserve its attachment to the GCC and to monarchism is lower than for its other members, while the cost is currently much higher. Qatar's carefree attitude to regime security was also possibly one of the causes of the Qatar Crisis in the first place: being unencumbered by domestic unrest and opposition, Qatar was free to support revolutionary movements and actors across the Arab world, which its neighbors saw as a threat to their own systems (Bianco and Stansfield 2018). It is therefore possible that the crisis might trigger a process of disentanglement of Qatar's ontological security from those of its fellow monarchies and thus lead to the emirate's disidentification with them.

Notes

1 The Sultanistic isolationism practiced by Imam Yahya and to some extent Ahmad parallel that of Sultan Said bin Taimur of Oman, and resulted in the same international isolation. The shah's advisor, Asadollah Alam, commented on the Sultan: "Diehard reactionaries like this are doomed – and good riddance say I" (Goode 2014, 446). Once Sultan Qaboos took over power and started reforming the country, making it more similar and accessible to other monarchs (at a time when monarchism had long become salient), he was supported by his neighbors in his war against Dhofari rebels.
2 Own translation.
3 E.g. in 2018, then-Saudi Foreign Minister Adel al-Jubeir proclaimed Saudi policy as a vision of "light" against Iran's "vision of darkness" (Paul and Ali 2018).

References

Al-Haida, Abdullah. 2019. "The Real Test for the GCC: Dealing with Qatar's Crisis Skilfully." *Asharq Al-Awsat*. https://aawsat.com/english/home/article/2027911/real-test-gcc-dealing-qatars-crisis-skilfully (January 28, 2020).

Al Jazeera. 2017. "Morocco Offers to Mediate Qatar-GCC Crisis." *Al Jazeera*. www.aljazeera.com/news/2017/06/morocco-offers-mediate-qatar-gcc-crisis-170611190417048.html (January 15, 2020).

BBC Arabic. 2017. "Al-Kuwait: Qatar musta'idda li-tafahhum wa hawajis ashiqqa'iha fi l-khalij." *BBC Arabic*. www.bbc.com/arabic/middleeast-40240092 (January 28, 2020).

Bianco, Cinzia, and Gareth Stansfield. 2018. "The Intra-GCC Crises: Mapping GCC Fragmentation After 2011." *International Affairs* 94(3): 613–35.

Cafiero, Giorgio, and Andreas Paraskevopoulos. 2019. "GCC Dispute Pushes Iran and Qatar Closer but with Caveats." *Atlantic Council*. www.atlanticcouncil.org/blogs/iransource/gcc-dispute-pushes-iran-and-qatar-closer-but-with-caveats/ (January 28, 2020).

DeYoung, Karen, and Ellen Nakashima. 2017. "UAE Orchestrated Hacking of Qatari Government Sites, Sparking Regional Upheaval, According to U.S. Intelligence Officials." *Washington Post*. www.washingtonpost.com/world/national-security/uae-hacked-qatari-government-sites-sparking-regional-upheaval-according-to-us-intelligence-officials/2017/07/16/00c46e54-698f-11e7-8eb5-cbccc2e7bfbf_story.html (January 26, 2020).

Emmons, Alex. 2018. "Saudi Arabia Planned to Invade Qatar Last Summer. Rex Tillerson's Efforts to Stop It May Have Cost Him His Job." *The Intercept*. https://theintercept.com/2018/08/01/rex-tillerson-qatar-saudi-uae/ (January 31, 2020).

The limits of SPSP 227

Gambrell, Jon. 2017a. "Qatar Restores Diplomatic Ties to Iran amid Regional Crisis | The Times of Israel." *The Times of Israel*. www.timesofisrael.com/qatar-restores-diplomatic-ties-to-iran-amid-regional-crisis/ (January 28, 2020).

———. 2017b. "UAE Official Says Qatar Giving Up World Cup May End 'Crisis'." *Bloomberg*. www.bloomberg.com/news/articles/2017-10-09/uae-official-urges-qatar-to-give-up-world-cup-to-end-crisis (January 28, 2020).

Gause, F. Gregory, III. 1990. *Saudi-Yemeni Relations: Domestic Structures and Foreign Influence*. New York: Columbia University Press.

Gengler, Justin, and Buthaina Al-Khelaifi. 2019. "Crisis, State Legitimacy, and Political Participation in a Non-Democracy: How Qatar Withstood the 2017 Blockade." *The Middle East Journal* 73(3): 397–416.

Goode, James F. 2014. "Assisting Our Brothers, Defending Ourselves: The Iranian Intervention in Oman, 1972–75." *Iranian Studies* 47(3): 441–62.

Hamid, Nadeem. 2019. "Qatar Says Holding Talks with Saudi Arabia to End Gulf Crisis." *Bloomberg*. www.bloomberg.com/news/articles/2019-12-06/qatar-says-holding-talks-with-saudi-arabia-to-end-gulf-crisis (January 28, 2020).

Katzman, Kenneth. 2019. *Qatar: Governance, Security, and U.S. Policy*. Washington: CRS Report for Congress.

Kirkpatrick, David D., and Sheera Frenkel. 2017. "Hacking in Qatar Highlights a Shift Toward Espionage-for-Hire." *The New York Times*. www.nytimes.com/2017/06/08/world/middleeast/qatar-cyberattack-espionage-for-hire.html (January 28, 2020).

Mekhennet, Souad, and Greg Miller. 2018. "Jamal Khashoggi's Final Months as an Exile in the Long Shadow of Saudi Arabia." *Washington Post*. www.washingtonpost.com/world/national-security/jamal-khashoggis-final-months-an-exile-in-the-long-shadow-of-saudi-arabia/2018/12/21/d6fc68c2-0476-11e9-b6a9-0aa5c2fcc9e4_story.html (January 28, 2020).

O'Connor, Tom. 2017. "Saudi Arabia Shoots Down Qatar Plane in Animated Warning." *Newsweek*. www.newsweek.com/saudi-arabia-shoot-down-qatar-plane-animated-warning-651584 (January 28, 2020).

Orkaby, Asher. 2015. "Saudi Arabia's War with the Houthis: Old Borders, New Lines." *WINEP*. www.washingtoninstitute.org/policy-analysis/view/saudi-arabias-war-with-the-houthis-old-borders-new-lines (May 8, 2017).

Paul, Katie, and Idrees Ali. 2018. "Saudi Arabia Says It Is Beacon of 'Light' Against Iran Despite Khashoggi Crisis." *Reuters*. www.reuters.com/article/us-bahrain-summit-idUSKCN1N10DD (February 1, 2020).

Perper, Rosie. 2018. "Saudi Arabia Is Planning to Turn Its Rival Qatar into an Island." *Business Insider*. www.businessinsider.com/saudi-arabia-wants-to-turn-qatar-into-an-island-2018-6 (January 28, 2020).

Rogan, Eugene L., and Tewfik Aclimandos. 2012. "The Yemen War and Egypt's War Preparedness." In *The 1967 Arab-Israeli War: Origins and Consequences*, Cambridge Middle East studies, eds. Avi Shlaim and William Roger Louis. Cambridge: Cambridge University Press, 149–64.

Rubin, Lawrence. 2019. "Jordan and Qatar Restore Diplomatic Ties, but Why Now?" *IISS*. www.iiss.org/blogs/analysis/2019/07/jordan-qatar-restore-ties (January 28, 2020).

Salama, Samir. 2014. "Qatar's History of Turbulent Relations with UAE." *GulfNews*. http://gulfnews.com/news/uae/government/qatar-s-history-of-turbulent-relations-with-uae-1.1312739 (February 19, 2017).

Sunik, Anna. 2017. "The UAE: From Junior Partner to Regional Power." *GIGA Focus Nahost* (6).

228 *The limits of SPSP*

———. 2019. *Reform Ohne Liberalisierung: Die Präsidentialisierung Saudi-Arabiens.* Hamburg: GIGA.

Ulrichsen, Kristian Coates. 2018. *The Gulf Impasse.* Gulf International Forum. https://gulfif.org/app/wp-content/uploads/2018/05/The-Gulf-Impasse%E2%80%99s-One-Year-Anniversary-the-Changing-Regional-Dynamics.pdf.

———. 2019. "Could the Gulf Crisis with Qatar Be Winding Down?" *Washington Post.* www.washingtonpost.com/politics/2019/12/12/could-gulf-crisis-with-qatar-be-winding-down/ (January 15, 2020).

□Uqāb, □Abd al-Wahhāb Ādam A□mad. 2011. *Taṭawwur Al-'alāqāt al-Yamanīyah al-Sa'ūdīyah, 1900–1970.* Dimashq: Dār Raslān.

Zabarah, Mohammed Ahmad. 2001. "Yemeni-Saudi Relations Gone Awry." In *Iran, Iraq and the Arab Gulf States*, ed. Joseph A. Kechichian. New York: Palgrave, 263–80.

7 Conclusion

Toward a peace among similar political systems

Despite Huntington's assessment 50 years ago, the present and future of monarchies is not bleak at all. Monarchies are a rewarding subject of study because they represent a phenomenon that is theoretically and empirically interesting: not only have they survived, but they have also been successful at avoiding war, at least among themselves.

The prism of monarchism also allows us to take a fresh look at the dynamics following the Arab Spring. The comparative case studies support a conceptualization of the monarchic peace as a subtype of a similar political systems peace (SPSP) and provide a "building block" (George and Bennett 2005, 76) of the theory, showing how ingroup dynamics operate between similar political systems. It seems neither democracies nor monarchies, for that matter, are "exceptional" in their foreign policy behavior. Consequently, the phenomenon usually described as the democratic peace should be reframed as a subtype of a broader pattern of war avoidance that can lead to "zones of peace" between similar political systems of different kinds.

What does it mean that monarchies also seem to have a similar political systems peace? Statistical data on interstate conflict indicate meaningful patterns of peace between monarchies. The theory-guided comparative case studies of ingroup identification between Middle Eastern monarchies confirmed that monarchic foreign policy behavior is different indeed – at least if it is directed toward another monarchy. Monarchies do not wage war against each other, although they do against other states. The reason for this can be traced back to the fact that monarchies recognize each other as part of the same "community" or ingroup that is governed by specific behavioral norms, of which nonviolence is of prime importance. A study of monarchies in periods of shared threat established the regional context of monarchic ingroup favoritism and epitomized the causal mechanism. Four case studies, in which the mechanism was traced, illuminated the dynamics and function of ingroup identification as a conflict-management and war-prevention mechanism.

The analysis of these cases also clarified the preconditions for the emergence of a shared identity, namely a *degree of independence and border stability*, which corresponds to key features of the modern nation-state. Once the basis for ingroup identification is laid by it and structural similarities, the identification is catalyzed

230   *Conclusion*

by a *low or decreasing share of monarchies* in the regional system and the presence of a *common threat*. It is impeded by a *divisive ideology* that calls for a system of hierarchy among nation-states. These three factors affect the *salience* of monarchism as a defining condition of group identity.

Three clusters of core ideas were derived from the research questions formulated in the introduction. The first and second cluster related to general patterns of foreign policy by focusing on the nexus between political system structure and foreign policy behavior.

There following are the core ideas here:

1   **Monarchies recognize each other as equal and part of the same ingroup, which encourages distinct types of behavior for monarchies toward one another and toward other regimes.**
2   **This ingroup identity leads to ingroup favoritism (but not necessarily outgroup hostility).** This, in turn, leads to **de-escalation of severe conflicts and crises and thus prevents war.** In a particularly strong version, it can lead to **monarchic alliance or solidarity beyond ad hoc coalitions.**
3   The third cluster is concerned with **changes in foreign policy behavior**: monarchic ingroup identification varies over time and so does the interaction between the monarchies. This variance is shaped by the *salience* of the monarchic identity. Three factors affect salience: when monarchies **are the minority and/or are decreasing** in numbers and when there is a **common threat** against them, salience is raised. When there is a **divisive ideology** among them, salience is lowered. However, **even during periods of low salience, the ingroup bond precludes military action in intra-monarchic conflicts.**

7.1 Monarchic ingroup identification

The various social processes for ingroup identification show that throughout many decades, there was a recognition as equals by Middle East monarchies that shaped their foreign policy behavior. Foreign policy restraint markedly differed among monarchies on the one hand and between monarchies and republics on the other hand, as suggested by the study of monarchic foreign policy in crisis and further established by the "quasi-experiments". The case studies also showed that **outgroup hostility (toward republics) was most pronounced in the presence of a common threat**, e.g. during the period of the Arab Cold War or against Iraq and Iran after they became republics and began fostering anti-monarchic ideologies and policies. **Monarchic favoritism, on the other hand, was present at all times**: monarchs and other regime elites recognize their counterparts as parts of the same community, with similar aims, interests, and fears, often threatened by similar forces and bound together by highly personalized ties. These ties serve as the basis on which to affirm and signal their commonalities and contributed to a restrained foreign policy during conflicts and a mostly cooperative foreign policy in less-tense periods.

Conclusion 231

This bond of ingroup solidarity is pervasive. Although it may vary in impact, it persistently discriminates between monarchies and non-monarchies. Among monarchies, the norm of nonviolence is deeply ingrained. This does not eliminate conflict, but it shapes *reactions* to conflicts and engenders restraint in foreign policy decision-making. Monarchic ingroup identity is meaningful for foreign policy behavior, especially concerning matters of such major importance as war and peace. The "quasi-experiments" also supported the idea that the change was driven by the political system difference rather than shared ethnicity, confession, or oil wealth, as those remained constant for Iran and Iraq after their revolutions.

The case studies also showed that not institutional similarity per se but mainly the *perception of similarity* shaped ingroup favoritism among monarchies. When monarchism was not a defining category, intra-monarchic relations did not differ significantly from relations with republics. The *personalization of relations* and the *affirmation of commonality* served as indicators for intense and significant personal relationships. *Personalization*, the basis for ingroup identification, was brought about through regularized social interaction via shared education and socialization and via bonds of intermarriage, kinship, and friendship that formed the basis for the development of an ingroup.

Once this basis had enabled the establishment of ingroup identification, it then became the foundation to perpetuate, reaffirm, and deepen the connection as the *commonality was affirmed and reaffirmed*. A deep connection that acknowledged equality among monarchs and ruling elites, often framed in metaphorical family terms, was signaled and strengthened in official and unofficial proclamations, statements, speeches, and memoirs. The reification of this identity in common rituals and ceremonies helped to overcome existing differences. The similarities of the systems meant that some ceremonies or occasions for meetings were more widespread among monarchies, e.g. coronations, royal successions, and weddings. The reification of identity strengthened the perception of similarity beyond mere institutional parallels. Even when there was no clear feeling of belonging to a family, there was always an emphasis on the similarities rather than on the divisions between the countries.

Restraint and alliance

The outcome of this identification was *restraint* in times of crisis. Sometimes this restraint meant not only non-aggression but also active cooperation and alliance. Both core ideas are explored by looking at *foreign policy restraint (or escalation)*. While not a question explicitly asked by this book, its analysis also gave first hints to the answer of *when* non-war turns into solidarity.

The higher the perceived similarity between monarchies, the greater the trust, solidarity, and willingness to reach mutually acceptable nonviolent dispute resolutions. In harmonious times, there might not be any reason for provocation and escalation, regardless of regime type.

However, during *crises*, these mechanisms become more meaningful, and here the discriminatory influence of ingroup identification is seen most clearly.

232 *Conclusion*

Whereas severe crises escalated into wars or militarized aggression against or between republics, monarchs attempted to de-escalate tensions inside the monarchic community. There was a consistent preference for cooperation over confrontation, unlike in republican or mixed dyads, a pattern seen across all case studies. Even in the tense times of the Qatar Crisis, monarchies – Oman, Kuwait, and Morocco – attempted to provide a mediating platform to solve the conflict between monarchies.

The most important finding in that regard was **that confrontation rarely reached the threshold where use of force was even considered, much less deployed**. In the rare cases that it was (the seven intra-monarchic MIDs in the region), the crises were quickly diffused before they could lead to war. While conflicts outside the ingroup might become existential and slide into war, a family-like community understands that conflicts can be mediated peacefully. After all, differences of opinion "even happen between brothers", as Zayed Al Nahyan, the ruler of the UAE, said about his country's relations with the Saudis in 1972 (cited in: Alkim 1989, 118). Being based on norms and identity, ingroup favoritism proved more robust. After all, **not wanting to risk war is not as strong a deterrent as not wanting war at all**.

The restraint went deeper than merely eschewing war initiation, as captured by the analysis of *non-military restraint*. Foreign policy decision makers in monarchies generally refrained from destabilizing the opponent's regime, even though campaigns to destabilize the position of individual monarchs, like in the case of the former Qatari Emir, Hamad bin Khalifa Al Thani, occasionally occurred. Even on the rhetorical level, threats of violence and rhetorical escalation by othering, demonization, or securitizing the conflict issue remained the exception, most remarkably during the confrontation between Bahrain and Qatar when Bahrain rebuked its neighbor for breaking "family norms of behavior" without othering it or stripping it of the shared identity. Communication lines were practically always upheld – though sometimes, boycotts of meetings were employed to signal disagreement. Although the feedback loop could not be adequately captured by the theoretical framework, foreign policy restraint during crises in turn clearly led to stronger bonds in post-conflict periods – just as strong bonds in "normal" periods fostered restraint in crisis, creating a feedback loop.

Apart from eschewing military conflict, in some periods, a more demanding norm of intra-monarchic interaction was activated, leading to *active mutual support (or solidarity) and long-term alliance and solidarity*, which sometimes even transformed into attempts to *institutionalize interstate bonds*. The most successful of these attempts resulted in the creation of the GCC, although the union between the Hashemite sister kingdoms of Jordan and Iraq was another, albeit short-lived, instance. As a form of positive ingroup favoritism (in contrast to "negative" non-war), alliance and solidarity are more-demanding and more-costly norms than mere restraint is and therefore not always observable.

Mutual support or intra-monarchic solidarity was activated mostly under two conditions: in the presence of a **common threat** (like the pan-Arabist revolutionary republics during the 1950s and 1960s) and **among especially close and**

Conclusion 233

especially similar monarchies, such as the GCC states. When particularly close and similar monarchies formalized existing alliance bonds, they could even lead to their institutionalization in formal intergovernmental organizations. It remains to be seen after the Qatar Crisis if the absence of a common threat might also drive the dissolution of such institutions, but so far, there is no hint that it does. Although Qatar left the Yemen War coalition and OPEC, there was never any suggestion of it leaving the GCC.

However, there were some contradictory findings whether alliance is triggered only by a common threat or also comes about without it, such as in the case of pre-existing groupings based on entrenched and enduring patterns of similarity and proximity. For instance, alliance and solidarity were more pronounced in the Bahraini-Qatari case even in periods without a strong mutual threat – but were propelled to salience during the period of the Arab Cold War, where the common threat was strong. Monarchic alliances were not as pronounced at the beginning of the formation of an ingroup or between highly dissimilar monarchies as in the Iran–UAE case or throughout the early period of the Saudi-Hashemite relations.

Similar caveats apply to the institutionalization of alliance, as seen most visibly with the GCC and the AFU between the Hashemite kingdoms of Jordan and Iraq. Institutionalization attempts failed in cases when no additional kinship or ethnic bonds existed – like the Gulf Security Pact propagated by the shah. This pattern may have also frozen any plans for extending GCC membership to Jordan and Morocco so far.

The findings thus illustrate how **identity can forge and cement alliances that go beyond ad hoc coalitions that are based on "material" interest-based politics and deterrence**. Alliances shaped by identity are more durable than ad hoc coalitions driven by common interests are. While a common threat might induce both, ad hoc coalitions break down when interests start to diverge again. In contrast, monarchic ingroup identification remains largely intact even after the departure of an immediate threat. Without such a sense of shared identity, Iraq felt free to attack Kuwait, previously joined into an ad hoc coalition with it against Iran. In contrast, the end of the Arab Cold War did not herald the end of intense and special monarchic relations (and joint peacefulness), although the level of mutual support decreased significantly. The alliance within the GCC persisted even when Bahrain and Qatar were at odds over the Hawar Islands conflict. Even Iran and the Gulf monarchies continued to ally despite the shah's seizure of islands claimed by UAE emirates.

The analysis strongly suggests that **monarchic restraint is indeed dyadic** and that **there is no general monarchic peacefulness**, based on the comparison with monarchic behavior toward republics provided by the case studies: subversion campaigns aimed at regime change, assassinations or support of militant groups are measures reserved against hostile republics. These measures were deployed by Saudi Arabia and Jordan against Egypt, Syria, and Iraq in the 1950s and 1960s, and the same policies were adopted by republics against each other or against monarchies, like the Iranian campaign against the GCC states in the 1980s or the Syrian campaign against Iraq in the 1970s. In addition, monarchies did not

234 *Conclusion*

hesitate to even deploy military measures against republics, most prominently during the Gulf War of 1990/1991. The same systematic cooperation preference that could be found among monarchies had no effect on monarchy–republic interactions wherever political interests diverged. Despite strong disagreements among the dynasties, the spectrum of acceptable and legitimate behavior among monarchies was different from those toward republics like Egypt and Syria. Once states changed their regime, this pattern changed accordingly, as demonstrated by the two case studies of "quasi-experiments". **Two sets of standards were valid for conflict resolution with monarchies on the one hand and conflict resolution involving republics on the other.** This supports the constructivist SIT interpretation rather than an institutionalist one.

Salience of ingroup identity

Another key finding is related to the *salience* of monarchy, the main factor behind *changes in the relations* between monarchies over time. Salience affects the mutual perception of monarchic elites as being part of a community. As illustrated by the case studies, intra-monarchic cohesion waxed and waned according to external circumstances. In brief, when salience was low because some of the driving factors behind it were weak or absent, social processes of ingroup identification declined, resulting in lower levels of ingroup favoritism and consequently weaker monarchic cohesion. In general, **no salience meant that military conflict was a possibility because there was no recognition as equals and no formation of a special community** (as was the case up to the 1930s). **Low salience meant weak ingroup identification and weak ingroup favoritism – non-war but also little to no instances of monarchic solidarity** and mutual support (as in the outset of Saudi-Hashemite relations). **High salience usually meant alliance and/or solidarity among monarchies**, sometimes leading up to attempts to institutionalize these alliances (as during the period of the Arab Cold War).

However, the case studies did not clearly establish a hierarchy between the different factors affecting salience and did not settle the question whether some might cancel others out. The findings support the interpretation that the strength of this intervening factor has a stronger explanatory power for monarchic alliance than for monarchic non-war. In other words, **a low salience might be enough to preclude war, but a higher salience is necessary for further monarchic favoritism.** However, given that the analysis is set in the postwar (post–world war) period, when monarchies had been declining for a long time, a basic level of monarchic salience had been present at all times since the 1940s, although its level varied strongly.

Two factors are identified as catalysts for ingroup identification: a common threat and a low and/or decreasing share of monarchies in the regional system. In addition, a divisive hierarchic ideology could be shown to obstruct ingroup identification: this was a main stumbling block for the cohesion of the republican camp during the Arab Cold War, as illustrated in the initial case study of monarchic intergroup conflict: the Nasserist and Ba'thist variants of pan-Arabism called for a

Conclusion 235

unification under a strong leadership, thereby dividing the revolutionary republics instead of uniting them against the monarchies. The case studies of monarchic foreign policy during periods of intragroup conflict provided additional evidence for this mechanism. Although Middle East monarchies are marked by their proclivity to pragmatism, during the rare episodes when a divisive ideology emerged (whether Hashemite irredentism or Persian supremacy), these ideologies either weakened ingroup identification (in the latter case) or precluded it altogether (in the first case). The Saudi-Hashemite and the Iran–UAE case studies thus provide some evidence for its influence on monarchic salience. The monarchic variants of divisive ideologies, however, also went hand in hand with imperialist foreign policies or occurred during the early period of state and regional system consolidation, and both factors impede ingroup identification and are therefore *scope conditions* for this analysis.

Since the inception of the modern Middle East state system, the share of monarchies in the regional system has continuously been on the decline (with the exception of a small bump due to the independence of the small Gulf monarchies). Monarchies never again reached majority status after 1962, when North Yemen imploded into civil war and Algeria became an independent republic. Taken together with the typical monarchic "pragmatism" that made them less susceptible to strong ideologies of any kind, the salience of monarchism as a defining characteristic for foreign policy actors remained prevalent to different degrees throughout the decades from this point on. Consequently, the **main parameter of change for monarchic salience** and thus monarchic foreign policy behavior throughout the period **was a common threat directed against monarchies**. This should not be confused with the conclusion that common threat has a stronger impact on salience than on other factors per se (although that could also be the case); it means merely that it has varied more widely than the other two factors affecting monarchic salience.

While the analysis showed that the presence of a direct threat heightened the salience of monarchism by intensifying the social processes of ingroup identification, increased threat levels also led to more-demanding norms of intragroup conduct – alliance and solidarity in addition to mere non-war. This effect could be observed, for instance, after the breakdown of the Egyptian and the Iraqi monarchies in the 1950s or during the Iraqi invasion of Kuwait. Sometimes, it even triggered military action in support of other monarchies, as in the Gulf War 1990/1991 or the Peninsula Shield operation in Bahrain in 2011.

If the monarchic system comes under threat, it becomes a strong politically relevant characteristic that might trump larger (Arab world) or smaller (tribal, personal, confessional, etc.) identification frames. If the option is "hanging together or hanging separately", the answer for foreign policy decision makers is clear. A feeling of immediate and often-existential threat also creates "communities of fate" by, in Wendt's words, "*identification* with the fate of the other" (Wendt 1994, 385, emphasis in original) through "shared norms and political culture" (1994, 386). A threat to one becomes a threat to all and triggers a joint response. These communities of fate are then transformed from ad hoc coalitions of "collective

236 *Conclusion*

security" into more-enduring alliances of "collective defense". Inside them, violence becomes both unacceptable and unfathomable, while alliances are created for joint action in order to defeat external threats.

Nonetheless, a common threat is neither a necessary nor a sufficient condition for long-term cooperation or alliance. The lack of republican cohesion in times of a monarchic threat during the Arab Cold War shows that it is not sufficient. The case of Bahrain and Qatar, on the other hand, shows that the preference to cooperate and engage in foreign policy restraint can be ingrained even without a shared threat as long as the ingroup is sufficiently developed.

The fact that there has been **no intra-monarchic war and only seven MIDs (out of 444) between Middle East monarchies in the examined period** (of which only three actually involved any use of force)[1] supports the conclusion that even low salience might preclude war – although it does not necessarily trigger mutual support. The absence of military conflict cannot serve as a confirmation of the hypothesis beyond doubt, although it makes a solid case for its plausibility, especially given the analysis of the causal mechanism. However, salience is not a trivial condition, because the historical context of the case studies also showed that when monarchy is not salient at all, war or at least militarized altercations can happen – as in the pre-World War II period of Saudi Arabia and the Hashemite states. **Salience, we can deduce, is key – and not the existence of monarchies per se. Only both combined can explain the patterns that we see in the case studies**.

Alternative and complementary factors

The combination of the different cases helped make the findings more robust, especially concerning the rival explanations discussed in Chapter 2. While the mechanism of ingroup identification could be seen most clearly in the case of Bahrain and Qatar, the other cases showed similar processes, thereby supporting the conclusion that the MP is not merely a *khaleeji* (Gulf) peace.

The different case studies also demonstrated that this peace is more than merely the consequence of *small-state* dynamics. Both "quasi-experiments" pitted a large state against a small neighbor who would have figured as easy prey (and indeed did in the republican period, especially in the Iraq–Kuwait case). As long as the involved states were all monarchies, however, they showed a high level of restraint. The Saudi-Hashemite case also pitted larger, more-powerful states against each other – with similar results.

Except for Jordan (and possibly Saudi Arabia in the early post-independence period), all countries covered are major *oil* (and gas) exporters. Oil, or rather wealth, played a significant role. While the case of Bahrain and Qatar showed the clearest signs of ingroup identification based on political and cultural similarity, Bahrain was also strongly incentivized to find a solution by compromise through promises of Qatari investment and financial support, as acknowledged by Bahraini politicians. Although the presence of oil enhances the states' resources and shapes its preferences, once a crisis situation has been reached, it can work as an

Conclusion 237

incentive to make peace (as for Bahrain vis-à-vis Qatar) or to make war (as for Iraq against Kuwait). In addition, there was no significant effect of militarism or a militarized political system. While this might shape the general proclivity toward war – across more (Jordan, Oman) or less "militarized" states (the Gulf monarchies) – the preference for cooperation and the inability to imagine war against a fellow monarch remained constant.

Perhaps the greatest caveat is that given that all monarchies of the past and present were Western allies, it was not possible to find a case to establish the independent effect of *Western alliance*. British influence and its role as a security guarantor was crucial in different time periods even after decolonization. British involvement probably deterred Saudi Arabia in 1956 (and Iraq in 1938), and Britain was an important mediator between Iran and the shaikhs that controlled the Trucial states' territories. US influence presumably played a similar role in more-recent times and may have had a similar effect in the Qatar Crisis (along with Turkey).

However, British (and US) influence alone cannot explain the phenomenon of the monarchic peace: Britain did not deter Iran from seizing the Tunbs while the Trucial States were still under its security umbrella and then failed to challenge Iran's fait accompli. The US could not prevent the Iraqi invasion of Kuwait – despite the fact that both states had long been supported by the US (although intermittently in the case of Iraq). Clashes occurred under a *Pax Britannica* as well as under a *Pax Americana*, but regional alliances among monarchies persisted and were even strengthened after British withdrawal. For instance, following the British withdrawal from the Persian Gulf, the 1970s were a period of intense Iranian-Arab monarchic cooperation until the fall of the Iranian monarchy; and Saudi-Jordanian relations grew more intense and friendlier *after* British retrenchment from the region. In addition, because Western alliance seems linked to the monarchic political system, its effects cannot be clearly separated.

This points to another major influence for monarchic interaction that cannot be discarded: the institutional aspects of *monarchism*. As stated earlier, there were clear differences between ingroup and outgroup foreign policy behavior. However, some traits linked to the monarchic political system either supported the mechanism of ingroup identification or worked alongside it in the same direction. This relates especially to the aforementioned Western alliance but also to monarchic pragmatism and to a potential monarchic proclivity for strong intragroup bonds. The absence of a foreign policy–oriented ideology that so often complicated the foreign relations of republics is intrinsically linked to the concept of monarchy. However, the Iran–UAE case also demonstrated that even the most omnipotent monarchs have to consider public opinion if they want to stay in power – which implies that their freedom in foreign policy is smaller than expected. The shah of Iran and the shaikhs of Sharjah and Ras al-Khaimah all claimed that they would have to cling to their territorial claims because they might otherwise be overthrown. Nonetheless, some features of ingroup identification dynamics are intrinsically tied to monarchic institutions – e.g. intermarriage and the long "tenures" of monarchs and other ruling family members in positions of

238 *Conclusion*

power. Royal ceremonies such as coronations all made intragroup bonds easier and more intense. In addition, in the two case studies that compared joint monarchic periods with mixed periods after the regime change of a member of the dyad, mostly the republics changed their foreign policy to a more confrontational level.[2]

In general, an institutional approach does not necessarily compete with a SIT-centric explanation. It can also create better conditions for it to work, but this might have implications for the generalizability of the theoretical model when it comes to non-monarchies. Another implication of a parallel institutionalist effect would be a possible explanation of why MP patterns are so similar to the DP: both could be institutionally predisposed to (dyadic) peacefulness. Only further research on other possible groups of "similar systems" can yield answers to these questions.

The advantage of a comparative case framework, consisting of multiple cases selected for difference, lies in the strengths of some of the cases being able to balance the weaknesses of others to some extent. This makes the findings more robust and helps to filter out the independent effect of joint monarchism among the plethora of other factors. Dynamic and fluid concepts, such as common identification, are difficult to capture, and the process of ingroup building takes time, a consolidated state, and political institutions. The case setup itself complicates the findings: per definition, most instances of "nearly missed war" take place in times when relations were not consistently close and greater tensions persisted, e.g. regarding the Saudi-Hashemite case, before or early on in the process of consolidation of both the regional system and monarchic ingroup identity. In this case, the relations grew even closer after the rivalry had ended, i.e. after the end of the analyzed period. After the 1950s, a military confrontation between Saudi Arabia and the remaining half of the Hashemite realms, i.e. Jordan, became immensely unlikely, as foreshadowed by their dynamics during the Arab Cold War period. However, these caveats also made for hard tests of the theory. Because the cases were different and featured ingroups at various stages of development while exhibiting the same main mechanisms, the resulting findings are more robust.

The quasi-experimental cases were particularly significant in that regard since they showed a marked contrast in bilateral relations when dyadic monarchism shifted to a relationship between a monarchy and a republic. Consequently, the transformation of the political system could be shown to have a significant impact on the processes of ingroup identification.

Despite all important caveats to the analytical findings, their importance lies in the establishment of a **mostly independent effect of joint monarchism that might work under diverse circumstances** – provided that there is a sufficiently developed salience of monarchy.

7.2 Monarchic peace as a building block study

The results of the theory-guided comparative case studies contribute to several research literatures. The book draws from research traditions embedded in comparative politics (CP) like Middle East monarchy research as well as research

Conclusion 239

grounded in the discipline of international relations (IR)/foreign policy analysis (FPA), such as the democratic peace theorem (DPT). Combining these traditions helps balance the respective biases of the various disciplines and enables the further development of the emerging field of study of the foreign policy of authoritarian regimes.

The theoretical framework presented here adds the study of monarchic foreign policy to the research on Middle Eastern monarchies and broadens the scope of the field. As for the FPA and IR literature in general, the case study combines the DPT literature and research on autocratic foreign policy by analyzing the conflict behavior of the monarchic subtype of autocracy, thereby dispelling the notion of a unique peacefulness among democracies. Probably the most important contribution is the insight that the democratic peace might simply be a subset of the SPSP, which includes other dyads, such as monarchies.

Transferring concepts that were created inside a democracy-centric research tradition to a region and a type of state not usually examined helps us to reach more-wide-ranging conclusions than either tradition did on their own. **It crushes two "exceptionalisms" at once: it turns out that neither the Middle East and its monarchies nor democracies is unique.** Democracies (mostly in the West) and monarchies (mostly in the Middle East) can behave similarly, by avoiding war and forging durable bonds and alliances among each other. The causal mechanism examined here can just as well be applied to other "similar political systems", including, of course, democracies.

Paradoxically, this narrowing of the gap between democracies and at least some types of autocracies is a result of taking authoritarianism seriously. Only by deconstructing the catch-all category of autocracies, by differentiating the subtypes and redefining "political similarity" can we produce meaningful insights into the way different autocracies behave in the international or regional system and why they do so.

The finding that the monarchic peace is not inherently tied to monarchism but rather to similarity, salience, and ingroup identification allowed us to make the case for an SPSP based on a social identity theory pathway. The SPSP thereby forms a bridge between the DPT tradition and autocracy research. **This does not make research on the democracy-specific aspects of the DP or the monarchy-specific aspects of the MP obsolete; rather, it merely complements them with an overarching framework that combines both.**

If the DP is reframed as a subset of the SPSP alongside the monarchic peace – and possibly also the Confucian peace (Kelly 2012), militarist peace (Martín 2006), republican peace (Weart 1994), and socialist peace (Oren and Hays 1997) – the theorem attains a greater explanatory power and enables us to uncover additional novel facts. It would thus fulfill Lakatos's criteria for a "progressive research program" (Lakatos 1970).

In addition, the book addresses the role of identity and foreign policy, as set on the agenda by earlier studies of their relationship (Telhami and Barnett 2002). It further delineates the conditions in which identity affects foreign policy and supports the "middle ground" between primordial and instrumental approaches – meaning

240　*Conclusion*

that identity is neither infinitely malleable, because more institutional similarities give the monarchic elites more to "latch on", nor simply primordial, because monarchic salience changes over time (cf. Saideman 2002, 186–187).

7.3 "Zones of peace" and similar political systems

After having closed some research gaps, the results of the case studies leave other gaps open and establish new ones. The main avenues for future research are, first, to intensify the study of SPSP, both within institutionalist and social constructivist frameworks; second, to deepen the study of the specific monarchic variant inside and outside of the provided framework; and third, to address other questions on the margins of this study that have been left unanswered.

First, having provided one building block of the SPSP, future studies should look at other possible cases under even-more-diverse conditions, ideally also in cross-regional comparisona. The "zones of peace" that could form part of the same typology as the MP and the DP mentioned earlier are prime candidates. Studies comparing these "zones of peace" to the MP and DP might flesh out and make the SPSP more robust on the basis of a stronger definition of "political similarity", which could in turn be operationalized for large-n studies.

Second, since this work focused on the most striking elements of foreign policy – war and peace – further studies should look at other elements that characterize interaction among states, regimes and rulers, including different forms of cooperation, trade and cultural relations, or membership in international fora. While this book focused on a psychological and social constructivist approach (SIT), further studies should probe the institutionalist account with other subtypes of the SPSP. SIT and institutional approaches might have an additive effect. For instance, as argued earlier, specific institutional features might make some groups of states more predisposed to develop an ingroup identification than others. While SIT-based approaches claim that peaceful group members are peaceful because they are *similar to each other*, institutionalist approaches instead state mostly that they behave in a peaceful way because they are *similar to democracies*. Maybe some subtypes of autocracy, like monarchies or single-party regimes, are indeed more similar institutionally to democracies and therefore behave in a similar way, as previous research suggested (Mattes and Rodríguez 2014; Sirin and Koch 2015; Weeks 2012). In short, although institutionalist arguments have been presented in the theoretical section as an alternative or rivaling explanation, they might in fact be complementary and as such a stepping stone toward further analytical precision.

Institutionalist arguments might also open up the way to examine whether the emergence, preservation, and deepening of an ingroup is shaped by the same drivers. The case studies suggested that a common threat might be more important at the outset of ingroup formation but that it might not be as essential for affirming and deepening the ingroup. There should also be further studies to answer the question under what conditions such ingroups develop. This book has shown how three main factors affect the salience of monarchy (overall share of monarchies,

Conclusion 241

common threat, and divisive ideology), but other groups of states might work under slightly different conditions.

Third, further questions concern more-detailed aspects of the causal mechanism that arose over course of the investigation. For one, what is the relative importance of regime type vis-à-vis other dimensions of similarity? For instance, the attempted integration of the ties of some core groups of monarchies in the case studies (especially the GCC and AFU) indicated that political system similarity goes a long way to explain non-war, but for deepening alliance and integration, cultural or linguistic similarity might be necessary. This points to an additive relationship between the different dimensions of similarity, but the question remains whether and under what conditions one could supplant the other. This aspect is also linked to the question of how exactly some similarities relate to regime type, like worldview, a conservative mindset, or a particular set of preferences. The argument that more similarity apart from regime type leads to a stronger ingroup might not be surprising, but it confirms that instead of Policy IV values, the study of "similarity" needs to be grounded in much-deeper analyses of history and culture.

Another question concerns the tipping point that determines when exactly a community of peace becomes a community of active solidarity or an institutionalized alliance. The case studies hinted at but did not systematically examine that this process might be shaped by two factors: the intensity of similarity (including more dimensions of similarity apart from the political system) and the intensity of a common threat.

7.4 Salience, threat, and mutual recognition in global comparison: implications for generalizability and policy

How far does the analysis of the foreign policy behavior of Middle Eastern monarchies in the postwar period stretch and travel? What insights can we gain beyond the 20th century and early 21st century, the Middle East, and beyond monarchies? And what does it mean for the actual conduct of foreign policy?

Because the logic of monarchic peace is based on developed nation-states that are governed by sovereignty and territorial integrity norms instead of the logic of authority and empire, the framework is not applicable to most periods before 1945. But what about the future, assuming that the trend of decreasing interstate war continues (Malešević 2014)?

While the theoretical framework was developed for the analysis of war and war avoidance, this study gives some preliminary answers to this question as well. Ingroup dynamics between similar states not only prevent war but also might foster durable cooperation, alliance, and even integration. The overview over the Arab Spring period shows how monarchic solidarity, consisting of mutual support and institutionalization attempts, can play out even if interstate war is not on the horizon. Further patterns connected to monarchic identification might be established in future studies.

242 *Conclusion*

Of course, even though interstate war has become almost obsolete in the past decade or so, this does not make the study of war and peace irrelevant. There is roughly one interstate war per decade, and even if that number were to go down, that does not mean that it will disappear completely. Even if interstate war were to be completely replaced by intrastate war, some of the implications of this book might be applicable to the subnational level. This is true for the SIT mechanism: monarchic solidarity will remain highly relevant amid highly sectarianized conflicts, such as those that we can observe in the contemporary Middle East. Even with interstate war gone, interstate conflicts remain. This book shows that specific instruments, like subversion policies vis-à-vis another regime, are linked to an antagonistic foreign policy that does not recognize the other as part of a salient ingroup. Subversion might replace open war making outside of interstate wars, but the mechanism would still apply.

If the phenomenon is not confined to one particular time frame, what about regional bias? To what extent is the monarchic peace relevant only in the Middle East? Clearly the region of the Middle East remains the strongest case for monarchic peace given that it is the only remaining regional system containing a significant number of monarchies. While the initial descriptive statistical overview of the features of interstate war includes other authoritarian monarchies as well, they are mostly too few and dispersed to warrant any sweeping conclusions. However, core findings might be replicated in other regions and time periods.

Some regional concentrations of monarchies can be found at different times in the past, such as between Cambodia, Laos, and Vietnam in their jointly monarchic period or between Swaziland and Lesotho (before the latter democratized). Outside the World War II scope, some periods of monarchic peace thrived under the right conditions. Kelly's Confucian peace between China, Korea, Japan, and Vietnam in 1644–1839 (2012) might be such an example of a monarchic peace among culturally similar political entities. The dwindling number of monarchies between the world wars in Europa might also provide a fertile ground for where monarchic salience might have been high enough to become a politically relevant driver of foreign policy. Stronger tests of the monarchic peace can look at the relations of monarchies that straddle cultural or linguistic regions apart from Iranian-Arab relations, like Afghanistan and Iran before 1973 or Ethiopia and possible Saudi Arabia or Yemen until 1974.

One major factor that might obstruct the traveling of the concept to another region and possibly time is *ideology*. As the comparative case studies established, the salience of monarchism highly depends on factors that are not intrinsically tied to monarchic institutions, such as the absence of a divisive hierarchical ideology. Obviously, ideology was never confined to the Middle East, but it has historically been a region where it had a particularly strong impact on regional politics (cf. Telhami and Barnett 2002). Middle East monarchies by design and for reasons of regime security were less affected by transnational and rigorous ideologies, but that might not necessarily be the case for monarchies in other regions and time periods.

Because the MP is merely a subtype of the SPSP, the framework does not have to be confined to other monarchies at all: it can be applied to other types of similar political systems. A main strength of the SIT mechanism is that it is general enough to be applicable to any group of states with similar political systems, be they different sorts of monarchies or other types of states altogether, like democracies or military juntas.

Apart from empirical and theoretical implications, the patterns of the MP matter for makers of foreign policy. First, the refocusing of the DP as part of an SPSP further buries the ill-fated notion of peace through democratization. Although previous studies have already pointed to the destabilizing effect of democratization, mostly because of the heightened risk of conflict in the transitional period from autocracy to democracy (Cederman, Hug, and Wenger 2008; Mansfield and Snyder 1995), this has still left the possibility open that it is worth the risk once the transition has finished (Ward and Gleditsch 1998). If, however, it is not democracies but rather similar systems in general that are peaceful toward each other, democratizing individual members of the community might lead to conflict in regions where interstate war has been nonexistent, thereby disrupting regional stability instead of fostering it – even in the long run. Also, a regime change or transition lowers the number of monarchies (or other types of similar systems), which heightens the salience of the pre-existing ingroup. Because this might induce a feeling of threat, it would strengthen opposition to regime change and liberalization, because such moves could lead to further destabilization. However, this destabilization potential must still be weighed carefully against the potential benefits of democratization or liberalization for *intrastate* peace and prosperity.

In addition, the findings emphasize once again the necessity for broad and diverse channels of communication between political elites in order to foster regularized interaction that leads to familiarity and trust and thereby more cooperative relations. While institutionalists see institutions as information hubs that reduce complexity, this analysis showed how institutions function as community hubs and facilitators of ingroup identification. In contrast to many institutionalist accounts, the SIT narrative emphasized that the best international institutions for that purpose are small and intimate.

It is easy to overlook the handful of hereditary regimes that have clung to power until today. But monarchies, it seems, are far from being "an anachronism in the modern world of nations" (Hudson 1977, 166). Instead, the focus on monarchies can serve to uncover broad and meaningful patterns of interstate relations that might have been neglected but that could easily become relevant to our understanding of many other regions and types of states.

Notes

1 A Jordanian-Egyptian clash during the First Arab–Israeli War in 1948, Qatar against Bahrain in April 1986 and Saudi Arabia against Qatar in 1992.

244 *Conclusion*

2 Although that might also be due to the fact that the monarchies in these cases (Kuwait and the UAE) were much smaller and militarily weaker states than were the republics (Iraq and Iran).

References

Al Alkim, Hassan Hamdan. 1989. *The Foreign Policy of the United Arab Emirates*. London: Saqi.

Cederman, Lars-Erik, Simon Hug, and Andreas Wenger. 2008. "Democratization and War in Political Science." *Democratization* 15(3): 509–24.

George, Alexander L., and Andrew Bennett. 2005. *Case Studies and Theory Development in the Social Sciences*. Cambridge; London: MIT Press.

Hudson, Michael C. 1977. *Arab Politics*. New Haven [u.a.]: Yale University Press.

Kelly, Robert E. 2012. "A 'Confucian Long Peace' in Pre-Western East Asia?" *European Journal of International Relations* 18(3): 407–30.

Lakatos, Imre. 1970. "Falsification and the Methodology of Scientific Research Programmes." In *Criticism and the Growth of Knowledge: Proceedings of the International Colloquium in the Philosophy of Science, London, 1965*, eds. Imre Lakatos and Alan Musgrave. Cambridge: Cambridge University Press, 91–197.

Malešević, Siniša. 2014. "Is War Becoming Obsolete? A Sociological Analysis." *The Sociological Review* 62(2_suppl): 65–86.

Mansfield, Edward D., and Jack Snyder. 1995. "Democratization and the Danger of War." *International Security* 20(1): 5–38.

Martín, Félix. 2006. *Militarist Peace in South America: Conditions for War and Peace*. 2006 edition. New York: Palgrave Macmillan.

Mattes, Michaela, and Mariana Rodríguez. 2014. "Autocracies and International Cooperation." *International Studies Quarterly* 58(3): 527–38.

Oren, Ido, and Jude Hays. 1997. "Democracies May Rarely Fight One Another, but Developed Socialist States Rarely Fight at All." *Alternatives: Global, Local, Political* 22(4): 493–521.

Saideman, Stephen. 2002. "Conclusion: Thinking Theoretically About Identity and Foreign Policy." In *Identity and Foreign Policy in the Middle East*, eds. Shibley Telhami and Michael Barnett. Ithaca: Cornell University Press, 169–200.

Sirin, Cigdem V., and Michael T. Koch. 2015. "Dictators and Death: Casualty Sensitivity of Autocracies in Militarized Interstate Disputes." *International Studies Quarterly* 59(4): 802–14.

Telhami, Shibley, and Michael Barnett. 2002. *Identity and Foreign Policy in the Middle East*. Ithaca: Cornell University Press.

Ward, Michael D., and Kristian S. Gleditsch. 1998. "Democratizing for Peace." *The American Political Science Review* 92(1): 51–61.

Weart, Spencer. 1994. "Peace Among Democratic and Oligarchic Republics." *Journal of Peace Research* 31(3): 299–316.

Weeks, Jessica. 2012. "Strongmen and Straw Men: Authoritarian Regimes and the Initiation of International Conflict." *The American Political Science Review* 106(2): 326–47.

Wendt, Alexander. 1994. "Collective Identity Formation and the International State." *The American Political Science Review* 88(2): 384–96.

Index

Abu Dhabi 83, 92, 184, 188, 223; relations with Dubai and other UAE emirates 15n12, 187–8, 205; relations with Iran 75, 176–7, 194–5, 199, 202–3

Abu Musa and the Tunb Islands 72, 177–80, 185–91, 197–206, 210, 212n14

Affirmation of commonality 33–5, 53n16, **118**, **143**, **174**, **209**, 231

Al Alaoui, Hassan II 72–3, 185

Al Alaoui dynasty 72, 78, 128

Al Bu-Said, Qaboos bin Said 41, 66, 75, 106, 185, 194, 226n1

Al Bu-Said, Said bin Taimur 65, 75, 226n1

Al Bu-Said dynasty 64

Al Hashemi, Abd al-Ilah bin Ali 127, 130, 133, 137, 158, **174**

Al Hashemi, Abdallah of Transjordan 67, 73–4, 84n2, 121–4, 126–33, 140–1

Al Hashemi, Faisal (I) bin Hussein of Iraq 123–7

Al Hashemi, Faisal (II) bin Ghazi of Iraq 71, 78, 133–5, 138, 158

Al Hashemi, Ghazi bin Faisal 127, 133, 155–62, 175, 211nn1–2

Al Hashemi, Hussein bin Ali 62, 121, 123–5, 127–8

Al Hashemi, Hussein bin Talal 42, 71–5, 106, 133–9, 145, 185; relations with Egypt and Syria 67, 69, 73–5; relations with Iraq 167, 170–1, 202

Al Hashemi, Talal bin Abdallah 65, 133

Al Khalifa 81, 92–6, 99, 105–7, 117, 119

Al Khalifa, Hamad bin Isa 65, 84n2, 93–5, 111

Al Khalifa, Isa bin Salman 105, 109–10

Al Khalifa, Khalifa bin Salman 108–10

Al Khalifa, Mohammed bin Mubarak 98, 208

Al Maktoum, Rashid bin Said 178, 183

Al Nahyan, Muhammad bin Zayed 221

Al Nahyan, Zayed bin Sultan 66, 195, 197, 210, 232; and Iran 75, 184, 186–7, 204, 206

Al Qasimi, Khalid bin Muhammad 179–80, 185–8, 199, 212n14, 212n20

Al Qasimi, Saqr bin Muhammad 179–80, 186–8, 204, 212n14, 212nn19–20

Al Qasimi dynasty 212n20

Al Sabah, Abdallah (III) as-Salim 67, 155–9, 169

Al Sabah, Ahmad 154

Al Sabah, Jabir al-Ahmad 167

Al Sabah, Nasir Muhammad 80, 194

Al Sabah dynasty 95, 154–7, 159, 170–1

al-Said, Nuri 48, 126, 132–4, 138, 154–9, 161

Al Saud, Abdallah bin Abd al-Aziz 42, 145, 198

Al Saud, Abd al-Aziz bin Abd al-Rahman (Ibn Saud) 121–5, 127–33, 135, 140, 144, 153, 219

Al Saud, Fahd bin Abd al-Aziz 168, 170–1

Al Saud, Faisal bin Abd al-Aziz 66, 78, 134, 137, 189

Al Saud, Khalid bin Abd al-Aziz 66, 72, 102, 190, 202

Al Saud, Nawaf bin Abd al-Aziz 75, 185

Al Saud, Saud al-Faisal 102, 116, 193, 201

Al Saud, Saud bin Abd al-Aziz 73, 77, 133–8, 169, 219

Al Saud, Talal bin Abd al-Aziz 68

Al Saud dynasty 63–4, 95, 121–30, 167

Al Thani, Abdullah bin Jassim 93

Al Thani, Hamad bin Jassim (coup participant) 99

Al Thani, Hamad bin Jassim al Jabir (foreign minister) 106–8, 113–14, 194

246 *Index*

Al Thani, Hamad bin Khalifa 92, 94, 104, 112–14, 232
Al Thani, Jassim bin Muhammad 95
Al Thani, Khalifa bin Hamad 102, 105, 113–14, 145n5
Al Thani, Tamim bin Hamad 221, 223, 225
Al Thani dynasty 66, 92–6, 99, 111, 117–19, 225
Arab Cold War 68–77, 114, 140, 145, 154, 158, 233–8
Arab Federation *see* Arab Union (AFU)
Arab nationalism 68, 76–7, 134, 141, 161, 173
Arab Spring 1, 45–6, 77–84, 145n4, 241
Arab Union (AFU) 71, 128–31, 137–40, 158–9, 233, 241
Arif, Abd ar-Rahman 163
Arif, Abd as-Salam 139, 162–3
autocracy 8, 18, 26, 46, 240; autocracy-democracy difference 9, 20, 243; research on 21–2, 239

Bahrain 91–121; and Iran 178–81
Bani Sadr, Abdul Hasan 195, 204
Ba'th 70, 76–7, 96–7, 141, 166–7, 176, 234
Bishara, Abdallah 80, 194, 204
Black September 1970 68–9
building block study 49–50, 229, 238, 240

Decisive Storm 82–3
democratic peace 2, 9, 18, 29, 229, 239; criticism 18–22; theorem (DPT) 5, 7–8, 10, 239
Dhofar 66, 75–6, 181, 189, 212n17, 226n1
Dubai 65–6, 97, 205, 224; relations with Iran 178, 181, 184, 188, 202, 212n17
dyadic peace 5, 8–10, 18–23, 41–6, 233, 238

Egypt 44, 68–77, 82, 130–40, 144, 158–61; monarchic period 11, 14n6, 47, 63–8, 122–6; in Qatar crisis 220–2; war participation 3–5, 170–3

family: references 33–4, 67, **118**, **143**, 156, 163, **174**, **209**; rhetoric 33, 53n17, 66, 111, 119, 223–5
Faruq, King of Egypt 66, 128, 130
First Gulf War 3–4, 41, 97, 101–5, 165, 211n5, 234–5; Jordan's role 170–2, 212n12
Foreign Policy Analysis (FPA) 7–9, 21, 239

Free Officers 68, 132, 160
Free Princes 68, 132

Gaddafi *see* Qadhafi, Mu'ammar
Gamal Abdel Nasser 70–7, 131–8, 182, 219, 234
Great Britain 64, 75, 93, 126, 134–5, 153, 156–7, 163, 169, 237
Greater Syria 73, 126–7, 130, 133, 161
Gulf Cooperation Council (GCC) 93, 97, 102–16, 120, 170, 196–203, 233; foundation 70, 72, 203; Jordan and Morocco 79–82, 85n13, 233; Qatar Crisis 220–6

Hamid ad-Din, Ahmad bin Yahya 75, 219
Hamid ad-Din, Muhammad al-Badr bin Ahmad 74
Hamid ad-Din, Yahya bin Muhammad 219, 226n1
Hamid ad-Din dynasty 63, 66, 218–20
Hashemite dynasty 121–41, 158, 161
Hijaz 62, 121–33, 167, 171
Hoveida, Amir Abbas 179–80
Hussein, Saddam 3, 38, 40–1, 160–1, 164–71, 201; personality 84n4, 168, 211n8

Ibn Saud *see* Al Saud, Abd al-Aziz bin Abd al-Rahman
Ikhwan 122–5, 129
Imam Ahmad *see* Hamid ad-Din, Ahmad bin Yahya
Imam Muhammad al-Badr *see* Hamid ad-Din, Muhammad al-Badr bin Ahmad
Imam Yahya *see* Hamid ad-Din, Yahya bin Muhammad
International Relations (IR) Theory 7, 18, 21, 239
Iran 77–80, 96–7, 176–218
Iraq 68–77, 80, 96–7, 134–8, 188, 192; and Kuwait 152–76; in monarchic period 62–8, 124–6; war participation 3–5; *see also* Arab Union (AFU); First Gulf War; Hussein, Saddam
Israel 44–6, 69, 72, 125, 139, 160, 182, 197; Arab-Israeli wars 3–4, 41, 74–5, 77, 127–30, 134

Jordan 40–5, 63–5, 80–1, 158; and the Al Saud 121–45; in the Arab Cold War 68–77, 138–40; war participation 3–5; *see also* First Gulf War, Jordan's role

Index 247

Khalatbari, Abbas Ali 180
khaleeji 82, 95–6, 103–5, 120–1, 145, 225, 236
Khatami, Mohammad 198, 205
Khomeini, Ruhollah 72, 97, 192–3, 195
King Abdallah of Jordan *see* Al Hashemi, Abdallah of Transjordan
King Abdallah of Saudi Arabia *see* Al Saud, Abdallah bin Abd al-Aziz
King Faisal of Iraq *see* Al Hashemi, Faisal (I) bin Hussein of Iraq; Al Hashemi, Faisal (II) bin Ghazi of Iraq
King Ghazi *see* Al Hashemi, Ghazi bin Faisal
King Hamad *see* Al Khalifa, Hamad bin Isa
King Hassan *see* Al Alaoui, Hassan II
King Isa *see* Al Khalifa, Isa bin Salman
Kuwait 41, 63, 70–2, 81, 211n10, 221–4; and Iran 185, 194, 203; and Iraq 138, 152–76; war participation 3–5; *see also* First Gulf War

Libya 40, 70–2, 76–9, 83, 99, 180, 187; monarchic period 62–6, 125, 137–8; war participation 3–5

MIDs (Militarized Interstate Disputes) 5–6, 77, 136, 145n8, 164, 185, 198; operationalization 35–6, 53n18
monadic peace 5, 10, 43, 46, 52n9; *see also* dyadic peace
Monarchic Peace (MP) 18–19, 30, 43, 46, 67, 83, 180; as a subtype of the SPSP 2, 5–12, 49, 218–20, 229, 233, 238–42
Morocco 62–8, 71–2, 128, 137, 170, 186; and the GCC 78–82, 221, 224, 232–3; war proneness and participation 3–4, 11, 40–2, 45, 49
Muslim Brotherhood 73, 81, 221, 224–5

Najd 66, 95, 121–4, 128, 166–7; Najdi *ulama'* 146n15

oil: and conflict 7, 40–1, 164, 167, 199, 202, 210; wealth and exploitation 92–4, 116, 121, 146n13, 154, 179, 192, 236
Oman 39, 53n19, 66, 82, 113, 170, 186, 212, 232; Dhofar insurgency 75–6, 189, 212n17; *see also* Dhofar
othering 33–4, 37, 48, 232; among monarchies 99, 122, 130, 224–5; between monarchies and republics 167, 195

Pahlavi, Shah Reza 54n26, 66–72, 75–8, 128, 177–91, 193, 202
Pahlavi dynasty 64, 67, 206
Palestinian Liberation Organisation (PLO) 69, 170
perception 23, 64, 68, 119, 132, 175; of similarity 25–30, 145, 220, 231, 234
Persepolis celebrations 35, 75–6, 184–5, 191
Persian nationalism *see* Persian supremacy
Persian supremacy 183, 188, 190–1, 235
Popular Front for the Liberation of the Occupied Arabian Gulf (PFLOAG) 166

Qadhafi, Mu'ammar 70, 75, 78, 202
Qasim, Abd al-Karim 77, 139, 158, 160–9, 175
Qatar 91–121; Qatar crisis 220–6

Rafsanjani, Ali Akbar Hashemi 194, 196, 203
Ras al-Khaimah 179–80, 185–8, 202–5, 212nn19–20, 237
royal club 8, 75, 79, 139, 218, 220, 225

salience 12, 27–31, 68, 76, 230, 234; in case studies 96, 105, 125, 131, 154, 160, 181, 192, 218, 223
Salih, Ali Abdallah 81
saming *see* Affirmation of commonality
Sandhurst (Royal Military Academy) 65, 67, 104, 107, 135, 156
Sanoussi, Idris 64
Sanoussi Dynasty 63, 66
Saudi Arabia 45, 63, 68–77, 82, 121–31, 218–20
scope conditions 13, 31, 38, 46–9, 121–4, 141, 218–19, 235
Sharif (religious legitimacy) 63–4, 125, 167, 171, 211n7
Sharif Hussein *see* Al Hashemi, Hussein bin Ali
Sharjah 178–80, 184–8, 198–9, 202–3, 206, 212n20
Similar Political Systems Peace (SPSP) 8–11, 18, 21–31, 120, 177, 218, 229–43
Six-Day War 1967 3, 68, 74, 189
small states 39–40, 50, 53n20, 236
social identity theory 8, 11, 22–5, 31, 36–9, 43, 234, 239–43

Syria 68–77, 99, 126–7, 130, 137, 201, 233; Kingdom of 62, 123; war participation 3–5; *see also* Greater Syria

Tunisia 4–5, 54n27, 62, 79, 137, 173

UAR *see* United Arab Republic (UAR)
United Arab Emirates (UAE) 14n11, 66, 75, 81, 178–81, 212n15
United Arab Republic (UAR) 69, 71, 73, 76–7, 127, 219; and AFU 137–9, 158, 164
'Utub tribe 66, 92, 95

Velayati, Ali Akbar 103, 194, 197

Wahhabism 45, 122–3, 125, 141, 146n16

Yemen 80, 82–3, 222; Federation of Southern Yemeni Emirates 62; North 40, 62–4, 66, 73, 181; South 75, 186, 189; war participation 3–5; Yemeni Civil War 70–1, 74–5; Yemeni-Saudi War 218–19

Zahedi, Ardeshir 180
zones of peace 19, 27, 42, 183, 229, 240–1